新时代商务英语专业系列教材
New Era Business English Series

总主编 / 翁凤翔　郭桂杭

Elements of International Business

国际商务概论

翁凤翔 / 编　著

重庆大学出版社

内容提要

　　作为商务英语专业国际商务知识类主干课程教材,本书系统地介绍了国际商务主要领域的基本知识和发展的最新动态,注重实用。除了商务英语专业学生以外,本书还适合国际商务、经济、管理、金融等涉外专业的大学生、研究生及工商管理硕士生(MBA)使用。本书用简单的英语写成,通俗易懂。通过使用本书,学生既能获得国际商务核心知识,又能提升国际商务英语水平,可谓一举两得。

图书在版编目(CIP)数据

　　国际商务概论:英文/翁凤翔编著.—重庆:重
庆大学出版社,2016.8(2021.1重印)
　　商务英语专业系列教材
　　ISBN 978-7-5689-0069-0

　　Ⅰ.①国… 　Ⅱ.①翁… 　Ⅲ.①国际商务—高等学校—
教材—英文　Ⅳ.①F740

　　中国版本图书馆 CIP 数据核字(2016)第 194192 号

国际商务概论
GUOJI SHANGWU GAILUN
翁凤翔　编　著

责任编辑:杨　敬　韩　鹏　　　版式设计:高小平
责任校对:邬小梅　　　　　　　责任印制:赵　晟

*

重庆大学出版社出版发行
出版人:饶帮华
社址:重庆市沙坪坝区大学城西路 21 号
邮编:401331
电话:(023) 88617190　88617185(中小学)
传真:(023) 88617186　88617166
网址:http://www.cqup.com.cn
邮箱:fxk@cqup.com.cn(营销中心)
全国新华书店经销
重庆市正前方彩色印刷有限公司印刷

*

开本:787mm×1092mm　1/16　印张:25.75　字数:611 千
2016 年 9 月第 1 版　　2021 年 1 月第 5 次印刷
ISBN 978-7-5689-0069-0　定价:49.50 元

总　序

　　商务英语作为本科专业获得教育部批准进入我国大学本科教育基本目录已经好些年了。商务英语本科专业的身份与地位获得了我国官方和外语界的认可。迄今为止，据不完全统计，有 300 所左右的大学开设了商务英语本科专业。各种商务英语学术活动也开始活跃。商务英语专业与英语语言文学专业、翻译专业成为我国英语教学的"三驾马车"。商务英语教学在全国已经形成较大规模，正呈良性发展态势，越来越多的大学正在积极准备申报商务英语本科专业。可以预计，将来在我国，除了研究性大学外的大部分普通本科院校的外语学院都可能开设商务英语本科专业。这是大势所趋，因为随着我国加大力度改革开放和经济全球化、世界经济一体化进程的加快，各个融入经济一体化的国家和地区急需有扎实英语功底的，熟悉国际商务基本知识的，具备国际商务领域操作技能的跨文化商务交际复合型、应用性商务英语人才。

　　高校商务英语专业教育首先必须有充足的合格师资；其次，需要有合适的教材。目前，虽然市面上有很多商务英语教材，但是，完整的四年商务英语本科专业教材并不多。重庆大学出版社出版的商务英语本科专业系列教材一定程度上能满足当前商务英语本科专业的教学需要。

　　本套系列教材能基本满足商务英语本科专业 1—4 年级通常开设课程的需要。商务英语专业不是商务专业而是语言专业。所以，基础年级的教材仍然是英语语言学习教材。但是，与传统的英语语言文学专业教材不同的是：商务英语专业学生所学习的英语具有显著的国际商务特色。所以，本套教材特别注重商务英语本科专业教育的特点，在基础阶段的英语技能教材中融入了商务英语元素，让学生在学习普通英语的同时，接触一些基础的商务英语语汇，通过听、说、读、写、译等技能训练，熟悉掌握商务英语专业四级和八级考试词汇，熟悉基础的商务英语篇章，了解国际商务常识。

　　根据我国《高等学校商务英语本科专业教学质量国家标准》（以下简称《标准》），本套教材不仅包含一、二年级的基础教材，还包含高年级的继续夯实商务英语语言知识的教材，如《高级商务英语教程》1—3 册等。此外，还包括英语语言文学专业学生所没有的突出商务英语本科专业特色的国际商务知识类教材，如《国际商务概论》《国际贸易实务》《国际贸易法》《市场营销》等。本套教材的总主编都是教育部商务英语专业教学协作组成员，参与了该《标准》的起草与制定，熟悉《标准》的要求，这为本套教材的质量提供了基本保障。此外，参与编写本套教材的主编及编者都是多年从事商务英语教学与研究的有经验的教师，因而，在教材的内容、体例、知识、练习以及辅助教材等方面，都充分考虑到了教材使用者的需求。教材的编写宗旨是：力求传授实用的商务英语知识和国际商务有关领域的知识，提高学生的商务英语综合素质和跨文化商务交际能力以及思辨创新能力。

　　教材编写考虑到了以后推出的全国商务英语本科专业四级和专业八级的考试要求。在教材的选材、练习、词汇等方面都尽可能与商务英语本科专业四级、八级考试对接。

　　本套教材特别适合培养复合型、应用性的商务英语人才的商务英语本科专业的学生使用，也可作为商务英语爱好者学习商务英语的教材。教材中若存在不当和疏漏之处，敬请专家、学者及教材使用者批评指正，以便我们不断修订完善。

翁凤翔

2016 年 3 月

Introduction

The world is changing so fast. Are you changing yourself to meet the requirements of the changing world? What do you dream of when you imagine your future? A fascinating top job with an international company or with companies concerned with international business? Economic analyses, combined with an interest in people and different cultures? If that is what you have in mind, you will want to study international business.

The aim of *Elements of International Business* is to provide students with a thorough understanding of the factors that make international business activities different from domestic business transactions.

Elements of International Business is for enthusiastic, energetic and ambitious internationally oriented students and/or company clerks and any others interested in international business. A thorough knowledge of international business linked with a keen insight into the legal, social and ethical environment of companies is important and necessary.

Besides, it is likewise important to constantly study the latest developments in the international business community. All through your studies you will have to solve problems and cases from the field of international business administration, using your knowledge of finance, accounting, marketing and management. *Elements of International Business* is intended to give readers a feel for the field of international business.

Further, reading this book is quite beneficial to those who are studying international business English and who are going to take part in business English certificate examinations such as BEC (Cambridge Business English Certificate), which is acknowledged by international companies.

The main features of this book are as follows:

1. This book is written in simple English, except for some special terms. Therefore, readers will find it easier to read this book than the fatter books on international business published abroad.

2. There are objectives in Chinese at the beginning of each chapter and a summary in Chinese at the end of each chapter to help readers better understand the essence of international business.

3. As the book covers most fields of international business, readers with different backgrounds can review their own subjects and learn more about the relevant subjects. Besides, readers can learn the English expressions of international business, which is very important, since in China subjects of

international business such as finance, marketing, and trade are normally taught in Chinese.

4. This book includes the latest developments in international business which keeps changing all the time, such as TPP, AIIB, etc.

5. The writer has included some sections related to China's business with the outside world. Learners of international business should know something about the development of China's international business. In addition, since China has joined the WTO, some policies, laws, and regulations have to be changed accordingly to meet the requirements of the WTO. Learners of international business must keep informed of these changes, some of which are included in this book.

6. The book is quite practical. Readers from schools or companies will find the book both very useful and practical in their studies and work, as the writer of this book, who has rich experience in teaching international business and who has working experiences in international businesses, has paid much attention to practical as well as academic value.

Each chapter provides the most essential points of the areas of international business and contains analytical studies combined with extensive application to the real world problems of managing international business activities.

The book provides a good grounding for undergraduates of international business and will be very useful for studies in international trade, finance, human resource management and so on. It is also intended to be beneficial to MBA students as it introduces a background to the research literature in the field. The practical knowledge of international business makes this book likewise very useful for postgraduates who need an understanding of international business as a background for studying management and business issues.

After reading the book, readers are sure to have a clear picture of international business.

The author welcomes any suggestions or comments on this book and will be very much grateful to those who provide such suggestions and comments.

Weng Fengxiang March 7, 2016

Contents

Chapter 1 | General View of International Business 国际商务概述

Objectives
学习目标

To understand what international business covers.

了解国际商务所涵盖的范围。

To explain why companies tend to engage in international business.

解释公司倾向于从事国际商务的原因。

To illustrate globalization.

阐述全球化。

To provide an overview of the GATT and the WTO.

概述关税和贸易总协定及世界贸易组织。

To describe the advantages and disadvantages of China's entry into the WTO.

阐述中国加入世界贸易组织之利弊。

1.1 What Is International Business? 何谓国际商务?

International business, an attractive term to the public, especially to the young, is normally understood to refer to all commercial transactions (private and governmental) between two or more countries or the transactions that take place across national borders for the purpose of satisfying the need of individuals and organizations.

Generally speaking, private companies undertake transactions so as to obtain profit while governments may or may not do the same in their transactions. In other words, international business involves commercial activities that cross national frontiers. International business is usually related to the following:

(1) The international circulation of goods, capital, services, employees and technology;

(2) Importing and exporting;

(3) Cross-border transactions in intellectual property by means of licensing and franchising;

A. patents;

B. trade marks;

C. know-how;

D. copyright materials;

E. and so on;

(4) Investment in physical and financial assets in foreign countries;

(5) Contract manufacturer or assembly of goods abroad for local sale or for export to other countries;

(6) Buying and selling in foreign countries;

(7) The establishment of foreign warehousing and distribution systems;

(8) The import to one country of goods from a second foreign country for subsequent local sale.

In a word, the transactions involved in international business chiefly include sales, investment, and logistics.

1.2 Why Do We Study International Business? 为何学习国际商务？

Needless to say, learners of international business are going to engage in any one of the above-mentioned international business activities or to make research on or to teach international business. No matter whether an individual may engage in international business in future or not, to study it enables him or her to be more competitive, as globalization is increasing all over the world.

Since China has entered into the WTO, more and more foreign investments have been coming into this country, and thus more chances are available. On the other hand, Chinese enterprises have increased their overseas investments. Therefore, more people familiar with international business are needed, who are sure to have more opportunities to extend their range and have their ideals realized.

The study of international business helps a person supplement his or her knowledge of general business functions such as accounting, finance, marketing, logistics, and so on through examining issues, practices, problems and solutions relating to these functions in foreign states. Besides, to study international business can help develop a person's sensitivity to foreign cultures, values and social norms. Further, studying international business enables individuals and firms to recognize the opportunities and risks of extra-territorial operations, the process of internationalisation of business and the management of these businesses in complex environments.

It can be seen that the study of international business can help a person a lot to develop himself or herself, adopt broader perspectives, and improve his or her overall business managerial efficiency.

▶ 1.3　International Business and International Trade　国际商务与国际贸易

International business and international trade differ in that international business has a broader sense.

International business refers to the transactions that are devised and carried out across national borders to satisfy the objectives of individuals and organizations. The transactions are concerned with different types. Primary types of international business are international trade (export-import trade) and foreign direct investment. International trade is one of the sections in international business.

In other words, international business refers to the business whose activities involve the crossing of national borders. It includes not only international trade and foreign manufacturing but also the growing service industry in such fields as transportation, tourism, banking, advertising, construction, retailing, wholesaling, insurance, education, mass communication and other related activities. On the other hand, international trade is chiefly concerned with sales and purchases of goods. The foundations of international trade are linked to the following four aspects:

(1) International trade and payments;

(2) Cargo insurance;

(3) Transportation and documentation;

(4) Elements of export law.

International business, however, concerns a number of aspects as mentioned above in "1.1".

Therefore, it can be seen that international trade is within the scope of international business. Or we might say that, relatively speaking, international business is on a more macro level while international trade is on a more micro level.

Some economists may focus more on the study of international trade and finance and they pay more attention to the flow of goods across the boarders of countries. Others think that multinational firms play a key role in international business and they focus chiefly on the firms in their analysis, as they look outwards at an assumed external economy. They examine functions and operations of the firms. The basic principles are linked to such functional areas as marketing, management, finance, accounting, and so on. Multinational enterprises are headquartered in one country but have operations in other countries and they account for the majority of the world's investment and trade.

International business, however, is not limited to international trade and international finance, or to specific theories of the multinational firm. Environmental conditions influence international business operations to a great extent.

From Figure 1.1, we may better understand the relationship between international business and international trade.

International trade can be in the form of exporting, importing or strategic global alliances. But no matter what form international trade may be in, it is only one of the much larger picture of international business, which is more concerned with global trade issues.

Figure 1.1

Therefore companies doing international trade should realize the global issues that can affect trade and should also identify ways of ensuring that their overseas activities really take the wider forces of international business into account. This is especially true when we have entered a new century in which globalization is a main trend.

From the perspective of practice of international trade, international trade can be further illustrated in Figure 1.2.

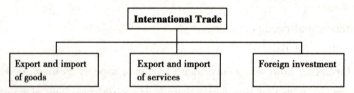

Figure 1.2　International Trade

➤ 1.4　Modes of International Business　国际商务形式

There are a number of modes of international business. A company may choose one of them. What mode of operation is to be chosen depends on the companies and governments themselves. Figure 1.3 illustrates the modes of international business.

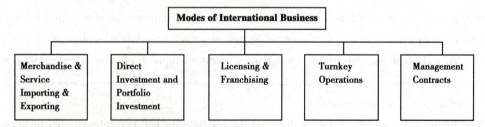

Figure 1.3　Modes of International Business

Here are some explanations about the above Figure 1.3.

（1）Merchandise exports and imports are normally the most common international economic transactions of a country. Merchandise exports or imports are tangible products. They are the goods that can be seen and are concrete objects. Services are non-product auxiliary functions and they are non-product international earnings of a nation. Services refer to the following aspects:

A. Tourism;

B. Transportation;

C. Banking;

D. Insurance;

E. Engineering and management services;

F. Education;

G. Information technology;

H. Hotelling;

I. and so on.

International tourism and transportation are important sources of revenue for airlines, shipping companies, travel agencies and hotels.

(2) Direct investment means the one that gives investor a controlling interest in a foreign company, i.e., foreign direct investment (FDI). Control need not be a 100-percent or even a 50-percent interest. A portfolio investment refers to a non-controlling interest in a company or ownership of a loan to another party. For example, stock in a company or loans to a company in the form of bonds, bills, and so on.

(3) Licensing means that such assets of companies as trademarks, patents, copyrights, or expertise are allowed to be used by foreign companies under licensing agreements. Earnings (Royalties) are earned through licensing. Franchising is a mode of business in which one party (the franchiser) allows another party (the franchisee) to use a trademark that is an essential asset for the franchisee's business.

(4) Turnkey operation means an operation facility that is constructed under contract and transferred to the owner when the facility is ready to begin operations. For example, a company may pay fees for engineering services that are often handled through turnkey operation.

(5) Management contracts refer to arrangements in which one company provides managers to carry out general or specialized management functions to another company.

Besides, BOT (Build—Operation—Transfer) is also a commonly-used mode in international business practice. BOT refers to the investment in building and operation of infrastructure facilities. It is normally a deal between a government and a foreign business. The former provides the latter with special license to undertake the BOT project and operates it after it is finished. The customer has to transfer the title to the finished project (which has been operated by the customer for some period of time) to the government in accordance with the agreement signed by and between the government and the customer.

▶ 1.5 The Need for Conducting International Business 从事国际商务的必要性

Since we have entered the new century, international business appears more and more important and exciting to nations, companies, and individuals as well.

International business is important and necessary because economic isolationism has become impossible. If a nation fails to become a part of the global market, this nation will surely be left behind in terms of its national economy. As a result, its citizens' living standard will decline, not to mention its science and technology. Successful participation in international business, however, is likely to improve quality of life and to bring about a better society, and even a more peaceful world.

International business is especially important and necessary to companies and it offers them more markets. International business brings new ideas, services and more capital across the world. So human capital can be used better and new technology can be shared by the global mankind. Besides, companies may reinforce themselves by and joining their hands with foreign companies and a combination of domestic and international business can present more opportunities for companies to expand, grow and obtain income than does domestic business alone.

As international business develops quickly in a country, the consumers can have more choices. A wider range of products produced by joint ventures or imported are available. Further, it is just because there are more choices of goods that the prices, the quality and the service will be much better through international competition. Meanwhile, international business offers more employment opportunities to individuals. The more investment flows into a country, the more employees will be needed. Those good at international business with professional and entrepreneurial skills may find a lot more opportunities.

From the above discussion it can be seen that international business, both as an opportunity and a challenge, is particularly important and necessary to countries, companies, and individuals.

▶ 1.6 Modern International Business Study 现代国际商务研究

After the World War Ⅱ, many nations were beginning to consider rebuilding their countries. They showed more interest in rebuilding than in investing abroad.

The field of modern international business started to develop in the 1950s. There were not so many MNEs as today. Most of the MNEs of that time were American.

Early textbooks of international business were often written by USA professors and they just offered a general, descriptive approach to this field. It was hard to find international research studies to provide substantive information at that time. The cases involved are more concerned with international divisions rather than true MNEs.

During the 1970s and 1980s the field of international business changed a lot. The economy of Europe and Japan grew quickly. Besides, there appeared great strides of newly industrialized countries. Then more and more attention was paid to international business. Professors became more research-oriented. International economics and finance became primary areas of interest.

In the latter part of the 1980s efforts were beginning to be made to bring together much of what was happening into a meaningful composite. The developments of the 1970s and 1980s were being studied in too micro a fashion, and a more macro approach to the field was needed.

In the 1990s, there appeared a strategic management focus to draw together the field of international business. The earlier interdisciplinary and functional approaches were being supplemented by a multidisciplinary approach that drew on information from a wide variety of disciplines that affected international business.

However, in today's international business study, cases from MNEs are becoming more and more important. This is because international business study is just based on the actual international business activities of the world today.

At present, the study of international business focuses more on economic globlizaiton and world economic integration.

▶ 1.7 Why Do Companies Engage in International Business? 公司介入国际商务之原因

As all businesses' original intention is to survive, they have to obtain profit. The reasons why companies engage in international business can be stated as follows:

(1) To expand sales and acquire resources from foreign countries;

(2) To diversify their activities;

(3) The domestic markets are saturated;

(4) To discover lucrative opportunities in other countries;

(5) To obtain materials, products or technologies that are not available in their own countries;

(6) To spread commercial risk across a number of countries;

(7) The competition in the home markets is too intense;

(8) Involvement in international business can facilitate the "experience curve" effect, i.e. cost reductions and efficiency increases attained in consequence of a business acquiring experience of certain types of activity, function or project;

(9) Economies of scope (as opposed to economies of scale) might become available;

(10) With the development of science and technology, especially electronic technology, international trade is much easier to organize than before. Communication means and facilities for international business travel are more extensive. The world has become "smaller" than before. Accordingly, it is easier to engage in international business.

1.8 Globalization 全球化

1.8.1 What Is Globalization? 何谓全球化?

Globalization is very much in the news today. Numerous companies have engaged aggressively in internationalization, propelled by the conviction that this is an irreversible market trend.

Globalization normally means a decoupling of space and time, emphasizing that with instantaneous communication, knowledge and culture can be shared around the world simultaneously.

But, from the perspective of international business, globalization refers to a primarily economic phenomenon, involving the increasing interaction or integration of national economic systems through the growth in international trade, investment and capital flows.

Without doubt, globalization is a capitalist process and the rapid increase in cross-border economic, social, technological exchange under conditions of capitalism.

Globalization is, however, not a speedy process, despite the rapid increases in global capital and trade flows. Nevertheless, globalization has given rise to permanent changes in the markets affected. Besides, globalization brings lots of opportunities for economic expansion. It is a trend of development of international business. Realizing this is helpful for us to conduct international trade. Today, the corporations in the world trade market are competing with other corporations from across the world. So they are seeking global profits.

Globalization is often cited as a factor accelerating competitive pressure. It has also been studied at length from the intercultural relations and organizational angle. Strangely enough, however, few authors have focused upon its strategic implications. The way to recognize the stakes of globalization can lead companies to completely rethink their strategy. They also explain how managers can help the company find the most promising path.

Globalization refers to the shift toward a more integrated and interdependent world economy. Globalization has two main components: the globalization of markets and the globalization of production.

The globalization of markets refers to the extent to which a market is characterized by broadly similar customer need, global customers and global market segments. In other words, the globalization of markets refers to the fact that in many industries historically distinct and separate national markets are merging into one huge global marketplace.

The globalization of production refers to the tendency among many companies to source goods and services from different locations around the world in order to take advantage of national differences in the cost and quality of factors of production (such as labour, energy, land, and capital). In this way, companies are likely to reduce costs and risks so that they can compete more effectively.

From the perspective of administration, globalization means that managers must adopt a global strategy underpinned by a global vision and global objectives.

The overall strategic vision or mission of the corporation must be based on the resources and competence of the organization and the extent of industry and market globalization. To a large extent, globalization is a business philosophy or a way of thinking which emphasizes the similarities rather than the differences between national markets.

1.8.2 The Development of Globalization 全球化的发展历程

When did globalization start? It is hard to decide the starting point. But the following can help understand the development of globalization.

In the 16th century, the first great expansion of European capitalism took place.

In the late 19th century, there appeared a big expansion in world trade and investment. But this was brought to a halt by the First World War and the bout of anti-free trade protectionism which resulted in the Great Depression in 1930s. It is thought that this period was an interruption to the process of globalization that started in the late 19th century.

As the Second World War came to an end, there was another big expansion of capitalism with the development of multinational companies interested in producing and selling in the domestic markets of nations around the world. The emancipation of colonies brought a new world order. Fast air travel and IT development enhanced the progress of international business.

The roots of globalization lie in the 18th, 19th and 20th centuries.

Since we have entered the new century and with the fast development of science and technology (especially the fantastic development of IT), international business has been increasing fast, which can be, in some way, considered the result of globalization.

1.8.3 Reasons for Globalization 全球化之原因

Globalization is driven by economic factors and it promotes trade and investment in poorer nations. But on the other hand, global corporations are thought of as polluters and environmentally irresponsible entities that consider themselves above national regulation and control.

Globalization as a process in the internationalisation of business is more fully explained by the "Global Shift Theory" by P.Dickens. In his new work *GLOBAL SHIFT*, he says that the world has changed, and that economic activities have become not just internationalized but also increasingly globalized. According to Dickens, globalization depends on the following key factors:

(1) The existence of appropriate technology to overcome geographical distances for standardization and the possibility of fragmenting the production process.

(2) The role of countries in regulating and controlling international business.

(3) The pursuit of global profit.

What's more, major technological, economic, social and political forces, some recent and others more distant, have caused businesses to become internationalized and then globalized.

The forces that facilitate globalization of industries and markets can be concluded as follows:

（1）Technical forces—industrialization, transport revolution, information and communications revolution;

（2）Economic forces—increasing incomes, world trade, world financial markets, market forces, and world competition;

（3）Political forces—reduced trade barriers, intellectual property right, privatization, development of trade blocs and technical standards;

（4）Social forces—consumerism, convergence in customer tastes, and education and skills.

To sum up, it seems that two macro factors underlie the trend toward greater globalization. The first is the decline in barriers to the free flow of goods, services, and capital that has occurred since the end of the Second World War. The second factor is technological change, particularly the dramatic developments that have occurred in recent years in communications, information processing, and transportation technologies.

1.8.4　The Present Status of Globalization　全球化现状

As mentioned above, globalization is a trend of international business. It is very clear that the world has not really become a global economy and that its industries and markets are not already fully globalized.

Different countries have been affected by global trends to some extent. World trade still remains dominated by the "Triad" (the EU, the USA, and the Pacific Rim). The Triad, which accounts for about 80% of the world's output and only about 20% of its population, are at the heart of global business. The rest of the world are in a disadvantageous position in terms of economy and technology. The spread of global business is far from geographically complete. There exist many localized markets and industries. And even within global industries some businesses operate successfully either locally or regionally.

Nevertheless, the overall trend is still towards the increasing globalization of business.

1.9　Internationalization　国际化

1.9.1　Internationalization, Globalization and Localization　国际化、全球化与本地化

Globalization is a way to be global, worldwide, international, intercontinental. Internationalization is supposed to refer to the process. It can be seen that globalization has a broader sense. Sometimes the term "internationalization" is abbreviated as "i18n", because there are 18 letters between the first letter "i" and the last "n".

Today globalization has become identified with a number of trends, most of which have been particularly evident in the period since World War Ⅱ. These include:

（1）an increase in a number of standards applied globally, e.g.: copyright laws;

(2) an increase in international trade at a faster rate than the growth in the world economy;

(3) increase in the share of the world economy controlled by multinational corporations;

(4) greater international cultural influences, for example, through exports of Hollywood movies;

(5) reduction in global cultural diversity;

(6) greater international travel and tourism;

(7) greater sharing of information by the spreading of technology such as the Internet and telephone;

(8) greater immigration, including illegal immigration.

Many of these trends are seen as positive by supporters of various forms of globalization, and in many cases globalization has been actively promoted by governments and others. For example, there are economic arguments such as the theory of comparative advantage suggesting that free trade leads to a more efficient allocation of resources, with all those involved in the trade benefiting.

There is much academic discussion about whether globalization is a real phenomenon or only a myth. Although the term globalization is widespread, many authors argue that the characteristics of the phenomenon have already been seen at other moments in history. Also, many note that those features that make people believe we are in a globalization process, including the increase in international trade and the greater role of multinational corporations, are not as deeply established as they first appeared. Thus, many authors prefer the use of the term "internationalization" rather than "globalization". To put it simply, the main difference between them is that with internationalization, the role of the states and the importance of nations are greater. That is, globalization is deeper than internationalization. So, these authors see that the frontiers of countries, in a broad sense, are far from being dissolved, and therefore this radical globalization process has not yet happened, and probably won't happen, considering that in world history, internationalization never turned into globalization.

Internationalization refers to the process of increasing involvement in international operations. This process includes the whole range of methods of undertaking business across national frontiers, some of which involve flows of goods and services between countries, some of which do not.

Localization refers to the process of adapting, translating and customizing a product for a specific market (for a specific locale). Localization involves taking a product and making it culturally appropriate to the target locale (country/region and language) where it will be used and sold. So far as international business administration is concerned, localization involves local national managers in all key managerial positions.

Both internationalization and localization are ways to adapt things to non-native environment, mostly other nations.

As an alternative to economic globalization, localization has been used to describe the process of concentrating production of goods nearer their end-users, rather than wherever the lowest costs are. The idea is to cut down environmental and other external costs that can occur with the extra transportation and regional specialisation that globalization encourages.

So far as a software product is concerned, globalization is used for the internationalization and the localization process together or the concept to produce software that works globally. Globalization addresses the business issues associated with making a product global. Globalization of high-tech products involves integrating localization throughout a company, after proper internationalization and product design, as well as marketing, sales, and support in the world market. The process of internationalization enables your source to be qualified for the international market. Internationalization is the design and development of software in a way that allows it to be localized (translated) to other locales (languages) without the need to alter the source code.

As the results of globalization, many companies and products find themselves in many countries worldwide. This has given rise to increasing requirements for localization of products and services.

1.9.2　The Internationalization Process　国际化进程

The process of internationalization by firms is central to the concept of international business education, and has rightly received consideration in the literature. It seems that the main reason for internationalization is the growth of the firm. It is believed that through expansion, growth and interaction in the world economy, firms ensure long-term survival and growth which ultimately brings benefits to the host nation and the home country as well.

Some think that the internationalization of the firm involves a logical and sequential process of acquisition, integration and use of knowledge about foreign markets. This idea may not always be true. All firms may not follow this approach in their internationalization process by means of exporting, licensing and investing directly in a foreign market. But it is very obvious that firms often intend to achieve the aims of their operations in the host country by exporting, licensing, franchising, joint venture, and a wholly-owned subsidiary.

A company's first experience of international business might be the receipt of an overseas order. Afterwards, the company may deal with more and more overseas orders. Accordingly, an export or import department is established to meet the need. This establishment is for many firms the first step towards wider internationalization of operations. To meet the need, more staff become expert at international trade, international trade finance, shipping business and other transportation documents. Staff engaged in the export department must be familiar with different international markets and some other knowledge concerned with international business.

As the transactions grow bigger and bigger, it is necessary for the company to set up branches, subsidiaries and perhaps production operations in other countries. The company may start its international marketing research, do advertising directly in foreign media, organise transport to or from foreign destinations, and raise finance from foreign sources.

Then the company may license foreign companies to produce its brands, or engage in franchising or local manufacture. Thus the company becomes a real international business.

The following stage in the international process might involve the firm undertaking joint ventures with foreign partners and/or establishing substantial permanent presences in foreign countries. By establishing subsidiaries in foreign countries, the company is able to project local images in foreign nations, to acquire know-how and technical skills only locally available, reduce production costs, obtain investment grants from foreign governments, and perhaps reduce its worldwide tax liability.

As time goes by, the company business activities take place regularly in foreign countries and its sales and profits become critically dependent on world market. The company, therefore, is moving towards becoming a genuinely multinational enterprise (MNE). That is to say, the company owns production, distribution, service and other units in many nations and plans the utilisation of its resources on the global scale.

1.9.3　Sources of Risk in the Internationalization Process　国际化进程中的风险因素

Risk is a problem of perceived uncertainty. Businesses have a good knowledge of their home country conditions but are less certain about the operating environment of foreign markets. Risk in international business can be categorized into three groups.

(1) Risk associated with generating profits in the host country such as:

A. Economic factors—decreasing GDP growth rates, increasing inflation rates, reduced local purchasing power (all reducing market size), and negative balance of payments (which may lead to "hard currency" repatriation restrictions, especially in developing countries) are examples of worsening economic risk which may suppress profits.

B. Political factors—strikes, dramatic tax hikes, changes in government (or key personnel in government), changes in legislation, war, military coups, social unrest and public demonstrations are examples of political risk which may impact negatively on sales or sales potential.

(2) Risk associated with transferring (or repatriating) earned profits back into the home country such as:

A. Exchange rate risk of which there are three types:

a. Transaction risk, the risk of not achieving the planned profit margin on sales due to an adverse movement in exchange rate from the rate used in the pricing decision.

b. Economic risk, the risk that a sustained, real rise of currency against the currencies of competitors will adversely affect a company's cost and therefore sales, margins and market share, which in turn, decreases the firm's return on capital employed.

c. Translation risk, the risk of loss of net worth of the company which arises from the legal requirement that all firms annually consolidate, in a single currency, their financial statements (balance sheets and income statements) of all world-wide operations.

B. Exchange regulations and restrictions limiting or taxing profit repatriation. These are often used by less developed countries, developing countries, and transition economies (e.g.: those of the former Soviet bloc) when "hard currency" reserves are low.

(3) Expropriation (the seizure of foreign assets by host country government).

This is generally uncommon, as most governments now recognize the net benefits of inward investment. Nowadays, countries seek to attract greater inflows of FDI, rather than seize foreign assets, which, naturally, would have the opposite effect.

Although the risks described above may not occur in practice, they can nevertheless have a profound influence on the decision making of international firms. It can be argued that the lower the psychic distance between home and host countries, the easier it is for firms to perceive more accurately their exposure to risk in international business. The degree of trust between the MNE and the firms it deals with (joint venture partners, licensees, agents, customers) may also shape managers' perceptions of risk.

1.10   The GATT and the WTO   关税与贸易总协定及世界贸易组织

International business activities are conducted by people across the borders of countries which have many differences in terms of political system, law, culture, history, economic level and so on. Different nations have their own policies to do international business. Unfortunately, the policies of different nations differ from one another. In order to promote international business, especially international trade, organizations such as the World Trade Organization (WTO) came into being. In this way, countries that engage in international trade can observe the same "game rules".

The WTO originated from the General Agreement on Tariffs and Trade (GATT).

The GATT was an association founded in 1947 with 23 member countries in the beginning. In the following year, the GATT started to operate. Those countries formed the association to negotiate reductions in trade restrictions and work toward common procedures in doing international trade.

Generally speaking, the GATT's key function was to establish a basic set of rules under which international trade could take place, to regulate international business conduct and to provide a forum for tariff negotiation, bargaining and international trade dispute settlements.

The GATT's most important activity was sponsoring rounds (sessions) which were named after the place where the round took place. For example, the Tokyo Round, the Uruguay Round. The rounds led to some multilateral reductions in tariffs and non-tariff barriers for its members. Most-favoured nation status for its members and non-discrimination in any new restrictions were included. Countries agreed to reduce tariffs on all products from all countries by a given percentage over some specified time period. But not all countries lowered their tariffs by the same percentage.

Besides tariff concerns, negotiating rounds deal with complex non-tariff barriers, especially in the following five areas:

(1) Industry standard;

(2) Government procurement;

(3) Subsidies and countervailing duties (duties in response to another country's protectionist measures);

(4) Licensing;

(5) Customs valuation.

The GATT had many accomplishments, but it had inherent weaknesses. In 1986, the Uruguay Round of negotiations of the GATT started and it was concluded in December 1993. One of the main achievements of the Uruguay Round was the agreement to found the World Trade Organization as an international body with permanent existence with effect from 1st January, 1995.

Conclusion of the Uruguay Round created the most significant trade agreement in the GATT's history, estimated by the OECD (Organization for Economic Cooperation and Development) to be sure to increase income by at least US $259 billion annually. The United States and the EU cut tariffs on the other's products by 50% immediately, with more cuts to follow.

Despite its occasional difficulties, there can be no doubt that since 1947, the GATT has reduced tariff levels significantly across a wide range of products throughout the world, has encouraged "good behaviour" in international trade practice and has led to much useful dialogue and communication among countries.

The WTO was founded in order to replace the GATT and deal with its shortcomings. Today, the WTO is enforcing the provisions of the GATT. The WTO is the legal and institutional foundation of the multilateral trading system. It provides the principal contractual obligations determining how governments frame and implement domestic trade legislation and regulations. Further, the WTO is the platform on which trade relations between countries evolve through collective debate, negotiation and adjudication.

The WTO is now responsible for providing a framework for trading relationships between countries and it plays a similar part to that of the International Monetary Fund and the World Bank.

The WTO provides the institutional framework for the multilateral trading system. It administers rules for international trade, provides a mechanism for setting disputes, and offers a forum for conducting trade negotiations, as set forth in the WTO agreements, which refer to some international trade agreements such as the WTO's predecessor, the General Agreement on Tariffs and Trade.

Under the WTO, there is a clearly defined dispute settlement mechanism. Disputes among the member countries may bring charges to a WTO panel whose rulings are binding. The WTO's dispute-settlement body has had a much heavier caseload than that under the old GATT's system. By bringing cases to the panel, accused countries may agree to settle before a ruling is made. For example, the trade conflicts between the EU and the USA over bananas, beef hormones, and export subsidies were referred to the WTO for settlement.

The WTO members are required to grant the same favourable trade conditions to all WTO members. But in the cases of regional trade agreements, the WTO allows exceptions from the principle. Nearly all of the WTO members have signed regional agreements with other nations.

The WTO rules cover 90 percent of world trade and those rules are based on the following principles.

(1) Non-discrimination: It means that each member nation must use the same rates of tariff to imports from all member nations. This principle is sometimes known as the application of Most

Favoured Nation Treatment to all WTO members.

(2) Resolution of disputes via consultation: The disputes among the member nations are to be solved through consultation though dumping (selling goods below the cost of production) may be counteracted by retaliatory measures targeted at the offending country.

(3) Non-legality of quantitative restrictions on imports unless a country is "underdeveloped" or/and experiencing severe balance of payments difficulties, or an agricultural or fisheries product is involved.

Countries in dispute first try to settle their problems bilaterally. If this fails, a WTO working party investigates the matter and makes a recommendation. If the offending country should ignore the recommendation, the aggrieved country is permitted to retaliate.

1.10.1　Differences Between the GATT and the WTO　关税与贸易总协定与世界贸易组织之差异

The GATT is not an organization but a treaty which countries signed to become contracting parties but not members. The GATT lacks permanence, as it offers only provisional application. This reduces its effectiveness as the basis for a rule-based system of world trade.

A member of the WTO has to adhere to all and not just some of these agreements while GATT agreements allowed countries to comply only with those agreements that they were contracted to.

The GATT applied only to trade in merchandise goods; the WTO covers trade in goods, services and trade in "ideas" or intellectual property.

In 1998 the WTO started to focus attention on potential international trade gains from electronic commerce.

1.10.2　Problems with the WTO　世界贸易组织存在的问题

The WTO is certainly playing a very important role in international business. Problems, however, exist with the WTO. The main problems with the WTO are as follows (Roger Bennett & Jim Blythe, 2002, p.74):

(1) Rule changes require a two-thirds majority of members. There is "one vote, one country" regardless of the size of the voting countries.

(2) Policing the use of hidden non-tariff barriers has proved difficult. As soon as one variety of hidden barrier is outlawed, another might be invented.

(3) An increasing number of governments outside the major trade blocs are currently advocating bilateral trade treaties as a means for counteracting the power of the regional trade groupings. To the extent that bilateral agreements are concluded, they undermine the WTO's position and influence.

(4) The wording of the main WTO agreement is vague and complicated, making it quite easy to circumvent commitments.

(5) The WTO itself cannot impose sanctions.

1.10.3 China and the WTO 中国与世界贸易组织

On December 11th, 2001, China officially became one of the members of the WTO after a long period of 15 years' negotiations with the WTO member countries. During that period, China had gradually liberalized most of her trade and improved her investment policies, making the official admission largely symbolic. It is quite significant for China to join the WTO. It will certainly facilitate China's international trade. And this should reinforce moves towards market liberalization. The WTO membership signals China's commitment to establish clear and enforceable non-discriminatory rules to conduct business within this country and with other countries as well.

It is well-known that China is among the developing countries. But China is becoming relatively powerful in the world's economy. By joining the WTO, China can enjoy many favourable rights in doing international business, but in the meantime, China has to perform her obligations. There are more advantages than disadvantages for China to join the WTO though China's national industries may meet great impact.

Since China has already become one of the WTO members, its economic growth will greatly increase and its legal and governmental reforms will be facilitated.

According to a WTO report, which was released on October 10, 2002, China has become the fourth largest trade body in the world following the Triad: the United States, the European Union and Japan. The improved trade environment following its entry into the WTO resulted in the rapid growth in China's trade volume. Therefore, it can be seen that China's entry into the WTO has great positive impact on China's international business.

Since China became one of the members of the WTO, more foreign investments have been flowing into this country, which is opposite to the prediction that foreign investment would decrease after China's entry into the WTO. This is because China has rich, low-cost labor resources and a vast market, both of which provide much scope for profit and make foreign investors more confident in China. Besides, the stable and promising political and economic situations attract foreign investors.

China must observe the same "game rules" as the other members of the WTO do, which will speed up its step to integrate its economy into the global economic framework. Besides, China's entry into the WTO will help private businesses to improve their growth. The Chinese government must also grant equal rights to all enterprises no matter whether they are state-owned or private ones according to the WTO equal treatment principle.

The functions of the Chinese government will change to some extent. In order to meet the requirement of its WTO membership, the government has initiated a campaign to clarify and unify governmental regulations to meet the WTO rules. More than 2,300 regulations were abolished or revised by 30 departments under the State Council.

Joining the WTO would commit China to a path that would engage more and more of its citizens in international business. Their livelihood would increasingly depend on China's attracting foreign investors and maintaining friendly relations with most of the world's nations.

On the other hand, however, the entry also has great impact on China's economy. Chinese products with comparative advantages have been seriously affected owing to an increase in anti-dumping allegations and the block of green barriers—import restrictions on the grounds of environmental and food safety.

What's more, the increased anti-dumping allegations resulted in the price disorder of Chinese enterprises.

Moreover, the agreement between China and the United States on China's entry into the WTO allows for the United States to adopt emergency measures to limit imports from China if those imports are deemed to be increasing too rapidly and may potentially jeopardize local production.

The entry into the WTO will inevitably make some people lose their jobs because of intense competition.

It is not likely that foreign companies or foreign capital will be able to absorb all the unemployed. It is also feared that China's environmental situation, which is precarious, will not benefit from WTO accession.

1. What Should China Do After the Entry into the WTO?

After fifteen years of negotiations, on November 10, 2001 at the World Trade Organization (WTO) Ministerial Conference in Doha, Qatar, WTO members formally approved the accession package for the People's Republic of China. China became a full member, the WTO's 143rd, on December 11, 2001.

The negotiations with China, as was the case with all WTO accession negotiations, consisted of three parts. China provided information to the WTO Working Party pertaining to its trade regime, which was updated throughout the 15 years of negotiations. Next, each interested WTO member negotiated a bilateral agreement with China concerning market access concessions and commitments for goods and services. These concessions and commitments were then formulated into two documents, *China's Goods and Services Schedules*, which apply to all WTO members. Simultaneously, China participated in multilateral negotiations with Working Party members on the rules that would govern trade with China. These documents are available at www.wto.org.

China has agreed to implement systematic reforms designed to establish a more transparent and predictable regime for business dealings.

To promote transparency, China will regularly publish those laws and regulations in official journals with relevant information including the responsible government entity and the effective date of the measure. In addition, China will create inquiry points, which will operate on 30-day-response times, to permit companies to obtain information about these laws and regulations. Furthermore, China has agreed to provide notice of laws and regulations, allowing reasonable time for comment, prior to implementation or enforcement. China plans to translate all trade laws and regulations into one or more of the WTO languages (English, French and Spanish), including those that will have to be drafted or revised as China comes into compliance with its WTO obligations. China has committed to the maximum extent possible to provide translated versions of trade laws and regulations prior to implementation, but in no case later than 90 days post-implementation.

China has also made a commitment that will help foster predictability in business dealings. It agreed to apply, implement and administer all of its laws and regulations relating to trade in goods and services in a uniform and impartial manner throughout China. China will have to do something about the following:

(1) Tariffs

China has committed to significantly reducing its tariffs on industrial products. These reductions had already begun in preparation for China's accession to the WTO. China's industrial tariffs will decline from a 1997 average of 25 percent to 8.9 percent. Nearly all of these reductions will be and have been completed. For a few products, reductions will continue until 2010.

China will completely eliminate its tariffs on beer, furniture and toys. The 1997 tariffs on these products averaged 70 percent, 22 percent and 23 percent respectively. Other product sectors where China has agreed to substantial tariff reduction are: cosmetics, distilled spirits, medical equipment, motor vehicles, paper products, scientific equipment and textiles. Additionally, China will join the *Information Technology Agreement* (ITA).

(2) Service Commitments

China has agreed to significant liberalization in a broad range of service sectors through eliminating market access restrictions, particularly in sectors of importance to the United States, including banking, insurance, telecommunications and professional services, accounting, legal and management consultancy services.

(3) Trading Rights and Distribution

China restricts the number of companies that have the right to import and export goods and the products that can be imported by these companies. China has agreed to eliminate any export performance, prior experience requirements and trade or foreign exchange balancing as criteria for obtaining or maintaining the right to import and export. Chinese enterprises will now have full trading rights, subject to certain minimum registered capital requirements. Joint ventures with minority foreign ownership will be granted full trading rights within one year and joint ventures with majority foreign ownership will be granted full trading rights within two years after accession. All enterprises in China will be granted full trading rights within three years after accession (except for limited products reserved for trade by state enterprises). According to the new trade law that became effective on the 1st of July 2004, even individuals are granted to engage in international trade.

(4) Trade-related Intellectual Property Rights

China's implementation of the WTO *Agreement on Trade-Related Aspects of Intellectual Property* (TRIPs) is an important step toward improving its intellectual property environment. Pursuant to the 1992 and 1995 bilateral intellectual property agreements and 1996 action plan, China has made steady progress in improving its intellectual property regime. However, the United States looks to China for continued improvement concerning the enforcement of intellectual property rights. The USA has developed a strong dialogue with China on this issue and China's officials recognize the need for more effective action to address this continuing problem.

(5) Import Licensing

China's import licensing system can no longer function as a trade barrier and must comply with the principles of national treatment and nondiscrimination.

(6) Importation and Investment Approvals

Importation and investment approvals can no longer be conditioned on whether competing domestic suppliers exist or on performance requirements of any kind, such as export performance, local content, technology transfer, offsets, foreign exchange balancing, or research and development. China has further agreed that it will only impose, apply or enforce laws, regulations or other measures relating to the transfer of technology that are consistent with the *WTO Agreement on Trade-related Investment Measures* and the *TRIPs Agreement*.

(7) Technical Barriers to Trade

In accordance with the *WTO Technical Barriers to Trade* (TBT) Agreement, China cannot use technical regulations, standards and conformity assessment procedures as unnecessary obstacles to trade. China will now base technical regulations on international standards. These regulations must now be developed in a transparent manner and applied equally to domestic and foreign products.

(8) Taxes

China has agreed to ensure that its laws, regulations and other measures relating to internal taxes and charges levied on imports comply with WTO rules and are applied in a nondiscriminatory manner. This obligation applies not only to national taxes but also to provincial and local taxes.

(9) Subsidies

China has agreed to eliminate, upon accession, all subsidies on industrial goods that are prohibited under WTO rules, i.e. export and import substitution subsidies.

2. Implications of Membership in the WTO for China

Due to the huge population of the country, China holds a certain fascination for international business. China is destined to become a major player in the world, both for manufacturing and potential sales. The pros and cons of WTO membership for China and how that impacts the rest of the world are studied as follows:

(1) Positives

The membership will deny other countries the ability to discriminate against China on trade matters. WTO membership will allow China to be heard in the international economic arena and to enjoy the privileges, like having access to the WTO mechanism for trade disputes.

There will be a shot in the arm for Chinese goods with free access to world markets. The main beneficiary will be those industries in which China has competitive advantages, like textile, home appliances, bicycles and motorcycles, food, and toys. There will be restructuring in the economy and many jobs will be created in those industries that have the ability to capitalize on the opportunities to export to the world markets.

China will be forced to upgrade its economy to international standards and eliminate unacceptable practices. These include respect for intellectual property, free access to markets, non-discriminatory and unfair practices, and respect for the rule of law.

One main beneficiary is Hong Kong, which traditionally serves as a conduit between China and the rest of the world. The China's boom will enable Hong Kong to sustain and increase its economic role.

Chinese consumers will enjoy the fruits of a capitalist economy, with more choices of goods and services. In addition, prices will be lower and customer service will improve owing to more competition.

(2) Negatives

Many state-owned enterprises (SOEs) that were used to the centrally-planned economic system will be eliminated. They are struggling with archaic machinery and old production methods, shoddy products, disregard for customers, heavy debt, and a stubborn, undisciplined, old workforce. They will be unable to survive open competition.

Chinese farmers, who lack modern farming techniques, machinery, and economy of scale, will be overwhelmed by foreign agricultural produce.

Enormous labor restructuring will happen, which is unprecedented in the modern world. Labor will migrate from rural to urban centers to seek job opportunities. Millions of employees in the lower skill categories, including a high proportion of older people, will be jobless without skill retraining. At the same time, there will be shortage of people needed to fill New Economy positions, like IT, telecommunication, law, finance, foreign trade, biotechnology, etc.

Many industries will be affected. One of the biggest industries to suffer in China will be the car industry. It is protected by high tariffs and lacks the economy of scale to be competitive. It will be attacked by imports at lower prices but of better quality.

Under WTO rules, tariffs will eventually be eliminated, and there will be no requirement for export quota and transfer of technology for local production. China will be under pressure to develop its own technology.

(3) Rights and Obligations

China has accepted the rights and obligations that are embodied in the WTO Agreements, including the fundamental principles of national and most-favored-nation treatment. Trade disputes involving China can now be settled under the WTO's integrated dispute settlement mechanism, a central element in providing security and predictability to the multilateral trading system. In addition, China has made a large number of specific commitments to bring its trade regime into conformity with WTO obligations.

Transparency will be substantially improved and all trade-related laws and regulations will be published and available upon request for comment before they are implemented.

China will establish procedures for companies, both domestic and foreign, which are affected by trade-related judicial or administrative decisions to request formal reviews by independent and impartial tribunals.

Product standards and standards-related procedures will be improved and brought in line with international practice.

China will eliminate requirements to export, produce foreign exchange, and transfer technology previously imposed on foreign investors. China will not introduce new or maintain existing export subsidies; and the protection of intellectual property rights will be strengthened.

WTO membership will require changes in the structure of China's economy, in the relationship between government and industry, and in government structures, procedures, legal and regulatory frameworks. These changes will take some time. However, the benefits for China will be substantial. China's export industries will obtain secure and predictable access to foreign markets, generating further job opportunities and promoting economic growth. Liberalized investment rules, a more transparent regulatory framework, and better export market access will attract foreign investors and bring technology and jobs as well. Greater competition within China will improve economic efficiency and productivity in the long run.

1.11 China in International Business Arena 国际商务舞台上的中国

China has already become a major economic force in the international business arena. With nearly one quarter of the world's population, China has experienced remarkable growth since it began to liberalize its economy in 1979. It is forecasted that China will become the largest economy in the world by 2020 (World Bank forecast). Now it is well known that China has become the second largest economy of the world.

Since 1990 annual GDP growth has easily exceeded that of any of the former "Four Asian Tigers" economies. This has been accompanied by rapid increases in international trade and inward investment through a variety of vehicles including bonds, equity investment and joint ventures. This has been accompanied by a massive restructuring of China's economic system including its financial institutions and accounting system. New accounting laws, largely based on IASs, are being introduced and the accounting system is currently undergoing substantial changes.

China is a rapidly growing economic power, which increasingly offers tremendous opportunities for international business ventures in the areas of manufacturing, investment, technology transfer and trade. As the world's most populous nation, China is considered a huge market for international business. China is still a poor country, but it is hoped that access to the global economy will change that.

China has emerged as the fastest growing economy in the world since opening its door in the late 1970s. With economic growth averaging 7.8 percent annually, China has quadrupled the size of its economy. It has vastly outperformed India in terms of economic development and forced many of its neighbouring countries to re-evaluate their positions in today's global economy. China is transforming itself from a rural society to an urban society, from an agricultural economy to a manufacturing economy, and from a centrally planned economy to a state-managed market economy "with Chinese characteristics".

During the 1980s, the rise of skyscrapers in Shenzhen and in Shanghai was an indication that China was beginning to engage in international business, making a slow and smooth transition from a planned economy to a socialist market economy. Along with the skyscrapers came the establishment of global brand names such as McDonald's and Coca-Cola. This led to the prevailing belief that China was beginning to open the door to the outside world. In other words, China intended and was ready to be involved in international business.

Since the gradual deregulation of state industries, China has made the transition from a planned economy to a socialist market economy. The elements of a free market that China has adopted led to Gross Domestic Product growth of seven to eight percent annually. This growth held steady. While some other countries were concentrating on increasing their exports, China focused on domestic industries. With a population of 1.3 billion, China was able to sustain strong domestic demand despite export declines while other economies in the region floundered.

Around that time, major foreign corporations started to invest in China. For example, US businesses recognized the diversity of China's economic spectrum and the country's wide range of markets, including both the prosperous and the impoverished.

China's accession to the World Trade Organization is quite significant to both China and the outside world. It also shows the important role China plays in international business. It provides foreign businesses with opportunities for the expansion in China. On the other hand, China reaps enormous benefits from the vitality of the business relations with other nations. It can also infiltrate other markets as a result of more international respectability in the economic arena. It has been estimated that, by the year 2020 China will be not only the world's most populous nation, but also the world's largest economy, a superpower in every sense of the word and that China's economy will be worth $10 trillion by the year 2050.

Economically, China has been progressing impressively over the last two decades, and by winning the 2008 Olympics bid, it has also hauled itself out of the political doldrums. This international spectacle will hoist the red flag of China to an even higher level in both the economic and political arenas. China is playing a very important role in international economy.

The beginning of this new century proved to be a new start for China's economy to mount up, and the whole world is attracted by its vigorous economic and trade growth. With China's entry into the World Trade Organization and the all-round exploitation of its West and North-East, China is now advancing into a new economic era, integrating simultaneously into the international market.

In the past ten to fifteen years, China's international position has been greatly enhanced. China is now a very important country in the world's affairs. It is predicted that China will become the most powerful economic country soon or later.

Summary of This Chapter
本章概要

1. 国际商务是不同国家政府及其企业、个人之间所进行的商务活动。全球的经济正在发生巨大的变化。国与国之间的商务活动更加频繁。尽管不同国家之间有种种差异，但是全球经济趋于大同是不可逆转的趋势。从微观上来说，国际商务主要涉及的范围有：对外直接投资、组合投资、特许经营、许可证贸易、交钥匙工程、管理合同、进出口贸易、第三产业贸易等。此外，国际商务所涉及的领域主要有：国际营销、国际人力资源管理、国际金融、国际经济、国际企业会计、国际物流、国际企业文化等。

2. 公司、企业寻求国际商务的主要原因有：(1)扩大销售额，获取外国资源；(2)拓展业务范围；(3)国内市场已经饱和；(4)从国外寻找谋取利润的机会；(5)获取国内缺乏的原材料、产品、技术；(6)分散商业风险；(7)国内竞争过于激烈；(8)大势所趋(全球经济一体化)；(9)获得国际竞争经验以适应未来的挑战。

3. 全球化：全球化意味着突破空间和时间概念，视整个世界为一个整体，全球共同享有信息、文化和知识等。从国际商务的角度来看，通过国际经济、国际贸易、国际金融、国际投资等向全球辐射和交叉，形成一个打破区域的国际商务系统。

4. 市场的全球化意味着整个世界从传统的分离市场逐渐形成一个国际大市场。生产的全球化意味着各个公司、企业在世界范围内寻求商品和服务，以充分利用各个国家的优势。从管理的角度来看，全球化意味着公司要从全球的高度来制定策略和管理企业。

5. 商务全球化是促使公司、企业发展的动力，一旦条件成熟，公司的管理层必须考虑向国外拓展。对许多公司来说，生产技术及通信技术的迅猛发展使全球化变得更容易控制和管理。

6. 推动全球化的两个重要因素：(1)第二次世界大战后，商品、服务及资本的自由流动的障碍减少了；(2)科学技术的迅猛发展，尤其是最近一些年来通信、信息处理和运输技术的飞速发展。第二次世界大战后，在美国的倡导下，联合其他一些西方国家，签订了《关税与贸易总协定》(GATT)。后来，在该协定的基础上成立了世界贸易组织(WTO)。成员国之间的关税率逐步下降。此外，许多国家逐步取消了对外直接投资的限制，这样公司更容易进入国外市场。其结果是促进了生产全球化和市场全球化。减少贸易壁垒也促进生产全球化。

7. 技术创新促进了市场全球化。集装箱化大大降低了运输成本。低成本的通信网络有助于创建电子全球市场。由于旅行的便利，世界变得越来越小，缩短了各国文化的距离，使消费者的购买习惯和倾向趋于相似。全球化引起专家、学者的争议，主要围绕着全球化对就业、工资、环境、工作条件和国家主权的影响等方面。

8. 关税与贸易总协定(GATT)(简称"关贸总协定")是一项调整各国在国际贸易政策方面的相互权利与义务的多边条约，是一个贸易谈判的场所，也是一个调节与解决各国之间国际贸易争端的机构。关贸总协定从1948年1月1日临时实施，一直到1996年12月31日与世界贸易组织并存1年结束，共存在了48年。关贸总协定在国际贸易中发挥了历史性的重要作用，它一直致力于各国国际贸易政策的协调，成功地主持了8轮世界范围的多边关税和贸易谈判,其涵盖面几乎涉及国际贸易领域的各个方面,既有传统的货物贸易,又有服务贸易、知识产权及与国际贸易有关的投资措施等三大新议题。关贸总协定不仅调整国际贸易政策,还协调各国贸易关系。关贸总协定和国际货币基金组织及世界银行一起,构成了第二次世界大战后世界经济的三大支柱。

9. 世界贸易组织(WTO)是国际贸易体制发展至今所形成的一种较高层的国际贸易体制。1990年意大利提出建立多边贸易组织(MTO)。1993年12月15日乌拉圭回合结束时根据美国的动议将"多边贸易组织"改为"世界贸易组织"(WTO)。1995年1月1日,世界贸易组织正式成立。世界贸易组织源自关税和贸易总协定(GATT),但不是对GATT的扬弃,而是在GATT基础上的发展和创新,不是简单照搬,但也不是完全否定。世界贸易组织有责任仲裁贸易争端和监督成员国的贸易政策。关贸总协定和世界贸易组织在许多方面是相同的,如提高生活水平、保证充分就业、保证实际收入和有效需求扩大、促进生产和贸易等方面。两者之间所不同的是,世界贸易组织在下列两个方面将关贸总协定的有关理念向前推进了一步:(1)《建立世界贸易组织的协定》提出了"寻求对环境的保护和维护"。(2)《建立世界贸易组织的协定》表明,协定各成员国认识到发展中国家在全球经济和社会发展中的重要性,因而提出给予发展中国家和最不发达国家"根据它们各自需要和不同经济发展水平的情况加强采取各种相应的措施"的待遇。

10. 世界贸易组织的宗旨是:(1)提高生活水平,保证充分就业和有效需求;(2)扩大生产和商品交易,扩大服务贸易;(3)倡导全球经济、社会和环境相协调的可持续发展之路;(4)重视发展中国家利益,谋求世界经济整体发展。世界贸易组织实行一系列重要原则:无歧视待遇原则(Non-discrimination)、最惠国待遇原则(Most-Favoured-Nation Treatment)、国民待遇原则(National Treatment)、贸易自由化原则(Free Trade)、互惠原则(Reciprocity)、一般取消数量限制原则(General Elimination of Quantitative Restrictions)、透明度原则(Transparency)、市场准入原则(Market Access)、对发展中国家优惠待遇原则(Preferential Treatment towards Developing Countries),公平、平等处理贸易争端原则(Settlement of Disputes in Justice and Equity)。

11. 中国加入世界贸易组织是大势所趋,总的来说,入世是利大于弊,既有机遇,又有挑战。入世后,中国可以享受以下权利:(1)中国的产品可以在世界贸易组织的其他成员国中享有多边的、无条件的最惠国待遇;(2)中国出口到所有发达国家的制成品和半制成品可享受"普惠制"待遇,以及其他给予发展中国家的特殊照顾;(3)中国可以利用世界贸易组织的多边争端解决机制来维护本国的合法权益;(4)中国可以在多边贸易组织中参与制定经济全球化规则。另一方面,入世后中国须承担以下义务:(1)进一步减让关税;(2)进一步取消非关税措施;(3)取消被禁止的出口补贴;(4)开放服务市场;(5)扩大对知识产权的保护范围;(6)放宽和改善外资政策;(7)增加贸易政策的透明度。

12. 入世对中国的意义和影响都非常大。入世后,国家必须调整外贸政策,改革外贸体制,将有关的法律、法规作相应的调整,政府有关部门也需要进行改革、调整以适应国际贸易组织的原则要求。(1)入世给中国的农业带来冲击(政府农业管理体制冲击、农产品价格冲击、农业生产结构影响、农民就业和收入的冲击,等等)。(2)入世后,中国的民族产业面临严峻挑战和冲击,中国工业必须作调整。不过,入世后的工业对外开放中我国仍有一定的产业保护政策。(3)入世后,给中国的纺织业带来机遇:相对宽松的出口环境、出口地区的多元化态势、竞争机制的引入。但是,入世对中国纺织业也带来挑战:保护结构解体,缺乏竞争力的行业受到冲击,配额制的保护功能将被自由竞争所取代。(4)入世后,中国的汽车行业受到冲击:汽车市场部分失去,汽车的销售和服务体系受到很大冲击,等等。(5)入世后,中国的石油石化工业和经济利益受到很大冲击,市场占有率将可能进一步下降,投资风险增加,利用外资和引进技术的难度将增大。(6)入世后,中国的信息产业受到影响:《信息技术产品协定》受到影响,外国信息技术企业进入中国市场所带来的影响,产业结构影响,信息技术交流与信息技术封锁并存。(7)入世后,中国银行业受到冲击:争夺市场,争夺人才,银行资信和资产质量受到影响。(8)入世后,中国的保险业受到影响:中国的保险业资本竞争势力薄弱,经营技术薄弱,保险资金投资渠道狭窄,因而很难和外国同行业竞争。(9)入世后,中国的电信业面临挑战:给民族通信设备制造业带来巨大压力,中国国内电信业务领域竞争形势将更加严峻,影响中国电信企业的有序发展,加剧中国电信业发展的不平衡态势。(10)入世后,中国的运输业迎来机遇和发展机会,但也带来挑战。中国的运输业体制、政策必须作出相应的调整以适应世界性的运输业激烈竞争。此外,入世后对中国的专业服务也有冲击,如法律服务业、会计/审计服务业等行业将迎接挑战。

13. 当前世界格局在大调整中加剧分化,世界经济正处于弱增长中低通胀阶段,市场不确定性增多。中国已经成为世界第二经济大国。中国经济今后一段时间,始终还会在一定增长速度的基础上继续前行。中国经济的发展只是到了某个阶段。未来中国很有可能成为世界第一经济大国。随着中国经济在世界地位中的不断上升,中国国际地位的提升比以往任何时候都显著。目前中国是世界上最大、综合实力最强的发展中国家,在国际事务中的影响力不断增大,已经成为国际政治、经济舞台上的一支重要力量。

New Words and Expressions

abrogate v. 取消;废除

accession n. (对条约等的)正式接受(或加入);就职;同意

agrifood n. 农业食品

allegation n. 断言;(尤指提不出证明的)辩解

alliance n. 联盟,同盟

allocation n. 分配;分派

approach n.& v. (处理问题的)方式,方法;途径;靠近;(着手)处理(问题等)

archaic a. 过时的

at length 详尽地;最后

bout n. 回合;较量

bring to a halt 使……停止

capitalize on 利用

circumvent v. 围绕;回避

composite v. & n. & a. 混合;合成物;复合的

convergence n. (异族文化等的)趋同;汇合点

copyright n. 版权

countervail v. 补偿;抵消

decouple v. 拆开;使分离

deregulation n. 撤销管制;规定

discipline v. & n. 使有条不紊;控制;行为准则;学科

doldrums n.(pl.) 忧郁;低潮;无生气

emancipation n. 解放

enhance v. 增大(价值、吸引力);增强;提

高……的价值

expertise *n. & v.* 专门知识（或技能）；专长；（进行）专业鉴定

expropriation *n.* 没收财产；征用土地；侵占

extend one's range 发挥才能

flounder *v. & n.* 挣扎

foster *v.* 培养；促进；抱（希望等）

franchise *v. & n.* 给……以特许权（使用等）；（经营）特权

give rise to 引起；导致

globalization *n.* 全球化

hike *v. & n.* 抬高（价格等）；提高；增加

impartial *a.* 公正的

impoverish *v.* 使贫困

infiltrate *v.* 渗入；渗透

infringement *n.* 违反；侵害

instantaneous *a.* 瞬间的

interdiscipline *v.* 跨学科

irreversible *a.* 不可逆转的；不可挽回的；不可撤销的

know-how *n.* 专有技术；技术秘密

license *v. & n.* 准许；发许可证；许可证；执照

lucrative *a.* 生利的；挣钱的

merchandise *n.* 商品

nullify *v.* 使……无效；废除；取消

outlaw *v. & n.* 剥夺；取缔；被剥夺公民权的人

panel *n.* 陪审团；评判小组；一组调查对象

patent *n. & v.* 专利；专利权；给予……专利

权；取得……的专利权

pertain to 符合；关于

propel *v.* 推动；推进

pros and cons 赞成者和反对者；正面和反面

protectionism *n.* （贸易）保护主义

psychic *a. & n.* 精神的；心灵的；超自然的；通灵的人

recompilation *n.* 再编制

rectification *n.* 修改；修正

reinforce *v. & n.* 增援；支援

retaliatory *a.* 报复性的

royalties *n.* 版税；专利权使用费

sanction *v. & n.* 认可；批准；赞许；鼓励；法令

saturate *v.* 使……饱和

shoddy *a. & n.* 假冒的；假货

strategy *n.* 策略；战略

stride *v. & n.* 迈进；进展

substantive *a.* （法律）实体的，规定权利和义务的

supplement *n. & v.* 增补（物）；增补；补充

tangible *a. & n.* 有形的；明确的；有形资产

trade mark 商标

turnkey operation 交钥匙工程

underpin *v.* 加强……的基础；支持；证实

unfurling *n.* 打开；展示

vehicle *n.* 运载工具；车辆；媒介物

vitality *n.* 生命力；活力

watchdog *n.* 监察人

> Discussion Questions

1. What is the difference between international business and international trade?

2. Why do companies engage in international business?

3. Why do we say that globalization is the trend of international business?

4. What are the advantages and disadvantages of China's joining the WTO?

5. China has become the second largest economic country, is it true?

Chapter 2 // The Framework of International Business 国际商务框架

Objectives
学习目标

To describe economic integration.

讲述经济一体化。

To provide an overview of the layout of international business.

概述国际商务之框架。

To present different regional trading groups like the EU and the NAFTA.

讲述世界主要经济联盟（如欧盟和北美自由贸易区）。

International business learners must know, among other things, the framework of international business. It is beneficial and necessary to keep in mind the global picture of international business. In addition, international business practitioners also need know the whole picture of the world in terms of international business, with specific reference to the part of the world in which they conduct international business.

International economic integration makes the member nations interdependent on each other and the fortune of each member country depends on the performance of the body as a whole. The main consequence for international management of the formation of regional trading blocs is that business decisions increasingly need to relate to (at least) several countries as a whole and not just as individual nations. Decisions with regard to extents and locations of the subsidiary activities of international business will be affected as much by the following desires as by any other consideration (Roger Bennett, 1999, p.11).

(1) To avoid high common external tariffs.

(2) To obtain local investment grants and subsidies.

(3) To satisfy the requirements of regional (rather than national) consumer segments.

The following discussion is based on the regional, rather than national, and economic integration.

2.1   Levels of Economic Integration   经济一体化的层次

Some nations integrate themselves into an economic organization (a kind of trading bloc) for their common and respective interests. They can be formed at different levels.

2.1.1   The Free Trade Area (FTA)   自由贸易区

The first level of economic integration is the free trade area. It involves the elimination of tariffs on trade among the countries in the regional group. Each member country of the group expects to gain by specializing in the production of goods and services in which it possesses comparative advantages and by importing from other member countries in the group products and services in which it faces comparative disadvantages. In other words, in a free trade area, all barriers to trade among member countries are removed. They can trade freely in much the same way they trade in their own countries. No discriminatory taxes, quotas, tariffs, or other barriers to trade are allowed.

A free trade agreement is signed by and between the FTA member countries. The agreement normally begins modestly by eliminating tariffs on goods that already have low tariffs, and there is usually an implementation period over which all tariffs are eliminated on all products. While the tariffs are being eliminated, the member countries of an FTA might explore other forms of cooperation, such as the reduction of non-tariff barriers or the trade in service and investment. The main focus of an FTA is on tariffs, though. The member countries may maintain their own external tariff against non-FTA countries.

The key free trade areas in the world, which will be discussed in detail later, are as follows:

A. The European Free Trade Association (EFTA);

B. The Central European Free Trade Agreement (CEFTA);

C. The North American Free Trade Agreement (NAFTA);

D. The Association of South East Asian Nations (ASEAN).

It is necessary to point out that a free trade area differs from a free trade zone.

A free trade zone (a foreign trade zone) is a designed area where importers can defer payment of customs duty while further processing of products takes place. The free trade zone is a certain area which is normally located at or near an international port of a country. It acts as an offshore assembly plant. In the free trade zone, local people are employed and local financing for a tax-exempt commercial activity is used.

Most free trade zones are in developing countries. Free trade zones have the following advantages.

(1) Free trade zones attract private companies: firstly, the company pays the tariff only when the goods are going to be launched into the markets; secondly, manufacturing costs are lower because companies need not pay taxes; thirdly, the producer can repackage the goods, grade them, and check for spoilage.

(2) Free trade zones enable the domestic importing companies to compete more readily with foreign producers of subsidiaries of multinational enterprises (MNEs). In this way, participation in international trade is increased.

(3) Relatively speaking, there is a good climate for business because there is not so much bureaucracy in a free trade zone.

Free trade zones are a step toward free trade. Besides, free trade zones are a must if a nation hopes to be very competitive in international business.

2.1.2　The Customs Union　关税同盟

The second level of regional economic integration is the customs union. It is one step further along the spectrum of economic integration. Like a free trade area, it involves the elimination of tariffs among member countries. But, unlike a free trade area, the customs union also involves establishment of a common external tariff structure toward non-member countries. In other words, member countries of the customs union establish common tariff and quota barriers against non-member countries. Therefore, imports from non-member countries are subject to the same tariff when sold to any member country of the customs union. For example, the North American Free Trade Agreement (the NAFTA) member countries are Canada, the United States, and Mexico. The three countries trade with one another freely without tariffs, but each country maintains a separate tariff with non-member countries (In contrast, customs union member countries have the common tariff.). If a Chinese company exports a product to the USA, it will enter the USA at a different tariffs rate than if the product were exported to Canada or Mexico because each member country of the NAFTA can set its own external tariff rate. But if a Chinese company exports a product to Germany and France, the tariff rates of the two countries are the same to the Chinese company, because the two countries are both members of the European Union, which is also a customs union. Thus, there would be no tariff advantage to the Chinese company to enter the EU by exporting to Germany versus France.

2.1.3　The Common Market　共同市场

A common market has all the elements of a customs union. Besides, a common market removes restrictions on the movement of the factors of production—labour, capital, and technology—across borders. This means that labour is free to work in any country in the common market without any restriction (workers need not apply for a visa, in case of immigration). To put it simply, a common market has three characteristics:

(1) No barriers to trade among member nations;

(2) A common external trade policy;

(3) Mobility of factors of production among member countries.

A common market allows reallocation of production resources such as capital, labour, and technology, based on the theory of comparative advantage. In a common market, business methods, procedures, rules on competition, etc., are harmonized among member nations and there is free movement within the market of capital and labour as well as goods. Commercial laws drafted by the authorities of the common market override domestic national legislation. The best example of a successful common market is the European Union (EU) although this group has progressed beyond a common market and is now focusing on political integration.

2.1.4   The Economic Union   经济联盟

An economic union is a deep form of economic integration and is characterized by free movement of goods, services, and factors of production between member countries and full integration of economic policies. Besides, an economic union has the following characteristics:

(1) Unifying monetary and fiscal policy among the member nations;

(2) Sharing a common currency (or a permanently fixed exchange rate among currencies);

(3) Employing the same tax rates and structures for all members.

In addition, most of the national economic policies of each member nation are ceded to the group at large. So it is clear that the formation of an economic union requires nations to surrender a large measure of their national sovereignty. In fact, there is no true economic union existing today. But, as is known to all, the EU has created a common currency: the euro. And there is a common Central Bank as well. This level of cooperation creates a degree of political integration among member nations, which means they lose a bit of their sovereignty. Therefore, it can be said that the EU is moving towards a complete economic union.

Table 2.1 illustrates more about the four economic integration forms.

Table 2.1   Forms of International Economic Integration

Stage of Integration	Abolition of Tariffs Among Members	Common Tariff and Quota System	Abolition of Restrictions on Factor Movements	Harmonization and Unification of Economic Policies and Institutions
Free trade area	Yes	No	No	No
Customs union	Yes	Yes	No	No
Common market	Yes	Yes	Yes	No
Economic union	Yes	Yes	Yes	Yes

2.1.5   The Political Union   政治联盟

A political union has a single government with all economic policies unified. So a political union goes beyond full economic integration. Only when countries give up their national powers and are led under a single government can a real political union come into being. A good example is the United States of America, in which fifty independent states are integrated into a political union. Another example is the unification of West and East Germany in 1991. The two nations now have one government and one set of overall economic policies. The EU, as just mentioned above, is moving towards a political union in that the European Parliament is directly elected by citizens of the EU countries and the Council of Ministers of the EU is composed of government ministers from the member countries.

So far we have discussed the five levels of economic integration. Further, it is necessary to draw attention to the following four points.

(1) It is not necessary for a country to pursue economic integration by starting with a free trade area and then working up to a common market or an economic union.

(2) Economic integration in the form of free trade typically results in a winning situation for all group members, since each member can specialize in those goods and services it makes most efficiently and relies on others in the group to provide the remainder. However, when a bloc of countries imposes a tariff on non-members, this often leads to a win-lose situation instead of a win-win one.

(3) Complementary to the above, bloc members often find that their business is able to achieve internal economies of scale because of lower production costs and other savings within the firm.

(4) In the short run, some bloc countries may suffer because other member countries are able to achieve greater increases in efficiency and thus dominate certain industries and markets in the bloc.

To sum up, the five levels of economic integration discussed above present strategic alternatives for groups of countries that seek to increase their international (intragroup) trade and thus benefit from the larger market created by the integration group. It is necessary to know that the five levels of economic integration do not necessarily represent a sequence of steps toward political and economic union.

▶ 2.2 The Triad 三足鼎立(三大区域)

"Triad" refers to a group of three very important trading and investment blocs. The Triad refers to the USA, the EU and Japan. Quite a lot of international trade transactions are conducted by the Triad and most foreign direct investments (FDI) are from the Triad as well.

Some think of the Triad from a different perspective: the Triad comprises the EU, the signatories of the North American Free Trade Agreement (NAFTA) and the Pacific Rim. The European element of the Triad is based on the EU, the North America element on the USA, and the Asian element on Japan as Figure 2.1 illustrates.

Most international trade involves at least one member of the Triad.

The USA has the largest economy in the world. The USA, together with Canada and Mexico,

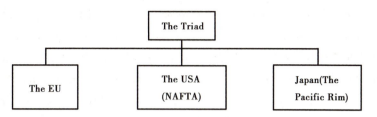

Figure 2.1　The Triad

implemented the North American Free Trade Agreement (NAFTA) in 1994. The USA economy is so large that it constitutes an entire segment of the Triad.

When we examine the current state of international business, it is worthwhile to pay close attention to the Triad. Every year countries from the Triad account for more trade and foreign direct investment (FDI) than the countries outside the Triad. Therefore, in the new century, the Triad will be the focus of international study. Lucrative markets exist in all three pillars of the Triad. To ignore any of them could result in great loss of potential sales. Besides, there are stratums of relatively homogenous customer types in all three regions of the Triad. As a result, the same products can be sold internationally in an essentially similar way. Further, there are some similarities of the core nations of the Triad, such as aging populations, common tastes and buying habits among the young, high consumers and so on.

It is supposed that during the first ten years of this new century, the Triad will still dominate the international business scene.

It is very necessary to point out that the Triad frame is changing. With China's rapid increase of her international position, China has replaced Japan in the Triad. Just as the international military Traid frame is made up of China, Russia and USA, the economic Triad is formed of the EU, USA and China.

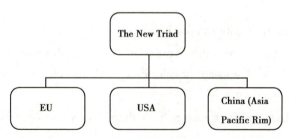

Figure 2.2　The New Triad

2.2.1　The European Union (EU)　欧盟

The EU is a group of 27 nations in Europe: Austria, Belgium, Denmark, Finland, Grmany, Greece, Ireland, Italy, Luxembourg, the Netherlands, Portugal, France, Spain, Sweden, Poland, Czech Republic, Hungary, Slovakia, Estonia, Latvia, Lithuania, Cyprus, Slovenia and Malta, Romania and Bulgaria. The last two nations joined the EU at the beginning of the year 2007.On July 1st,2013, the Republic of Croatia became the 28th member nation of the EU. After the UK's June of 2016 vote to leave the EU, it cannot be counted as a member of the EU. It will take the UK at least two years to eventually exit from the EU. Therefore, in this sense, the UK is still a member of the EU. Until Article 50 (of *the Lisbon Treaty*, the process by which a member state can leave the EU) is invoked, the UK will continue to engage with EU business as normal and be engaged in EU decision-making in the usual way. Once *the Lisbon Treaty* is invoked, the UK will remain bound by EU law until the terms of the UK's exist have been determined.

The period of the Great Depression from the late 1920s through World War Ⅱ was characterized by isolationism, protectionism, and fierce nationalism. Due to the economic chaos and political disorder of the period, no serious attempts at economic integration were made until the end of World War Ⅱ. From the devastation of the war, however, a spirit of cooperation gradually emerged in Europe.

The EU was founded in 1957. There were only six countries at that time (Belgium, France, Italy, Luxembourg, the Netherlands and West Germany). They signed the *Treaty of Rome*. The organization was originally called the European Economic Community (EEC). The following is a brief development of the EU.

(1) In 1946, Winston Churchill called for a United States of Europe.

(2) In 1947, the Marshall Plan for the economic revival of the Europe devastated by war was announced.

(3) In 1948, the Organization for European Economic Cooperation (OEEC) was created to coordinate the Marshall Plan.

(4) In 1949, the North Atlantic Treaty was signed.

(5) In 1951, the six countries (Belgium, France, German, Italy, Luxembourg, and the Netherlands) signed the Treaty of Paris establishing the European Coal and Steel Community (ECSC).

(6) In 1952, the ECSC Treaty entered into force.

(7) In 1957, the Six signed the *Treaties of Rome* establishing the European Economic Community (EEC) and the European Atomic Energy Community (Euratom or EAEC). They became effective on January 1,1958.

(8) In 1958, the basis for the Common Agriculture Policy was established.

(9) In 1959, the first steps were taken in the progressive abolition of customs duties and quotas within EEC.

(10) In 1960, the *Stockholm Convention* established the European Free Trade Association (EFTA) among seven European countries (Austria, Denmark, Norway, Portugal, Sweden, Switzerland, the United Kingdom). The OEEC became the Organization for Economic Cooperation and Development (OECD).

(11) In 1961, the first regulation on free movement of workers within the EEC came into force.

(12) In 1962, the Common Agriculture Policy was created.

(13) In 1965, a Treaty merging the ECSC, EEC, and Euratom was signed. The Treaty came

into force on July 1, 1967.

(14) In 1966, agreement was reached on a value-added tax (VAT) system; a treaty merging the Executives of the European Communities came into force; and the EEC changed its name to European Community (EC).

(15) In 1967, all remaining internal tariffs were eliminated and a common external tariff was imposed.

(16) In 1972, the "currency snake" was established where the Six agreed to limit currency fluctuations between their currencies to 2.25%.

(17) In 1973, Denmark, Ireland, and the United Kingdom became members of the EC.

(18) In 1974, the Council set up a European Regional Development Fund (ERDF) and Regional Policy Committee.

(19) In 1979, European Monetary System came into effect; European Parliament was elected by universal suffrage for the first time.

(20) In 1980, Greece became the tenth member of the EC.

(21) In 1985, commission sent the Council a White Paper on completion of internal market by 1992.

(22) In 1986, Spain and Portugal became the eleventh and twelfth members of the EC. Single European Act (SEA) was signed, improving decision-making procedures and increasing the role of the European Parliament, and came into effect on July 1, 1987.

(23) In 1989, collapse of the Berlin Wall; German Democratic Republic opened its borders.

(24) In 1990, the first phase of European Monetary Union (EMU) came into effect. Unification of Germany.

(25) In 1992, European Union was signed in Maastrict and adopted by member countries on November 1, 1993.

(26) In 1993, the Single European Market came into force (January 1, 1993). Council concluded agreement creating European Economic Area, effective on January 1, 1994.

(27) In 1994, European Monetary Institute came into effect.

(28) In 1995, Austria, Finland, Sweden became the thirteenth, fourteenth, and fifteenth members of the EU.

(29) An EU summit named the 11 countries that would join the European single currency.

(30) The euro, the single European currency, came into effect (January 1, 1999).

Figure 2.3 shows the brief development of the EU.

The EU is the largest and most comprehensive of the regional economic groups. It was a customs union when it was founded. The formation of the EU Parliament and the establishment of a common currency, the euro, make the EU the most ambitious of all the regional trade groups.

The EU is a very big market in terms of both population and income that companies should pay attention to. However, when compared with the USA, the market in Europe is still fragmented and inefficient. Therefore, it is thought that mergers, takeovers and spin-offs will continue in Europe in

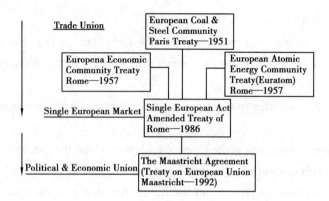

Figure 2.3   Development of the EU

the following years.

The total GDP of the EU is bigger than that of the USA or Japan. In terms of import and export, the EU accounts for more than 34% of all world imports and more than 35% of all world exports.

1. Institutions of the EU

The European Union comprises 25 Member States united in an effort to safeguard peace and promote economic and social progress, and incorporates three Communities which have common institutions. The Coal and Steel Community was the first to be set up (by the *Treaty of Paris*, 1951), followed by an Economic Community and an Atomic Energy Community (*Treaties of Rome*, 1957). Under the *Single European Act* (1986), the Communities finally dismantled all internal borders to establish a single market. The Treaty on European Union, signed in Maastricht in 1992, created a European Union combining a Community moving towards economic and monetary union with intergovernmental cooperation in certain areas.

The Union is managed by these institutions: a democratically elected Parliament, a Council representing the Member States and composed of government ministers, a European Council of Heads of State or Government, a Commission which acts as guardian of the Treaties and has the power to initiate and implement legislation, a Court of justice which ensures that Community law is observed and a Court of Auditors which monitors the financial management of the Union. In addition, there are a number of advisory bodies, which represent economic, social and regional interests. The European Investment Bank was set up to facilitate the financing of projects, which contribute to the balanced development of the Union. The bodies of the EU are as follows:

(1) The European Commission;

(2) The European Parliament;

(3) The European Council;

(4) The Council of the European Union;

(5) The Court of Justice and the Court of First Instance;

(6) The European Court of Auditors;

(7) The Economic and Social Committee and the ECSC Consultative Committee;

(8) The Committee of the Regions;

(9) The European Investment Bank;

(10) The European Central Bank.

2. The EU vs Asia

The EU trade and investment relations with Asia have expanded substantially in recent years, notwithstanding the substantial medium-term impact of the East Asian Crisis from 1997. In 2000, Asia accounted for 21.2 % of EU exports, making the region the EU third largest regional trading partner after Europe outside the EU (30.9%), and NAFTA (28.4%), but ahead of the Mediterranean, South and Central American, Gulf and ACP countries combined (17.1%). Asia is also the fourth largest regional destination for outward investment from the EU, accounting for 6.8% of total EU outward FDI in 1999 and coming after NAFTA (67.5%), Central and South America (15.1%) and Europe outside the EU (7.5%).

In addition, new programs in mutually-beneficial economic cooperation have been introduced since 1992, with a view to strengthening economic relations between Europe and Asia. Overall, the EU and its member states account for some 30% of global ODA flows going to Asia—after Japan (50%) but well ahead of the USA (9%).

3. The EU vs South Asia

The countries of South Asia (Afghanistan, Bangladesh, Bhutan, India, the Maldives, Nepal, Pakistan, Sri Lanka) have a total population of 1.33 billion, and an average per capita income of some $430 (ranging from $220 in Nepal, through $450 in India, to $1,160 in the Maldives). Some 522 million people in the region live on incomes of less than $1 per day, representing 44% of the world's poor. Four countries in the region (Afghanistan, Bangladesh, Bhutan and Nepal) are classified as least-developed countries by the UN.

Economically, South Asia accounts for 2.0% of world GNP, and for 2.2% of the EU's external trade. India is a significant investment destination for European companies (0.4% of EU external FDI in 1999), and with its own internal diversity has a very modern high-tech sector, offering much potential for economic cooperation with Europe.

Regional cooperation efforts in South Asia began in 1985, with the establishment of SAARC (South Asian Association for Regional Cooperation), in which all countries of the region, with the exception of Afghanistan, take part.

4. The EU vs South-East Asia

The countries of South-East Asia (Brunei Darussalam, Burma/Myanmar, Cambodia, Indonesia, Laos, Malaysia, the Philippines, Singapore, Thailand, Vietnam) have a total population of 512 million, and an average per capita income of $1,020 (ranging from $260 in Cambodia, through $3,400 in Malaysia, to $29,610 in Singapore). Three countries in the region (Burma/Myanmar, Cambodia, Laos) are classified as Least-Developed countries by the UN.

Economically, the countries of South-East Asia account for 1.8% of world GNP, and for 5.6%

of EU external trade. The region has also been a major investment destination for the EU, though the Asian Crisis has substantially impacted on these investment flows (the region accounted for 5.8% of EU external FDI in 1996, but 0.6% in 1999).

Regional cooperation efforts in South-East Asia have been substantial since the establishment of ASEAN (the Association of South-East Asian Nations) in 1967. ASEAN's economic efforts have taken on an increasing political dimension in recent years, with the establishment of the ASEAN Regional Forum (ARF) in 1994. Seven of the ten ASEAN countries also play an active part in ASEM and in APEC.

5. The EU vs North-East Asia

The countries of North-East Asia have a total population of 1.5 billion, and an average per capita income of $4,000 (ranging from $780 in China, through $8,490 in South Korea, to $32,230 in Japan).

The region has been undergoing significant changes in recent years. In Japan events of the last decade have highlighted the need for economic restructuring and attention is currently focused strongly on what the new Prime Minister Koizumi will do to revive the economy. The economic crisis of 1997 and 1998 has led South Korea to launch a process of economic and structural reform. China has seen significant economic modernization and has joined the WTO. Therefore, there is considerable cumulative change in the region.

In political terms, the smooth integration of China into the regional economy and polity, and relations between Japan and its neighbours, will be major determinants of the shape of the region in the coming years.

Economically, North-East Asia accounts for 20.2% of world GNP, and for 17.4% of the EU's external trade. Japan alone accounts for 14.0% of world GNP, and 6.6% of EU external trade (while China accounts for 3.4% of world GNP, and 4.8% of EU external trade).

Regional cooperation efforts in North-East Asia have in the past been very limited, partly in reflection of the heritage of World War II and the Cold War. Recently however, there has been greater interest in the creation of regional free trade areas.

6. The EU vs Eastern Europe and Central Asia

The European Union, together with its Member States, is the largest provider of technical assistance.

Furthermore, the EU is the most important external trading partner, aside from economic ties between these countries themselves.

With the collapse of the former Soviet Union, the European Union decided to support the transition process towards market economies and democratic societies in countries of Eastern Europe and Central Asia.

Thus, since the beginning of the nineties, the EU has developed a much more formal and political relationship with 13 countries of the region: Armenia, Azerbaijan, Belarus, Georgia,

Kazakhstan, Kyrgyzstan, Moldova, Mongolia, Russia, Tajikistan, Turkmenistan, Ukraine and Uzbekistan.

Building strong trading links is a major objective of the EU, but the overall aim is to foster enduring political, economic and cultural links so as to ensure peace and security.

In addition, with the EU enlargement process eastwards, the number of EU countries sharing a border with the partner countries will indeed sharply increase. This will certainly influence the dialogue between the European Union and countries from Eastern Europe and Central Asia.

7. The EU vs Australia and New Zealand

Australia and New Zealand have a total population of 23 million, and average per capita incomes of $20,050 (Australia) and $13,780 (New Zealand).

Both countries play an active part in regional security issues (for example through the ARF), and in regional economic cooperation (for example through APEC).

Australia accounts for 1.5% of world GNP, and accounts for 1.5% of EU external trade.

2.2.2　The North American Free Trade Agreement (NAFTA)　北美洲自由贸易协定

In January 1994, Canada, the United States and Mexico launched the *North American Free Trade Agreement* (NAFTA) and formed the world's largest free trade area. The Agreement has brought economic growth and better living quality to people in all the three countries. In addition, NAFTA has established a strong foundation for future growth and has set a valuable example of the benefits of trade liberalization.

In other words, NAFTA went into effect in 1994. It originated with the Canada-US Free Trade Agreement. The extended treaty from August 1992 not only includes Mexico, but also tries to implement a common market for goods and services within 15 years. Since July 1995, Chile has talked about membership. But the Mexican economic crisis made southern extensions of NAFTA unlikely.

NAFTA, a trilateral treaty between the North American countries: Canada, Mexico and the United States, creates the world's biggest tariff-free trade area with a combined economy of $6.5 trillion and 370 million people. NAFTA is a powerful trading bloc.

NAFTA covers the following areas.

(1) Market access: tariff and non-tariff barriers, rule of origin, governmental procurement.

(2) Trade rules: safeguards, subsidies, countervailing and antidumping duties, health and safety standards.

(3) Services: provides for the same safeguards for trade in services (consulting, engineering, software, etc.) that exist for trade in goods.

(4) Investment: establishes investment rules governing minority interests, portfolio investment, real property and majority-owned or controlled investments from the NAFTA countries.

(5) Intellectual property: the three countries pledge to provide adequate and effective

protection and enforcement of intellectual property right, while ensuring that enforcement measures do not themselves become barriers to legitimate trade.

1. The Aims of the Three Governments to Sign the Agreement

The aims of the three Governments to sign the Agreement are as follows:

(1) To strengthen the special bonds of friendship and cooperation between their nations;

(2) To contribute to the harmonious development and expansion of world trade and provide a catalyst to broaden international cooperation;

(3) To create an expanded and secure market for the goods and services produced in their territories;

(4) To reduce distortions to trade;

(5) To establish clear and mutually advantageous rules governing their trade;

(6) To ensure a predictable commercial framework for business planning and investment;

(7) To build on their respective rights and obligations under the General Agreement on Tariffs and Trade and other multilateral and bilateral instruments of cooperation;

(8) To enhance the competitiveness of their firms in global markets;

(9) To foster creativity and innovation, and promote trade in goods and services, which are the subject of intellectual property rights;

(10) To create new employment opportunities and improve working conditions and living standards in their respective territories;

(11) To undertake each of the preceding in a manner consistent with environmental protection and conservation;

(12) To preserve their flexibility to safeguard the public welfare;

(13) To promote sustainable development;

(14) To strengthen the development and enforcement of environmental laws and regulations;

(15) To protect, enhance and enforce basic workers' rights.

2. The Objectives of NAFTA

The objectives of the Agreement include national treatment, most-favored-nation treatment and transparency. The objectives are as follows:

(1) To eliminate barriers to trade in, and facilitate the cross-border movement of, goods and services between the territories of the parties;

(2) To promote conditions of fair competition in the free trade area;

(3) To increase substantially investment opportunities in their territories;

(4) To provide adequate and effective protection and enforcement of intellectual property rights in each party's territory;

(5) To create effective procedures for the implementation and application of the Agreement, and for its joint administration and the resolution of disputes;

(6) To establish a framework for further trilateral, regional and multilateral cooperation to

expand and enhance the benefits of the Agreement.

3. Implications of NAFTA on Corporate Strategy

A number of predictions were made when NAFTA was signed.

Firstly, it was predicted that companies would perceive NAFTA as one big regional market, allowing companies to rationalize production, products, and financing. That has largely happened in a number of industries, especially automotive products and electronics, such as computers. Employment has increased in the auto industry in the USA since NAFTA was signed. NAFTA is actually causing MNEs to look at the region differently in terms of trade and investment.

Secondly, it was predicted that sophisticated US companies would destroy Canadian and Mexican companies once the markets opened up. In general, US companies have not run Canadian and Mexican companies out of business. In fact, US companies along the border of Canada find that Canadian companies are generating more competition for them than low-wage Mexican companies. NAFTA has forced companies from all three countries to re-examine their strategies and determine how to operate in the market.

And finally, it was predicted that Mexico can be considered a consumer market rather than just a production location. In fact, Mexico is being regarded more as a market for US and Canadian exports than just a location for low-cost production.

4. Impact of NAFTA

In public opinion, NAFTA is a debatable issue. Supporters claim that during the past years of its application, NAFTA has shown its predicted positive effect on the three countries' economies. Supported by many statistics, its critics, however, claim that the impact of the agreement contradicts the original aims of NAFTA, especially the intended effect on the labor market. The adversaries of NAFTA believe that in specific areas like the automobile and textile industries, 40% of existing jobs in the US are endangered. The cause for this apprehension is easy to follow. Due to the lower wages in Mexico it is favourable for US firms to migrate to northern Mexico in order to reduce production costs. Besides, trade unions are less powerful in Mexico, allowing for greater flexibility for the firms due to severed regulations in the field of labor rights. Furthermore, the ecological and safety standards are less prohibitive in Mexico. It is observed that firms most frequently set up factories in the Mexican counties that are close to the US border. Goods are shipped over the border to the Mexican plants for cheap assembly and then return to the US.

As a trade agreement, NAFTA delivered its principal objective of more trade. Since 1993, the value of two-way US trade with Mexico has almost tripled, from $81 billion to $232 billion, growing twice as fast as US trade with the rest of the world. Canada and Mexico are now America's number one and two trading partners, respectively, with Japan a distant third.

One reason why NAFTA remains controversial today is that advocates and opponents alike were guilty a decade ago of exaggerating its impact. Advocates claimed it would create hundreds of thousands of jobs due to a dramatic rise in exports; opponents claimed far more jobs would be destroyed by a flood of imports and swarms of US companies moving to Mexico to take advantage of cheap labor.

In reality, NAFTA was never going to have much of an impact on the US economy. America's GDP at the time was almost 20 times larger than Mexico's, and US tariffs against Mexican goods already averaged a low 2 percent. Its biggest dividend for the United States has been in foreign policy.

So far as trade is concerned, NAFTA members have become much more significant trading partners with each other; and overall trade of NAFTA members has increased faster than trade with the rest of the world, and exports to NAFTA members have increased, but imports have increased faster. On the other hand, the impact of NAFTA has been difficult to measure. More jobs have probably been created than lost to NAFTA, but there are too many confounding variables to measure the impact accurately.

By every reasonable measure, NAFTA has been a public policy success. It has deepened and institutionalized Mexico's drive to modernize and liberalize its economy, society, and political system. It has spurred trade, investment, and economic integration in North America. And it has enhanced American productivity and prosperity—refuting the critics. With the *North American Free Trade Agreement* being well under way, and with other countries negotiating their own free trade accords, trade between most countries is most definitely on the upswing.

2.2.3　The Asia-Pacific Economic Rim　亚太经济圈

1. Japan

Japan also plays an important part in international business. Japan's economy is the largest in Asia. It is also a major investor in the other two groups of the Triad.

Japan is one of the most affluent countries in the world. It has a population of about 126 million. Population and economic activity are concentrated on the eastern coast, particularly in the conurbations around Osaka and Tokyo. A 900 km coastal region running south-west from Tokyo contains half of Japan's total population and 80% of its manufacturing capacity.

Japan is often criticized for unfairly blocking the importation of foreign goods. Another problem is the relatively small number of independent buying firms. In Japan, there are quite a lot of collaborative agreements among Japanese firms that create problems for foreign companies which wish to enter the Japanese market and which would be illegal under the monopoly and competition laws of many other nations. Grouping of firms occurs by means of financial links, sharing common suppliers, or through joint control of distribution outlets. These groups of Japanese businesses exert powerful influence on the Japanese economy.

It is a timely reminder that, despite all Japan's current problems passing, the country remains an important international political and economic power.

Japan is obviously important in terms of its economic role and its relationships with the United States and East Asia.

The above discussion is mainly based on the information of the Internet. The following discussion is chiefly based on a report of an American professor from the Internet.

(1) Japan vs the USA

Despite Japan's recent recession, it is believed by many Americans that Japan's economy is equal to or even stronger than that of the USA. Such beliefs result in some Americans buying the conspiratorial arguments about the "Japanese Threat", found in recent fiction by such authors as Tom Clancy and Michael Crichton. While Japan is a world economic power, the Japanese face problems that are unparalleled since the end of World War Ⅱ.

It is believed by many that the United States was once the greatest economy in the world, but the Japanese "caught" the Americans from the beginning of the 1970s. Today, the Japanese are superior and America is on a downward economic spiral. Many Americans also believe that through such practices as permanent employment and the seniority system, Japanese business managers have caused the productivity to surpass the US. First of all, Japan never "caught" the US in an economic sense. From the early 1950s to the Arab oil shocks of the 1970s, Japan experienced one of the most impressive periods of economic growth in recorded history. Still, when Japanese output, per capita income, and productivity are compared to those of the US, the latter country is much stronger in most respects.

While the US and Japan together are responsible for between 30% and 40% of world output, the overall output of the Japanese economy is only approximately 42% that of the US. Japanese per capita income is 83% that of the US. Greater US output of goods and services per labor hour, or higher productivity is a major reason why the American economy is stronger than that of Japan. The American workers continue in the 1990s to be the most productive in the world, as has been true throughout the previous century.

Recently in one of the most accurate measures of productivity, GDP per capita, Germany took Japan's place as second to the US. Japan's overall productivity rate is 82% that of the US. The United States' biggest productivity lead is in services, but even in manufacturing, Japanese levels are significantly lower than in the US. While Japan is more productive in machine tools, consumer electronics, and motor vehicles, estimates are that Japan is a generation behind the US in the telecommunications and software industries.

(2) A Brief Look at Japan's Productivity and Regulation Impact

Productivity problems are a major reason why Japanese manufacturers now have some of the world's highest production costs. The irony is that many of the practices that have made the Japanese economy so successful in the past, including strong government involvement in the economy and the permanent employment/seniority system, are now hindering Japan's future international competitiveness.

During the Meiji Restoration, government policy-makers, while recognizing the superiority of private markets over public production, nevertheless, guided Japan's economic development. Now the Japanese must compete against the US, other already successful East Asian countries, and a host of newly emerging economic powerhouses such as the People's Republic of China, Thailand, and Vietnam. An increasingly competitive environment calls for maximum flexibility in the private sector, but Japan suffers from a stifling level of regulation. Over-regulation is a major reason why Japanese consumers pay on average one-third more for goods and services than Americans. Government regulation also drives productivity down as individuals and companies devote an inordinate amount of time to satisfy bureaucrats.

Too many regulations directly contribute to Japan's large trade surplus. While Japan has low official tariffs, many other regulations are written so as to favor Japanese manufacturers and specifically prevent foreign access to domestic markets. This type of so-called "informal trade barrier" will often take the form of environmental or consumer safety regulations that are impossible for foreign manufacturers to satisfy. Regulations, such as the large-store-opening-laws, while not intentionally designed to keep foreign goods out, nevertheless, have this effect.

(3) Asia-Pacific Perspective

The Asia-Pacific region, particularly East Asia, is one that is experiencing rapid economic growth while grave concerns related to the worsening of the region's environmental problems such as air and water pollution are being expressed. The primary motor for this region's economic growth is the export-oriented industrialization of developing countries and the boom in intra-regional trade. For these reasons, the Asia-Pacific is the region where interlinkages of environment and trade are particularly relevant and need to be watched closely.

Direct foreign investment by Japanese firms as well as Japan's import of products and semi-finished products have played an important role—with considerable amount of production capacity shifting from Japan to Asian countries—in deepening the mutually dependent relationship between Japan and other Asian countries. At the same time, Asian countries remain a large provider of primary commodities to Japan. Japanese companies have many direct investments in those countries to extract and import natural resources.

Asia is also the region to which technologies are actually being transferred from Japan in the form of intra-industry vertical trade as well as intra-company transfer. Taking these factors into account, Japan, through cooperation between the government and private sector, needs to make a positive contribution to the protection of the environment of this region and to take care not to produce negative effects on the environment in its economic cooperation and development of investments with those countries.

To sum up, it is important to point out that Japan is a triad power. The country has experienced the fastest and longest period of sustained economic growth in world history over the last 40 years. Although the rate of growth began to slow in the 1990s, Japan's momentum will keep it competitive in the new century. It is thought that the new century may be the Pacific century, with other Asian nations following the Japanese model of rapid growth and development.

2. "The Four Little Tigers (Four Little Dragons)"

The Four Little Tigers, which are also called "Four Little Dragons", refer to the four relatively industrialized countries or regions of the Pacific Rim: China Hong Kong, Singapore, South Korea, and China Taiwan.

With a projected annual increase in its gross national product, the Asia-Pacific region is at the core of the world economy. In terms of the quality of their products, the Four Tigers are on a par with the leading industrial nations. More importantly, the entire region is being positively influenced by China's increasingly market-oriented approach to economic development, which is in the grip of unprecedented, and seemingly unstoppable, economic activities. It seems that everyone in the Western World has been talking about the Asia-Pacific region as the economic centre of the 21st century.

An essential element for the continued rapid transformation of the Asia-Pacific region is the deployment of an efficient telecommunications infrastructure. Asia's Internet development has benefited substantially from the rapid growth in the telecommunication infrastructure within the region. The deployment of efficient submarine fibre cables has prompted the growth of the Internet within Asia. This rapid growth has been accompanied by a strong demand from the commercial and business world which identifies the benefits of tapping into the global Internet.

The Four Tigers, all of which base their economies on either exports or the service industry, experienced record lows in economic growth in the past mainly as a result of a collapse of the world's high-technology markets and a downturn in the US economy caused by the September 11 terrorist attacks on New York and Washington, D.C.

(1) China Taiwan

Taiwan's economy, which has bottomed out from its lowest level in a decade, posted the second-best performance among the four "Asian Tigers" in the first quarter of the year 2002.

Taiwan posted 0.9 percent growth in its overall economy in the first quarter of the year 2002, second only to South Korea's growth of 5.7 percent but better than Singapore's negative 1.7 percent growth and Hong Kong's negative 0.9 percent growth.

Taiwan suffered the deepest upset in foreign trade among the Four Tigers in 2001, with its exports falling 17.2 percent and imports plummeting 23.4 percent. By comparison, Singapore's exports slid 11.7 percent, while imports were down 13.8 percent. South Korea posted a decline of 12.7 percent and 12.1 percent in its export and import trade respectively while Hong Kong recorded a fall of 5.9 percent and 5.8 percent respectively in its export and import trade.

In terms of unemployment, unemployment rate in the Four Tigers remained relatively high. Hong Kong toped the list with an unemployment rate of 7 percent posted for the first five months of the year 2002, compared with Taiwan's 5.1 percent and South Korea's 3.4 percent. Singapore posted a jobless rate of 4.5 percent in the first three months of the year 2002.

(2) Singapore

Singapore has the second highest per capita GDP in Asia after Japan. Its population is mostly Chinese. The country is a self-contained business centre with state-of-the-art facilities and ancillary business services; many joint ventures and distributorship arrangements in neighbouring countries are organized from the territory. Business is conducted in English language. However, a big problem for Singapore is its heavy dependence on external trade.

Singapore government has been encouraging foreign investment, and restrictions on equity, licensing, and joint ventures are negligible. Singapore has been a major target for investment by MNEs in recent years, especially for US firms.

Productivity has been rising rapidly in Singapore, and this has put a strain on the country to recruit the needed personnel. Unemployment is extremely low and the tight market has been producing average wage increases of 7%—8% annually through most of the 1990s. Singapore is also trying to increase its manufacturing and research and development expertise, and to let others handle the low-skill work.

（3）South Korea

South Korea's economy is one of the most open in the world, with 75% ratio of trade to national income. Since 1965, its average growth rate has exceeded 6% every year. South Korea has experienced rapid economic growth over the last two decades. The free enterprises system is well entrenched and the private sector dominates business, although government influence is considerable. GDP grew by 8.6 percent in the year 2002, but in 2001 growth fell to 2 percent. Some major investments in recent years have come in chemicals, electronics, and machinery.

South Korea's MNEs are some of the largest in the developing world and include such household names as Samsung, Hyundai, and Daewoo. These large MNEs are family-run conglomerates.

Some major advantages of doing business in South Korea include a growing economy and increasing disposal income. Some disadvantages include the difficulty of breaking into the market and of developing alliances that can effectively compete with the local conglomerates.

South Korea companies and their workers are trying to put aside their differences and to regain productivity ground that was lost in the late 1980s. Many companies are trying to find out ways to protect local markets and generate exports. In this way, South Korea may continue to remain a competitive market for MNEs, and the country is likely to continue linking strongly to the Triad.

（4）China Hong Kong

Hong Kong was only a trading port in the beginning. It has now developed into a significant manufacturing territory, with about a quarter of its GDP deriving from industry (especially textiles, machinery, plastics and consumer electronics). The whole territory is, effectively, a free trade zone with very few controls on imports or exports. Today, Hong Kong's workers are among the most productive in the world.

The Hong Kong government levies no import tariffs. However, domestic consumption taxes (referred to as duties in Hong Kong) are imposed on certain goods, such as tobacco (including cigarettes), alcoholic beverage, methyl- alcohol and some fuels. These taxes are levied equally on local manufactures.

Besides, Hong Kong government imposes restrictions on the import and export of high technology products, mirroring the control lists of the multilateral export control regimes. This includes restrictions on unlicensed re-exports to mainland China.

Most of Hong Kong's trade is with mainland China, which takes up 36% of the Territory's exports and provides nearly one-third of its imports. About 80% of Hong Kong's exported goods are in reality re-exports from mainland China.

On average, Hong Kong consumers are no wealthier than many others in Guangdong Province, but their tastes are essentially Western, and they are totally familiar with the Western approach to sales promotion and the presentation of goods.

Of the Four Little Tigers, the Chinese dominate the population. Together with the fast developing economy of the mainland of China, the Chinese are playing a very important role in international business.

In addition, the highest rates of economic growth in the Pacific Rim are currently occurring in Indonesia, Malaysia, the Philippines and Thailand, although per capita national incomes are much lower than in the Four Little Tigers.

2.3　Outside the Triad　三大区域之外

Although the Triad dominates the international business, other regional integrated organizations also play an important role in the international business. The following discussion is around these regional integrated organizations.

2.3.1　Latin American Integration Association (LAIA)　拉丁美洲联盟

The Latin American Integration Association (LAIA), which is also known as ALADI (the abbreviation of Spanish), is an organization formed in 1980 by Argentina, Bolivia, Brazil, Chile, Colombia, Ecuador, Mexico, Paraguay, Peru, Uruguay, and Venezuela, taking over the duties of the Latin American Free Trade Association (LAFTA), which was created in 1960 to establish a common market for its member nations through progressive tariff reductions until the elimination of tariff barriers by 1973. In 1969 the deadline was extended until 1980, at which time the plan was scrapped, and the new organization, LAIA, was created by the Treaty of Montevideo. It became operational in March 1981. It seeks economic cooperation among its 11 members. Trade between LAFTA members increased after 1961, but problems arose by the mid-1960s between the less-developed countries and the more prosperous ones. LAIA has the more limited goal of encouraging free trade, with no deadline for the institution of a common market. Economic hardship in Argentina, Brazil, and many other member nations have made LAIA's task difficult. LAIA's headquarters are in Montevideo, Uruguay. Members approved the *Regional Tariff Preference Scheme* in 1984 and expanded upon it in 1987 and 1990.

2.3.2　The Caribbean Community and Common Market（CARICOM）　加勒比共同体及共同市场

The Caribbean Community and Common Market（CARICOM）was established by *the Treaty of Chaguaramas*, which was signed by Barbados, Jamaica, Guyana and Trinidad & Tobago and came into effect on August 1, 1973. Subsequently the other eight Caribbean territories joined CARICOM. The Bahamas became the 13th Member State of the Community on July 4, 1983. Suriname became the 14th Member State of the Caribbean Community on July 4, 1995. In July 1991, the British Virgin Islands and the Turks and Caicos became Associated Members of CARICOM.

The purpose of CARICOM is to promote economic integration and development, especially in less-developed areas of the region. CARICOM aims at the creation of a common market. Besides managing a common market, CARICOM formulates policies regarding health, education, labor, science and technology, tourism, foreign policy, and the environment.

From its inception, the Community has concentrated on the promotion of the integration of the economies of Member States, coordinating the foreign policies of the independent Member States.

CARICOM members are: Antigua and Barbuda, Belize, Grenada, Montserrat, St. Vincent and the Grenadines, Turks and Caicos Islands, the Bahamas, British Virgin Islands, Guyana, St. Kitts and Nevis, Suriname, Barbados, Dominica, Jamaica, Saint Lucia, Trinidad and Tobago.

2.3.3　MERCOSUR　南美共同市场

MERCOSUR is the major trade group in South America. It is a customs union between Brazil, Uruguay, Paraguay, and Argentina. It has been slow in developing a common external tariff, and economic problems of member countries have hampered progress.

The four original members generate 80% of South America's GNP. Besides, MERCOSUR has signed free trade agreements with Bolivia and Chile and is negotiating with other countries to do the same.

2.3.4　The Association of South-East Asian Nations（ASEAN）　东南亚国家联盟（东盟）

ASEAN is a relatively successful free trade area in South-East Asia that relies more on the US market for exports than on each other. The member nations include: Brunei, Cambodia, Indonesia, Laos, Malaysia, Myanmar, the Philippines, Singapore, Thailand, and Vietnam.

ASEAN is a regional group, the total population of which is bigger than that of the EU or NAFTA, but their per capita GDP is smaller. Nevertheless, economic growth rates of ASEAN members are among the highest in the world.

Its key position in the Asia-Pacific region, its dedication to peace and stability in the region and its important economic weight have made ASEAN an essential partner for the EU in Asia. ASEAN was established on August 8, 1967 in Bangkok, Thailand with the signature of the Bangkok declaration by the five original member nations (Indonesia, Malaysia, Philippines, Singapore, and Thailand). In 1984, Brunei Darussalam was admitted as the sixth member. In 1995, Vietnam also joined ASEAN. Lao People's Democratic Republic and Burma/Myanmar became members in 1997. Cambodia joined in 1999.

1. The EU-ASEAN Partnership

The EU has been a longstanding Dialogue Partner of ASEAN. The political dialogue entails regular Ministerial meetings, participation in the Post Ministerial Conferences which take place immediately after ASEAN's annual ministerial meetings and in the ASEAN Regional Forum. In September 2001 the European Commission presented its Communication "Europe and Asia: A Strategic Framework for Enhanced Partnerships", which identified ASEAN as a key economic and political partner of EC and emphasized its importance as a locomotive for overall relations between Europe and Asia.

2. Trade Relations Between the EU and ASEAN

In 2001, the EU was ASEAN's second largest export market and the third largest trading partner after the United States and Japan. EU exports to ASEAN were estimated at 42.7 billion, while EU imports from ASEAN were valued at 66.2 billion, demonstrating that the EU maintained its commitment to keeping its market open to ASEAN after the 1997 Asian Financial Crisis.

As a region, ASEAN has benefited significantly from the EU's Generalized System of Preferences. ASEAN countries such as Thailand and Indonesia have "graduated" a number of sectors where they have become competitive in the last few years, losing the benefit of the GSP for important products—in particular, fishery products for Thailand. Singapore, due to its advanced level of development, is excluded from the system. European investment was high in the region before the crisis and although the trend is rising again, it has not yet reached pre-crisis level.

2.3.5　The Asia Pacific Economic Cooperation (APEC)　亚太经济合作组织

APEC was founded in November 1989 in order to promote multilateral economic cooperation in trade and investment in the Pacific Rim. It is made up of 21 countries and/or regions that border the Pacific Rim—both in Asia and in the Americas. APEC is a largely ineffectual organization compared with the EU and the NAFTA. APEC's main objectives are as follows:

(1) To resist protectionist pressure and maintain the momentum of trade liberalization;

(2) To counter inward-looking regionalism elsewhere, such as in the EU and NAFTA;

(3) To provide ways to deal with economic conflicts in the region.

APEC is the premier forum for facilitating economic growth, cooperation, trade and investment in the Asia-Pacific region. APEC has a membership of 21 economic jurisdictions, a population of over 2.5 billion and a combined GDP of 19 trillion US dollars accounting for 47 percent of world trade. It is a unique forum operating on the basis of open dialogue and equal respect for the views of all participants.

As the primary regional vehicle for promoting trade and investment and practical economic cooperation, the end result of APEC's activities includes increased employment opportunities and community development.

APEC is working to achieve what is referred to as the "Bogor Goals" of free and open trade and investment in the Asia-Pacific by 2010 for developed economies and by 2020 for developing economies.

APEC has identified three specific areas that are crucial to achieving the Bogor Goals. These three pillars are:

(1) Trade and Investment Liberalization;

(2) Business Facilitation;

(3) Economic and Technical Cooperation.

Since its inception in 1989, APEC has helped to reduce tariffs and other barriers to trade in the Asia-Pacific region. APEC has also worked to ensure the safe and efficient movement of goods, services and people across the borders in the region through facilitating practical policy formulation in APEC economies and by facilitating economic and technical cooperation.

In 2001, Shanghai successfully hosted ministerial and leaders' meetings of APEC. APEC Trade Ministers Meeting opened in Shanghai on June 6 and closed on June 7. Mexico hosted it in 2002.

On Nov.10 and Nov.11, 2014, the Summit of APEC was held in Beijing, which indicates that China is becoming more and more important in APEC.

In recent years, the trading volume between China and other member nations of APEC has accounted for more than half of the total trading volume of China. The total economic scale of APEC member nations accounts for 57% of the world' economic scale.

APEC Organization

APEC operates by consensus. In 1991, members committed themselves to conducting their activities and work programs on the basis of open dialogue with equal respect for the views of all participants.

1) Ministerial and Senior Officials Meetings

The APEC Chair, which rotates annually among members, is responsible for hosting the annual ministerial meeting of foreign and economic ministers.

2) APEC Business Advisory Council

In 1995 APEC Economic Leaders established a permanent council composed of up to three senior business people from each member economy to provide advice on the implementation of APEC action plans and on other specific business/private sector priorities. Chairmanship of APEC rotates each year according to which economy chairs APEC. The 2002 APEC Chair is Mr. Javier Prieto, Senior Vice President for External Affairs for CEMEX of Mexico.

3) APEC Fora

At each year's Ministerial Meeting, members define and fund work programs for APEC's three committees, eleven working groups and other APEC fora.

The Members of APEC

When APEC was established in 1989, there were 12 founding members, namely Australia, Brunei Darussalam, Canada, Indonesia, Japan, Republic of Korea, Malaysia, New Zealand, Republic of the Philippines, Singapore, Thailand and the Unites States. In November 1991, APEC accepted three new members: People's Republic of China, Hong Kong (its designation has been changed to Hong Kong, China since 1 July 1997) and Chinese Taipei. In November 1993, APEC accepted Mexico and Papua New Guinea as new members. At the same time, APEC decided that Chile would become a full member in November 1994. In November 1997, APEC Economic Leaders welcomed Peru, Russia and Vietnam as new members of the APEC community. Their formal membership started in November 1998.

2.3.6　The Organization of Petroleum Exporting Countries (OPEC)

OPEC is an example of a producer cartel. It is a group of commodity-producing countries that have significant control over supply and that band together to control output and price. It is part of a larger category of energy commodities, which also includes coal and natural gas. It is not confined to the Middle East. OPEC controls prices by establishing production quotas on member countries.

OPEC is an international organization of a number of developing countries which are heavily reliant on oil revenues as their main source of income. Membership is open to any country which is a substantial net exporter of oil and which shares the ideals of the organization. The current members are Algeria, Indonesia, Iran, Iraq, Kuwait, Libya, Nigeria, Qatar, Saudi Arabia, the United Arab Emirates and Venezuela.

Since oil revenues are so vital for the economic development of these nations, they aim to bring stability and harmony to the oil market by adjusting their oil output to help ensure a balance between supply and demand. Twice a year, or more frequently if required, the Oil and Energy Ministers of the OPEC Members meet to decide on the Organization's output level, and consider whether any action to adjust output is necessary in the light of recent and anticipated oil market developments. All OPEC's members collectively supply about 40 per cent of the world's oil output, and possess more than three-quarters of the world's total proven crude oil reserves.

OPEC is a permanent, intergovernmental organization, created at the Baghdad Conference on September 10-14, 1960, by Iran, Iraq, Kuwait, Saudi Arabia and Venezuela. The five Founding Members were later joined by eight other Members: Qatar (1961), Indonesia (1962), Socialist Peoples Libyan Arab Jamahiriya (1962), United Arab Emirates (1967), Algeria (1969), Nigeria (1971), Ecuador (1973—1992) and Gabon (1975—1994). OPEC had its headquarters in Geneva, Switzerland, in the first five years of its existence. This was moved to Vienna, Austria, on September 1, 1965.

OPEC's objective is to co-ordinate and unify petroleum policies among Member Countries in order to secure fair and stable prices for petroleum producers, an efficient, economic and regular supply of petroleum to consuming nations, and a fair return on capital to those investing in the industry.

2.3.7　The Shanghai Cooperation Organization（SCO）

On June 15, 2001, the Shanghai Cooperation Organization was established in Shanghai by the heads of state of the six countries of China, Russia, Kazakhstan, Kyrgyzatan, Tadzhikistan and Uzbekistan on the basis of the original "Shanghai Five," signifying the birth of a new regional cooperation organization aiming to seek security through mutual trust and to seek cooperation through mutual benefits. The purpose of the Shanghai Cooperation Organization is to strengthen the mutual trust and good neighborly friendship between the member countries, encourage their effective cooperation in political affairs, economy, trade, science and technology, culture, education, energy, communications, environmental protection and other fields, devote jointly to maintaining and safeguarding regional peace, security and stability, and establish a democratic, fair and rational international political and economic new order. The heads of state of the Shanghai Cooperation Organization member countries will meet formally once a year and their heads of government will also meet regularly, in the member countries by turns.

SCO's predecessor, the Shanghai Five mechanism, originated and grew from the endeavor by China, Russia, Kazakhstan, Kyrgystan and Tajikistan to strengthen confidence-building and disarmament in the border regions. In 1996 and 1997, their heads of state met in Shanghai and Moscow respectively and signed the *Treaty on Deepening Military Trust in Border Regions* and the *Treaty on Reduction of Military Forces in Border Regions*. Thereafter, this annual meeting became a regular practice and had been held alternately in the five member states. The topics of the meeting gradually extended from building up trust in the border regions to mutually beneficial cooperation in the political affairs, security, diplomacy, economy, trade, and other fields among the five states. The President of Uzbekistan was invited to the 2000 Dushanbe Summit as a guest of the host state. As the first meeting of the five heads of state took place in Shanghai, the cooperation mechanism was later known as the "Shanghai Five".

On September 23, 2003, prime ministers of the member states of the Shanghai Cooperation Organization held talks in Beijing. The talks attained substantial achievements, symbolizing that the SCO has put an end to its initial stage of work and is now stepping into a new era for an all-round, stable development and will play independently a role in the international community.

On the 10th of July, 2015, the 15th meeting of SCO Executive Council was held in Russia. SCO is considering welcoming India and Pakistan to join SCO, which indicates that SCO will open its door to take in new members.

2.3.8　TPP

TPP (*Trans-Pacific Partnership Agreement*), signed in 2015, is an important international multi-lateral economic negotiation organization. It came from the *Trans-Pacific Strategic Economic Partnership Agreement*. TPP was initiated by the four countries, namely, New Zealand, Singapore,

Chili and Brunei, aiming to promote the liberalization of trade in Asia-Pacific region.

TPP is about free trade but is more than that, because it involves not only free trade between member nations but also involves intellectual property, labor force, environmental protection, free conversion of currencies, etc.

The negotiation of TPP started in March of 2010. The negotiation involves two parts: one is about the rules of intellectual property protection and issues of other aspects which are to be negotiated and decided by the 12 negotiation nations and the other is about the reduction of tariffs and other aspects through bilateral negotiation.

On Oct. 5th, 2015, TPP reached some agreement with the USA, Japan and other 10 Pan-Pacific countries. The 12 countries account for 40% of the world economy. The tariffs of about 18,000 types of goods will be reduced or removed.

In accordance with TPP, the member nations of TPP shall respect freedom, democracy, legal system, human rights etc. Besides, the Agreement requires: freedom of trade and service, free conversion of currencies, fair taxation, privatization of state-owned enterprises, protection of labor force, protection of environmental resources, information freedom (including journalism and Internet news freedom), etc.

China has not signed the TPP, as there are many obstacles for China to do so. For example, it is hard presently for China to privatize all her state-run enterprises and to carry out zero tariffs in international trade, and so on. Of the TPP member nations, USA is an activist, who intends to control the TPP. In this sense, TPP is more political. The "ABC" (Anyone But China) drives China into a seemingly difficult situation. Contries concered will not continue to import product from China, as China's products are not as competitive as before. As a result, China's BOP will be negatively impacted on. However, China is facing the situation and effectively finding out strategies to deal with it. For example, China initiated Asian Infrastructure Investment Bank, which will be discussed in 7.9 of Chapter Seven.

TPP and WTO have somenting in common: both concerns free trade but TPP differs from WTO in that TPP not only regards free trade but also regards such fields as free conversion of currencies, environmental protection, etc. In other words, TPP includes free trade of traditional commodities and comprehensive free trade that covers service trade.

2.3.9   BRIC

In economics, BRIC is a grouping acronym that refers to the countries of Brazil, Russia, India and China, which are all deemed to be at a similar stage of newly advanced economic development. It is typically rendered as "the BRICs" or "the BRIC countries" or "the BRIC economies" or alternatively as the "Big Four". A related acronym, BRICS, includes South Africa.

The acronym was coined in 2001 by Jim O'Neill from investment bank Goldman Sachs in a paper entitled "Building Better Global Economic BRICs". The acronym has come into widespread use as a symbol of the apparent shift in global economic power away from the developed G7 economies towards the developing world.

Projections on the future power of the BRIC economies vary widely. Some sources suggest that they might overtake the G7 economies by 2027. More modestly, Goldman Sachs has argued that, although the four BRIC countries are developing rapidly, it was only by 2050 that their combined economies could eclipse the combined economies of the current richest countries of the world.

In 2010, however, while the four BRIC countries accounted for over a quarter of the world's land area and more than 40% of the world's population, they accounted for only one-quarter of the world gross national income.

According to a paper published in 2005, Mexico and South Korea were the only other countries comparable to the BRICs, but their economies were excluded initially because they were considered already more developed, as they were already members of the OECD. The same creator of the term "BRIC" endorsed the term MINT, that includes Mexico, Indonesia, Nigeria and Turkey.

Goldman Sachs did not argue that the BRICs would organize themselves into an economic bloc, or a formal trading association, as the European Union has done. However, there are some indications that the "four BRIC countries have been seeking to form a 'political club' or 'alliance'", and thereby converting "their growing economic power into greater geopolitical clout". On June 16, 2009, the leaders of the BRIC countries held their first summit in Yekaterinburg, and issued a declaration calling for the establishment of an equitable, democratic and multipolar world order. Since then, they have met in Brasília in 2010, met in Sanya, on China's Hainan Island in 2011 and in New Delhi, India, in 2012.

Some other developing countries that have not yet reached the N-11 economic level, such as South Africa, aspired to BRIC status. South Africa was subsequently successful in joining the bloc, despite the fact that economists at the Reuters 2011 Investment Outlook Summit dismissed the prospects of South African success. South Africa, at a population of under 50 million people, was just too small an economy to join the BRIC ranks. However, after the BRIC countries formed a political organization among themselves, they later expanded to include South Africa, becoming the BRICS.

Several of the more developed of the N-11 countries, in particular Turkey, Mexico, Indonesia and South Korea, were seen as the most likely contenders to the BRICs.

In recent years, the BRICs have received increasing scholarly attention. Brazilian political economist Marcos Prado Troyjo and French investment banker Christian Déséglise founded the BRICLab at Columbia University, a Forum examining the strategic, political and economic consequences of the rise of BRIC countries, especially by analyzing their projects for power, prosperity and prestige through graduate courses, special sessions with guest speakers, Executive Education programs, and annual conferences for policymakers, business and academic leaders, and students. This shows that BRICS is playing an important role in the global affairs.

2.3.10 "One Belt and One Road" "一带一路"

The "Silk Road Economic Belt" and "21st Century Maritime Silk Road," or "One Belt and

One Road" for short, were development strategies put forward by China's President Xi Jinping in 2013. The "One Belt" will link China with Europe through Central and Western Asia. The "One Road" represents a maritime route through the Straight of Malacca to India, the Middle East and East Africa. One road on land and one ruote at sea will consolidate China's relations with the countries and regions on the "road" and on the "route".

The Maritime Silk Road dates back to 2,000 years ago, when ancient merchants sailed from China's eastern coast, passing Southeast Asia, the Southernmost tip of India and East Africa, all the way to the Persian Gulf and the Red Sea, strengthening economic ties and cultural communication.

China has highlighted the geographic and strategic importance of Xinjiang Uygur autonomous region, the starting point of the Silk Road economic belt. The Central government will formulate a series of preferential policies for the autonomous region.

China's "one belt and one road" initiative could usher in a new era that sees China as the undisputed geopolitical powerhouse in the region. The initiative will establish new routes linking Asia, Europe and Africa. It has two parts—a new "Silk Road economic belt" linking China to Europe that cuts through mountainous regions in Central Asia; and the "maritime Silk Road" that links China's port facilities with the African coast and then pushes up through the Suez Canal into the Mediterranean Sea.

The idea of "one belt and one road" is based mainly on the economy, but has political and strategic components and implications. It aims for the joint development, common prosperity and for energy security, too.

China will have to establish security for these new routes, since many of them snake through potentially dangerous areas such as Africa's coast (maritime piracy) and the "wild west" of Central Asia (Islamic extremism).

The routes will require logistics hubs, communication networks, airports, railway lines, modern highways, ports and a military component that allows for a rapid response to a crisis.

The China-backed Asian Infrastructure Investment Bank (AIIB)—established in 2013 can assist regional neighbors in infrastructure development and to help facilitate the creation of facilities to support the "one belt, one road" initiative.

2.3.11　China (Shanghai) Pilot Free Trade Zone　中国(上海)自由贸易区

The China (Shanghai) Pilot Free Trade Zone was founded at Waigaoqiao Area, Pudong, Shanghai, on September 29, 2013 and it is the first free-trade zone in mainland China. Since 21 April 2015, Shanghai FTZ's areas have been expanded, including Lujiazui Finance and Trade Zone, Shanghai Jinqiao Economic and Technological Development Zone (former Jinqiao Export Processing Zone) and Zhangjiang Hi-Tech Park. The total area of the zone is 120.72 square kilometers.

It was a major move China took to promote further reform and opening up to the outside world in the new situation, and it was designed to explore a new path and gain new experience for comprehensive deepening reform and opening China wider to the outside world and to promote development for all regions. The new strategy is to expedite the functional transformation of government, expand the opening up of service sectors and promote the reform of the foreign investment administrative system, and develop the headquarters economy and new trade forms. Besides, it is to explore RMB convertibility under capital account items and opening up of financial services, to improve Customs' supervision efficiency, to create a framework to support investment and innovation activities to cultivate an internationalized law-based business environment, and to pilot a free trade zone, as measured by international standards, with convenient investment and trading procedures, full convertibility of currencies, effective and efficient goods supervision, and investor-friendly regulatory environment.

The experience hence gained shall serve nationwide with new ideas and approaches for opening up the economy and deepening the reform further. The major task of the Zone is, by taking the lead to experiment step by step with risks under control and improving gradually, and to develop a framework in line with international norms for investment and trade:

(1) to accelerate the transformation of government functions;

(2) to open up investment sectors;

(3) to promote the transformation of trade development approach;

(4) to deepen innovation and opening up of financial services;

(5) to improve regulatory supporting systems.

The zone is being used as a testing ground for a number of economic and social reforms. For example, the sale of video game consoles, banned in China since 2000, will be allowed within the zone. Consoles and individual games will still be subject to a case-by-case approval by the Shanghai Municipal Administration of Culture, Radio, Film & TV for manufacturing and sales in China.

Within the zone, the following sectors enjoy special policies:

(1) Arbitration

The FTZ features a distinctive mechanism for dispute resolution than exists elsewhere in China. Arbitration in the zone is governed by a separate set of Arbitration Rules issued by the Shanghai International Arbitration Center (SHIAC). These introduce several reforms favourable to foreign investment in the FTZ, including emergency arbitration, hybrid mediation/arbitration, and lower barriers to summary procedure. Additionally, arbitrators may be chosen from outside of the official roster maintained by SHIAC, provided they satisfy certain qualifying criteria.

(2) Corporate establishment

The zone cancels out a number of financial requirements for setting up a company in China, including the minimum registration capital of RMB30,000 for limited liability companies, the RMB100,000 minimum for single shareholder companies, and the RMB5 million minimum for joint stock companies. Moreover, under the FTZ's new capital registration system, foreign investors are no longer required to contribute 15-percent capital within three months and full capital within two years of the establishment of a foreign invested enterprise (FIE).

Instead, shareholders of companies established in the zone may agree upon the contribution amount, form, and period of contribution at their own discretion. However, shareholders are still liable for the authenticity and legality of capital contributions and will be held accountable to the company within the limits of their respective subscribed capital or shares.

In addition to these financial reforms, the FTZ also introduces a simplified procedure for foreign investors to establish a company in China. The "one-stop application processing platform" unique to the zone requires that all application materials be submitted to and handled by the Industry and Commerce Authority (AIC) in the zone. The relevant approval and filing procedures are then conducted via inter-departmental circulation, after which the various licenses and certificates (including the business license, enterprise code certificate, and tax registration certificate) are issued to the applicant(s) by the AIC.

This means that applicants may obtain all the necessary documents for company establishment in one place, in contrast with outside the zone where applicants must run around between different authorities for the issuance of various certificates.

(3) Foreign exchange

As announced by the State Administration of Foreign Exchange (SAFE) Shanghai Branch on 28 February, 2014, the Free Trade Zone will permit yuan convertibility and unrestricted foreign currency exchange, and a tax-free period of 10 years for the businesses in the area as a means to simplify the process of foreign direct investment (FDI) and facilitate the management of capital accounts.

Under the new regulations, foreign invested enterprises (FIEs) registered in the FTZ may now make foreign exchange capital account settlements at their own discretion, as opposed to under the previous rules, where settlements were restricted to those deemed to be "actual needs" by SAFE. FIEs in the FTZ may also now open RMB special deposit accounts to hold RMB funds obtained from foreign exchange settlements, which may then be used to effect payments for real transactions.

(4) Foreign investment

The zone introduces a number of reforms designed to create a preferential environment for foreign investment. On 18 September 2013, the State Council of China published a list of 18 service industries to receive more relaxed policies in the zone, including medical services, value-added telecommunications, ocean freight & international ship management and banking. Another important feature of the zone is found in its "negative list" approach to foreign investment, which is permitted in all sectors unless explicitly prohibited by the inclusion of a given sector on the Negative List published by the Shanghai Municipal Government. The 16 sectors thus named as restricted or prohibited for foreign investment are organized as follows:

1) Agriculture, forestry, animal husbandry and fishery

2) Mining

3) Manufacturing

4) Production and supply of power, gas and water

5）Construction

6）Wholesale and retail

7）Transportation, warehousing and postal services

8）Information transmission, computer services and software

9）Finance

10）Real estate

11）Leasing and commercial services

12）Scientific research and technical services

13）Water conservancy, environmental, and public facilities management

14）Education

15）Health and Social Industries

16）Cultural, sports and entertainment industries

Since it was established on September 29, 2013, the China (Shanghai) Pilot Free Trade Zone (FTZ) has carried out institutional reform and innovation in areas of investment, foreign trade, finance and post-filing supervision to form a legal framework for investment and trade within the zone. It has adopted the negative list for investment management, simplified foreign trade supervision procedures, promoted financial system reform to realize RMB capital account convertibility, and advocated post-filing supervision as a way to transform government functions. The Negative List was updated in July 2014, further relaxing restrictions on foreign investment in the financial industry, manufacturing, and transportation services.

The expanded Shanghai Free Trade Zone will continue to take the national lead in reform and innovation, guard against risks in experiments, cater to the needs of enterprises, make good use of advantages of Pudong New Area, speed up government transformation, make breakthroughs in reform and opening-up, formulate rules for investment and trade that comply with international practices, and contribute to the realization of the Chinese Dream of national rejuvenation.

The FTZ is characteristic of being copiable. The State Council decided on December 28, 2014 to introduce the practices of Shanghai FTZ nationwide and established free trade zones also in Guangdong, Tianjin and Fujian. More FTA will emerge with the successful practices of the exisiting FTZs. It is predicted that with more and more FTZs coming into being, China economy will even powerful and will near her dreams.

Summary of This Chapter
本章概要

1. 区域经济一体化成了当今世界经济的一个发展趋势。区域经济一体化指的是：一个地理区域内的所有国家经过磋商、谈判达成共识，一致同意减少并最后完全消除国与国之间的关税和非关税壁垒，以达到相互之间的商品、服务和生产要素的自由流动之目的。区域经济一体化分几个层次。(1)自由贸易区:自由贸易区内的成员国之间的商品和服务贸易的所有壁垒都被完全取消。此外,自由贸易区内不允许实行歧视性关税、配额、补贴等。(2)关税同盟:关税同盟更前进了一步,它不但消除了成员国之间的贸易壁垒,而且联合采取统一的对外贸易政策,例如欧盟最初就是一个关税同盟。(3)共同市场:共同市场的成员国之间的贸易壁垒也被取消,并且实行统一的对外贸易政策。但是,共同市场允许生产要素在成员国之间自由流动,这与关税同盟有所不同。(4)经济联盟:经济联盟和共同市场一样,成员国之间的产品和生产要素可以自由流动并联合一致对外采取统一的贸易政策。但是,经济联盟与共同市场不同的是:经济联盟需要有统一的货币,成员国税率要协调,要采取统一的财政和货币政策。(5)政治联盟:只有成员国放弃了政治权利、经济完全一体化的情况下才形成了政治联盟。政治联盟需要有协调机构对各个成员国的公民负责。欧盟正逐步走向政治联盟。

2. 当今世界经济布局形成了"三足鼎立"(the Triad)状态:欧盟(The European Union)、北美自由贸易协定(The North American Free Trade Agreement)(以美国为主)、太平洋经济圈(The Pacific Rim)(日本在东方是主要发达国家。此外还有"四小龙",中国大陆也正逐步崛起,已经成为世界第二大经济体)。世界500强企业主要来自这三大"经济区域"。

3. 欧盟:欧盟包括欧洲煤钢共同体(The European Coal and Steel Community,ECSC)、欧洲经济共同体(The European Economic Community,EEC)和欧洲原子能共同体(The European Atomic Energy Community)。其中,欧洲经济共同体最重要。至2015年7月欧盟有28个成员国,19个成员国使用统一的货币(英国、瑞典、丹麦等国除外)。欧盟的先驱是1951年4月18日成立的欧洲煤钢共同体。签约国有法国、联邦德国、荷兰、比利时、卢森堡、意大利。该六国于1957年3月25日签订了建立欧洲经济共同体条约和成立欧洲原子能共同体条约。这两个条约统称为《罗马条约》。1994年《马斯特里赫条约》签订后,欧洲共同体更名为欧洲联盟,简称为"欧盟"。欧盟是和美国、日本抗衡的经济、政治超级实体,其国内生产总值比美国还高。欧盟的政治机构有欧洲理事会、部长理事会、欧洲委员会、欧洲议会及欧洲法院。2004年5月1日10个东欧国家加入欧盟,它们分别是匈牙利、波兰、捷克、斯洛文尼亚、斯洛伐克、爱沙尼亚、立陶宛、马耳他、塞浦路斯、拉脱维亚。2007年初,罗马尼亚和保加利亚加入欧盟。2013年7月日,克罗地亚加入欧盟。

4. 北美自由贸易协定:经过历时一年零两个月的反复磋商,美国、加拿大和墨西哥三国外贸部长会议最终于1992年8月1日晚就北美自由贸易协定的最后文本达成了一致意见。1994年8月12日,美国、加拿大及墨西哥三国签署了一项三边自由贸易协定——北美自由贸易协定。1994年1月1日,该协定正式生效。根据该协定,三个签约国将在15年内逐步取消货物和劳务贸易及资本流动的所有关税和壁垒。协定内容包括市场准入、贸易、法规、服务业、投资和知识产权等方面。美国和加拿大之间早在1988年就签订了自由贸易协定,其目的是取消有关加拿大和美国双边贸易的所有关税。北美自由贸易协定的签订对世界经济和国际贸易的影响较大,这标志着世界最大的自由贸易区的最终形成不可逆转。北美自由贸易协定目前面临的问题是区域扩大。从1994年12月起,美、加、墨、智4国领导人决定开始就智利加入北美自由贸易协定进行谈判。1996年11月18日,加拿大和智利在渥太华正式签署了两国自由贸易协定。该协定从1997年6月2日起正式实施。

5. 日本是东方经济上强大的发达国家。日本是欧盟和北美自由贸易协定国的主要投资国。日本日益感觉到了以中国为首的发展中国家的经济崛起及迅猛发展对其形成的压力。尽管目前中国的经济水平不能和日本相提并论,但是,未来的东方经济强国是否仍然是日本还是未知数。

6. 在世界三大经济体(TRIAD)之外,形成了一些区域经济一体化联盟。(1)加勒比共同体(CARICOM):1991年,在加勒比共同体的主持下,加勒比地区的英语国家创建了一个关税同盟。(2)东南亚国家联盟(ASEAN):东南亚国家联盟于1967年成立。该联盟和亚太经合组织(APEC)是东方两大有影响力的经济联盟。东盟的基本目标是:促进成员国之间的自由贸易,在产业政策方面相互合作。东盟的经济合作计划主要包括:制订共同工业计划,粮食、能源有限供应计划,优惠关税。(3)亚太经合组织(APEC):该组织在澳大利亚的提议下,于1989年11月在澳大利亚首都堪培拉成立。12个成员国参加了第一次会议。1991年中国以主权国家加入该组织,香港和台北以地区经济体名义参加该组织。该组织现有成员国21个。该组织的世界贸易额构成了世界经济增长的主要部分。亚太经合组织的主要目标是:促进该地区的多边经济合作。亚太经合组织是一个成员国之间就经济贸易问题进行协商的论坛,而不是一个政策谈判机构。从组织成立起,贸易和投资自由化一直是主线,贯穿于该组织的发展进程中。(4)上海合作组织(SCO):该组织是诞生于21世纪初的欧亚大陆的一个新型的区域性多边合作组织。"上海合作组织"是在"上海五国"基础上形成的。"上海五国"机制是该组织的前身。自从1996年五国元首在上海首次会晤以来,"上海五国"便成为中、俄、哈、吉、塔五国合作机制与进程举世公认的专有代名词,通过5年来分别在五国轮流举行的5次峰会,五国合作的需求和愿望不断增强,领域和范围不断拓展,深度和层次不断提升,从而为新组织的诞生奠定了坚实的基础。上海合作组织的宗旨是:①加强各成员国之间的相互信任和睦邻友好;②鼓励各成员国在政治、经贸、科技、文化、教育、能源、交通、环保及其他领域的有效合作;③共同致力于维护和保障地区的和平、安全与稳定;④建立民主、公正、合理的国际政治、经济新秩序。成员国将严格遵循《联合国宪章》的宗旨与原则,相互尊重独立、主权和领土完整,互不干涉内政,互不使用或威胁使用武力,平等互利,通过相互协商解决所有问题,不谋求在相毗邻地区的单方面军事优势。奉行不结盟、不针对其他国家和地区及对外开放的原则,与其他国家及有关国际和地区组织开展多种形式的对话、交流与合作,在协商一致的基础上吸收认同该组织框架内合作宗旨和任务、该组织宣言第六条阐述的原则及其他各项条款,其加入能促进实现这一合作的国家为该组织新成员。上海合作组织目前共有6个成员国:中国(1996)、俄罗斯(1996)、哈萨克斯坦(1996)、吉尔吉斯斯坦(1996)、塔吉克斯坦(1996)、乌兹别克斯坦(2001)。上海合作组织峰会2005年7月5日在哈萨克斯坦首都阿斯塔纳举行。上海合作组织成员国国家元首和该组织观察员国家领导人出席了会议。在本次峰会上,上海合作组织成员国家签署了多项重要声明和文件,并正式接纳印度、巴基斯坦和伊朗为观察员。这是继2004年塔什干峰会通过《上海合作组织观察员条例》并接纳蒙古国为观察员后的又一次的扩员。印度、巴基斯坦和伊朗加入后,上海合作组织已由6国增加到10国,其覆盖的地域范围也空前扩展,从东亚、中亚延伸到南亚、西亚,其地域面积占据了欧亚大陆的近70%,人口占到世界总人口的40%,上海合作组织已成为欧亚大陆人口最多、面积最大的区域性国际组织。

有人预计,到 2050 年,随着世界主要经济强国的不断发展,世界经济格局将发生重大变化,全球新的六大经济体很可能变成中国、美国、印度、日本、巴西、俄罗斯。

7. "亚洲四小龙":指亚洲经济相对发达的四个国家和地区:新加坡、中国台湾、中国香港、韩国。"四小龙"在亚太地区经济上属于更发达的国家或地区。就它们的产品质量而言,可以与发达工业国家的产品质量相媲美。近年来,由于中国的崛起,西方世界特别关注亚太地区的发展。有人预测,亚太地区可能成为 21 世纪的经济中心。"四小龙"的经济发展主要依靠出口和服务业。"四小龙"在亚太地区仍然是令人瞩目的、较发达的和有实力的国家或地区。不过,随着中国大陆经济新的崛起和其他国家的经济快速发展,世界的注意力更多关注的是中国大陆。

8. 随着中国改革开放,中国的经济大国地位已经获得世界认可,成为了第二经济大国。这样就改变了世界三大经济板块的格局,亚太地区的领头国已经由中国将日本取而代之。甚至有人认为,同如世界军事三大板块的构成,美国、俄罗斯和中国,当今世界经济三大板块由美国、欧盟和中国构成。

9. 跨太平洋伙伴关系协定(Trans-Pacific Partnership Agreement),也被称作"经济北约",是目前重要的国际多边经济谈判组织,前身是跨太平洋战略经济伙伴关系协定(Trans-Pacific Strategic Economic Partnership Agreement,P4)。是由亚太经济合作会议成员国中的新西兰、新加坡、智利和文莱等四国发起,从 2002 年开始酝酿的一组多边关系的自由贸易协定,原名亚太自由贸易区,旨在促进亚太地区的贸易自由化。

2015 年 10 月 5 日,泛太平洋战略经济伙伴关系协定(TPP)终于取得实质性突破,美国、日本和其他 10 个泛太平洋国家就 TPP 达成一致。12 个参与国加起来所占全球经济的比重达到了 40%。TPP 将对近 18,000 种类别的商品降低或减免关税。

跨太平洋伙伴关系协议将突破传统的自由贸易协定(FTA)模式,达成包括所有商品和服务在内的综合性自由贸易协议。跨太平洋伙伴关系协议将对亚太经济一体化进程产生重要影响,可能将整合亚太的两大经济区域合作组织,亦即亚洲太平洋经济合作组织和东南亚国家联盟重叠的主要成员国,将发展成为涵盖亚洲太平洋经济合作组织(APEC)大多数成员在内的亚太自由贸易区,成为亚太区域内的小型世界贸易组织(WTO)。

目前中国尚未加入该协定,但未来不排除中国在适宜的时候提出加入。从短期看,该协定或对中国的对外贸易形成某种程度的冲击,但从长期看,在经济全球化的大背景下,任何一个多边贸易安排都无法将非协定国家和地区排除于国际贸易体系之外,否则其自身发展将大为受限。

TPP 与 WTO 不尽相同。它从传统、单一、狭义的贸易协定拓展成为现代、广义、综合的贸易协定。除了经济元素以外,TPP 包含了许多非经济元素。TPP 成员不仅要受到贸易机制的制约,而且还要受到法律法规、社会团体、生态环境、商业模式和公众评判等制约。这可以说是西方国家,对于"自由贸易"的全新注解。这是整体、多层次发展的自由贸易新模式。(Source:百度百科)

10. 金砖五国(BRICS),金砖五国来自"金砖四国"这一概念,特指新兴市场投资代表。"金砖四国"(BRIC)是俄罗斯(Russia)、中国(China)、巴西(Brazil)和印度(India)的英文首字母缩写。BRIC 与英语单词的 brick(砖)类似,所以被称为"金砖四国"。2008—2009 年,相关国家举行系列会谈和建立峰会机制,拓展为国际政治实体。2010 年南非(South Africa)加入后,其英文单词变为"BRICS",并改称为"金砖国家"。金砖国家的标志是五国国旗的代表颜色做条状围成的圆形,象征着"金砖国家"的合作,团结。

11. "一带一路"(One Belt, One Road Intiatives),"一带一路"是我国政府提出的 21 世纪经济发展的新战略。"一带"指丝绸之路经济带,"一路"指 21 世纪海上丝绸之路。"一带一路"沿线总人口约 44 亿,经济总量约 21 万亿美元,分别约占全球的 63% 和 29%。"一带一路"作为中国的国家战略,对中国未来的经济发展有着重大的战略意义,是我国进一步改革开放的新的举措。该战略给中国未来的发展确定了新的思路与前进方向。另外,对所涉及的国家和地区的发展也是一个契机,建立了中国与这些国家经济、文化等领域的合作新平台。

12. 中国(上海)自由贸易试验区,中国(上海)自由贸易试验区于 2013 年 9 月 29 日在上海浦东外高桥挂牌成立,包括七个区域,总面积达 120.72 平方千米。这是中国在新形势下推进改革开放的一项重大举措,旨在为全面深化改革和扩大开放探索新路径、积累新经验,促进各地区共同发展。

试验区的总体目标是:经过两至三年的改革试验,加快转变政府职能,积极推进服务业扩大开放和外商投资管理体制改革,大力发展总部经济和新型贸易业态,加快探索资本项目可兑换和金融服务业全面开放,探索建立货物状态分类监管模式,努力形成促进投资和创新的政策支持体系,着力培育国际化和法治化的营商环境,力争建设成为具有国际水准的投资贸易便利、货币兑换自由、监管高效便捷、法制环境规范的自由贸易试验区,为中国扩大开放和深化改革探索新思路和新途径。试验区的主要任务是按照先行先试、风险可控、分步推进、逐步完善的方式,形成与国际投资、贸易通行规则相衔接的基本制度框架,涉及加快政府职能转变、扩大投资领域开放、推进贸易发展方式转变、深化金融领域的开放创新、完善法制领域的制度保障等五方面。同时,试验区还致力于营造相应的监管和税收制度环境。

➤ New Words and Expressions

accentuate v. 强调;增强
affluent a.& n. 丰富的;富裕的;富裕的人
apocalyptic a. 重大实践的
appropriation n. 拨款;拨付;占用;盗用
as of 在……时;到……为止;从……时起
asuncion n. 亚松森(巴拉圭首都)
at large 详尽地;充分地;随意地
auditor n. 审计师
bureaucrat n. 官僚(主义者)
bureaucracy n. 官僚;官僚主义
cartel n. 卡特尔;企业联合

catastrophe n. 大灾难
cede v. 转让;割让;放弃
censure n. & v. 指责;责备
chaos n. 混乱;一团糟
compatible a. 适合的
comprise v. 包含;构成
condiment n. 辛辣调味品
conductive a. 传导性的
conformance n. 依照;符合
conglomerate n. & a. & v. 聚合的;联合大企业;(使)聚合

conspiratorial *a.* 阴谋的；共谋的

conurbation *n.* 集合城市（拥有卫星城市的大都市，如伦敦等）

countervail *v.* 补偿；抵消

deindustrialize *v.* 去工业化

deployment *n.* 施展；调动；利用

determinant *n. & a.* 决定因素；决定性的

devastation *n.* 破坏；压倒

directorate-general *n.* 总主管；（部门等的）全体行政工作人员

dismantle *v.* 拆除（设备）

disparity *n.* 不同；不等

dissemination *n.* 传播

earmark *v. & n.* 标记；特征

endow *v.* 捐赠；给予

enter into force 生效

entrench *v.* 对（法律保障的权利等）实施额外保证

envisage *v.* 想像；设想

exodus *n.* （成群的）出去；（大批人）移居国外

fall within 被纳入……范畴

fiscal *a.* 财政的

fora *n.* （复数）论坛；讨论会

foremost *a.* 首要的；杰出的

grip *v. & n.* 掌握；支配；控制

harmonise *v.* 协调；成为一致

hindsight *n.* 事后的聪明；事后的认识

homogeneous *a.* 同类的；同族的；均一的

impartial *a.* 公正的；无偏见的

impetus *n.* 促进；推动力

inaugural *a.* 就职的；创立的

ineffectual *a.* 无效果的

infringement *n.* 违反；侵害

initiate *v.* 创始；发起

in rotation 轮流地

institutionalize *v.* 使制度化

integration *n.* 结合；整体；成为一体

inter alia *ad.* [拉]除了别的因素以外，首先，特别

isolationism *n.* 隔离主义

legislation *n.* 立法；法规

linear *a.* 按发展顺序的

loot *v. & n.* 值钱的东西；掠夺

maladministration *n.* 管理不善

methyl *n.* 甲基

monetary *a.* 钱的；货币的；金融的

monitor *v. & n.* 监视；监督；监控器

narcotics *n.* 麻醉

nationalism *n.* 民族主义；国家主义；工业国有主义

notwithstanding *ad. & prep. & conj.* 尽管

ombudsman *n.* （调查官员渎职的）特派调查官

on a par with 和……同等/同价

override *v.* 撤销；使无效

per capita *ad. & a.* 每人；按人计算地/的

petition *n. & v.* 诉状；请求

pharmaceutical *a.* 制药的；药剂的

pledge *v. & n.* 诺言；抵押（品）；典当（品）；保人；保证

plenary *a. & n.* 完全的；充分的；全体出席的；全体会议

plummeting *n.* 骤然跌落

post *v.* 宣布；把（某项目）过账；把……入账；向……提供最新消息

powerhouse *n.* 权势集团；发电厂；强国

primus inter pares *n.* [拉]同事（或同辈）中位居首位者（或年最长者）；（团体的）发言人

premier *n. & a.* 首相；总理；首位的；最早的

proceedings *n.* 诉讼（程序）

rationalize *v.* 合理化改革工业或农业等

refer...to 向……提交

renounce *v.* （声明）放弃；拒绝承认

revive *v.* 使再生效

rotate *v.* 轮流

scrap *v.& n.* 敲碎；报废；碎片；废料

secretariat *n.* （作为行政机构的）部，处；书记（或秘书、部长、大臣）的职务

see to it that ……保证使……；务必使……；将……搞定、落实

seniority *n.* 资深；职位高

spectrum *n.* 系列；范围

spur *v.* 疾驰

stifle *v.* 抑制

stratum *n.* 阶层

subscription *n.* 签署（同意）；（债券等的）认购（额）；捐助

subsidy *n.* 补贴；津贴；（一国给另一国的）财政援助

substantive *a.* 实体的；规定权利和义务的；实质的

suffrage *n.* 投票权；投票

summit *n.* 最高级会议；峰会；最高官阶

surpass *v.* 超过；胜过

swarms of 大量的；许多的

tap *v.* 开发；发掘

term of office 任职期限

unilateral *a.* 单方面

unanimity *n.* 一致（同意）

unify *v.* 使成一体；联合的；单边的

unparalleled *a.* 无比的；空前的

unprecedented *a.* 史无前例的；前所未有的

vis-à-vis *n.& prep.* （职位上的）对等人物；相应地位的人；关于；和……相对

▶ Discussion Questions

1. How many levels of economic integration are there? What are the differences between them?

2. What is a political union? Is EU a political union? Why or why not? Please give an example of a political union.

3. What does the Triad mean? What functions does the Triad perform in the world economy?

4. Why are the "Four Little Tigers" not so often mentioned as before?

5. How does TPP differ from WTO?

6. What is ths great significance of China (Shanghai) Pilot Free Trade Zone?

Chapter 3 | Culture and International Business 文化与国际商务

Objectives
学习目标

To understand the nature of culture.

理解文化的性质。

To understand the impact of culture on international business.

理解文化对国际商务的影响。

To learn to avoid cultural conflicts in conducting international business.

学会在国际商务活动中避免文化碰撞。

To learn how to resolve the problems arising from the cultural conflicts in international business.

学会解决国际商务活动中由文化碰撞引起的问题。

3.1　What Is Culture?　何谓文化?

Culture is around us everywhere and we are affected by it all the time before we can realize it. But what is culture? There are more than 160 definitions of it. The following are only a few of them.

（1）Culture is always a collective phenomenon, because it is at least partly shared with people who live or lived within the same social environment, which is where it was learned. It is the collective programming of the mind which distinguishes the members of one group or category of people from another. (Hofstede G. *Cultures and Organizations*. London: HarperCollins Business 1994:5)

（2）Culture is the sum total of the beliefs, rules, techniques, institutions, and artefacts that characterized human populations. In other words, culture consists of the learned patterns of behaviour common to members of a given society—the unique lifestyle of a particular group of people. (Ball D A, McCulloch W. H, Jr. *International Business*. 6th ed. London: Richard D. Irwin, 1996)

(3) A national culture is the set of beliefs, perspectives, motivations, values and norms shared by the majority of the inhabitants of a particular country. (Bennett R. *International Business*. London: Pitman Publishing, 1999)

(4) Clifford Geertz (1926—present) is best known for his ethnographic studies of Javanese culture and for his writings about the interpretation of culture. In attempting to lay out the various meanings attached to the word "culture", Clifford Geertz refers to the important anthropological work, Clyde Kluckhohn's *Mirror for Man*, in which the following meanings are suggested:

A. "The total way of life of a people"

B. "The social legacy the individual acquires from his group"

C. "A way of thinking, feeling, and believing"

D. "An abstraction from behaviour"

E. "A set of standardized orientations to recurrent problems"

F. "Learned behaviour"

G. "A mechanism for the normative regulation of behaviour"

H. "A set of techniques for adjusting both to the external environment and to other men"

I. "A precipitate of history"

J. "A behavioral map, sieve, or matrix"

In addition, John H. Bodley, Chairman of the Department of Anthropology at Washington State University, says: "I use the term 'culture' to refer collectively to a society and its way of life or in reference to human culture as a whole."

After studying many other explanations about culture, we find that:

(1) culture is a learned human behaviour, a way of life, and it is not innate. Culture is social heritage, or tradition, which is passed on to future generations;

(2) the various aspects of culture are interrelated;

(3) culture defines the boundaries of different groups;

(4) culture consists of everything on a list of topics, or categories, such as social organization, religion, or economy;

(5) culture is ideals, values, or rules for living;

(6) culture is the way human beings solve problems of adapting to the environment or living together;

(7) culture is a complex of ideas, or learned habits, and it inhibits impulses and distinguishes people from animals;

(8) culture consists of patterned and interrelated ideas, symbols, or behaviors;

(9) culture is based on arbitrarily assigned meanings that are shared by a society.

3.2 Layers of Culture 文化层面

As is mentioned at the beginning of this chapter, culture is around us and has been affecting us all the time. Everyone must be in a certain culture. As culture consists of different layers which are interrelated to each other, it is possible that a person might be exposed to culture at different layers at the same time. We can divide culture into the following layers.

(1) A national level according to one's country (or countries for people who migrated during their lifetime).

(2) A regional and/or ethnic and/or religious and/or linguistic affiliation level, as most nations are composed of culturally different regions and/or ethnic and/or religious and/or language groups.

(3) A gender level, according to whether a person was born as a girl or as a boy.

(4) A generation level, which separates grandparents from parents and from children.

(5) A social class level, associated with educational opportunities and with a person's occupation or profession.

(6) For those who are employed, an organizational or corporate level according to the way employers have been socialized by their work organization.

From the above, we can see that it is quite possible that a Chinese manager who works in the UK is at several cultural levels: first, he carries the Chinese traditional culture which all Chinese people share; secondly, as he is working in a business, he carries the corporate culture which is shared by business people in general and which is shared by his colleagues in particular, because the company where he is working has its own business culture. And what's more, the Chinese manager has masculine culture which is shared by the male and differs from the feminine culture.

The layers of culture, however, can be divided in a different way. It can be categorized into the outer layer: explicit products, the middle layer: norms and values, and the core: assumptions about existence. Figure 3.1 shows the relationship between them.

Explicit culture is the observable reality of the language, food, buildings, markets, fashions and so on. They are the symbols of a deeper level of culture. For example, if we see a group of Japanese managers bowing, we are actually seeing explicit culture as the sheer act of bending.

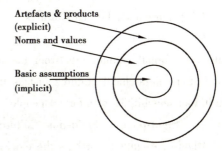

Figure 3.1   A Model of Culture

Norms are the mutual sense which a group has of what is "right" or "wrong". Values, on the other hand, determine the definition of "good and bad", and are therefore closely related to the ideals shared by a group. The norms, consciously or subconsciously, give us a feeling of "This is how I normally should behave". Values, however, give us a feeling of "This is how I aspire or desire to behave."

For example, in one culture, people might agree to the value: "Hard work is quite important to a prosperous society." The behavioural norm of the people in another culture, however, might be: "Do not work harder than the other members of the group because if so we would all be expected to do more and would end up worse off." In this point the norm differs from the value.

Once I asked my MBA students of an international class a question "What is the purpose of an enterprise?" Interesting enough, I got different answers: " to obtain more profits", "to compete", "to produce goods", "to enlarge sales", and so on. We cannot arbitrarily say that those answers are wrong. The core of human existence is to survive. Likewise, the core of culture is related to existence. The basic value human beings strive for is to survive. So is a business. Historically and presently, we have witnessed civilizations fighting daily against nature. The word "culture" originates from the same root as the verb "to cultivate", meaning to till the soil: the way people act upon nature. Therefore, we can see that the core of culture is actually related to nature. A specific organizational culture or functional culture is nothing more than the way in which groups have organized themselves over the years to solve the problems and challenges presented to them.

So far as international business is concerned, we can categorize four sorts of patterns of cross-cultural business behaviors.

(1) Deal-focus vs. Relationship-focus

This is the "great divide" between business cultures. Deal-focused (DF) people are fundamentally task-oriented while relationship-focused (RF) people are more people-oriented. Obviously, the two sorts of cultural business behaviors conflict with each other. For example, when deal-focused export marketers try to do business with prospects from relationship-focused market, many RF business people find DF types of business people pushy, aggressive and offensively blunt. In return, DF types often consider their RF counterparts dilatory, vague and inscrutable.

(2) Informal vs. Formal Cultures

Problems occur when informal business travellers from relatively egalitarian cultures cross paths with more formal counterparts from hierarchical societies. Breezy informality offends high-status people from hierarchical cultures just as the status-consciousness of formal people may offend the egalitarian sensibilities of informal people.

(3) Rigid-time vs. Fluid-time Cultures

Rigid-time culture worships the clock while fluid-time culture is more relaxed about time and scheduling, focusing instead on the people around them. So conflict may occur when business people of the two sorts of cultures meet. Some rigid-time visitors regard their fluid-time customers as lazy, undisciplined. Whereas, the fluid-time culture business people often regard the rigid-time customers as arrogant martinets enslaved by arbitrary deadlines.

(4) Expressive vs. Reserved Cultures

Business people of expressive culture communicate in radically different ways from their more reserved counterparts no matter whether they are communicating verbally, para-verbally or nonverbally. The confusion resulting from these differences can spoil our best efforts to market, sell, source, negotiate or manage people across cultures. The expressive/reserved divide creates a major communication gap.

3.3   Reasons for the Differences Between Cultures   文化差异的原因

To study the reasons for the differences between cultures is very useful and important for differentiating international business relationships between nations because culture may become an obstacle between the international businesspeople if they are not familiar with the culture of the country from which their customers come.

There are three chief factors that result in differences between cultures.

（1）Language

Language plays a particularly prominent role in the way culture is transmitted. Without language, there would be no real culture. Language helps people think and communicate. It is agreed by most people that people encode things in memory in terms of a particular language, and language defines the way they view the world. In other words, language determines the content of a society's mental representation of their environment. People use language for interaction with others, so language has a powerful role in shaping people's behaviour and in forming beliefs and habitual patterns of interaction, hence, culture. Language, therefore, is an artefact of culture that helps to form its values, attitudes, beliefs, and behavioural routines. For example, when a British employee who has finished a job beautifully is praised by his boss "Well done!" he usually responds by saying "Thank you!" But in China, the employee may say "没什么", which literally means "nothing".

A language is inextricably linked with all aspects of a culture, and each culture reflects in its language what is of value to the people. Culture is largely inculcated through language: either spoken or written. Very little of what man learns is actually learned from his individual experience. Language, then, becomes the embodiment of culture.

Language is a factor that greatly affects cultural stability. When people from different areas speak the same language, culture spreads more easily and they can communicate better. The language diversity has created problems for companies in integrating their workforces and marketing products at a truly national level. In an international business the management might include managers from different cultures who speak different languages. More often than not, those people meet problems because of culture conflict.

There are thousands of languages spoken in the world. But only a few dominate. The English, French, and Spanish languages have widespread acceptance. They are spoken prevalently in 44, 27, and 20 countries, respectively. Commerce can more easily occur with other nations that share the same language.

Of all the languages in the world, the English language is regarded as "international language", with which we can do business with business people from any nations.

People speaking the same mother tongue share the same culture no matter whether they are living in the same country or not. So business people need to pay attention to the culture conflict originating from this.

It is necessary to point out that a new trend is worth paying attention to. The Chinese language is being learned by an increasing number of nations. This is because China is becoming more and more influential in economy and politics. What's more, the Chinese language is second only to English in terms of the number of the people speaking it.

(2) Survival

Many cultural characteristics originally developed to help the survival of groups in their environment. For example, many Western cultures shake hands with their right hand as a form of greeting. Initially, this was probably an indication that no weapon was being held or about to be drawn with the dominant right hand. Further, people in different climates seem to have different attitudes towards time. For example, the lack of urgency often observed in tropical climates might have originally reflected the lack of seasonality related to agriculture. Because crops can be grown all the year round, there is no need to plant and harvest at certain times and therefore people there pay little attention to deadlines.

(3) Religion

Religion, an important component of culture, is responsible for many of the attitudes and beliefs that affect human behaviors. So people of different religions differ in culture. To know the basic tenets of some of the more popular religions will contribute to a better understanding of why people's behaviors and attitudes vary so greatly from country to country.

Religion reflects beliefs and behaviors shared by groups of people that cannot be verified by empirical tests. So religious values are closely related to cultural values. There are three chief religions: Buddhism, Christian and Muslim. Besides, there are a number of other religions such as Hindu.

Religion is a strong shaper of values. Almost all regions have people of various religious beliefs, but a region's culture is most influenced by its dominant religion. Some religion areas of dominance transcend national boundaries. The dominant religion usually influences legal and customary business practices. The extent to which religion affects the cultural profile of a society depends on the extent to which a particular religion is dominating or state sanctioned, the importance that society places on religion, the degree of religious homogeneity in the society, and the degree of tolerance for religious diversity that exists in the society.

Since religion affects culture, we have to pay attention when doing international trade. For example, if we sell beef to India we may meet criticism from Hindu. For the same reason, Muslims will never buy your pork no matter how hard you try to market it and consequently you offend them, which might influence your future business relationship.

(4) Environment

Environment refers to the surroundings one lives in. It includes the material life, the education system, the political system, the traditional modes of thoughts and so on. It is said that man is an outcome of the environment. It means that the environment a person lives in will shape him or her in some way. In other words, if a person stays in a certain environment in a relatively long period of time, he may modify himself to some degree. For example, a manager who used to be a professor in a university might appear different from what he used to be because of his long time business career.

3.4   Cultural Conflicts in International Business　国际商务中的文化碰撞

Doing international business is a cross-cultural activity. In communicating with each other, business people from different cultures bring their own cultures which might be in the way here and there between them.

As human beings, people from any culture have a lot in common. Therefore, in general, if language is not a problem for us, we can communicate with verbal language or nonverbal language. But in particular, since there exist differences between cultures, there occur some cultural conflicts between international business people, which is quite possible and natural. In a way, understanding the cultural conflicts and knowing how to tackle them is of vital significance to international businesspeople, which will be discussed in the following.

3.4.1   Cultural Conflict in Negotiation　商务谈判中的文化碰撞

Negotiation is a common and necessary process in concluding an international transaction. Businesspeople from different cultures may sometimes find themselves in an awkward position owing to the cultural conflict. As a matter of fact, when two parties of different cultures sit at the negotiation table, two cultures are conflicting. Cultural conflict may result in a failure of a deal or loss of opportunity or loss of profits. For example, foreigners with some knowledge about Chinese culture will avoid making an appointment with Chinese businesspeople to negotiate during the traditional Chinese Spring Festival, especially on the New Year's Eve and in the three following days, as Chinese people think that it is not the time to make money during the Festival. On the other hand, they need relaxation after a whole year's hard work.

Cultural elements influence the style, method, pace, and goal of negotiators. The negotiators must remain alert to not only the culture of the society represented but the personal views and outlook of the negotiator across the negotiation table and even across wire (when talking on the phone).

Negotiation between businesspeople is an activity of cross-cultural communication, and closely linked with communication is the accommodation of differences in negotiating styles. Some cultures are more formal than others, others more confrontational; some tend towards understatement, others inclined to exaggeration; some more conscious of status and far less egalitarian than Americans, others so circumspect (to save face and preserve harmony) as to leave a typical Western businessman baffled in trying to find out the intent.

Understanding manners and customs is especially important in negotiations because misunderstanding manners or customs of another culture may result in poor outcomes or even disasters.

To negotiate effectively in cross-culture environment, all types of communication should be read correctly. For example, Americans often interpret inaction and silence as negative signs. Japanese managers tend to expect that their silence can get Americans to lower prices or sweeten a deal. Even a simple agreement may take days to negotiate in the Middle East because the Arab party may want to talk about unrelated issues or do something else for a while. The aggressive style of Russian negotiators and their usual last-minute change requests may cause astonishment and concern on the part of ill-prepared negotiators. The following examples may further show how culture conflicts damage international trade transactions.

At the negotiation table, the Western business negotiation group leader found the Japanese negotiation leader nodding his head after he made his offer to the Japanese negotiators, so he thought the Japanese business counterpart agreed to their offer, and he took out the contract, hoping to conclude the negotiation by signing the sales contract. But, to his great astonishment, the Japanese counterpart did not show any sign of signing the contract. The Western business negotiation group leader, however, felt offended. He thought the Japanese counterpart was not serious. The negotiation then ended resultless.

The process of decision making is varied. The time taken to make one decision will depend on whether such authority is centralized, assigned to a committee of technical people, routed through a network within the organization, or entirely delegated to the negotiator. For example, it is also concerned with the negotiation between the Japanese businesspeople and an American group. After being offered the price, the Japanese negotiators habitually remained silent for some time. The American negotiator, however, thought that the price he had offered might be not competitive. So he reduced the offered price, which surprised and very much pleased the Japanese negotiators.

From the above two examples, we can see that cultural conflicts are quite worth paying attention to.

Businesspeople from the West and the East differ a lot in culture. Even among Europeans whose cultures are nearer to each other, if two partners have not taken the trouble to get acquainted or complete their homework, the result might be terrible. For example:

Once an Italian director of a construction company went to a German company to negotiate for a project. He began the discussion with a presentation of his company that vaunted its long history and its achievements. Hearing this, the German managers first looked startled, then they excused themselves and left without even listening to the offer. The Italian director was not wrong in doing in that way. On the other hand, the German managers were not purposely rude by leaving without even listening to the offer. Cultural conflict was responsible for all that. Germans typically do all the necessary background research before walking into the door. They thought the Italian director was engaged in idle boasting about his company, and they found that offensive. Yet the Italian director thought that he was engaged in a vague preliminary of any real negotiations. Real negotiating, as far as he was concerned, would not start at least for another day.

The above example illustrates how cultural conflict affects business negotiations even between business people whose cultures are somewhat similar. As mentioned previously, differences between cultures arise from such factors as religion. For example, Chinese businesspeople from Guangdong

Province normally believe in Buddhism. They rely more on fortune in negotiating. In Northern Europe, with its Protestant tradition and indoor culture, people tend to emphasize the technical, the numerical, and the tested. Southern Europe, on the other hand, with its Catholic background and open-air lifestyle, tends to favour personal networks, social context, innovation, and flair. Meetings in the south are often longer, but the decision process may be faster. So when negotiating with businesspeople from the south of Europe, you need more patience.

It can be seen that cultural differences exist between regions, which is reflected in negotiation. For example, in approaching negotiations, Nordics embrace win-win styles, while the British and Germans prefer position-based tactics in which the parties act as adversaries who stake out their positions and fight aggressively to defend them.

In France there is not such north-south differences. One study shows that the style of French negotiators is the most aggressive of thirteen diverse cultures. In a way, the French still embrace the art of diplomatic negotiating invented in France in the fourteenth century. French managers will have carefully prepared for negotiations, but they normally will begin with some light, logical sparring. Throughout the preliminary and middle stages of negotiation, the French managers will judge the partners carefully on their intellectual skills and their ability to reply quickly and with authority. French businesspeople may be impressed more by brilliant savvy than by a well-reasoned argument. This is because the French education system stresses mathematics and logic. Doing business is a highly intellectual process for French managers. This reflects the fact that education is one of the factors that affect culture.

Only when the negotiation process is conducted within the cultural context of both parties does the transaction become possible. This quest is ongoing because negotiations are a recurring activity. Further, it is not the agreement but what happens afterwards that determines whether the participants of the negotiation will satisfy their objectives. In this, the cultivation of cultural compatibility not only makes the deal but also preserves it. Therefore, the art of cross-cultural negotiation must not simply be learned and forgotten; it will of necessity support the foundation of the commercial arrangement.

3.4.2　Cultural Conflict in Marketing　国际营销中的文化碰撞

In order to export its products, an international corporation has to make marketing strategies and has them carried out. Marketing is one of the important elements for an exporter to compete and survive. Before we start to discuss cultural conflict in marketing, it is quite essential to define marketing.

Some think that marketing is a company-driven function concerned only with getting goods to the consumer at the most advantageous price for the producer. Others think that marketing is driven by the needs of the customer, and that its main aim is to satisfy consumers by giving them the products they demand, when they want them and for the price they are willing to pay.

Marketing is actually a series of activities which are intended to draw profitable demands for products or services by such means as advertising, promotion, direct selling, pricing, positioning, carrying out market research, developing and testing new products. Above all, marketing is a strategic process that identifies competitive advantages and potential threats, and effective marketing planning is an essential part of any business strategy.

Cultural conflict may occur in international marketing. Great attention must be paid to this. Basically, exporters encounter culture at two distinct levels.

(1) The individual level, where they negotiate and communicate with their direct contacts in the market.

(2) The market level, where they satisfy the needs of their customers by modifying products and approaches to appeal to the population at large. Despite the influence of one on the other, anticipating individual behaviour premised entirely on the inclinations of society is to deny the strong influences of one's family, profession, social class, generation, and many other influences. In the same way, anticipating market behaviour based on single individual is equally spurious, as the collective experience of the society might bear little resemblance to the model.

International trade marketers must be clear about the two levels so that they may contact business partners of other cultures more easily and market their products better.

Products (service is also a kind of product) are the core of marketing. As far as products are concerned, industrial products are less impacted on by culture than consumer goods.

To market products, international business managers must be concerned about differences in the ways products are used in different cultures. Usage differences have to be translated into product forms and promotional decisions. General Foods' Tang is positioned as a breakfast drink in the USA; in France, where fruit juices and drinks are not usually consumed at breakfast, Tang is positioned as a refreshment. To improve powdered-soup domination in Argentina, Campbell markets its products as "the real soup", stressing its list of fresh ingredients. In Poland, where most soup consumed is home-made, Campbell promotes to mothers looking for convenience.

If attention is not paid to the cultural conflict, marketing program may not go as well as it was expected. Take Disney as an example:

Differences between European and US catering culture played a supporting role in bringing the Disney theme park near Paris to the verge of bankruptcy. Disney, one of the world's most successful global marketers, initially refused to adapt its food and beverage service formula to the European customers.

When Euro Disney's restaurants started to operate in 1993, there was no sufficient seating capacity. Whereas Americans visiting Disneyland and Disney World in the USA eat lunch anytime the spirit moves them, while the French and other European visitors wanted lunch at the same time, around 1 p.m. Nor did European visitors accept standing in queue for an hour or so. What's more, Euro Disney restaurants offered no wine or beer. That was because Disney's US eateries are "family restaurants" where alcoholic beverages are out of place. What did it matter if European traditions and expectations are totally different? By late 1993 Euro Disney had suffered a lot of losses approaching one billion dollars. Faced with the terrible fact, the management of Disney amended the marketing strategy and put a European in charge of the operation. Among the modifications made was an important addition to the menu: visitors can now enjoy beer or wine at what is now called Disneyland Paris.

For the management at Disney, the European fiasco was a temporary blip in a brilliant record of success in marketing across cultures. Therefore, cultural conflict can never be ignored. The following further strengthens this point.

Cultural conflicts which can affect international business operations arise in all aspects of business activity and have their impact within each of traditional functions. Differences in the behaviour of customers must be taken into account in product policies and marketing strategies. For example, a German housewife values convenience and can be rather easily persuaded to buy packaged soup. A French housewife, however, prefers homemade soup because it fulfils her image of herself as the mother. For another example, an American area manager, John Watson of an international cosmetics company was instructed by the headquarters to sell soaps in Malaysia. The fragrance of the soap, however, is not popular in Malaysia, so the sales were very poor.

Many aspects of a product such as packaging, colour, and advertising message, should be changed to fit the local culture without changing the product's basic nature; otherwise, cultural conflicts may cause unexpected outcomes.

For example, in China, the battery whose trade mark is "白象" is famous and sells well. But when the trade mark was literally translated into "White Elephant" and exported to the western world, the sales were stuck. The marketer later found out the cause: "white elephant" in English culture refers to something that is stupid and useless; thus, a burden. Nobody wants to buy a product which indicates uselessness. Here is another example, lotus is a delicate flower favoured by Chinese people, but in Japan, lotus is associated with funeral. So products with lotus pattern or a product whose brand name is concerned with lotus cannot be exported to Japan.

Here is another example: the famous company GM tried to market the car whose brand name was "Chevy Nova" in Mexico. But the translation of "Nova" in Mexico means "won't go". Are consumers willing to buy a car that "won't go"? Consequently, the sales of this car in Mexico were poor. The translation must be changed just because of cultural conflict resulting from the language. Another interesting example, Kentucky Fried Chicken's translation of advertisement slogan "It's finger licking good!" into "It's so good, you will eat your fingers." in Persian. What marketing effect will be obtained then?

More examples will show how important it is to know the cultural conflicts in marketing. The example of Kentucky Fried Chicken in India illustrates the difficulties that marketers may have in entering culturally complex markets. Even though the company opened its outlets in two of India's most cosmopolitan cities (Bangalore and New Delhi), it found itself the target of protests by a wide range of opponents. Of all the reasons for this protection, the culture conflict was chiefly responsible. American catering culture is quite different from Indian's. KFC should have tried to appear more Indian rather than using high-profile advertising with Western ideas. Indians are ambivalent towards foreign culture, and its ideas may not always work well there.

3.4.3　Cultural Conflict in Business Administration　企业管理中的文化碰撞

Cultural conflicts often occur in the administration of an international company where employees are from different cultures. As more and more investment goes to foreign countries, the number of subsidiaries, joint ventures and other affiliated businesses is increasing worldwide. Those businesses include people from different cultures at all levels. Especially the senior managers might be made up of mixed cultures. In an international company, the general manager may come from the UK where the headquarters of the company are located, the sales manager may be from the host country, and the accounting manager may come from Japan. These managers may find themselves encountering conflicts resulting from culture. Besides, the foreign managers may likewise encounter cultural conflicts when they deal with problems with the employees.

For the multinational enterprise the impact of cultural conflicts affects management at two levels, the national and the multinational.

At the national level, the situation is largely of "we and they" type. The manager of a subsidiary must be aware of possible conflicts between local conditions and the cultural assumptions underlying the business practices being imported. Essentially these problems are two-sided and management personnel of subsidiaries must be the bridge between the local situation and the international enterprise.

At the multinational level, or more specifically at the global or regional headquarters of the international enterprise, the task is to coordinate and integrate business activities that are operating in many different cultural environments. Managers must deal with many languages and many cultures. The problems are both horizontal—across many cultures—and vertical—between each subsidiary and headquarters. And the organizational structure and policies of the global enterprise must facilitate communications and the implementation of policies across many cultures in order to achieve global goals.

It is well known that markets are becoming globalized and the need for standardization in organizational design, systems and procedures is increasing. Yet international managers are also under pressure to adapt their organization to the local characteristics of the market, the legislation, the fiscal regime, the socio-political system and the cultural system as well.

To survive, the international enterprises have to try to accept the values of local culture patterns and seek to work within the limits of the accepted behavior patterns and customary goals that underlie these beliefs.

In all circumstances, local traditions and habits are respected and, as often as possible in foreign operations, local concepts are permitted to continue in preference to substituting those of another culture pattern. As a general rule, foreign firms find it wise to adjust to local standards with less deviation than is permitted for native companies because of nationalistic sensitivity to foreign influences.

Any business operating within a single country must adjust to the culture within which it operates, but the need for cultural sensitivity and adjustment is much greater for the international company. For the international company, cross-national transfer of any one of its old products or conventional practices may represent an innovation. When a company has an existence outside a culture, many of its actions will introduce something new, which might be accepted or not accepted because of cultural conflicts or for some other reasons.

Differences in behavior and values of employees can have a major impact on the effectiveness of production-management policies. The Chinese worker may find that lunch break is so important for the following afternoon work, while the German workers may have their lunch by eating bread and drinking beer while working. Further, the African factory worker may find paternalism a desirable practice because it helps him replace security feelings that he loses when he leaves his traditional group. The American factory worker, on the other hand, tends to feel that paternalistic management is outdated because it restricts his current need to express his individuality.

The external relations of the international company can also be affected by cultural conflicts. In dealing with local business firms in a specific national environment, the international enterprise may have to recognize that agreements and accommodations among potential competitors, rather than aggressive competition, are the accepted norm. And bribery might be a traditional means that influences official actions in one culture while it is not in another culture. In raising money from local banks or security markets, personal reputation may be the key requirement in one culture whereas a high degree of financial disclosure may be the more important element in another.

The international manager might not be a professor who is expert at culture. But he should become generally familiar with the key cultural elements that are likely to affect international business activities.

One of the principal differences among cultures is in assumptions and attitudes relating to man's ability to influence the future. For example, an assumption that people may substantially influence the future underlies much of US management philosophy. This belief in self-determination contrasts sharply with a fatalistic viewpoint in some Moslem cultures that the future is not in man's hands.

Variations among cultures in the dominant views toward achievement and work can be a vital determinant of management performance and productive efficiency. The achievement motivation of an individual refers to a basic attitude toward life. An achievement-motivated person makes accomplishment an end in itself. But, in some cultures, there are people who may not be achievement-motivated. They are more material-motivated: they are more interested in the rewards. The manager should be clever enough to differentiate the people who differ in this respect.

So far as an international business is concerned, the management of the business is, to some extent, management of cultures. International managers operate in a brand new culture. In every culture in the world such phenomena as authority, bureaucracy, creativity, good fellowship, verification and accountability are experienced in different ways. Take the American international cosmetics company for example again. In 1992, Richard Sanford was the general manager with Peter Schuster as his assistant. The former was not familiar with Chinese culture while the latter was and his wife was a Chinese. Mr. Schuster was greatly influenced by Chinese culture and knew that Chinese people pay more attention to relationship in management. So he even tried his best to ask the management not to dismiss an employee. In contrast, Mr. Sanford stuck to his idea that American culture is superior. He thought management should be based on American culture. Then cultural conflict sometimes happened even between the two Americans.

Therefore, international managers have to adapt themselves to the new culture and learn to deal with cultural conflicts which might occur at any time.

3.4.4　Cultural Conflicts in Business Public Relations　商务公共关系中的文化碰撞

The process of doing business is actually an art of how to deal with the relationship between people. This is especially true of doing international business, because more than one culture is involved in the whole process. A businessman who is expert at dealing with public relations is more likely to succeed. But, when he is in a strange culture or when he is dealing with public relations linked to different cultures, he has to be careful with the cultural conflicts. It is quite likely for a man who is not familiar with the cultural conflicts to offend other people before he can realize it.

Man with some knowledge about western world may know that it is not proper to ask a female's age. So, when you are at a cocktail party with business partners, you may start a conversation by asking something unimportant such as "You look so beautiful with this dress on today!", "Today's weather is so fine, don't you think?". But if you ask a young girl "Are you married?" She may feel very surprised and might be offended by your question.

Body language sometimes differs greatly in different cultures. For example, disagreement is indicated by shaking the head from side to side in such countries as the UK and China, but in some other cultures, they may nod the head or perhaps wave their hand in front of the face.

Once an American businessman was talking excitedly with his foreign customers at dinner after a successful negotiation between them. The American businessman made a circle with his thumb and forefinger to indicate "OK". His foreign customer felt astonished when seeing his gesture. The next day, the contract was cancelled by his foreign partners because in their culture, the circle refers to a special organ of man's body. It is considered to be very rude to do so.

Dealing in China, international managers need know that making deals has more to do with cooperation than competition. The Chinese businessmen believe that one should build the relationship first and, if successful, transaction will follow.

Therefore, we can see that international businessmen have to be careful in dealing with public relations in terms of culture.

Further, different cultures have different senses of punctuality. In Germany, Switzerland, the Netherlands and other rigid-time cultures, it is imperative to be on time for the scheduled meeting.

On the other hand, in some other cultures the visitor is expected to arrive on time in order to show respect. In some cultures, a woman may not like to shake hands with a man. So never reach out your hand before a lady offers hers.

Non-European visitors tend to be perplexed by the variety of kissing rituals in the multicultural mixture that is in Europe. But don't worry about kissing or being kissed the first time you meet. Of course do not kiss the people whose culture you are not sure of.

When exchanging business cards, the side with English version must face foreign businessmen. It is very respectful to offer a business card with two hands in China and Japan. But, in the UK, British businessmen may not realize it. Many visitors to the USA are struck by how casually Americans treat business cards. An American businessman is likely to stuff the card in his back pocket, toss it onto the desk, scribble on it or even pick his teeth with it at the lunch table.

When we give business gifts, cultural conflicts must be paid attention to. In some cultures, if you give a sharp object like a knife as a gift, that means the end of the relationship. In Europe, when an agreement is signed, it is time to give the gifts, but in some Asian countries, at the end of the meeting. You must know that North America is not a gift-giving culture. Many companies have strict policies concerning gifts, especially for people with purchasing responsibilities.

In China, people normally do not open the package of the gift the moment the gift is received. In the western cultures, however, the package will be opened as soon as the gift is received together with compliments like "How beautiful it is!", "I like it very much!".

In addition, as businessmen often entertain each other, table manners are also very important. Different cultures have different catering customs, to which enough attention must be paid to avoid awkwardness.

3.4.5   Culture and Accounting   文化与会计

It is believed by many people that culture has a significant influence on accounting. Culture, in the sense of how people think and feel and their values, beliefs and attitudes, affects their behaviour. Accounting regulations and practices are an outcome of human behaviour.

Culture modifies the influence of ecological or environmental and external factors. It also influences the values or subculture of accountants and the institutions of a society. These in turn both influence accounting system.

Social culture influences the organizational structures. This has obvious implications for both management and financial accounting. One example is Japanese companies. Japanese corporate groups are often based on a multitude of relationships such as supplier, customer and debt relationships and common directorships. Rather than there being majority share-ownership by a clearly defined parent company there are often relatively small share cross-holdings throughout the group.

Besides, decision-making processes of companies should be considered. These, in turn, will influence the accounting system. But culture also has a more direct impact on financial accounting.

The financial accounting system is set up and run by and for various groups of people, in particular auditors, management accountants or other statement preparers, accounting regulators (who may or may not also be accountants) and statement users. Each of these groups may be thought of as a distinct sub-cultural group with its own subculture. Some of these groups are not very homogenous and will not have a well-defined subculture. For example, shareholders range from private individuals to companies holding shares in associates and subsidiaries, to investment trusts and pension schemes. They have little in common beyond perhaps sharing a belief in private ownership of industry, profit maximization by companies and personal wealth maximization.

3.5 Corporate Culture and National Culture 企业文化与民族文化

3.5.1 The Development of Corporate Culture 企业文化的形成

Corporate culture, which is also called "organizational culture", is a new concept proposed in the second half of last century. The term "organizational culture" first appeared casually in English-language literature in the 1960s as a synonym of "climate". The equivalent "corporate culture", coined in the 1970s, began to become popular and accepted by businesses.

In recent years, the word "culture" seems to be fashionable. Talking about culture seems to be a fad. We can hear "campus culture", "wine culture", "tea culture", etc.

"Corporate culture" has already become a widely accepted term in mainstream business. Many executives pay as much attention to culture as to strategy in shaping a business plan. Some mergers are shunned because of cultural differences; others proceed because the cultures of the merging partners line up.

It is not difficult to understand this phenomenon as culture is concerned with groups of people who share the same customs, values, norms and so on. Among those people, there gradually forms a certain specific common concept of conduct in their spirit and practice. For the same reason, in a company, a certain corporate spirit and specific mode of practices will develop and finally be formed, hence, corporate culture.

3.5.2 What Is Corporate Culture? 何谓企业文化?

Corporate culture is closely related to the management of businesses in terms of organizational structure, strategy, and control. It seems that there is no standard definition about corporate culture, but it is agreed by most people that corporate culture is:

(1) holistic, referring to a whole which is more than the sum of its parts;

(2) historically determined, reflecting the history of the organization;

(3) related to the things anthropologists study, like rituals and symbols.

In his work *Cultures and Organizations*, Geert Hofstede defines the "organization culture" as follows: the collective programming of the mind which distinguishes the members of one organization from another. (Geer Hofstede, 1994, p.180)

Corporate culture shares the characteristics of what we call "culture". The staff in a company are an independent group. Although an individual has his or her own sense of norms, values or outlook of life, they share the same norms, values, and rituals in their way of work. In other words, their behaviors in work are based on the same rules and regulations of the same company. Their conduct is normally based on the same ideal. Among them there is a common understanding about their conduct in the company.

Corporate culture is concerned with the management of the company. Edgar Schein, the author of *Organizational Culture and Leadership* says: "There is a possibility, under-emphasized in leadership research, that the only thing of real importance that leaders do is to create and manage culture and that the unique talent of leaders is to work with culture."

The strategies are made by the management. Those strategies contain the ideas of the founder or the founders and the successive leaders. The ideas are embodied in the strategies or plans they make and are carried out by the staff of the whole company. As time goes by, specific style of management is gradually formed. That is not enough so far as corporate culture is concerned. It is when there is a spirit shared by all staff of the company and there is a special atmosphere in which the staff work in accordance with the same criterion that a corporate culture may take its shape.

In 1995 the famous magazine *Fortune* reported the results of its corporate reputation survey. The report says: "There is growing concern that companies cannot live by numbers alone. The one thing that set the top-ranking companies in the survey apart is their robust cultures." A robust culture in a cohesive enterprise is committed to a deep and abiding shared purpose. Its robustness is highly dependent on a unifying colourful cultural picture woven over time as people cooperate and learn together.

As a matter of fact, each company has its own specific culture. The problem is that nobody notices the formation of the culture to which the staff of the company have been contributing. To a large extent, this depends on the management of the company. Clever managers will purposely try to find out the underlying culture in the company or try to create their specific culture for the sake of management. A corporate culture moves in months and years, not days and weeks. Values focus on the future and the importance of investing in it, as is best symbolized by the slogans of some famous companies.

"Progress is our most important product." (GE)

"Better living through chemistry." (DuPont)

"Alcoa can't wait for tomorrow."

"IBM means offering you services."

With clear corporate cultural orientation, the company will be more cohesive and may keep energetic even when the company goes through a difficult period.

From the above discussion we may define corporate culture as follows:

Corporate culture is a specific spirit commonly shared by a company and a specific atmosphere under which the whole company strive for the objectives. Both of the spirit and the atmosphere distinguish the company from others, and influence and guide the company staff's practices in their work.

3.5.3 Differences Between Corporate Culture and National Culture 企业文化与民族文化的区别

Every type of culture normally shares some characteristics of culture in general. So corporate culture and national culture have something in common in that both are concerned with the elements of culture. However, it is not right to say that the two cultures are identical phenomena. This is because a nation is not a company, and the two types of culture differ in nature. The differences between national and corporate cultures are due to the different roles played in each by the manifestations of culture shown in the following Onion Figure (Figure 3.2).

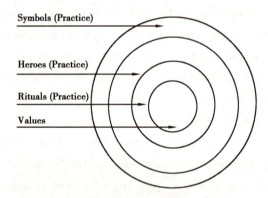

Figure 3.2 "Onion Figure": Manifestations of Culture at Different Levels of Depth

The above figure shows that symbols, heroes, and rituals have been subsumed under the term "practices". As such they can be observed by the outsiders; their cultural meaning, however, is invisible and lies precisely and only in the way these practices are interpreted by the insiders. On the other hand, the core of culture as shown in the figure, is formed by values. Values are broad tendencies to prefer certain states of affairs over others.

Corporate culture focuses on the given criterion or guidance in order to direct the practice of the staff of a company. National culture is linked with deeper levels such as values. It is found out that the roles of values versus practices are exactly reversed with respect to the national level. Comparing otherwise similar people in different companies showed considerable differences in practices but much smaller differences in values. This is shown in Figure 3.3.

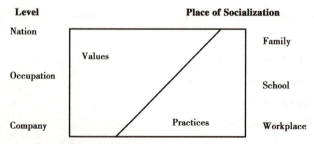

Figure 3.3 The Nature of Cultural Differences: the National, Occupational, and Corporate Level

A national culture is a set of beliefs, perspectives, motivations, values and norms shared by the majority of the inhabitants of a particular country. As the above figure shows, at the national level cultural differences reside mostly in values, less in practices. On the other hand, at the corporate level, cultural differences reside mostly in practices, less in values. An occupational cultural level has been placed halfway between nation and company. This is because values are acquired in one's early youth, mainly in the family and in the neighbourhood, and later at school. As a child grows up, most of his basic values have been programmed into his mind. Corporate practices, on the other hand, are learned through socialization at the workplace, which most people enter as adults, that is, with the bulk of their values firmly in place.

Generally speaking, the values of a company's founder and key leaders will shape corporate cultures, but the way these cultures affect ordinary staff is through shared practices. Founders-leaders' values become staff's practices. The shared perceptions of daily practices should be considered to be the core of a corporate culture.

So far as national culture is concerned, people observe the values which are passed on to them. It is understandable that in a company the employees share the corporate culture, but their values may differ more according to criteria like the nationality, age, and the education of the employees than according to their membership of the company.

▶ 3.6　Cultural Conflicts and Multinational Companies (MNCs)
　　文化碰撞与跨国公司

The following discussion actually is related to business administration. But we intend to discuss the topic from a different perspective.

Cultural conflicts happen between the multinational company and the host country. The international managers have to face a new culture round them. Normally a company will seek to work within existing local culture patterns, although this may not always be possible. MNCs may have a number of fresh subsidiaries in foreign countries. They need to introduce working methods that might conflict with the cultures of the host countries.

To survive, MNCs should try to build upon rather than destroy traditional values and practices, implement controversial measures only when there is a definite need for them, and communicate with employees as much as possible.

On the other hand, an MNC may have employees from different cultures. Those employees might find themselves involved in cultural conflicts because each of them carries their national culture although they work under the same corporate culture.

Further, more cultural conflicts will happen in a merged company, as it takes time for the culturally related management practices and policies to mix together. For example, when a multinational company employs American and British managers who have much in common as both share the same language tradition, there still exist cultural conflicts between them. In the USA, results are normally the criteria for the selection and promotion of executives. In the UK, an

American general manager complained that people were promoted because of the school they attended and their family background but not for their accomplishments. Likewise, school ties are important in France. It is the same with China. For example, a clerk who graduated from Beijing University may have more chances to get promoted than an employee who graduated from an ordinary university.

In China, there are numberless subsidiaries or joint ventures where managers are from different cultures. In the beginning, those foreign managers might not be accustomed to the Chinese culture. But if they want to succeed in his management in China, they should pay attention to the cultural conflicts and try to avoid the conflicts by learning Chinese culture. As a matter of fact, some foreign managers in China are used to Chinese culture and are doing well in their work.

As we all know, the Japanese are famous for their excellent teamwork spirit, but in the USA, individualism is very popular. So if a Japanese manager and an American manager work together, they might encounter cultural conflict. To cooperate better in their work, they have to learn to get used to each other's culture.

Nowadays, more and more Chinese companies start their operations overseas. They have to take into account cultural conflicts in their strategy program. Getting familiar with the local culture is the first step of their overseas investment project. The following tips might be helpful in avoiding cultural conflicts.

(1) A mentor is most desirable. Knowledge about the local culture can be obtained from the mentor.

(2) It is necessary to do extensive reading about social and business etiquette, history and folklore, current affairs (including current relations between the two countries), the cultural values, religion, political structure, and practical matters such as currency and hours of business.

(3) While in the multinational company, international managers need have some local close friends who may be either his colleagues or from other lines of business. From frequent contact with those friends, he can learn more about the local cultures. Besides, to take part in local people's activities can help to get some sense of local culture.

(4) Try to learn to speak the host country's official language. No matter how well you can speak, it is a way to get nearer to the local culture. At least, you are nearer to the local culture psychologically.

(5) Understand components of cultures. A region is a sort of cultural iceberg with two components: surface culture (fads, styles, food, etc.) and deep culture (attitudes, beliefs, values). Generally speaking, less than 15% of a region's culture is visible, and the foreign managers must look below the surface. For example, in the UK, British people have the habit to line up on the sidewalk when waiting for a bus. This is surface culture, which results from the deep cultural desire to lead neat and controlled lives.

(6) Respect the local culture. Pay attention to your manners. Some business managers, especially those from developed countries, may think their cultures are superior. Those managers will

often encounter cultural conflicts. Once a Saudi Arabian official said "Americans in foreign countries have a tendency to treat the natives as foreigners and they forget that actually it is they who are foreigners themselves."

（7）Never do what you are not sure of when you find there might be a cultural gap. Be sure that you will not offend others before you start to act.

（8）Try to get information from any sources, such as newspaper, TV programs and Internet.

Summary of This Chapter
本章概要

1. 国际商务人员绝不能忽略文化因素对交易的影响。文化影响人的行为方式和思维方式。只有了解客户所在国的文化传统，才能进一步了解客户其人，从而顺利地进行交易。

2. 文化是人类在社会历史发展过程中所创造的物质和精神的总和，特指精神财富，如文学、艺术、教育、科学等。文化和文明的内涵包括知识、艺术、道德、法律、习俗，以及作为社会成员的个人而获得的其他任何能力、习惯在内的一种综合体。文化是一个社会的信仰和实践的总和。

3. 不同的国家有不同的文化传统。文化的决定因素以文化准则和价值观体系为中心，它涉及宗教、语言、教育、社会结构、政治制度、科技发展水平等。东西方世界的文化迥然不同。即使是东方国家间，文化传统由于其决定因素之故，差异也很大。

4. 随着人类文明的发展，文化也发生变化。人类的价值观不断演变。科技的迅猛发展促进了文化的演变。此外，文化与语言有密切的关系。通过语言，社会的信仰才得以表达和传播。语言是文化的一部分，同时又是文化的载体。没有语言就没有文化，由此可见语言对文化的影响非常之大。

5. 一个国家有其独特的文化。一个企业也有其独特的文化。"企业文化"一词最早出现是在20世纪60年代。企业文化是近年来企业战略管理的一个重要方面。企业文化的形成需要企业领导对其重视，在制订企业策略时对本企业的文化特色需要有明显的方向性，使本企业全体员工在统一的管理策略下，形成企业的独特文化环境和文化氛围。企业文化的形成就是这样一个渐进发展、逐步形成的过程。企业文化一般指的是一个企业有别于其他企业的企业精神、独特的管理模式、独特的劳动价值观和团队敬业氛围。

6. 国际商务活动实际上是跨文化交际活动。不同国度的商人烙上了其祖国传统文化的烙印，同时又带有其独特的企业文化。所以，在进行国际商务活动中出现文化碰撞是很自然的事。文化碰撞发生的表现形式主要是人与人之间的文化隔阂和行为习惯、观念等的差异。文化碰撞反映在企业营运的各个方面，如营销、企业管理、公共关系、业务谈判等。

▶ New Words and Expressions

accessorize v. 用配件(或饰件)装备

adversary n. 对手;敌手

affiliation n. 联营;隶属

ambivalent a. 举棋不定的

anecdote n. 轶事

anthropological a. 人类学的

anthropologist n. 人类学者

arbitrarily ad. 武断地

artefact n. 人工制品

at large 详尽地;充分地

attire n.& v. 服装;使穿上

backslap v. 拍某人的肩膀

baffle v. 阻碍

banal a. 平庸的

beckon v. 召唤

blip n. 清脆短促的声音;信号

blunt a. 生硬的;钝的

bouquet n. 花束;(酒的)香味

breezy a. 轻松活泼的

cohesive a. 有凝聚力的

compatibility n. 和谐

contact n. 熟人

cosmetics n. 化妆品

deviation n. 偏离

dilatory a. 拖拉的;拖延的

egalitarian a.& n. 平等的;平等主义者

empirical a. 经验主义的;来自经验的

ethnic a.& n. 种族(上)的;异族的;人种学

ethnocentric a. 种族的

ethnographic a. 人种的

etiquettes n. 礼节;(行业中的)规矩

evasive a. 偷漏(税等)的

explicit a. (租金等的)需直接付款的;货币的;清楚的

facilitate v. 推进;促进

fad n. 时尚

fiasco n. 大败;长颈瓶

hierarchical a. 等级制度的

holistic a. 全盘的;全面的

impasse n. 僵局

indomitable a. 不屈服的

inextricably ad. 复杂地;(困境)无法摆脱地

in preference to 优先于

inscrutable a. 不可理解的;不可思议的

interrelate v. (使)互相联系

lager n. (浓度轻的)啤酒

manifestation n. 显示;证明

martinis n. (一种)鸡尾酒

matrix n. 基层;基质

merger n. (企业、公司等的)合并

niceties n. 细微的区别

orientation n. 向东;方向;倾向性;适应

para-verbally ad. 类似词语地

partake v. 参与;分担;吃;喝

perplex v. 使费解;使困惑

port n. 姿态;姿势;波尔图葡萄酒(原指葡萄牙产的一种深红色葡萄酒)

potted plant 盆景

precipitate v. 猛然下降;使下降

premise v. 以……为前提;预先提出

presumptuous a. 专横的;傲慢的

prop v.& n. 支撑;支持

pushy a. 粗鲁的;一意孤行的

recurrent a. 周期性发生的

repertoire n. 全部技能;所有组成部分;全套

rigid a. 刻板的;僵硬的

ritual n. 仪式;程序;礼制

robust a. 强健的;坚强的;醇的;浓的

savvy n.& v. 实际知识;理解;知晓

shun *v.* 避免；回避
sieve *v.& n.* 过滤（器）；精选
spurious *a.* 伪造的
stake out 流出；保留
subsume *v.* 把……归入（纳入）；把……包括

在内
underlie *v.* 位于……下面；构成（理论、政策、行为等）的基础；（权利、担保等）优先于
vaunt *n.& v.* 自吹自擂

▶ Discussion Questions

1. What are culture, national culture, and corporate culture? What are the differences between national culture and corporate culture?

2. Why should culture be paid attention to in international business?

3. What does cultural conflict mean?

Chapter 4 | International Business Environment 国际商务环境

Objectives
学习目标

To have knowledge about the international business environment.

掌握国际商务环境知识。

To outline the importance and the influence of various environmental factors.

概述各种环境因素的重要性及影响。

To understand the relations between the environmental factors.

了解各种环境因素之间的关系。

Business organizations are different in many ways. However, they have something in common: the transformation of inputs into outputs. This transformation process takes place against a background of external influences which affect the company and its activities. This external environment is complex, volatile and interactive, but it cannot be ignored in any meaningful analysis of business activity.

It is said that a person is a product of the environment. There is something in saying so. Any person is living within a certain environment, and so is a firm. Therefore a firm is surely affected by the environment in which it conducts domestic and international business.

Basically, organizations are entities which consist of interrelated parts that are intertwined with the outside world: the "external environment" in system language. This environment is concerned with a wide range of influences: economic, demographic, social, political, legal, technological, and so on. All this affects business activity to some extent. Figure 4.1 shows the environment around a firm.

International businesses do not operate in a vacuum. They cannot be isolated from the external environment within which they operate. Besides, as different countries differ in political system, economic development level, legal system, cultural orientation, and so on, international businesses have to be very careful when conducting international business. It is quite possible that external

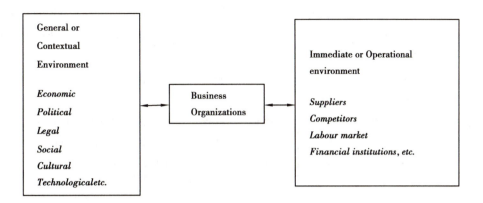

Figure 4.1   Two Levels of Environment

environmental factors can result in positive opportunities or in negative constraints. Therefore, it is very important and quite necessary for managers to identify all the relevant factors in the international business environment, understand their influences on the companies' operations and assess their weaknesses and strengths. The following aspects have impact on international business.

4.1   The Economic Environment   经济环境

Business organizations operate in an economic environment which shapes, and is shaped by, their activities.

The economic environment in which international business must be conducted is normally the most important aspect of the remote environment. In every nation and region in the world, the constant interplay of the factors of production (land, labour and capital) impacts on the activity of all firms, both domestic and multinational. The domestic economic environment affects business activities within a country, while the international economic environment affects business activities between and among nations.

Domestic economic environment is concerned with the following.

4.1.1   Population   人口

Market size is primarily a function of the population and purchasing power propensity. Generally speaking, the larger the population, the better the market. But it is rational to say that there is no correlation between population size and sales potential. Nevertheless, population is the primary indicator of the size of any market. International companies should consider the population size of the country where they are going to conduct business. Thus, China, the country with the largest population in the world, is always considered to be an important market.

Besides, the geographic distribution of population within a country is also important, because it has significant marketing and logistics implications for international marketing planning. Normally, urban centres tend to be more densely populated than the rural areas. This affects international business activity. Besides, a country may be made up of relatively developed areas and underdeveloped areas or developing areas. Population in different areas has different living standards and different demands. International businesses normally focus on those developed areas, as the population there is denser and the purchasing power is stronger. Those developing areas can never be ignored, though.

In addition, age distribution is an important consideration when the structure and composition of the population is being examined. People of different ages have different consumption ways. The different needs of those people affect the activities of international business.

4.1.2　Per Capita Income　人均收入

It is probably the commonest statistical indicator of a country's economic potential that international companies consider when they are going to make investment decisions. Per capita income measures the performance of an economy in relation to the size of the population. If a country's population is small but it is supported by high gross domestic product (GDP), the per capita income will be high. The size of China's population is very large, but the per capita is not high, as China is still a developing country. Attention should be paid to the fact that to rely entirely on per capita income in evaluating a country's marketing potential might be misleading.

4.1.3　Income Distribution　收入分配

Although per capita income can be an indicator of the basic economic potential of a country, it is generally misleading and perhaps dangerous for international companies to rely on this indicator in assessing any market, because the income distribution is not average. In a country, it is possible that wealth is concentrated in the hands of a tiny minority of the population. Therefore, it is not uncommon that 20 percent of the population enjoy 80 percent of the luxury products.

4.1.4　Types of Economy　经济形态

Different types of economy may show differences in the level of development, the predominant economic activities, availability of economic and technological infrastructures, and the degree of urbanization. It is important to identify the differences in evaluating the level of development, type of production techniques and the nature of consumption in a country, because those aspects are closely related to the marketing of certain products. There are economic types like central planned economy, free-market economy. They affect business activities in different ways.

Centrally planned economy is the economic type in which the central government plans and governs most economic decisions. This type used to be adopted in China. The disadvantages of this type are self-evident to most Chinese people.

In a free-market economy prices determine what goods companies need to produce; production costs and the availability of resources determine how they are produced (and the incomes that factors inputs shall receive); while consumer spending determines the market prices which themselves generate production. So goods in great demand command highest prices. Consequently, companies will try their best to provide products to meet the consumers' requirements. On the other hand, concerns for the environment, social justice, etc., are treated in much the same way as demands for particular products. The key features of free-market economy are as follows:

(1) Resources are in private ownership and the individuals owning them are free to use them as they wish.

(2) Firms are normally privately owned. They are free to make their own decisions on production without state interference.

(3) There is no blueprint (master plan) to direct production and consumption.

(4) Decisions on resources allocation are the result of a decentralized system of markets and prices, in which the decisions of millions of consumers and hundreds of thousands of firms are automatically coordinated.

(5) The consumer is sovereign. In other words, the consumer dictates the pattern of supply and hence the pattern of resource allocation.

In a word, market forces decide what to produce, how to produce, and how to distribute. Figure 4.2 illustrates the basic operation of a market economy.

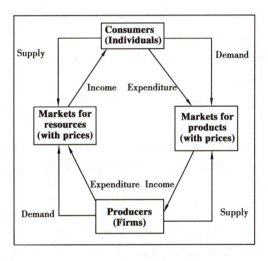

Figure 4.2   The Market Economy

>> 4.2   The Political Environment   政治环境

International business activities are often affected by political environment. A political ideology often plays an important role so far as political environment is concerned. A political ideology is a body of constructs (complex ideas), theories, and aims that constitute a socio-political program. Ideologies can help bring countries together. A good example is China. One reason why China wants Hong Kong back is because of ethnic Chinese ties. Further, mainland China, China Taiwan, China Hong Kong, and Singapore are considered as "Chinese Economic Area".

The political environment in which international business is conducted is made up of three important elements: the home country political environment, the host country political environment, and the global political environment. The three are generally complex and intertwined.

4.2.1 Home Country Political Environment 母国政治环境

If the political environment of the home country is favourable, a company's international business activities will not be affected much. But this is not likely to happen. Any nation has its political policies towards international business. This is particularly pertinent to certain product categories, such as frontier military and nuclear technology.

Governments usually have specific rules and regulations to restrict international business. Such regulations are based on political purposes. The restrictions are particularly sensitive when they address activities abroad.

On the other hand, the political environment in most countries normally offers general support for the international business efforts of companies headquartered within the country. For example, a government may try to reduce trade barriers or to increase trade opportunities through bilateral and multilateral negotiations.

Political environment is therefore closely related to government activity. International business managers must pay attention to the government activity which normally involves three main areas: embargoes or trade sanctions, export controls, and the regulation of international business behaviour.

(1) Sanction and embargo

Sanction and embargo are used to refer to governmental actions that distort free flows of trade in goods, services, or ideas for decidedly adversarial and political, rather than economic purposes. Economic sanctions and embargoes have become a principal tool of the foreign policy for many countries. They are often imposed unilaterally for the purpose of changing a country's government or at least changing its policies.

(2) Export control

Export control systems are designed to deny or at least delay the acquisition of strategically important goods by adversaries. Many nations have export control systems. There are regulations or laws to control all export of goods, services, and ideas from the country.

Many international business activities can be carried out with a general license which is used to provide blanket permission to export.

(3) Regulating international business behavior

A country may make special laws and regulations in order to assure that the international business activities are in agreement with the country's moral, ethical standards.

4.2.2 Host Country Political Environment 东道国政治环境

Host country politics are those of the foreign market in which a company may be conducting its activities away from home. Host country policies governing the activities of foreign companies can range from the welcoming and supportive to the outright hostile. The political atmosphere in the host country influences the activities of international companies. If the political situation of the host country is quite fine and stable, international businesses are more inclined to conduct business there; otherwise, they will turn to other international markets.

4.2.3 Global Political Environment 全球政治环境

Global political environment may be described as the combined politics of the home, host and third countries. The political atmosphere in a third country can have a major impact on the activities of international companies in ways that may not be immediately apparent. International companies must consider the following before they conduct business in a foreign country:

(1) The political structure of the country;

(2) The type of economic system of the country;

(3) Whether their own industry is in the public or private sector;

(4) How the foreign country considers their investment;

(5) The ways the foreign government controls the nature and extent of private enterprise;

(6) The policies of the foreign country towards overseas investment.

A country's political system influences how business is conducted domestically and internationally. For example, in Hong Kong, the political change from China taking control in 1997 worried many managers. But as the political situation remains stable, international business activities in Hong Kong are not so affected as expected.

4.3 The Legal Environment 法律环境

Businesses and individuals both live and conduct their activities within a certain framework of law based on customs and practice, on the judicial decisions of the courts and on statutes enacted by governments. The legal environment affects and regulates a company's activities. Besides, the legal environment also provides an enabling mechanism through which a company may meet its own needs and achieve profits through entrepreneurial activity.

The law of a country reflects the political and social attitudes of the country. Today, the society is becoming more and more litigious and business organizations must not ignore the legal implications of their actions. On the other hand, the legal environment in a country is always influencing the business activities of companies.

The legal environment in which international business is conducted could be considered as a subset of the political environment, as the two are completely intertwined. The legal system is another dimension of the external environment that influences business. Managers must be familiar with the legal systems in the countries where they do international business, the nature of the legal profession, both domestic and international, and the legal relationships that exist between countries.

4.3.1　Legal System　法律制度

Legal system can be classified as common law, civil law, and theocratic law.

Common law is based on tradition, precedent, custom and usage. The USA, Canada, and the UK are examples of this legal system.

Civil law is based on a detailed set of laws that make up a code. Rules for conducting business transactions are a part of the code. So, civil law system is also called codified legal system (Code Law). More than 70 countries operate on a civil law basis, such as most European countries, Japan, Russia, and so on. Civil Law (Code Law) is established by arbitrary methods and constitutes a comprehensive set of codes which clearly spell out the laws applicable in all possible legal situations. These are divided into three separate codes: commercial, civil and criminal. When dealing with business matters, commercial codes have precedence over other codes.

The main difference between the common law and civil law is that common law is based on the courts' interpretations of events, while civil law is based on how the law is applied to the facts.

Theocratic law is based on religious precepts. The best example of this law is Islamic law, which is found in Muslim countries. Islamic law is a moral rather than a commercial law and is intended to govern all aspects of life. An example of how Islamic law influences international business can be found in banking. Islamic law does not allow banks to pay or collect interest. Instead, banks have to structure fees into their loans to allow them to make a profit.

4.3.2　Three Aspects of the International Legal Environment　国际法律环境 的三个方面

The legal environment normally is concerned with three aspects: home country laws, host country laws, and international laws.

(1) Home country laws

Home country laws and regulations deal with two important issues: conduct of the company in the domestic market and trade with third countries.

The laws and regulations are made to protect the domestic consumers, national interest and security. Companies' activities are subject to those laws and regulations.

For the international operators, there are additional controls on exporting to third countries. Laws concerned are made to control the international activities of companies for the sake of the country. Many countries have established anti-trust laws and anti-corruption laws.

Anti-trust laws are used to prevent foreign business firms from engaging in anti-competitive practices such as price-fixing, producer collusion, taking over competitor through illegal means, and other activities considered harmful to local competition.

There is currently no international agreement regarding the control of corrupt practices. Governments and business firms have different definitions and interpretations of corrupt practices and policy standards.

（2）Host country laws

Multinational enterprises (MNEs) must observe the laws of the host country. Their activities are subject to the laws and regulations of the host country. The most important areas with strong control include investment regulations, tariffs and duties, anti-dumping regulations and the protection of local industries (the infant industry argument).

In developing countries there are always some laws and regulations to control foreign companies activities. Foreign companies may be excluded from competing with domestic companies in certain sectors of the local economy or their involvement is severely restricted to protect local industry.

（3）International laws

International law is defined as the collection of treaties, conventions and agreements between nations, which have, more or less, the force of law. They are normally multilateral among nations.

International laws are particularly related to such areas as patents and trademark protection, piracy laws, UN resolutions, multilateral trade agreements such as GATT and Codes of conduct for MNEs. International laws are made for MNEs to observe so that the business activities can be carried out more successfully. Registered intellectual properties and inventions are protected in international law under the auspices of the World Intellectual Property Organization (WIPO).

4.3.3 Legal Risk Analysis 法律风险分析

There exist legal risks in international business activities. It is quite important and necessary for business managers to conduct a legal risk analysis before signing any contract to start up a business in a foreign country. The legal risk analysis should include the following (Sonia El Kahal, 1994)：

（1）A detailed examination of the legal system in operation in the country considered (civil, code, or Islamic) and a thorough understanding of the laws themselves；

（2）A historical review of any discriminatory practices against foreign citizens and firms practised by that country；

（3）Familiarity with contract enforcement practices and appeal procedures；

（4）A clear identification of arbitration practices available；

（5）A study of the foreign country's consistency in implementing the law；

（6）An understanding of the compensation award system and its procedures；

（7）A current revision of administrative procedures；

（8）A consideration of relevant international law and international conventions and codes.

4.4 The Socio-cultural Environment 社会文化环境

4.4.1 Factors of the Socio-cultural Environment Influence 社会文化环境影响因素

The socio-cultural environment for international business refers to the set of factors which shape the material and psychological development of a nation, and represents the primary influence on individual lifestyle, attitudes, predisposition and behaviours.

The social dimension of culture is receiving serious attention as a critical determinant of international management behaviour. The socio-cultural environment is made up of the following:

(1) Physical variables;

(2) Demographic variables;

(3) Behavioural variables.

The variables all influence business activities in a given country. So it should come as no surprise that the socio-cultural environment of international business gives MNEs managers many problems in the new culture, which can be defined as the totality of the complex and learned behaviour of members of a given society. The elements of culture include beliefs, art, morals, law and customs.

Culture is, perhaps, one of the most important determinants of consumer behaviour. Besides, culture considerations are most important in marketing, with human resource management coming a close second. Therefore, managers must understand that socio-cultural environment greatly influences international business activities. Figure 4.3 illustrates the relationships in the socio-cultural environment and marketing implications.

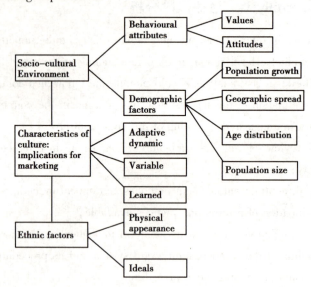

Figure 4.3   The Socio-cultural Environment and Marketing Implications

4.4.2   The Impact of the Socio-cultural Environment on International Business
社会文化环境对国际商务的影响

From the perspective of international marketing, international business is chiefly affected by the socio-cultural environment in the following aspects.

(1) Product

Because there exist differences in beliefs, values and lifestyles between countries, the utility value of a single product may be quite different. For example, branding and packaging of products are always subject to cultural influence. In China, consumers seem to be more interested in products with English version on the packaging.

(2) Price

Products are bought in markets on the basis of either perceived or real utility value. In some developing countries, if a product is marked with "Made in the USA", it will normally be considered as higher quality, hence, deserving higher price.

(3) Promotion

Culture is perhaps the most powerful influence in determining effectiveness and acceptability or otherwise of advertising copy, design and other elements of marketing promotion in international markets.

(4) Distribution

Certain distribution strategies may be affected by local norms and practices that derive from culture. For example, mail order business does not work in Spain, because packages cannot be delivered to private addresses by the post office.

In a world of globalization, cross-cultural understanding appears particularly important in conducting international business activities. MNEs managers should keep the following points in mind to cope with international differences in culture.

(1) Be culturally prepared.

(2) Learn the local language and its non-verbal elements.

(3) Mix with host nationals.

(4) Be creative and experimental without fear of failure.

(5) Be culturally sensitive; do not stereotype or criticize.

(6) Recognize complexities in the host culture.

(7) Perceive yourself as a culture bearer and ambassador.

(8) Be patient, understanding and accepting of your hosts.

(9) Be most realistic in your expectations.

(10) Accept the challenge of intercultural experiences.

4.5   The Technological Environment   技术环境

Technology and its application have become the key factors in determining the international competitiveness of the firm in international business.

The technological revolution in the 1980s and 1990s just means that no firm, and certainly no industry, can be insulated from its impact on both domestic and international business. As the impact of technology increases, the significance of local and regional differences is diminished.

Technology is a critical aspect of MNE operations, and represents the single most important competitive advantage that an international firm can possess. MNEs can internationalize the advantage throughout its network of subsidiaries at very little extra cost. Technological changes lead to new products and new processes.

In assessing the technological environment, the MNE has two difficult tasks: appraising the nature and extent of competitors' technology, and forecasting the rate and direction of technological advances. The former is normally carried out as part of the firm's normal strategic management process. The latter can be carried out in the following ways:

(1) Seeking expert opinions;

(2) Extrapolating from existing statistical trends;

(3) Forecasting with the aid of specially designed computer-based modes.

The concept of the global village is commonly accepted today and indicates the importance of communications in the technological environment. The rapid expanding use of fax machines, portable telephones, and personal communication devices points to the evolution of unrestricted information flows. The new technologies offer exciting new opportunities to conduct international business. Changes in other technologies will be likewise rapid and will have a major effect on business in general. For example, the appearance of super-conductive materials and composite materials has made possible the development of new systems in fields such as transportation and electric power, pushing the frontiers of human activity into as yet unexplored areas such as outer space and the depths of the oceans.

The evolutionary nature of technology implies that companies that are able to maintain their technological activities will remain competitive.

4.6 The Financial Environment 金融环境

When a company is going to internationalise its activities, it will inevitably encounter foreign financial markets. The financial environment also impacts international business. An international company will encounter the global foreign exchange market which has two main purposes: currency conversion and reduction of foreign exchange risk.

Besides, an international company may face transaction exposure whenever there is a significant time gap between an international transaction and the payment. Foreign exchange rates keep changing. Further, a government may impose exchange controls to restrict the use of its currency in international transactions.

Considering the close linkage among financial markets, shocks in one market will quickly translate into rapid shifts in others and easily overpower the financial resources of individual governments. Therefore, financial environment is likewise vital in conducting international business. International business activities are affected by the international financial environment. For example, a few years ago the financial crisis in the south-east Asian countries seriously affected other financial markets in the rest of the world and international business activities were consequently affected as well.

When considering individual foreign countries, MNEs will obviously be influenced by different tax regimes. And minimization of global tax payouts by declaring foreign profits in appropriate countries is a very worthwhile activity. An international company can also achieve a formidable competitive advantage by borrowing funds in countries with low interest rates and investing these funds in other parts of its global network, including the home country. It can then be seen that the different financial environment also influences international business activities.

4.7　The Information Environment　信息环境

Information is like a bridge between the organization and its environment and is the means by which a picture of the changing environment is built up within the organization.

It is said that we are in a world of information. Information plays a particularly important role in international business. The more quickly a firm gets information, the more chances it can obtain to succeed in its international business. Knowledge is one of the greatest assets of most organizations and its contribution to sustainable competitive advantage has been noted by many.

A firm's knowledge base may include, among other things, an understanding of the precise needs of customers, how those needs are likely to change over time, how those needs are satisfied in terms of efficient and effective production systems and an understanding of competitors' activities.

Information about the current state of the environment is used as a starting point for planning future strategy, based on assumption about how the environment will change. In turbulent environment, having access to timely and relevant information can give a firm a competitive advantage. For example, firms that got information about the potential financial crisis in the south-east Asian countries might not suffer as much as those not timely informed.

4.8　The Internal Environment　内部环境

Generally speaking, internal environment refers to those key aspects of the internal context of business such as the organisation's structure and functions and the way they are configured to achieve specified organizational aims.

Internal environment of a firm affects its operations to a great extent. Internally, the structure and policies of an organization affect the manner in which the organization responds to environmental change. Today, great attention is being paid to the internal features of business organizations when companies conduct international business. There are normally three areas of the internal organization:

(1) Understanding organizations;

(2) Organizations' structures;

（3）Key functions within the enterprise.

4.8.1　Understanding Organizations　认知组织

A central theme running through any analysis of the internal environment is the idea of "management". So the internal environment is closely related to business management.

The internal culture of a company can affect the way it responds to organizational change. Corporate culture concerns the social and behavioural manifestation of a whole set of values which are shared by its members.

In addition to its dominant culture, it is often possible that a company may have subcultures. It is found out that within many organizations, cultural attitudes are hard to change when the nature of an organization's business environment has significantly changed, leaving the established culture a liability in terms of managing change.

For many organizations, employees are the biggest item of cost and potentially the biggest cause of delay in responding rapidly to environmental change. Many organizations have been trying to improve the effectiveness of their employees through a program of internal marketing, which came to prominence during the 1980s. It describes the application of marketing techniques to audiences within the organization. Every organization can be considered to contain an internal marketplace. Diverse groups of employees engage in exchange between each other in this marketplace.

Organizations are actually open systems, interacting with their environments as they convert input into output. Inputs include people, finance, materials and information, provided by the environment in which the organization exists and operates. Output comprises such items as goods and services, information, ideas and wastes, discharged into the environment for consumption by end and intermediate users and in some cases representing inputs used by other organizations.

4.8.2　Organization Structure　组织结构

Normally business organizations are characterized by a division of labour which allows employees to specialize in particular roles and to occupy designated positions to achieve the organization's objectives. The resulting pattern of relationship between individuals and roles constitutes what is known as the organisation's structure and represents the means by which the purpose and work of the enterprise is carried out. Besides, it provides a framework through which communications can occur and within which the processes of management can be applied.

The essence of structure is the division of work between individuals and the formal organizational relationships that are created between them. These relationships will be reflected in individual job descriptions and also in the overall organization chart which shows how an organization is organised.

4.8.3　Key Functions Within the Enterprise　企业内部的主要职能部门

Most organization structures reflect a degree of functional specialization. There are a number of functional divisions in an organization and each specializes in a certain area, such as production, finance, marketing, personnel, and so on. To manage these functions and to deal with the relationships between them play an important role in achieving the organization's objectives. Figure 4.4 illustrates the relationships.

Figure 4.4   A Functional Organization Structure

The internal functions are interdependent. For example, when Sales Department needs more salesmen, it needs Personnel Department's help, and the latter will ask Advertising Department to advertise vacant positions. And when the sales volume is increasing, Production Department has to speed up production to meet the needs of the Sales Department. Meanwhile, Sales Department may need more funds to support the sales force's business travel. The extent to which all of these requirements can be met simultaneously depends on internal factors and external influences as well.

Summary of This Chapter
本章概要

1. 国际商务环境对国际商务运作十分重要,因为各种环境因素对国际商务的运作有直接影响。国际商务管理者必须充分了解各种环境给国际商务带来的影响,尤其是负面影响。国际商务环境可分为内部环境和外部环境。内部环境指企业内部组织结构、职能部门的功能、各部门之间的关系、公司文化氛围等。国际商务内部环境近年来备受企业管理者的关注。国际商务外部环境主要有:(1)政治环境;(2)社会文化环境;(3)法律环境;(4)经济环境;(5)金融环境;(6)技术环境;(7)信息环境;等等。国际商务的各种环境互为联系,也相互影响或相互制约。处理好国际商务内部环境和外部环境是企业生存和发展的重要任务。只有具备适应各种环境能力的人和企业,才能在激烈的竞争中立于不败之地。

2. 政治环境:政治环境以各种方式影响着国际商务。政治环境涉及一个国家的政治制度。不同政治制度的国家对国际商务所采取的控制手段有所不同。政治环境包括母国政治环境、东道国政治环境及全球政治环境。投资者在制定向他国投资计划之前,必须对该国的政治环境有充分的了解和预测,如政治体制是否健全、政治形势是否稳定,等等。政治体制的健全能促进经济贸易的发展,政治形势的稳定可减少投资方的风险。

3. 社会文化环境:文化的构成因素非常复杂,它包括知识、信念、法律、习俗等。文化对国际商务的影响不容忽视。不同国家有自己独特的文化、历史、习俗及人们作为社会成员所需要的其他能力,等等。国家的民族文化直接影响企业文化。如个人主义是西方市场经济的一个主要特征,西方倾向于以合同为准的市场惯例。在东方,国家之间的社会文化差异制约着国际商务从业者。造成社会文化差异的一个重要因素是宗教。宗教对文化产生强烈的影响。不同宗教信仰的人会有不同的价值观。一个国家的价值观体系和伦理准则能影响在该国从事商务的成本。跨国企业员工必须有较好的适应不同文化环境的能力。文化环境随着时间推移而变化。经济进步和全球化可以看作是推动社会文化环境改变的两个主要动力。

4. 法律环境:法律环境主要涉及一个国家的政治、法律制度。一个国家的法律体系或制度指的是国家的法令或法律。法律制度与国际商务有着很密切的关系,并且直接影响国际商务的运作。一国的企业在从事国际商务时,必定受到该国的法律制度的制约。法律制约商务实践,规定商务交易的行为方式,制定商务交易中各有关方的权利和义务。各国的法律环境各有特点。法律制度和经济制度皆受政治体制的影响。国际商务是在国家一定的法律框架中进行的。制约商务活动的法律反映出统治者的政治意识形态。目前世界上有两个主要法律、惯例体系:普通法体系和民法体系。英国、英国殖民地及美国是采用普通法体系的国家。普通法体系在英国有悠久的历史。普通法以惯例、先例和习惯为基础,法庭解释普通法时按这些特征判决案例。民法以一套非常详细的法律为基础,这些法律被写进法典。法典定义规定商务交易的法律条文。法庭判案时根据法典解释民法的法律条文。目前世界上有 80 多个国家采用民法体系,其中包括德国、法国、日本、俄罗斯等。良好的法律环境能在很大程度上促进国际商务,因为任何企业都希望,交易各方在遵守具有法律意义的合同的前提下从事国际商务活动。

5. 经济环境:一个国家的经济环境受政治、经济和法律制度的制约。经济环境涉及国家的经济发展水平和经济制度的影响幅度。各国的经济发展水平有所不同。一个国家的国民生产总值(GNP)可以用来衡量一个国家的经济发展水平。不过应该指出,GNP 有时不一定可靠,因为国民生产总值没有考虑到生活费用的差异。经济环境的改善和提高,首先是经济发展水平的提高,即经济必须稳定、持续、良好地向前发展。经济增长需要有创新,创新需要有市场经济。商务环境中,有助于创新和经济增长的一个重要因素就是健全的法律制度。法律必须能对财产权进行强有力的保护。否则,经济环境就将受到"污染"。

6. 金融环境:金融环境与外汇、国际货币体系及全球资本市场有关。另外,一个国家的银行体系的优劣影响该国的金融环境。金融环境涉及本国金融环境、东道主国金融环境和国际金融环境。国际金融环境的好坏直接影响国际商务活动。当某个国家或某个地区金融环境恶劣时,该国或该地区的国际商务活动必然呆滞。营造良好的金融环境能给一个国家带来更多的商机。

7. 技术环境:技术环境与科学技术关系密切。科技的发展水平决定技术环境的优劣。跨国企业必须掌握最先进的科学技术及科学的管理技术,才可能在激烈的竞争中取胜。当代科学技术的迅猛发展带来了更多的商机。就国际商务而言,一个国家的技术环境若能给外国投资者提供更多的便利,那么该国的国际商务形势必然看好。

8. 信息环境:信息环境是信息时代的主要特征。随着科技的发展,尤其是电子科学技术的更新和迅速发展,"地球村"的概念逐步为人们所接受。从某种程度上来说,信息是决定一个企业生存的关键要素。只有掌握了最新、最有价值的信息,企业才能制定出行之有效的经营策略。信息是企业与环境沟通的桥梁。商场如战场,谁有最通畅的信息渠道,谁就能掌握最新信息,并能占据商务的"制高点",这样才更有竞争力。

New Words and Expressions

adversarial *a.* 对抗性的,对手的

appeal *v.& n.* 上诉(to);指控;恳请

blueprint *v. & n.* 为……制定行动计划;为……制定详细规则;蓝图;计划

collusion *n.* 共谋;串通

configure *v.* 使成形;(按特定形式)安装,装配,配置

constrain *v.* 限制;制约;强行

correlation *n.* 相互关系;依存关系

decentralize *v.* 下放权力;分散

demographic *a.* 人口的

embargo *v.& n.* 禁运

extrapolate *v.* 推断

formidable *a.* 难对付的;可怕的

implication *n.* 含义;暗示;涉及;密切关系

infrastructure *n.* (社会、国家的)基础设施

insulate *v.& n.* 隔离

interdependentl *a.* 互相依赖的;相互依存的

interplay *v.& n.* 相互影响;相互作用

interrelate *v.* (使)相互联系

intertwine *v.* (使)缠结

litigious *a.* 诉讼的;关于诉讼的

negative *a.& n.& v.* 否定的;消极的;反面意见;否定;驳斥

outright *a.& ad.* 无保留的;全部的;不分批(或分期付款)的/地

payout *n.* 花费;支出

per capita income 人均收入

piracy *n.* 侵犯版权;侵犯专利权

positive *a.* 确定的;积极的;(协定、习惯)正式规定的;(政府)行使社会经济管理职能的

precedent *n.& a.* 先例;惯例;在先的

predisposition *n.* 倾向;意向;禀性

propensity *n.* (性格上的)倾向;习性

rational *a.* 理性的;合理的

sanction *v.&n.* 认可;批准;(为维护法律所做的)制裁

simultaneously *ad.* 同步地;同时发生地

statistical *a.* 统计的;统计学的

stereotype *n.& v.* 陈规;旧框框;把……弄得一成不变

subset *n.* (组成大套的)一小套

theocratic *a.* 神权的;神权政治的

transformation *n.* 转变;变革

unilaterally *ad.* 单方面地

urbanization *n.* 城市化;都市化

Discussion Questions

1. Why is environment important to international business?

2. What is global political environment? And how does it affect international business?

3. Why do we say the functional sections of a company are interdependent?

Chapter 5 | International Trade 国际贸易

Objectives
学习目标

To get to know the main features of international trade.
了解国际贸易的主要特征。

▶ 5.1 What Is International Trade? 何谓国际贸易？

It is necessary to discuss the meaning of "trade" before we come to "international trade". By "trade", we mean the transaction between two parties; in other words, "trade" means that one party sells goods or provides services to the other, who buys the goods or technology or accepts services by paying money or paying back to the seller in some other ways.

International trade refers to the transactions that take place between the sellers from one country and the buyers from another. From the perspective of one country, international trade is also called "foreign trade". International trade is the trade that is across the border. International trade is the branch of economics concerned with the exchange of goods and services with foreign countries. International trade can also be understood as export and import of goods or technology or services. In fact, in international trade, tangible goods (goods that can be seen and touched) account for the most percentage. The purchase and sales of goods are called "visible trade" as well. In the same way, the purchase and sale of services and technology are called "invisible trade", as the subject matter concerned is not tangible goods. Visible trade is trade in goods which can be actually seen passing through ports or airports, entering or leaving one country. Invisible trade is trade in services and technology. The services in question include such items as transport, banking, tourism insurance and education. As for technology, it is more closely concerned with visible trade. For example, if an American corporation licensed China to produce a new model of DVD, the American corporation would need to make available to China all the technological knowledge required to produce that product, which is a tangible product. The sum the Chinese manufacturer paid for the use of this know-how would be an invisible item of trade.

Trade in goods and services is one of the means by which a country is linked to another in economy. Countries that have mutual international trade relationship need the goods or services from each other. They are dependent on one another in some way. One party in a country needs something and is willing to buy while the other party in another country has the goods and is likewise willing to sell the goods. Either party gets its own benefits. It is a win-win deal.

Further, the term "international trade" is broadly defined as transactions between sovereign nations which include the purchase and sale of consumer services such as travel, industrial raw materials and services, producer and capital goods such as plant and machinery, securities in the form of promissory notes and stock-ownership certificates, and natural resources such as crude oil, gold and other minerals.

International trade has developed greatly under the influence of international agreements that began in 1944 at the Bretton Woods Conference. The agreements recognized that all nations, no matter what their economic organization may be, must trade if they hope to get economically powerful. Some countries have raw materials that others do not have; some countries have favourable climates to particular crops while others do not have, and some countries have skills and expertise or technology that other countries do not have. For this reason, international trade becomes inevitable.

The foundations of international trade are linked to the following four aspects:

(1) International trade and payments;

(2) Cargo insurance;

(3) Transportation and documentation;

(4) Elements of export law.

International trade keeps changing in terms of the laws, practices and systems of trade, as the situation of the world is changing fast. It is possible that some countries' political systems are undergoing shifting, so the policies and strategies of international trade of those nations will change to some extent.

We may well say that international trade is a necessity for the prosperity of the nations on the earth on the basis of a win-win idea. Some hold the idea that international trade creates value, increases the efficiency of resource allocation worldwide, reduces production costs through economies of scale, lowers input costs and, through the international division of labour, lowers prices paid by consumers and increases product variety and availability.

International trade can also be described as the branch of economics concerned with the exchange of goods and services with foreign countries.

Today, more countries have begun to move from state-run economies to market-run economies. International trade is therefore becoming even more important under the circumstances.

▶ 5.2　How Did International Trade Start?　国际贸易的起源

International trade started on the basis of a barter trade at the very beginning. That is to say, Party A sold something to Party B, but Party B did not pay Party A with money (no money existed at that time!) but bartered the goods of the same value to Party A. In other words, commodities or raw materials were exchanged for each other and for the limited number of manufactured goods available.

With the increase of the volume of the transactions, a medium of exchange had to be found, however. Coins, made of precious metals (normally gold or silver), were the medium widely adopted. Hence, universal acceptance of money was ensured. Coins were exchanged when people from different countries did business with each other. The exchange of coins was the forerunner of modern day foreign exchange dealing. In the West, this kind of exchange took place as early as Roman Times.

It was upon this early development that the acceleration of trade was made possible as travel opened up new opportunities. What's more, human beings have three basic necessities: food, clothing and sheltering for the sake of existence. It is because of the three basic necessities that people need different commodities to meet their demands. For example, in China, apples are produced in Yantai, Shangdong. But in Nanchang, Jiangxi, no apples are produced because of the climate conditions. So, if people in Nanchang want to have apples, they have to buy from other sources with RMB. Likewise, in international trade, one country needs commodities from the other country because that country is unable to produce them or because that country needs those commodities for other reasons.

▶ 5.3　The Benefits, Structure of, and Reasons for International Trade 国际贸易的利益、结构及原因

5.3.1　The Benefits of International Trade　国际贸易的利益

There are a number of benefits of international trade.

First of all, consumers can have a wide selection of goods in the market place. Those goods may be produced with low costs and so they are at the most competitive price to the consumers. Secondly, in the perspective of developing countries, goods of advanced technology and science can be introduced as well as the advanced production lines together with the advanced administration methods. Thirdly, in the perspective of developed countries, companies can buy or produce goods with low costs. Producers benefit from the economies in cost resulting from a wider market than that obtainable within their own country. This is also true of the developing countries. Fourthly, for the countries involved in international trade, different needs of the people and of the governments are met. The balance of payments is adjusted (which will be discussed later in this chapter). Finally, in a word, international trade brings the countries benefits economically as well as politically, as trade is linked to economy and economy is always concerned with politics. International trade is a win-win deal for countries doing international trade. There may be some other benefits that international trade may bring to us. Only a few are mentioned here.

5.3.2   The Structure of International Trade   国际贸易的结构

The international trade structure seems more complex than it might appear at first sight.

Speaking of international trade, we will often think of exporting. As a matter of fact, exporting does not form the whole picture of international trade. The selling and buying methods and sometimes the methods of exchanging goods are different according to the goods and markets concerned.

The structure of international trade is made up of direct exporting, counter-trade, commodity trading, multinational operations, subsidiaries and joint ventures. The structure of international trade should not be confused with the varying channels for distribution of goods, however.

Direct exporting certainly accounts for the most percentage of international trade. It is concerned with the shipment of goods by the seller to either its agent or distributor, who will on-sell the goods to the end buyer, or direct to that buyer. Payment will be made by the agent, distributor or buyer or through the banking system.

5.3.3   The Reasons for International Trade   国际贸易的原因

Some chief reasons why nations trade with each other are stated as follows:

(1) International trade can increase competition and prevent the monopolistic control of the home market by local producers.

(2) International trade can provide a stimulus to economic growth, develop technology and improve living standards.

(3) International trade can offer more opportunities to exchange ideas and develop the infrastructure of a country or region and its resources.

(4) International trade can also develop beneficial links between trading countries and encourage tourism and education. Therefore, it helps to stabilize a country's political and economic situations.

(5) People from different nations have different tastes, preferences and consumption patterns to be satisfied. International trade can help to meet the people's needs of a country.

5.4   International Trade in the Framework of the World Economy   世界经济框架中的贸易

Generally speaking, there are three main types of economies in this world:

(1) Free enterprise economies;

(2) Mixed economies;

（3）Controlled economies.

The three types of economies are closely related to the political systems of the nations.

Free enterprise economies are ones where the government almost has no control. The trade and industry are largely run by private firms. The best example of this type is the United States of America. In addition, some other countries that have mixed economies are getting closer and closer to free enterprise by means of privatization.

Mixed economies are ones where different types of economies exist side by side. In mixed economies there are industries that are run by the state, but a large number of industries and most trading activities are controlled by private firms. The best examples are the countries of the European Union（EU）. Many advanced nations and developing nations also have some state-run industries.

Controlled economies are ones where the government controls the whole economy. Besides, the trading activities are also controlled by the government. China used to be of this type of economy.

In a way, we may say all economies are mixed economies with some differences in the extent to which the economies are mixed. This is because mixed economies have the advantages of controlled economies and free enterprise economies but avoid their respective disadvantages.

With the appearance of multinational companies, the economies of the nations are more complex. Multinational companies operate within many nations and bring prosperity to many economies. They have to some extent made the picture of international trade less clear since they operate within many nations instead of just in their own countries.

International trade just operates within this kind of framework. When we do business with different economies, we have to adopt different policies and ways to adapt ourselves to different situations so that we can successfully conclude a deal in this framework of the world economy.

▶ 5.5　Incoterms　《国际贸易术语通则》

As world economy develops so fast, firms have more chances than ever before to conduct international trade. Goods are sold in more and more countries, in larger quantities, and in greater variety.

Incoterms are standard trade definitions most commonly used in international sales contracts. Devised and published by the International Chamber of Commerce（ICC）. They are at the heart of international trade. In other words, Incoterms are the official rules of ICC for the interpretation of trade terms and are used to facilitate the conduct of international trade. Reference to Incoterms 2010 in a sales contract defines clearly the parties' respective obligations and reduces the risks of legal complications.

Incoterms are international rules that are accepted by governments, legal authorities and practitioners worldwide for the interpretation of the most commonly used terms in international trade. They either reduce or remove altogether uncertainties arising from differing interpretations of such terms in different countries.

It is likely that the parties to a contract do not know the trading practices of the overseas partners. Therefore, misunderstanding, disputes and litigation will occur between them. That entails not only time but also money. In order to remedy these problems, the International Chamber of Commerce first published in 1936 a set of international rules for the interpretation of trade terms. These rules were known as "Incoterms('International Commercial Terms')1936". Since then, ICC expert lawyers and trade practitioners have updated them seven times to keep pace with the development of international trade. The rules were amended according to the actual practice of international trade in 1953, 1967, 1976, 1980, 1990, 2000 and the latest amendments and additions occurred in the year 2010 in order to bring the rules in line with current international trade practices.

Most contracts made after 1 January 2010 will refer to the latest edition of Incoterms, which came into force on that date. Versions of Incoterms preceding the 2010 edition may still be incorporated into future contracts if the parties so agree. However, this of course is not recommended because the latest version is designed to bring Incoterms in line with the latest developments in commercial practice.

The English text is the original and official version of Incoterms 2010, which have been endorsed by the United Nations Commission on International Trade Law (UNCITRAL). Authorized translations into 31 languages are available from ICC national committees.

Correct use of Incoterms goes a long way to providing the legal certainty upon which mutual confidence between business partners must be based. To be sure of using them correctly, trade practitioners need to consult the full ICC texts, and to beware of the many unauthorized summaries and approximate versions that abound on the web.

The scope of Incoterms is limited to matters relating to the rights and obligations of the parties to the contract of sale with respect to the delivery of goods sold, but excluding "intangibles" like computer software.

Each Incoterm is referred to by a three-letter abbreviation. It is necessary for the parties concerned with the international trade transaction to know "Incoterms 2010". These international consignment delivery terms are linked with a number of factors which include: air or sea freight plus transport costs, product costs, packing costs and so on.

Since the creation of the Incoterms rules by ICC in 1936, this globally accepted contractual standard has been regularly updated to keep pace with the development of international trade. The Incoterms 2010 rules take account of the continued spread of customs-free zones, the increased use of electronic communications in business transactions, heightened concern about security in the movement of goods in transport practices. Incoterms 2010 updates and consolidates the "delivered" rules, reducing the total number of rules from 13 to 11, and offers a simpler and clearer presentation of all the rules. Incoterms 2010 is also the first version of the Incoterms rules to make all references to buyers and sellers gender-neutral. The broad expertise of ICC's Commission on Commercial Law and Practice, whose membership is drawn from all parts of the world and all trade sectors, ensures that the Incoterms 2010 rules respond to business needs everywhere.

The thirteen terms in Incoterms 2000 have been changed into eleven terms in Incoterms 2010. Incoterms 2010 divides the terms into two types based on the transportation modes (rules for any mode or modes of transport and rules for sea and inland waterway transport only), and the former DAF, DEQ and DDU in Incoterms 2000 are replaced by DAT and DAP in Incoterms 2010. The following are the terms in Incoterms 2010:

Rules for Any Mode or Modes of Transport		
EXW	Ex Works	工厂交货
FCA	Free Carrier	货交承运人
CPT	Carriage Paid To	运费付至
CIP	Carriage and Insurance Paid To	运保费付至
DAT	Delivered At Terminal	指定终端交货
DAP	Delivered At Place	指定目的地交货
DDP	Delivered Duty Paid	完税后交货
Rules for Sea and Inland Waterway Transport		
FAS	Free Alongside Ship	装运港船边交货
FOB	Free On Board	装运港船上交货
CFR	Cost and Freight	成本加运费
CIF	Cost, Insurance and Freight	成本加运保费

5.6 Documentation of Export 出口单证

A wide range of documents passes between importers and exporters and intermediaries to record every element of their international trade transactions. They are used to identify the mode of transport, delivery terms and payment methods agreed, as well as the type of transaction being undertaken. As the documents are raised by all the parties involved in the transaction, from buyer and seller through to forwarder and bank, they fulfil a number of requirements. Firstly, commercial documents are used to provide specific information to the organizations involved in the physical distribution of the goods and are instrumental in ensuring that the international transactions proceed as quickly and efficiently as possible. The documents that relate to payment provide financial security to all parties, and the overall function of the various types of international trade documentation is to reduce risk and maintain evidence of the transactions.

The information provided in the documents must be wholly accurate and appropriate to the particular purpose of each individual document. Inaccurate documentation will result in delays in processing, shipping and receipt of goods, which in turn may lead to contract being breached through delivery times not being met. As a result, exporters will lose money on the contract, and importers will not be able to fulfil other orders relying on imported components. Therefore, all parties involved in the transaction hope to ensure that the documentation should be CLEAR, CORRECT and COMPLETE (3Cs).

Without documents, international trade can never be conducted. Basically, there are four types of international trade documentation:

Transport documentation, such as Bill of Lading, Air waybill, and so on.

Customs documentation, such as export declaration, import declaration, transit documents, invoices, and so on.

Insurance documentation, such as insurance policy, insurance certificate, insurance declaration, and so on.

Payment documentation, such as letter of credit, bill of exchange, promissory note, cheque, and so on.

In the export transaction such documents as follows are requisite and very important:

5.6.1　Bill of Lading (B/L)　提单

A bill of lading is a receipt for goods shipped on board a vessel, signed by the person (or his or her agent) who contracts to carry them, and stating the conditions in which the goods were delivered to (and received by) the ship. Bill of lading is a document of title to the goods which are the subject of the contract between the buyer (importer) and the seller (exporter). B/L is a document issued by the master of the vessel or by the agent of the master to evidence that goods have been shipped on the vessel and accepted. It is the most important commercial document in international trade, and is used to control delivery of goods transported by sea.

When we speak of B/L, we always refer to the maritime B/L, because more than 90% of the goods are transported by sea in international trade. So it is the most common transport document for the export of the goods. The factors that cause it to remain a chief document are numerous, and relate to the organization of payment through banking system.

(1) Functions of a Bill of Lading

The B/L has three major functions:

The B/L is a receipt for goods shipped on board a vessel.

The B/L is signed by the carrier as a receipt for goods which are entrusted to him for onward transportation. Bills of lading are made out in sets with either two or three originals and a variable number of copies. They are known as negotiable copies and each copy can give title to the goods. When the master of the vessel or his agent signs that the goods have been shipped on board in apparent good order and condition, he commits the shipowner to carry them safely to the destination.

The B/L is evidence of the contract of carriage.

It is evidence of the contract between the exporter and the shipping company. On the reverse side of the B/L there are the full terms and conditions of carriage which expressly stipulate the obligations and rights of both parties. And the disputes, if any, are based on the terms and conditions. It is issued after the contract has been signed.

The B/L is a document of title.

A document of title is one which the law recognizes as representing the goods so that the document can be transferred to a third party.

The B/L is quasi-negotiable. The B/L represents the goods. The important ingredient to the payment arrangement is that it describes ownership and when and where ownership is transferred. A B/L can be endorsed over to a third party in order to transfer the ownership of the goods to the transferee. Only one bill of lading in a set needs to be endorsed to transfer the property. When the B/L is transferred in this way, the buyer has effectively received the goods.

(2) Contents of a Bill of Lading

A B/L normally includes the following:

The name of the shipper (usually the exporter).

The name of the carrying vessel.

A full description of the cargo (provided it is not bulk cargo) including any shipping marks, individual packages numbers in the consignment, contents, cubic measurement, gross weight and so on.

The marks and numbers that identify the goods.

The port of shipment or dry port/CFS. The port of discharge or dry port/CFS.

Full details of freight, including when and where it is to be paid—whether freight paid or payable at destination.

The name of consignee or, if the shipper is eager to withhold the consignee's name, shipper's order.

The terms of the contract of carriage.

The date the goods are received for shipment and/or loaded on the vessel.

The name and address of the notified party (the person to be notified on the arrival of the shipment, normally the buyer).

The number of B/L signed on behalf of the Master or his agent, acknowledging receipt of the goods.

The signature of the ship's Master or his agent.

5.6.2 Air Waybill 航空运单

An air waybill is the consignment note used for the carriage of goods by air. Unlike a B/L, the air waybill is not a document of title or a transferable or negotiable instrument. It is not possible to use it as a negotiable instrument for L/C purposes. This is because the cargo would arrive at the destination some days or some weeks before the air waybill's arrival through the banking system.

The air waybill is a receipt for the goods for despatch and it is prima facia evidence of the conditions of the goods.

There are normally 12 copies of air waybill. Copies 1, 2 and 3 are the originals. The distribution of the 12 copies is listed as follows:

Original 1: for issuing carrier (airline)—green copy

Original 2: for consignee—pink copy

Original 3: for shipper—blue copy

Copy No.4: delivery receipt—yellow copy

Copy No.5: for airport of destination

Copy No.6: for third carrier

Copy No.7: for second carrier

Copy No.8: for first carrier

Copy No.9: for sales agent

Copy No.10: extra copy for carrier

Copy No.11: invoice

Copy No.12: for airport of departure

Not all these forms will be used in every consignment but the extra copies are just discarded. On the reverse of the air waybill are printed the conditions of carriage and they are subject to the *Carriage by Air Act 1961*. This is based on the Warsaw Rules and a number of other conventions. An air waybill must include the following items:

(1) The place and date of its execution.

(2) The name and address of the shipper.

(3) The names and addresses of the consignor and consignee.

(4) First carrier (airline), departure and destination airports and any special route to be followed, full technical description of cargo dimensions, commodity code, rate class, chargeable weight and freight rate.

(5) Total freight amount prepaid and/or to pay at destination.

(6) Details of any ancillary charges payable.

(7) Signature of the shipper or his agent. Signature of the issuing carrier (airline operator) or his agent.

(8) Details of booked flight and actual flight.

So far as international payments are concerned, under a documentary L/C, certain specific information or instructions to be shown on the air waybill may be requested. The items that might be included are:

(1) The names and addresses of the exporter, importer and the first carrier or airline, the names of the airports of departure and destination.

(2) Details of any special routes.

(3) The date of the flight.

(4) The declared value of the commodity for customs purposes.

(5) The number of packages with marks, weights, quantity and dimensions.

(6) The freight charge per unit of weight or volume.

（7）The technical description of the goods（not the commercial description）.

（8）The signature of the exporter or his agent.

（9）The place and date of issuance.

（10）The signature of the issuing carrier or his agent.

5.6.3　Packing List　装箱单

A packing list is provided and completed by the shipper at the time the goods are dispatched and it accompanies the goods and the carrier's documents such as B/L, sea waybill, and so on throughout the transit. The packing list gives details of the invoice, buyer, consignee, country of origin, vessel or flight date, port/airport of loading, port/airport of discharge, and so on. The packing list is also called a "packing note". It normally gives the following details of:

（1）The invoice.

（2）Buyer.

（3）Consignee.

（4）Country of origin.

（5）Vessel or flight date.

（6）Port or airport of loading and port or airport of discharge.

（7）Place of delivery.

（8）Shipping marks.

（9）Container number.

（10）Weight and/or volume（cubic）of the commodity.

（11）Other detailed information about the goods, including packaging information.

When the exporter goes to negotiating bank to negotiate the bill of exchange, he must provide a packing list together with other documents. In recent years, under documentary letter of credit system, the packing list is a must required by the banks and customs. Besides, the packing list is very much evidence in containerised shipments.

5.6.4　Commercial Invoice　商业发票

Basically the invoice is a document rendered by one person to another in regard of goods which have been sold. Its primary function is a check for the purchase against charges and delivery. The commercial invoice gives the details of the goods and is issued by the seller（exporter）. It forms the basis of the transaction between the seller and the buyer, and is completed in accord with the number of prescribed copies required.

Of the different kinds of invoices in international trade, the commercial invoice is the most important. The exporter issues the commercial invoice to give full details about the goods. He must issue the invoice in the right way, as any mistake in the invoice will result in the serious delay or trouble of the business. The commercial invoice's chief functions are listed as follows:

A check for the buyer against charges and delivery.

For insurance purpose.

For packing purpose.

Useful evidence to verify the value and nature of the goods and sometimes, it is evidence of the contract between the seller and the buyer.

A commercial invoice is not necessarily a contract of sale, but it may form a contract of sale if it is in writing and contains all the material terms.

Normally, a commercial invoice will include the following information:

(1) The names and addresses of the buyer (importer) and the seller (exporter).

(2) The buyer's reference: order number, indent number, etc.

(3) The number and types of packages.

(4) The weights and measurements of the consignment.

(5) The place and date of issuing the commercial invoice.

(6) Details of actual cost of freight and insurance if so requested.

(7) The total amount, including price of goods, freight, insurance, and so on.

(8) The export and/or import licence number.

(9) The contents of individual packages.

(10) The method of despatch.

(11) Shipment terms.

(12) L/C number and details (if so requested).

(13) Country of origin of goods.

(14) The signature of the exporter.

5.6.5　Pro-forma Invoice　形式发票

This type of invoice is prepared by the exporter and may be required in advance for licence or letter of credit purposes. The document includes the date, name of the consignee, quantity and description of the goods, marks and measurements of packages, costs of the goods, packing, carriage, freight, postage, insurance premium, terms of sale, terms of payment, etc. The pro-forma invoice is dispatched to the buyer to facilitate obtaining from the bank the requisite currency to buy the goods and subsequently issue a letter of credit. Additionally, it may be needed for an import licence.

5.6.6　Insurance Policy　保险证

In international trade, goods are normally insured in case that the goods might be damaged or get lost in transit. The insurance policy is the most important document in cargo insurance. The insurance policy is the insurance evidence of the goods insured. It is issued by the insurer (the insurance company). The insurance policy is a legal document which binds upon the insurer and the insured. It can be used as evidence in legal action. The insurance policy normally includes such items as follows:

(1) The names and addresses of the parties concerned.

(2) The name, quantity, weight and shipping marks of the insured commodity.

(3) The facility of transportation.

(4) The type of insurance.

(5) The insurance duration.

(6) The value that is insured.

(7) The premium.

(8) The date and place of issuing the insurance policy.

(9) The place at which the claim is payable.

(10) The signature of the insurer.

On the reverse of the insurance policy there are the terms and conditions concerning the rights and obligations of the insured and the insurer, which are very important as well.

5.6.7 Bill of Exchange (B/E) 汇票

The bill of exchange is a popular way of arranging payment. The most normal procedure is for the exporter (seller) to hand the bill of exchange together with the documents to the exporter's (seller's) bank who will send them to a bank overseas for "collection".

5.6.8 Certificate of Origin 原产的证明

The certificate of origin is required in some countries. The certificate must agree with specific conditions, which govern the format and layout of the document and specify the quality of the paper required. The certificate of origin specifies the name, quantity and value of the goods, etc. together with their place of manufacture. It states the country of origin of the goods shipped.

Normally, certificate of origin for non-preferential purposes is a trade policy issue with wider connotations than preferential origin. It may be required to identify favoured nation status goods, in order to reduce import duties or, from negative perspective, to identify commodities originating from certain regions or countries, the importation of which may be restricted or prohibited.

Summary of This Chapter
本章概要

1. 国际贸易又被称为世界贸易,它指国与国和地区与地区之间的商品和劳务交换的活动。换言之,这种国与国之间和地区与地区之间的商品和劳务交换活动,即各国的对外贸易构成世界范围的交易,也就是世界贸易。国际贸易还包括技术交易。传统的国际贸易由商品的进口和出口构成。商品的进出口被称为有形贸易。技术及服务的交易被称为无形贸易。国际贸易是国际商务活动中的主要部分之一。

2. 对外贸易也被称为进出口贸易或国外贸易。对外贸易包括货物进出口、技术进出口和服务进出口。国际支付是国际贸易中一个重要环节。

3. 从世界范围内来看,国际贸易格局主要由三大块组成:欧盟、北美自由贸易协定国家及日本。这三大地区国家的贸易量占了世界贸易量的绝大多数,并左右世界贸易。

4. 贸易术语(trade terms)又被称作贸易条件、价格术语(price terms),这些术语明确规定了买卖双方的义务。《国际贸易术语解释通则》对国际贸易中的贸易术语提供一套解释的国际规则,以避免各国的不同解释而产生争议。国际商会第一次于 1939 年颁布了一套解释贸易术语的国际规则,其名称为 Incoterms 1936,以后又于 1953 年、1967 年、1976 年、1980 年、1990 年、2000 年、2010 年不断修改和补充,逐步完善以适应国际贸易实践的发展。Incoterms 只涉及国际贸易中的销售合同,尤其是销售合同中买卖双方的关系,而且,只限于一些非常明确的方面。此外,Incoterms 所涵盖的范围只限于销售合同当事人的权利义务中,与已售的有形货物的交货有关的事项。另外,Incoterms 还涉及货物进出口的清关、货物包装的义务,买方接受货物的义务,以及提供证明各项义务得到完整履行的义务。2010 年 9 月 27 日,国际商会正式推出《2010 国际贸易术语解释通则》(Incoterms 2010),与 Incoterms 2000 并用,新版本于 2011 年 1 月 1 日正式生效。新版由原来的 13 个术语更新为 11 个术语。这11 个术语被分为两类:第一类中的七种贸易术语不用考虑所选用运输方式的种类。EXW,FCA,CPT,CIP,DAT,DAP 和 DDP 都属于第一类。它们甚至可以运用于没有海上运输的情况下。只要运输中一个部分运用过船只便可以适用此类术语。在第二类术语中,交货点和把货物送达买方的地点都是港口,所以只适用于"海上或内陆水上运输"。FAS,FOB,CFR 和 CIF 都属于这一类。最后的 3 个术语,删除了以越过船舷为交货标准而代之以将货物装运上船。这更准确地反映了现代商业现实,规避了以往风险围绕船舷这条虚拟垂线来回摇摆。

5. 国际贸易中的单证指的是:国际贸易中使用的单据和其他具有规章或法律意义的文件或文书,如海运提单、售货确认书、信用证等。出口单证指在出口业务过程中所涉及的单证,如汇票、原产地证书、出口许可证书等。这些单证非常重要,没有它们的参与,出口业务无法完成。单证具有法律意义。有的单证是货物买卖的凭证,如商业发票;有的是物权凭证,如提单。

New Words and Expressions

acceptance n. 承兑
address v. 使(口头或书面严词)针对……而发
as opposed to 与……对照之下;而非
comprise v. 包含;包括;组成;构成
contemplate v. 思忖;期待
creditworthiness n. 信誉可靠
dictate v. 口授;强制规定
diversify v. 增加产品的品种

economies of scale 规模经济
effect v. 实现、达到(目的等);实施
entail v. 需要;使人承担
evaluate v. 鉴定;对……进行评价
exploit v. 开拓;开发;开采;利用
facilitate v. 使容易;使便利;促进
forego v. 发生在……之前
in accordance with 与……一致
in compliance with 依从;遵照

incur *v.* 招致；引起

instinct *n.* 本能；直觉

justify *v.* 证明……为正当理由；是……的正当理由

mature *v.& a.* 使（计划）完善；成熟的

momentum *n.* 势头

nascent *a.* 尚未成熟的；开始成形的

nominate *v.* 提名；委托，任命

paymaster *n.*（发放薪饷的）出纳员

prescribe *v.* 规定；指定

provided that 以……为条件；假如

render *v.* 执行；实施；放弃；开出账单

requisite *a.* 必要的；必不可少的

slump *n.& v.* 暴跌；不景气；（市场等）萧条

solvent *a.* 有偿付能力的

sophistication *n.* 高精尖（技术）

stabilize *v.* 稳定；安定

surplus *n.* 过剩；盈余；公积金；顺差；过剩

▶ Discussion Questions

1. How important is international trade in the framework of international business?

2. Why does a country's government set up international trade barriers?

3. What are the functions of Incoterms?

4. Is Bill of Lading a document of title to the consignment? Why or why not?

Chapter 6 International Marketing 国际营销

Objectives
学习目标

Objectives
学习目标

To understand the ABC of international marketing.

理解国际营销的基本知识。

To recognize the differences between international marketing and domestic marketing.

掌握国际营销与国内营销的区别。

To get to know the new concepts of international marketing.

了解国际营销的新概念。

To outline the importance of E-marketing.

概述电子营销的重要性。

6.1 The Nature of Marketing 营销的本质

Marketing is closely related to products and services that are supposed to be used or be provided for certain purposes among which profits are the greatest concern.

Marketing is related to people because every effort is made by the marketing side to persuade people on the other side—customers, consumers, end-users (whatever they are called)—to buy the goods or to accept the services. So it can be seen that marketing is a double track activity. All marketing activities are intended to obtain active response from the marketing target. Figure 6.1 further illustrates this.

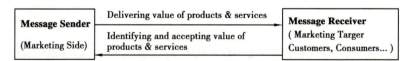

Figure 6.1   Marketing Nature

Therefore, marketing is a process of passing on messages to the receiver who is intended to give active response. Marketing is a process of matching the resources of a business with identified customer needs. In other words, marketing is concerned with customer satisfaction and with the focusing of the organization's resources to ensure that the customer is satisfied—at a profit to the business.

From the perspective of the marketing, marketing is the management process responsible for profitably identifying, anticipating and satisfying customer requirements. The process is also a kind of process of "value added". Value in marketing means delivering on a whole range of promises to the customer.

The fundamental management issue in marketing is to understand the customer's perception of value and to determine a superior value position from this perspective and to ensure that, by developing a consensus throughout the company, value is provided and communicated to the customer group.

The modern value orientation views marketing as a series of four delivery processes whereby the business system is designed in such a way that value is delivered by the company to the customer through a number of discrete stages.

(1) To identify society and customer values to be promoted by the company.

(2) To attempt to provide the value identified.

(3) To communicate the value to customers and potential customers through advertising, public relations and personal selling.

(4) To attempt to deliver the value to customers, which is done through distribution and logistics, direct marketing and sales promotion.

Marketing especially focuses on:

(1) the importance of customer;

(2) the importance of profit;

(3) the importance of a managerial, organization-wide approach.

Therefore, when the marketing concept is applied to a business we can say that it means at least the following three things:

(1) That every aspect of the firm's operations must be clearly based on the importance of the customer.

(2) That the firm must make an adequate "profit" for its efforts (but more on this point below).

(3) That all parts of the organization must co-operate enthusiastically and efficiently in the marketing process.

6.2 Domestic Marketing and International Marketing 国内营销与国际营销

Marketing is a collection of activities, including advertising, public relations and sales promotions, marketing research and new product development, packaging design and merchandising, personal selling and after-sales service, and the determination of selling prices.

Marketing is far more than selling: profitability and added shareholder value are the ultimate aims of all marketing pursuits.

International marketing is the process of identifying the goods and services that customers outside the home country want and then providing them at the right price and place. This process is similar to the process of domestic marketing, but there are some important modifications that are used to adapt marketing efforts to the needs of the specific country or region.

Domestic and international marketing principles are the same, but international company managers must take foreign environmental differences into account and interpret foreign information correctly. Owing to the environmental differences, managers apply those principles in a different way abroad. For international and domestic marketing, the basic tools and concepts of marketing are applied in order to satisfy consumer demand. But it is quite likely that the problems an international company manager encounters in international marketing and the techniques he uses to solve the problems are quite different.

Domestic marketing is relatively easier to carry out. For international marketing, however, the environment is quite different from country to country: services and facilities are priced differently and may not be available at all in some countries. Besides, cultural, legal, political, economic and other environments differ considerably among nations. Differences between domestic marketing and international marketing are listed as follows:

(1) Domestic marketing research data is available in a single language and is usually easily accessed while international marketing, research data is generally in foreign languages and may be extremely difficult to obtain and in interpret.

(2) Domestic marketing promotional messages need to consider just a single national culture while for international marketing, cultural differences must be taken into account.

(3) For domestic marketing, market segmentation occurs within a single country while for international marketing, market segments might be defined across the same type of consumer in many different countries.

(4) For domestic marketing, communication and control are immediate and direct while for international marketing, communication and control may be difficult.

(5) For domestic marketing, business laws and regulations are clearly understood while for international marketing, foreign laws and regulations might not be clear.

(6) For domestic marketing, business risks can be normally identified and assessed while for international marketing, environments may be so unstable that it is very hard to identify and assess risks.

(7) For domestic marketing, planning and organizational control systems can be simple and direct while for international marketing, the complexity of international trade often necessitates the adoption of complex and sophisticated planning, organization and control systems.

(8) For domestic marketing, distribution channels are easy to monitor and control while for

international marketing, distribution is often carried out by intermediaries, so it is much harder to monitor.

(9) For domestic marketing, competitors' behaviour is easily predicted while for international marketing, competitors' behaviour is harder to observe, therefore less predictable.

(10) For domestic marketing, new product development can be geared to the needs of the home market while for international marketing, new product development must take account of all the markets that the product will be sold in.

6.3 Reasons for Marketing Abroad   海外营销的原因

Of the many factors that induce a company to begin operating abroad, the most obvious, perhaps, are as follows:

(1) Economies of scale and scope as well as "experience curve" efforts resulting from increased outputs.

(2) The existence of lucrative markets in foreign countries that are not available at home.

(3) Saturated markets in the home country.

(4) Response to incoming competitive activity.

Scale economies might not be available if consumer' tastes in the foreign markets necessitate numerous product modifications. Likewise, the costs of market entry (advertising and promotion, establishment of distribution networks and so on) could outweigh production savings. Operating in foreign markets can also facilitate the "experience curve" effects, i.e, cost reductions and efficiency increases attained in consequence of a business acquiring experience of certain type of activity, function or project. These effects differ from economies of scale in that they result from longer experience of doing something rather than producing greater volume of output.

In addition, reasons for companies' becoming involved in international marketing may include the following.

(1) Today, new product development typically requires so much expenditure that in many cases companies intending to introduce new products must adopt an international perspective.

(2) The higher turnover derived from international sales might enable a firm to initiate new product research and development that in the long term will give it a competitive edge.

(3) Corporate plans can be anchored against a wider range of (international) opportunities.

(4) There might be less competition in some foreign markets.

(5) A sudden collapse in market demand in one country may be offset by expansion in others.

(6) Opportunities may be afforded by new trade agreements between nations, or by the opening up of new markets in countries that were previously closed to imports. A good example of this is the gradual opening up of trade with China.

(7) Consumers in some foreign markets might be wealthier than consumers in the company's own country.

6.4   Market   市场

Market refers to either the physical place where buyers and sellers meet to conduct business activities, or the demand or desire of the consumers to buy goods or to accept services. From the economic perspective, a market is described as a collection of buyers and sellers who transact over a particular product or product class (the housing market or grain market).

In any market, there will be a buyer and a seller, and somehow both have to be brought together so that a sale can take place. In the product market, the buyer is the household and the seller is the firm. In economic language the household demands the good or service and the firm supplies the good or service. Each of these will be considered separately first and then brought together.

A market is basically made up of all the potential customers who share a particular need or want and who might be willing and able to engage in exchange to satisfy that need or want. This proves it right that the concepts of satisfaction and exchange are at the core of marketing, as marketing is the process of planning and executing the conception, pricing, promotion, and distribution of ideas, goods, and services to create exchanges that satisfy individual and organizational objectives.

6.4.1   Three Elements of Market   市场三要素

The three fundamental elements of market are customer, purchasing desire of the customer, and purchasing power of the customer.

As mentioned at the beginning of this chapter, customers are of great concern in marketing. Without customers all activities of marketing will come to nothing. Before marketing a product to a foreign market, the customer should be first of all taken into account. The more a firm understands the customer, the more efficient marketing the firm will have.

Besides, the customer's desire and purchasing power must be paid great attention to. The demand for a good or a service depends on a number of factors, the most important of which include:

(1) the price of the good;

(2) the prices of other goods;

(3) disposable income;

(4) tastes.

The above factors (except for the fourth one) are also related to the customer's purchasing power. Besides, customer's purchasing power is concerned with the economic level of the country and the customer's own financial situation. From the perspective of international marketing, customer's purchasing power should be considered as a whole. In other words, the general purchasing power of the individuals and the organizations of a foreign country need to be considered as a whole.

All firms operate in markets, whether they are local, national or international. Although firms might be able to influence the market conditions that face them, they need to know their own markets and how markets fit together in the market economy. Firms also need to know the shape and position of the demand curve they face, including knowledge of the following aspects:

(1) The nature of the goods they manufacture;

(2) The way in which it is viewed by consumers;

(3) The factors which affect the demand for their goods;

(4) Any change likely in the future which will affect the market;

(5) Any likely government intervention in the market.

If the firm is quite familiar with this information, it is possible that the firm can retain markets, expand existing markets, and move into new ones.

6.4.2   Market Structure   市场结构

Market structure refers to the amount of competition that exists in a market between producers. The degree of competition can be considered as lying along a continuum with very competitive markets at one end and markets in which no competition exists at all at the other end. Please refer to Figure 6.2.

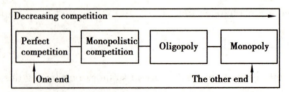

Figure 6.2   Market Structure

It is necessary to draw attention to the structural factors.

(1) Amount of actual competition: seller concentration, and buyer concentration.

(2) Existence of potential competition.

(3) Demand conditions.

(4) Existence of barriers to entry.

Market structure is important because it has the implications for conduct and because it has an impact on the strategic possibilities which face the organization, their ability to act strategically and the likely effects of such strategic behaviour.

6.4.3   The Globalization of Market   市场全球化

Today, a powerful force drives the whole world toward a converging commonalty. That force is technology. As science and technology develop so fast, communication, transport, and travel have become so convenient that we sometimes think the world is so small. As a result, there comes a new commercial reality—the emergence of global markets for standardized consumer products on a previously unimagined scale of magnitude. The accustomed differences in national or regional preferences are disappearing. The globalization of markets is at hand. The multinational corporation operates in a number of countries and adjusts its products and practices to each—at relatively high costs. The global corporation operates with resolute consistency—at relatively low costs—as if the entire world were a single entity; it sells the same thing in the same way everywhere.

In the long run, such technological forces may lead to the evolution of a global culture. Today, the continuing persistence of cultural and economic differences among nations acts as a major brake on any trend toward global consumer tastes and preferences. Besides, trade barriers and differences in product and technical standards also constrain a firm's ability to sell a standardized product to a global market. There may be a long way to go before the genuine global market comes into being, but the trend of the globalization of market is overwhelming.

6.4.4　Market Segmentation　市场细分

Segmentation is the strategy of developing different marketing programs for different customer groups or segments. Each customer segment has its own unique demand function based on price, physical product characteristics, and non-physical attributes reflecting image and performance.

A market segment is made up of a group of customers who share a similar set of wants, such as the car buyers who are primarily seeking low-cost basic transportation. Attention should be drawn, however, to the fact that young, middle-income car buyers are not a segment, but a sector, because they differ about what they want in a car. Some will want low-cost cars and others will want expensive cars.

Market segmentation is about subdividing a market into groups of consumers, each of which needs a separate marketing mix for maximum exploitation. The individual customer groups are likely to respond in clearly different ways to any particular marketing mix. Generally speaking, the bigger the difference in response, the better is the segmentation differential. Essentially, the segmentation exercise must identify customer characteristics that correlate closely with buying intentions.

The main reasons for segmenting a market are as follows:

(1) It helps the company to evaluate the positions of competitors and environmental opportunities.

(2) It develops a focus on product positioning and market strategies.

(3) It assists in identifying and allocating scarce marketing resources.

(4) It enables managers to adjust the marketing plan.

In addition, it is thought by some that segmentation allows:

(1) foreign firms to be selected on the basis of their individual potential;

(2) foreign markets to be treated independently, as elements of an overall foreign market portfolio to be increased or decreased depending on individual profitability;

(3) products and product lines to be tailored to the particular needs and requirements of local markets;

(4) products and product lines to be priced according to local demand and competitive conditions;

(5) channels to be developed according to local competitive conditions and market

circumstances;

(6) promotional themes and campaigns to be developed according to local competitive conditions and market circumstances.

The task of international marketing is to identify segments of particular country—markets that will react profitably to separate marketing treatments across international boarders. Naturally, this gives the MNEs the option of addressing a small segment over a number of international markets which, individually, would not give a satisfactory return. The segmentation process itself can be carried out with a broad focus using differentiating parameters like political system, economic system, level of development, religion, language, geographical location and climate.

Narrow-focus segmentation can make use of behavioural factors such as brand loyalty, choice of channel, benefits sought, and sensitivity to variations in product, price and quality.

In terms of actually carrying out the international segmentation exercise, it is suggested by some that:

(1) the MNEs marketer should be able to measure the size and the purchasing power of each segment;

(2) the MNEs should be able to reach each segment through available distribution channels and media;

(3) the identified market segments should be large enough to justify the change or modification of the marketing approach in order to reach them.

6.4.5 Target Market 目标市场

It's important to remember that the focus of marketing is on people. If marketers are concentrating their efforts on the product or profit only, they'll miss the market. The term "target market" is used because that market—that group of people—is the "bull's eye" at which marketers aim all their marketing efforts.

Therefore, it is important to remember that a market is people, people with common characteristics that set them apart as a group. The more statistics we have about a target market, the more precisely we can develop our marketing strategy. Figure 6.3 shows some examples of market segments (or groups).

Here are examples of target segments that can be created using Figure 6.3.

(1) Women business owners between the ages of 25 and 60 earning more than $25,000 annually form a demographic segment.

(2) People who drive compact cars due to their fuel efficiency form a benefit segment.

The target market plays an important role in designing marketing strategies.

The reason we're concerned with identifying a target market is that it makes strategies for designing, pricing, distributing, promoting, positioning and improving the product, service or idea easier, more effective, and more cost-effective.

For example, if research shows that a sturdy recyclable package with blue lettering appeals to

Types of Market Segment	Shared Group Characteristics
Demographic segment	**Measurable Statistics** such as age, income, occupation, etc.
Psychographic segment	**Lifestyle Preferences** such as music lovers, city or urban dwellers, etc.
Use–based segment	**Frequency of usage** such as recreational drinking, travelling, etc.
Benefit segment	**Desire to obtain the same product benefits** such as luxury, thriftiness, comfort from food, etc.
Geographic segment	**Location** such as home address, business address, etc.

Figure 6.3   Market Segments

our target market and if we're focused on that target market, we should choose that type of packaging. If, however, we're product-or profit-oriented—rather than people-oriented—we might simply make the package out of plain styrofoam because it protects the product (product-oriented) or because it's cheap (profit-oriented).

Here's another example: If we know our target market is 24-to 49-year-old men who like rhythm & blues, are frequent CD buyers, and live in urban neighborhoods, we can create an advertising message to appeal to those types of buyers. Additionally, we could buy spots on a specific radio station or TV show that appeals to this type of buyers.

6.5   International Marketing Environment   国际营销环境

International marketers can never ignore the international marketing environment, which is a complex mixture of macro and micro forces. The environment facing the international firm is made up of a number of demands and constraints to which the organization must adjust so as to survive and develop. This environment consists of a number of elements, the underlying characteristics of which are that they lie outside the control of the firm. Figure 6.4 illustrates the international marketing environment.

(1) Demographic environment influences marketing strategy because people, the core of marketing, make up markets.

(2) Economic environment influences marketing strategy because besides people, markets require purchasing power which in an economy depends on current income, prices, savings, debt, and credit availability.

(3) Natural environment influences marketing strategy because a country's natural environment affects its economic development.

(4) Technological environment influences marketing strategy because technology is one of the

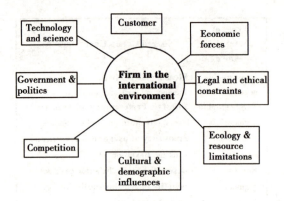

Figure 6.4   The International Marketing Environment

most important forces that shape people's lives and the economy's growth rate is affected by how many major new technologies are discovered. Besides, new technology brings long-run consequences that are not always predicted.

（5）Political-legal environment influences marketing strategy because this environment consists of laws, government agencies, and pressure groups that influence and limit various organizations and individuals. This environment may exert great impact on international marketing strategy.

（6）Social-cultural environment influences marketing strategy because the main element of society is people who share a culture, and society shapes people's beliefs, values, and norms.

（7）Competition environment influences marketing strategy because the extent of competition in a country affects people's demand.

6.6   Marketing Strategy   营销战略

Marketing strategy is concerned with finding sustainable ways for organizations to compete in a continuously changing world. A strategy is a plan of action designed to achieve the long-run goals of the organization. It means choosing a general direction for the firm, together with organizational deigns, policies, systems and a style of management best suited for beating the competitors.

Adoption of correct strategies causes the firm to offer the right products to the right markets at the right time with the right quality and at the right price.

"All marketing strategy is built on STP—Segmentation, Targeting, and Positioning." (Kotler, 2003, p.308).

Marketing strategies evolve from more general business objectives. Generally speaking, marketing strategies include the following dimensions：

（1）The product or service market in which companies expect to compete；

（2）The level of investment needed to grow, maintain, or milk the business；

（3）The production line, positioning, pricing, and distribution strategies needed to compete in the selected market；

（4）The assets or skills to provide a sustainable competitive advantage.

Successful marketing strategies are based on assets such as brand names that are strongly relative to those of competitors. Examples of strategic decisions related to international marketing are as follows:

(1) The products the firm will supply, in terms of positioning the firm against competition that already exists or is likely to exist in the overseas market.

(2) The markets in which the business is to operate, in terms of both target countries and market segments within those countries.

(3) Quality and price levels, based on available market niches.

(4) Legal forms of the parent enterprise and its subsidiaries (public company, private company, partnership, etc.) and how many departments and divisions to have within the firm. This will be relative both to the overall corporate strategy of the parent company and the local regulatory systems in the target country.

(5) Financing of international operations, and policy on repatriation and reinvestment of profits.

6.6.1 Benefits of Strategy 战略利益

Some successful managers do not pay much attention to the marketing strategies. This might be a potential danger to the businesses. There are in fact many real and significant advantages in having coherent and well-prepared strategies. The main benefits of excellent strategies include the following.

(1) The firm can thus realize its strengths and weaknesses and assess critically the feasibility of its aims.

(2) Reactions to change in competitors' behaviour can be decided in advance.

(3) Results may be compared against logically predetermined targets.

(4) Foreseeable pitfalls can be avoided.

(5) The existence of a strategy provides a focal point toward which all the company's promotional efforts may be directed.

6.6.2 Strategy Formulation 战略制定

The process of formulating and implementing strategies can be regarded as a continuous cycle, as shown in Figure 6.5. This begins with a statement of the mission of the business—its fundamental purpose. Mission statements cover the following five components.

(1) Purpose: the organization's reason for existing.

(2) Strategic goals: what it wishes to achieve.

(3) Values: how it relates to its stakeholders.

(4) Standard: organizational policies and norms of behaviour.

(5) Strategic pathway: the means it will use to achieve its goals.

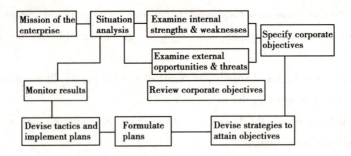

Figure 6.5   Formulating and Implementing Strategies

6.7   Integrated Marketing   整合营销

Integrated marketing means that all the departments of a company cooperate to work together for a common purpose of meeting the customer's needs. There are two forms of integrated marketing.

First, all the departments that have marketing functions work together. Such marketing functions are advertising, customer service, sales force, product management, marketing research, etc. It is not so easy for all the function sections to cooperate well. They must be coordinated in order to achieve the firm's purpose—to serve the customer.

Second, besides the function sections, other departments of the firm must also take part. They must also work together from the customer's point of view. All managers must realize that customers are "God" of the firm. The customer is the company's only true "profit centre". Without customers, all the efforts of the departments of the firm will come to nothing.

6.8   Direct Marketing   直接营销

Direct marketing is a tactic that closely resembles promotion, although there are key differences. Direct marketing tactics allow firms to communicate directly to potential customers (normally through multi media). Consumers, in turn, buy directly from the firm. No intermediaries such as wholesalers or retailers are involved. The widely used means of direct marketing communication is through mail catalogs. However, direct marketing by telephone and television companies is also common.

Strategic decisions in direct marketing include program scope (testing versus rollout of the full program), the basic offer (product, incentives, and premiums), the concept and theme, versioning and/or personalization, and media selection.

6.8.1   Publicity   宣传

Publicity is any form of non-paid commercially significant news or editorial comment on ideas, products, or institutions. Newspapers, television, radio stations, or magazines usually convey such information. Firms do not pay for publicity, but their products or services benefit from the coverage.

Besides, the firm typically provides most of the information through news releases or other documents.

6.8.2 Media Selection 媒体选择

Media selection involves various decisions.

(1) The type of media to use.

(2) The primary options include television, radio, magazines, newspapers, billboards, direct mails, the World Wide Web, and/or Yellow Pages.

(3) The choice of a medium is influenced by the number of people in the audience, their attributes, the cost of advertising there, and the ability of the medium to accomplish desired goals such as product demonstration, conveying facts, or stimulating emotions.

(4) The specific vehicle to use within each medium or media chosen. For example, if magazines are chosen, a technical advertiser might select a professional magazine, whereas a mass marketer might select *Time*.

(5) The schedule of media advertising. This is a timing issue of when and how often to advertise: a constant level, high level followed by decline, pulsing, and responsive tactics.

➤ 6.9 Positioning 定位

Positioning means finding out what customers think about the firm's products in relation to competing products, with a view either to modifying the product (plus associated advertising and other publicity) in order to make it fit in with these prescriptions, or to changing the product's position in consumers' minds.

"Positioning is the act of designing the company's offering and image to occupy a distinctive place in the mind of the target market" (Kotler, 2003, p.308). Or, "positioning is the act of designing the company's image and value offer so that the segment's customers understand and appreciate what the company stands for in relation to its competitors."

Product positioning focuses on buyers' perceptions about the location of brands within specific market segments. These positions are based on how well perceived product characteristics match the needs of the buyer. Positioning depends on the nature of the product, competing products and on how consumers see themselves (the life styles to which they aspire, role models, etc.).

A company's product is differentiated from those of its competitors partly by its quality and features, and partly by its positioning in the minds of consumers; these form the basis for achieving competitive advantage in the market. Therefore, a positioning strategy has to be based on the aggregate benefits that consumers seek from a product class. It is suggested by some that marketers have only two choices in developing their positioning strategy:

(1) To go head to head in direct competition with other firms, or

(2) To try to differentiate the product. In other words, they should make the product so unique that it has no direct competition.

The two approaches could be developed and exploited by using the following criteria:

(1) Product positioning could be achieved by emphasizing the attributes of the products or the benefits that consumers seek. This is the most frequently adopted positioning strategy. For example, Toyota launched its Lexus range as very luxurious cars.

(2) Positioning by product category. This involves pitching a product against similar products with a view to highlighting the differences in quality or price. For example, Unilever Company launched Radion in the UK as a detergent that removes stale odour in washed clothes and pitched it against other brands of washing powder.

(3) Positioning by use/user. Sometimes, products are positioned according to users' characteristics and lifestyle. Rolex wrist watches are positioned as exclusive products for the wealthy or for special occasions.

It is possible that a single product may be positioned differently in each market. This is because in each market international marketing environments may be different and unique. Therefore, it is necessary and important for marketers to strike a balance between a product's features, users' characteristics and culture, and the benefits sought from a product in order to determine an ideal positioning strategy for each market.

6.9.1　Where to Position　定位方向

Companies usually will position their brands to make the products more attractive to the consumers. Positioning in one country is very difficult, not to speak of positioning in several countries with quite different environmental factors. A number of factors influence the decision whether to go for a single position or different positions in various countries as follows (Roger Bennett, 2002):

(1) The extent to which a product's selling points are perceived similarly in different countries. Items close together on a perceptual scale may be seen by customers as being similar (even if by objective standards they are not) and hence might be expected to compete against each other more directly with other brands.

(2) Whether the item fulfils the same consumer needs in each market.

(3) The degree of direct and immediate substitutability between the advertised output and locally supplied brands (if this is high, the appropriate position for the product should be self-evident).

(4) Special advantages the advertised brand has to offer.

(5) Whether the brand name and/or product features need to be altered for use in different markets.

(6) The scope of the product's appeal: whether it sells to a broad cross-section of consumers (in relation to their age, sex, income level, lifestyle, etc.) or only within small market niches.

6.9.2　Positioning Methods　定位方法

The following are methods a company may adopt for positioning (Kotler, 2003).

（1）Attribute positioning：A company positions itself on an attribute, such as size or number of years in existence.

（2）Benefit positioning：The product is positioned as the leader in a certain benefit.

（3）Use or application positioning：Positioning the product as best for some use or application.

（4）User positioning：Positioning the product as best for some user group.

（5）Competitor positioning：The product claims to be better in some way than a named competitor.

（6）Product category positioning：The product is positioned as the leader in a certain product category.

（7）Quality or price positioning：The product is positioned as offering the best value.

6.10　Differentiation　差异化营销

Differentiation means making the product quite different from competitors' products or making the product quite unique.

For example, by marketing what is new, exclusive, lowest-priced, etc., a company can differentiate itself from the competition. In a sense, this is "avoidance behaviour" —the company is avoiding a direct competition.

Some products like chicken, steel, aspirin are not easy to be differentiated. Yet differentiation is still possible. A product can be differentiated by using unique packing means or with a separate brand identity. Other products such as automobiles, commercial buildings, and furniture are capable of high differentiation.

Market segmentation and product differentiation are often used together. However, there are situations where segmentation is used without product differentiation and where differentiation is used without segmentation. It is important to understand how segmentation's focus on customer groups interacts with product differentiation.

6.10.1　Differentiation Variables　差异化营销变异

There are a number of differentiation variables which are listed below in Figure 6.6 (Kotler, 2003).

6.10.2　Cost of Differentiation　差异化营销成本

Product differentiation can certainly help improve sales, but it is expensive. Some of the added costs of differentiation are as follows：

（1）Product modification；

（2）Shorter production runs；

（3）Larger inventories.

The high cost of differentiation raises the question of whether it is possible to gain the benefits of

Product	Services	Personnel	Channel	Image
Form	Ordering ease	Competence	Coverage	Symbols
Features	Delivery	Courtesy	Expertise	Media
Performance	Installation	Credibility	Performance	Atmosphere
Conformance	Customer training	Reliability		Events
Durability	Customer consulting	Responsiveness		
Reliability	Maintenance and repair	Communication		
Reparability	Miscellaneous			
Style				
Design				

Figure 6.6　Differentiation Variables

segmentation without actually changing the product. The answer is yes, but it requires careful planning.

6.11　Personal Selling　推销

Personal selling is the form of sales communication in which negotiations are conducted directly with potential customers, normally at the customer's premises or at exhibitions.

Personal selling is a direct form of promotion used to persuade customers to accept a particular point of view. Some goods, such as industrial products or goods that require explanation or description, rely heavily on personal selling. For example, Avon, the cosmetics company, relies mainly on personal selling and has been very successful with this approach even in countries where people are unaccustomed to buying cosmetics from a door-to-door salesperson.

6.11.1　Principles of Personal Selling　推销原则

There are normally three aspects of personal selling.

(1) Professionalism

A salesman should be an expert at selling. He is not just an order taker, but also an active order getter. A salesman should know the customers' needs. He should be able to answer the customer's questions about the product he sells and should be able to solve the problems of the customers. To achieve this aim, a salesman must be very much familiar with his products in terms of features, performances, strengths, weaknesses, and so on.

Besides, a salesman needs to know how to greet the buyer to get the relationship off to a good start. In other words, a salesman should know the art of how to deal with people.

Further, a salesman should be a kind of specialist of the product to such an extent that he is able to give a successful presentation or demonstration about the product. He should be able to present a whole picture of the product to the potential customer and give professional and satisfying answers to the potential customers.

（2）Negotiation

Negotiation is concerned with exchange activities and the manner in which the terms of exchange are established (Kotler, 2003). A lot of business-to-business (B2B) involves negotiation skills. Through detailed negotiation, the two parties reach an agreement of the transaction. Salesmen should also be excellent negotiators. To be a good negotiator, a salesman need not only be an expert at the product, he must also be a person who is able to read a person's mind. Negotiation involves a lot of skills. To be a good negotiator, a salesman must also have a wide range of knowledge, such as the competition environment, the other party's needs, the foreign exchange rates, and so on.

（3）Relationship marketing

Relationship marketing means that the salesmen should maintain good relationship with the customers. Therefore, a salesman should be very good at dealing with public relations. He need provide good after-sales service and provide immediate solutions to the problems of the customers. In order to maintain good relationship, salesmen may invite the customer to their company or entertain the customer with some good meals, chances to travel, and so on.

6.11.2　Process of Personal Selling　推销过程

The process of personal selling can be divided into three stages: pre-transactional stage, transactional stage, and post-transactional stage. Figure 6.7 illustrates the steps involved.

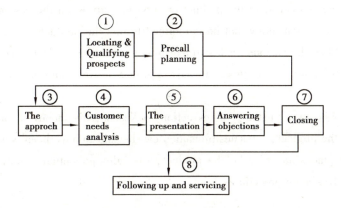

Figure 6.7   Personal Selling Stages

6.11.3　Aspects of Personal Selling Operations　有关推销的方方面面

（1）Face-to-face selling: It is very useful for products such as newly launched household electric appliances or services such as insurance that need detailed explanation or demonstration. Where the company is new, where the product is new, or where the company is entering new markets, the face-to-face interview is an important and powerful method of sales communication, if properly conducted by adequately prepared and knowledgeable salespeople. Face-to-face selling in the consumer goods field is often an important adjunct to other means of marketing communication.

(2) Telephoning selling：It is a relatively cheap method of making contact with potential customers and attempting to sell to them. Where the company is known to the potential customer and its products or services equally known and accepted, the telephone can be a low-cost, effective method of sales communication. Videophones provide more convenience or impressive sales communication.

(3) Direct selling by correspondence：It is often a vital aspect of the promotional mix. Information about the company or about products or services can be contained in the brochures or booklets which are posted to the potential customers.

6.12　AIDA "爱达"

AIDA stands for "Attention, Interest, Desire, and Action". Marketers should always keep AIDA in mind in marketing.

(1) Attention：If customers do not pay any attention to your products or services, how can the products be sold to them? In a market where similar products of the competitors are lying side by side with yours, the problem is how to draw customers' attention. Attention can be drawn by, say, holding a demonstration of the product.

(2) Interest：It is not enough to successfully draw customers' attention. It is an important step to arouse the customer's interest in the product or service. Only when the customer feels interested in the product or service is it likely that he is inclined to buy the product.

(3) Desire：When the customer starts to feel interested in the product or service, the marketer must lose no time in leading the customer to have a strong desire to buy the product or accept the service.

(4) Action：When the customer takes action—takes out his money to buy the product, or places an order for the product, the sales promotion can be said to have been concluded. In the case where the customer places an order for the product, the sales promotion is only half done, as the following stage involves more procedures.

6.13　FABV "发步"

FABV stands for "Features, Advantages, Benefits, and Value". When the marketers are giving presentations or demonstrations about the product or service, they must not ignore FABV. Besides AIDA, marketers must also use FABV approach.

(1) Features：Features describe physical characteristics of a market offering, such as the particular components in the TV set or new function of a mobile phone.

(2) Advantages：Advantages describe why the features provide an advantage to the customer. For example, marketers can tell the customer that the main components in the TV set are made in a famous company of Japan so as to show its features that the competitors' product may not have.

（3）Benefits：Benefits describe the economic，technical，service，and social benefits delivered by the offering. For example，the TV manufacturer may ensure the customer that the TV set can work efficiently for a longer period of time than the competitor's and after-sales service will certainly be first-class. Besides，the price might be a little higher than the competitors' product，but，in a long run，the TV set is not expensive because it can be used for a much longer period of time and it can produce better effect.

（4）Value：Value describes the summative worth（often in monetary terms）of the offering.

▶ 6.14　SWOT and PEST Analysis Templates　SWOT（态势）和 PEST（宏观环境）分析模型

6.14.1　SWOT Analysis Template　SWOT 分析模型

SWOT stands for "Strengths，Weaknesses，Opportunities，and Threats". Marketers must be quite familiar with the SWOT of their products or services and the SWOT of the competitors'.

（1）Strengths：Strengths refer to the strong points—the advantages over the competitors' products. For example，when giving a presentation about a new brand of mobile phone，marketers can emphasize the strong points of the new product. He may tell the customers that the new product can be used as a video phone when connected to a specific facility. On the other hand，to know the competitor's strength is very important so that it can be bypassed or neutralized.

（2）Weaknesses：Weaknesses refer to the disadvantageous points of a product. Marketers must also know the weaknesses of their product so that they may try to avoid them when introducing it. To know a competitor's strengths and weaknesses is likewise very important and can provide insights into how capable it is pursuing various types of strategies. It also forms an important input into the process of identifying and selecting strategic alternatives. One approach is to attempt to exploit a competitor's weakness in an area where the firm has an existing or developing strength. The desired pattern is to use a strength to compete with a competitor's weakness.

（3）Opportunities：Opportunities are self-explanatory. They refer to the opportunities of marketing products or services or any other opportunities that are favourable for the development of the business. Opportunities can be found anywhere；the problem is how to get access to them or to find them out. On the other hand，opportunities can refer to any opportunities that can be used for the development of a company's strategies.

（4）Threats：Threats refer to the competitive advantages of the competitors. Those advantages of the competitors are threatening the firm. To realize the threats is quite important so that a firm can be ready and find out ways to compete against the competitors better.

6.14.2　PEST Analysis Template　PEST 分析模型

PEST stands for "Political，Economic，Social and Technological"（environment）. The four aspects ouside a firm are out of the control of a firm. The PEST analysis template is a tool to evaluate the four external factors that may affet a firm's business. It is often helpful to complete a PEST analysis prior to a SWOT analysis, although it may be more useful to complete a PEST analysis as part of, or after, a SWOT analysis. A SWOT analysis measures a business unit; a PEST analysis measures trends and changes in the market.

The four factors have great influence upon any business decision in a given business environment. It is not easy to imagine the amount of hard work and research that is involved whenever a new product or commercial utility is launched. For that matter, any change in the business management and development strategy calls for minute scrutiny of the environment which would form the background for such change. It is with respect to this detailed dissection of the environment and the proper understanding of the verdict that is assimilated from such dissection that any decision pertaining to expansion, entry, exit or any other transition is reached.

PEST analysis is one tool of strategic management which scans the business and market environment to enable the firm to understand the surroundings in which it is operating or which it intends to enter. Before proceeding towards the example, let's get to know this strategic management tool better. Here are the details about PEST:

(1) Political environment

It refers to all those things pertaining to and perpetrated by the government that affect the economy and business scenario in general. Government regulations and policies that impact on the business environment the most may include trade and labor laws, tax policies, environmental laws and regulations, trade restrictions, commercial tariffs, infrastructure and development policies, etc.. The degree of political stability also has a huge impact upon business environment and the economy in general.

(2) Economic environment

It refers mostly to the macroeconomic factors as these factors may have a high impact upon the business environment but a firm does not have any control over them. The most it can do is to modify its business strategies and various commercial and financial policies accordingly to make the most of the economic situation at hand. These economic factors may include the currency exchange rate, interest rate, economic growth rate, rate of inflation, etc..

(3) Social environment

It refers to the social, religious and cultural aspects of the business environment that may be affected by, and may react to, the firm's transitional strategies either positively or negatively. These may include demographic aspects like age distribution, population growth rate, employment and income statistics, education and career trends, religious beliefs and social stigmas, overall general attitude (conservative or liberal), etc. These factors may have a huge impact upon the firm's operations within the business environment as any action by the firm which goes against or threatens the societal norms may face criticism, negative publicity and protests.

（4）Technological environment

It refers to the technical aspects of the business environment and may include the level of automation available in the current times, technical facilities and infrastructure, rate of technological progress and research and development activities. These factors may assume decisive proportions and may impact the cost, quality and scope of innovation for a product, service or commercial utility.

Two more categories were added to the above—Legal and Environmental (as in ecological factors)—turning PEST into PESTLE.

（5）Legal environment

It includes various laws and legislation pertaining to consumers, discrimination, employment, competition, public health and safety.

（6）Environmental factors

Environmenal factors include climate, weather, ecological balance, level of pollution, wildlife conservation, tourism, farming, etc.

⟫ 6.15　Branding　品牌策略

6.15.1　What Is a Brand?　何谓品牌?

A brand is an identifying mark for products or service. When a company registers a brand legally, it becomes a trademark. A brand gives a product or service instant recognition and may save promotional costs.

According to the American Marketing Association, a brand is a name, term, sign, symbol or design, or a combination of them, intended to identify the goods or services of one seller or group of sellers to differentiate them from those of competitors.

A brand is a complex symbol that can convey up to six levels of meaning (Kotler, 2003).

（1）Attributes: A brand brings to mind certain attributes. For example, Changhong suggests moderate price, but reliable quality TV sets. And Chunlan suggests air conditioners of competitive price and good quality.

（2）Benefits: Attributes must be conveyed in functional and emotional benefits. For example, "good quality" could translate into the functional benefit "I won't have to buy another air-conditioner for a number of years."

（3）Values: The brand also indicates something about the producer's values.

（4）Culture: The brand may represent a certain culture.

（5）Personality: The brand can project a certain personality.

（6）User: The brand suggests the kind of consumer who buys or uses the product.

MNEs must make four major branding decisions as follows:

（1）Brand versus no brand;

（2）Manufacturer's brand versus private brand；

（3）One brand versus multiple brands；

（4）Worldwide brands versus local brands.

It is believed that the most distinctive skill of professional marketers may well be their ability to create, maintain, protect and enhance brands. It is also believed that branding is the art and cornerstone of marketing. Branding is not simple at all. It is not just attaching a name to a product. Rather it is a process on which the organization can sharpen its strategic skills, entailing a consideration of the organization's patents, processes, history and experience, knowledge of raw materials, the skills of its labour force and, not least, the segments of the market in which it will operate.

Much international expansion takes place through acquisition of companies in foreign countries that already have branded products. For example, when Maytag, virtually unknown by consumers in China, formed a joint venture with the Chinese washing machine company Rongshida, it used the brand name Rongshida.

6.15.2 Brand Equity 品牌资产

Brand equity, the focal point of brand decisions, is defined as "a set of brand assets and liabilities linked to a brand, its name and symbol, that add to or subtract from the value provided by a product or service to a firm and/or to that firm's customers". (Richard P.Bagozzi, 1998).

To customers, brand equity facilitates information processing, leads to greater confidence in decision making, and creates enhanced satisfaction. Underlying the brand equity are five broad assets: brand loyalty, brand awareness, perceived quality, brand association, and other proprietary brand assets.

Brand loyalty encourages customers to buy a particular brand time after time and remain insensitive to competitors' offerings. Brand awareness means that a certain brand can help customer to realize the features of the brand name, which attracts attention, conveys images of familiarity, and so on. Brand names can also be abstract symbols of the quality of the product or service they represent. Brand association refers to ideas, values, and other information linked to a focal brand. Other proprietary brand assets include patents, trademarks, and marketing channel relationships.

In a word, brand equity provides value to customers by enhancing efficient information processing and shopping, building confidence in decision making, reinforcing buying, and contributing to self-esteem. On the other hand, brand equity helps sellers increase marketing efficiency and effectiveness, build brand loyalty, improve profit margins, gain leverage over retailers, and achieve distinctiveness over the competition.

Figure 6.8 provides an overview of branding decisions (Kotler, 2003).

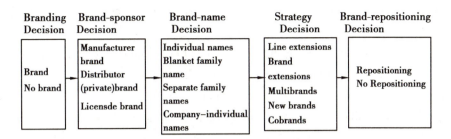

Figure 6.8   An Overview of Branding Decisions

6.16   Unique Selling Proposition（USP） 独特的销售方式

Unique selling proposition means the company develops a very special selling proposition for each brand. For example, the advertisement must make a proposition to the consumer, besides words and product puffery, but not just show window advertising. Each advertisement must say to each reader："Buy this product, and you will get this specific benefit." The proposition must be one that the competitor either cannot, or does not, offer. It must be unique—either a uniqueness of the brand or a claim not otherwise made in that particular field of advertising.

The USP chosen for a brand is often given a scientific character in an advertisement. By focusing on a specific product benefit (hopefully a unique one), it is felt that consumers' self interest will be stimulated and serve as the primary motivators of sales. Some very concrete, human elements are used in the USPs. For example, "Evergood Coffee, a triumph of taste over tradition." (Norway), "Safeway is the place to shop for families with young children." (Safeway, UK).

6.17   Word-of-mouth 口碑效应

Word-of-mouth means that the existing customer conveys information about the product he has bought in favour of the producer because of its good quality or excellent service. In other words, the existing customer recommends the product he has bought to others because, after he uses the product, he finds that the product is really worth buying.

6.18   Marketing Mix—the 4 Ps 营销组合：4 Ps

6.18.1   Elements of Marketing Mix 营销组合的要素

Marketing mix was first developed by E. Jerome MacCarthy about more than 40 years ago. He developed the four-factor classification, which has come to be known as the famous Four Ps of the marketing mix：Product, Price, Place, and Promotion.

（1）Product：It defines the characteristics of the product or service that meets the needs of the customers. It includes a study of the product features: packaging, branding and servicing policies, and style.

(2) Price: It decides on a pricing strategy. It refers to the money that customers have to pay for the product, such as a wholesale price or retail price, allowances and credit terms.

(3) Place (or route of distribution): This stands for various activities the firm undertakes to make the product accessible and available to consumers. This includes, for example, choosing retailers, wholesalers, physical distribution firms and intermediaries. But, some of the revolutions in marketing have come about by changing this P. Think of telephone insurance and the Internet!

(4) Promotion: This includes all the weapons in the marketing armoury—advertising, selling, sales promotions, public relations, etc., which the firms uses to persuade customers to buy the product or accept the services.

There are a number of circumstances that will dictate which elements of the marketing mix are to be employed and in which proportion. If you have put sufficient time into accurately defining your marketplace, your market segment, your product positioning, and your unique selling propositions, then it becomes much easier to carry out this task.

Taking time to think through your marketing strategy forces you to take some very difficult decisions. The most difficult ones are those where you decide NOT to do certain things, such as deciding certain market sectors are not key to your company's success due to the difficulty in competing effectively. The benefit of taking such decisions is that it really helps you to focus on a more limited (and achievable) set of objectives. It then becomes much clearer which elements of the marketing mix need to be used, and hence you achieve profitable results from your marketing budget.

The key elements of the international marketing mix are shown in Figure 6.9.

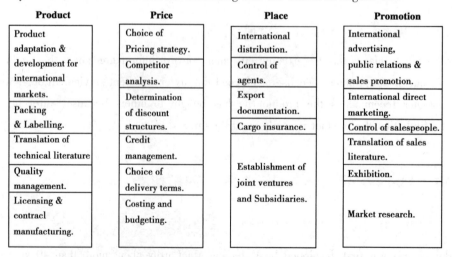

Figure 6.9   Key Elements of the International Marketing Mix

6.18.2   The First P—Product   第一个 P: 产品

Of the four Ps, product is the most important, as the following three Ps are just based on Product. In other words, the product is the basic ingredient upon which the marketing mix is constructed, without which the other ingredients are meaningless.

Products can be defined as goods and services that fill customers' needs. We often think of products as physical objects such as computers, TV sets, cars, wine, and so on. However, from the perspective of marketing, marketers are also concerned with promoting service-oriented products such as insurance, banking, movies, resort locations. Besides, products include people such as an international business professor, political candidates, and events such as trade fair. Further, organizations can also be regarded as products such as the American Cancer Society. Even ideas can be marketed, as in the case of recycling or seat belt usage.

Therefore, product is broadly defined and can include physical goods, services, events, organizations, people, and ideas.

A product has the following three obvious characteristics.

(1) Physical: shape, style, colour, size, weight, etc.

(2) Functional: its performance in use.

(3) Symbolic: based on the psychological and social satisfactions it delivers.

1. Product Classification

Products can be categorized into the following:

(1) Consumer products

A. Convenience products, which are low-cost, repeatedly bought and readily accessible, such as bread, milk and newspapers.

B. Shopping products, which are more highly priced, bought less often and after some thought and effort, such as furniture, domestic electrical equipment, personal computers.

C. Speciality products which are similar to shopping products in terms of purchasing patterns though more exclusive and highly priced because of the distinctive features they have.

(2) Industrial products

They range from capital equipment, accessories and components, raw materials, etc., to the consumable supplies which facilitate production and administrative operation.

2. Total Product

A total product is not just a collection of component parts or the result of fusing together various materials, but it also includes the following:

(1) Accessories;

(2) An installation service;

(3) An operating manual;

(4) A package;

（5）A brand name or trade mark;

（6）A user guarantee;

（7）After-sales service, and so on.

3. Product Mix

A product mix (also called product assortment) is the set of all products and items that a particular seller offers for sale. (Kotler, 2003) A product mix is normally described in terms of width, length and depth.

Width refers to the number of different products that are marketed by a single firm. Products lines are groups of similar items that are used together, sold to the same customer, or handled through the same distribution channels. For example, among other things, General Motors sells cars, trucks, and chassis, and each of these can be thought of as a product line.

Length refers to the number of items sold by a company within each product line. Depth suggests that, as in the case of General Motors, each of the car, truck, and chassis categories at GM is available in different shapes and model designations.

The three dimensions of the product mix provide useful starting points for determining product strategies for a firm. Companies can use them to expand in three basic directions. They can add new product lines to serve a broader range of customers. Besides, they can deepen their model offering by adding product variations. Further, they can lengthen their product line. In addition, a company's product mix has some consistency, which refers to how closely related the various product lines are in end use, production requirements, distribution channels, or some other ways. A company can pursue more product-line consistency.

4. International Product Lifecycle (PL)

Like a human being, a product is thought of as having a lifecycle. Products are conceived and born, mature, decline and eventually die. We can divide a product's lifecycle into four phases: introductory phase, growth phase, maturity phase, and decline phase.

（1）Introductory phase

This phase is characterized by high expenditures (for market research, test marketing, launch costs, etc.) and possibly financial losses. Customers will be interested in the new product. Typically these customers are younger, better educated and more affluent than the rest of the population. Technical problems are likely and realizing this, many potential consumers will delay purchasing the product. At this stage, there is usually no competition. Advertising is normally the most important elements of the marketing mix during the introduction. The aim is to impress the new brand on the consumers.

（2）Growth phase

During this stage, conventional consumers start to buy the product. Competition is starting. Therefore, advertisement should attempt both to reinforce customer loyalty and to broaden the product's appeal.

（3）Maturity phase

During this stage, the product reaches the climax. Efforts are made to stabilize market share and to make the product more attractive (through improvements in design and presentation) to new market segments. Extra features might be added, quality improved and distribution systems widened. Most consumers have by now either tried the product or decided not to buy. Competitions become intense. More strategies are used to make the product more competitive.

（4）Decline phase

Eventually, the market is saturated and the product enters its phase of decline. The customers' tastes may have changed, or the product may now be technically out of date. As a result, sales and profit start to fall.

There may be differences among countries in either the shape or the length of a product's lifecycle. A product facing declining sales in one country may have growing or sustained sales in another. For example, cars are a mature product in Western Europe and in the USA, and Japan. They are in the late growth stage in South Korea and in the early growth stage in China and India.

5. Reasons for Product Alteration

There are a number of reasons for companies to alter their products in order to meet the needs of customers in different countries.

（1）Legal reasons

Explicit legal requirements are the most obvious reason for altering products for foreign markets. The exact requirements vary widely by country but are usually meant to protect consumers.

Marketing managers must watch for the indirect legal requirements that may affect product content or demand. In some countries, companies cannot easily import certain raw materials or components, forcing them to construct an end product with local substitutes that may alter the final result substantially. Legal requirements such as high taxes on heavy automobiles also shift companies sales to smaller models, thus indirectly altering demand for tire sales and grades of gasoline.

（2）Cultural reasons

Marketing managers find it hard to determine in advance whether foreign consumers are willing to accept new or different products. The new products should meet the requirements of the culture of a nation. Therefore, the product has to be altered in some way so as to fit the new foreign market.

（3）Economic reasons

Personal income and infrastructures affect product demand. Companies have to change the product strategies to meet the requirements of different countries of different economic levels.

When a product comes to the stage of decline, it has to be altered; otherwise, the product is not even cost-effective, not to mention other costs of the product.

6. Packaging and Labelling

（1）Packaging

Packaging and labelling are both very important to a product, as most physical products have to be packaged and labelled. Both are thought of as an element of product strategy and many marketers even have called packaging a fifth P.

The main concern in designing packages for products, especially for new products, is to protect the merchandise on its journey from the factory to the customer. This is especially true of industrial goods and appliances whose sales are made from display models. From the perspective of marketing, packaging is of vital importance in sales promotion. Sales are enhanced by packages that are visible, informative, emotionally appealing, and workable.

Good packaging helps sell because items with high visibility are easier to find when they are displayed on store shelves. Design with good and useful information may help attract customers and make them more inclined to decide to buy the goods.

The emotional factor in packaging refers to the image that consumers form after viewing a product.

Workability in packaging means that the container not only protects the product but is also easy to open and re-close, is readily stored, and has utility for secondary uses once the product is used up. For example, in China, some goods are packaged in a special container—a real cup, which can be used as a cup after the goods within are used up.

As services are also products, the packaging of services are likewise important. When an insurance company decides that the opaque jargon of its policies will be replaced by easy-to-understand, "user-friendly" language, it is improving the "packaging" and presentation of its "product".

(2) Labelling

The label may be a simple tag attached to the product or an elaborately designed graphic that is part of the package. The label normally carries information about the brand name, manufacturer's name and address, price, specifications, and so on.

The design of the label must be fully in phase with the desired image of the product. In fact, it is the part of the package that carries the identification/promotion functions. For example, the label of the British black tea "Lepton" looks more attractive because the quality of the label is much better than some labels of teas made in China.

Companies must also pay attention to the legal requirements related to the contents of a label. In many countries, statutes are in force concerning false trade descriptions, weights and measures, and price marking.

6.18.3　The Second P—Price　第二个 P：价格

Within the marketing mix, price is always paid much attention to. From the perspective of international marketing, price does not only refer to the price of a commodity. It involves marketing strategies, such as international pricing strategies. It also involves the production cost, profit margins, taxes, logistics, and so on.

A price must be low enough to gain sale, but high enough to guarantee the flow of funds required to carry on other activities, such as R&D, production and distribution. The proper price will not only assure short-term profits but also give the company the resources necessary for achieving long-term competitive viability.

1. Factors Influencing Pricing

International pricing is a complex procedure: all the issues applicable to domestic price decisions might be relevant to foreign sales. Besides, there are additional problems of lack of information, uncertain consumer responses and foreign exchange rate influences. In parallel with domestic marketing, the prices a company is able to charge in foreign markets depend on:

(1) the total demand for the product in each country, which itself varies according to population, per capita income, tastes and fashions, seasonal factors, and so on;

(2) the responsiveness of consumer demand to price changes so that if a small reduction in price leads to a large increase in sales, then a price cut will be economically worthwhile because extra sales will more than compensate for reduced unit revenue;

(3) expected behaviour of competitors;

(4) market response to promotional activity.

Besides, pricing is more complex internationally than domestically because of the following factors:

(1) Different degrees of governmental intervention;

(2) Greater diversity of markets;

(3) Rising price for exports;

(4) Changing values of currencies;

(5) Differences in fixed versus variable pricing practices;

(6) Retailers' strength with suppliers;

(7) Costs of production and distribution;

(8) The product's brand image and the degree of consumer loyalty;

(9) Consumers' knowledge of the availability of substitute products;

(10) Consumers' perceptions of the attributes and quality of the product.

Figure 6.10 illustrates influences on international pricing decisions.

Choosing a price for the product that is entirely new to a particular national market is especially difficult. There are few guidelines to help with making a decision: consumer loyalty does not exist; consumers have little perception of the item's characteristics and quality, and there are no alternatives against which the product may be compared. Problems are compounded when a product is technically sophisticated and requires extensive after-sales service and customer care. Most firms introducing new products in fact determine their prices by first establishing their costs, adding a mark-up and then modifying the outcome in the light of market conditions. The process for international pricing decision-making is outlined in Figure 6.11(Source: Roger Bennett, 2002).

2. Pricing Strategies

There are a number of pricing strategies that are available.

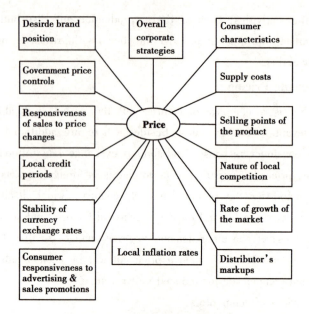

Figure 6.10　Influences on International Pricing Decisions

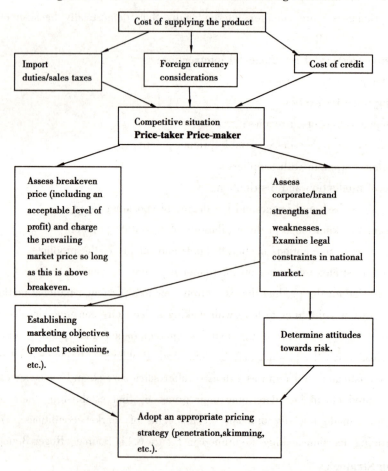

Figure 6.11　International Pricing Decisions

（1）Penetration pricing

A low price is combined with aggressive advertising aimed at capturing a large percentage of the market. The strategy will fail if competitors reduce their prices at the same time. This is a long-term strategy intended to build market share. It involves substantial expenditures on promoting the product. Pricing at low levels in some foreign markets might be for the following reasons:

1）Lower income levels of local consumers;

2）Intense local competition from rival companies;

3）Weak demand for the product.

（2）Skimming

Skimming is a high-price policy suitable for top-quality versions of established products. The firm must convince high-income consumers that the expensive model offers distinctive improvements over the standard version. This policy requires the existence in the local market of significant numbers of high-income consumers prepared to pay top prices. Products should be designed to attract the wealthy consumers who are able to realize that their purchases are worth the value of the product.

（3）Cost-plus

In cost-plus pricing the supplying firm predetermines the length of a production run, adds up all its anticipated costs—fixed and variable—and divides estimated total costs by planned output. Cost-plus pricing is problematic for firms producing several different products. Allocations of overheads to the various items will be arbitrary to some extent, so that individual products may be over-or under-priced. Besides, not all of a production run will necessarily be sold. Some units may have to be put into stock or scrapped, hence altering the unit production costs of the remaining items.

（4）Product lifecycle pricing

Here the price is varied according to the stage in the product's lifecycle. In the early stage, a high price may be set to cover development and advertising costs. The price might then be systematically lowered to broaden the product's appeal. The following are some pointers to pricing strategies.

1）Prices must be related to overall corporate policy, including the institutional "image" the organization wishes to develop and maintain, its philosophy toward price competition, etc.

2）Decisions on products and services, distribution, promotion, administration are all affected by decisions on price—cause and effect relationships within marketing objectives and "mix" strategies must therefore be carefully studied.

3）Price has a key influence on demand and therefore the market's perception of price and its implications for cost, volume, profit relationships must be closely examined.

4）Pricing strategy must take sufficient account of external constraints. For example, government economic measures (on inflation), price regulation and monopolies legislation, and the reactions of distributors, competitors, suppliers, etc., which may all act as important determinant on prices.

5）In most cases, price must be related to the requirements of the total product portfolio and hence to overall marketing objectives.

6) In developing strategy, future trends in costs, demand and competition must be carefully considered and policies on adapting prices to changed market conditions must be devised.

7) Most markets are in a constant state of change which heightens the risks of price decisions—wherever possible and, however informal, marketing research and any other relevant techniques should be employed in developing pricing strategy.

3. Promotional Pricing

In order to stimulate early purchases, companies may use some pricing techniques such as the following:

(1) Loss-leader pricing: The prices of products are reduced a great deal to attract the customers.

(2) Special-event pricing: Sellers sell the goods at different prices in different seasons or when certain events are taking place. For example, at the end of winter, some goods for the winter use such as leather coats, are sold at special low prices.

(3) Cash rebates: Rebates can help clear inventories without cutting the stated list price.

(4) Low-interest financing: Companies offer low-interest financing to attract customers.

(5) Longer payment terms: Companies offer long payment terms, such as mortgage, installments to stimulate the customers' purchases.

(6) Warranties and service contracts: Companies offer a free or low-cost warranty or service contract.

(7) Psychological discounting: This strategy involves an artificially high price and then offering the product at substantial savings. For example, the commodity is marked with "Was $488, now $288."

6.18.4　The Third P—Promotion　第三个 P：促销

Promotion is the presentation of messages intended to help sell a product or service and it is the process of stimulating demand for a company's goods or services. "International promotion" is used here in this book to connote a range of communication tools designed to influence consumers' attitudes and behaviors toward a product or service. These tools are advertising, sales promotion, sponsorship and publicity, direct marketing and trade exhibitions. The effectiveness of international promotion is based on the exploitation of cross-cultural similarities rather than differences. The marketers face a number of problems in planning international promotions, such as differences in culture, economy, tastes and attitudes, government regulations, marketing institutions and language.

1. Methods of International Promotion

(1) Advertising

Advertising is a non-personal form of promotion in which a firm attempts to persuade consumers to a particular point of view. Advertising is the most visible and documented form of marketing promotion and has generated most interest and attention among academics, professionals and consumers. In most marketing organizations, the bulk of promotion's budget is spent on various forms of advertising.

As companies begin to develop their international advertising campaigns, there are a number of strategies that can be pursued in each market depending on the nature of the product, how it is used, and the company's communication objectives. It is believed by some that there are some strategic alternatives that can be employed:

1) Same product, same message worldwide;

2) Same product, different communications;

3) Different product, same communications;

4) Dual adaptation;

5) New product, new message.

(2) Sales promotion

Sales promotion is short-term incentives such as discounts, quantity purchases discounts, coupons, money-back guarantees, in-store consumer promotions designed to increase trials, generate sales, deepen market acceptance and increase market penetration. In international markets, these activities are especially important at the introductory stage of the product lifecycle.

Typical dealer promotions include point-of-purchase (POP) displays, cash allowances, credits, gifts, bonuses, "2 for 1" deals, contests, prizes, free advice or information, etc.

(3) Sponsorship and publicity

Event sponsorship seeks to exploit a relationship between a firm and an event with a view to achieving specific marketing objectives such as enhancing corporate and brand image, and possibly avoiding severe controls or outright ban on advertising of certain products. For example, advertisements of the sponsors' products can be always found around the playground of a sports meet.

(4) Direct marketing

Direct marketing can be an effective marketing promotion tool whether used independently or in conjunction with other methods of promotion if it is carefully developed and implemented. Direct marketing has become necessary for firms to develop a system that enables them to acquire and maintain some form of database for analysis and tracking of customer behaviors, with a view to developing effective relationship marketing strategies. Direct marketing works on the principles of interaction, targeting, continuity and control. With advances in technology, it is now possible for international firms to coordinate their direct marketing activities across the world.

(5) Trade exhibitions

Trade exhibitions are also an effective tool in international marketing communication particularly for industrious products. Trade exhibitions help firms to come into direct contact with prospective customers who are either ready to buy or seriously considering a purchase. On the other hand, buyers can have more choices at the exhibitions. For example, in China, trade exhibitions are held twice in Guangzhou yearly. They attribute a lot to Chinese international trade.

2. Types of Promotion

Promotions can be categorized into the following.

(1) Consumer promotion

Consumer promotions aim at producing an action response. To do this, marketers may use one or more of a variety of stimuli, such as coupons, free samples, premium. However, there is a major drawback with customer promotions: they sometimes do not build brand preference or encourage repeat sales. Rather, they serve only as a free gift or price reduction.

(2) Dealer promotion

Dealers typically need incentive to carry and push a sponsor's brands. The most important dealer promotion is, perhaps, the point-of-purchase (POP) display. A POP promotion consists of a sign, poster, or other attention-getting device that dealers place next to merchandise or present conspicuously with related merchandise away from competitors' brands and other products. Other dealer promotions involve contest, prizes, free training or business advice, free vacations, and specialty advertising items. In fact, these displays act as consumer and dealer promotions.

(3) Sales force promotion

Firms often use incentives to motivate their own sales forces. The sales chiefly depend on the efforts of the sales forces. The incentives may include bonuses, commissions, raising salaries, free trips, and other forms of rewards.

3. International Promotional Strategy

Promotion consists of the whole communications package that presents information about product or service to potential customers. There are broad similarities with domestic promotional strategy in that the activities can be classified in to PUSH (methods involving direct selling) and PULL (depending on the use of mass media). The former is more useful for high-price goods, while the latter predominates where advertising can be used fruitfully. In international marketing, both PUSH and PULL methods can be used in combination, depending on product price relative to per capita income, accessibility and cost of appropriate media information, and the type of distribution system available.

The strength and recognizability of the brand name is a powerful determinant of promotional strategy. The ideal situation for a firm in global markets is to develop the brand name to the situation where it becomes generic. For example, Xerox is very popular in China. Sony is familiar to Chinese consumers.

The purpose of the international promotional strategy is to create a sustainable and favourable image for the product in all foreign markets served.

6.18.5　The Fourth P—Place　第四个 P：场所

Place refers to the distribution channels. A channel distribution is a series of intermediaries that handle, store and/or assume ownership of goods as they pass from the producer to the end-consumer.

In other words, distribution channels are groups of related organizations that help make goods and services available for use by customers.

Channels of distribution for international marketing can be very long, as there are channels both within and between countries. Therefore, international distribution decisions are inherently more complex than those for purely domestic distribution operations. In international physical distribution, goods are subject to multi modes of transport and possibly delays at borders, cover longer distance, involve higher costs, and require more extensive documentation. The importance of international physical distribution to the success of any international marketing operation cannot be overemphasized as it has a direct impact on how a market is served and the cost of doing so.

1. Distribution Systems

There are different distribution systems in different countries. It is often difficult to standardize the distribution systems and to use the same approach in every country. For example, in Finland, there is a predominance of general line retailers who carry a wide assortment of merchandise. In contrast, the wholesaler and retail structure in Italy is characterized by a wide array of stores, many of which specialize or carry limited lines of merchandise. So in distributing goods in these two countries, international firms need to employ different strategies.

Consumer spending habits can also negate attempts to standardize distribution. In the USA, many middlemen are geared to handling credit sales, but in China, most consumer purchases are on a cash basis.

The location where consumers are used to buying will likewise affect distribution. In economically developed countries where supermarkets have become commonplace, customers purchase a wide range of food and other products under one roof. But, in most countries, purchases are made in smaller stores and distribution requires the international firms or the local sales manager to deal with a large number of retailers, each of whom is selling a small amount of merchandise.

There are quite a lot of ways goods and services can be distributed to customers. No distribution system can actually satisfy the need of every firm, and many businesses use several distribution channels to reach different market segments. Generally speaking, there are four main categories of distribution systems as follows:

(1) Direct to consumers: for example, mail order or if the supplier owns and controls its own outlets.

(2) Producer to retailer: here the retailer bears the cost of storing goods awaiting sale.

(3) Producer to intermediary: The advantage of selling to an intermediary (export merchant, for example) includes less administrations and the transfer of the risk of product failure from the supplier to the intermediary.

(4) Through agents: agents operate on a commission basis and may be either brokers, who simply bring together buyers and sellers without ever taking physical possession of the goods; or factors who do possess the goods until customers are found and who sometimes sell under their own names at prices they think best.

2. Choosing the Best Distribution System

A number of criteria can be used in creating the most efficient distribution system. To carry the products, MNEs need find the best possible distributors. The possible distributors should be financially reliable and strong. Besides, the distributors must know well the right people and provide assistance in handling governmental red tapes. Another factor is the number and type of product lines the distributor carries currently so that the multinational can identify middlemen who are most likely to give its goods a strong marketing push. In a word, a company may choose a distributor according to:

(1) its financial strength;

(2) its good connections;

(3) extent of its other business commitments;

(4) current status of its personnel, facilities, and equipment.

Depending on the nature of the market and the competition, the MNEs may give exclusive geographic distribution to one local seller or may arrange to have a number of sellers jointly selling the product. From the perspective of exports, it is suggested that the following systems may be selected.

(1) Direct system: this is a distribution system that permits the centralization of stocks in the home country and where deliveries are made directly to foreign buyers. The main advantage is that it eliminates the need for foreign warehousing and allows for greater centralization of inventory.

(2) Transit system: with this system, exports are handled through a non-stockholding, bulk-breaking point in a particular foreign market for onward transfer to other countries. The aim is to ensure that freight is transported more economically in greater bulk to a distribution point in a given foreign location and disaggregated into individual orders much closer to the other foreign markets.

(3) Classical system: this system is the most common system of distribution, particularly with exporters who are actively engaged in a host country. With this system, stocks are distributed to depots in each foreign market; orders can be delivered more rapidly from the warehouse in the host market than from the factory; freight can be dispatched to the foreign market with less urgency, permitting the use of cheaper modes of transport and offering greater scope for load consolidation, and less documentation is required and smaller import duties payable.

(4) Multi-country system: with a multi-country system, a single warehouse which is centrally located in close proximity to the main export markets is used as a supply point to customers in several countries.

3. Differences Between International Distribution and Domestic Distribution

Although the international distribution and domestic distribution have something in common, they differ from each other in the following respects.

(1) The range of available options is more varied. An MNE can establish its own distribution system (purchasing or setting up from very beginning its own distribution subsidiaries in various

countries) or may opt to use locally controlled channels. Standardization of the methods and procedures used by an MNE for international distribution is very difficult because of the big differences that exist in national distribution systems. Domestic distribution is relatively easier because no national distribution system differences exist.

(2) Distribution channels are normally longer and more complex than domestic distribution channels.

(3) Delays and hold-ups at various points in international distribution systems are common. This is because the process of distributions is much more complicated while domestic distribution is less complex.

(4) Wholesaling and retailing systems differ markedly in different countries. In domestic distributions wholesaling and retailing systems are the same.

4. Distributions Alternatives

(1) Direct Distribution

This is the simplest channel that is directly from the producer to the consumer or business buyer. Direct distribution is also used by not-for-profit organizations to disperse literature.

(2) Adding retailers

Retailers have been a traditional part of distribution channels. They provide shopping convenience, local inventories, exchange services, and repairs. The use of retailers has proved effective and efficient for both consumers and manufacturers of food, tires, videos rentals, hardware, dry cleaning, and so on.

(3) Using wholesalers

Wholesalers are dealers who buy in large volume and resell to retailers in lots. They provide retailers with assortments of merchandise, backup stocks, credit, delivery, and promotional assistance.

(4) Agents and brokers

Brokers and independent representatives (reps) are used to sell goods in a channel of distribution. Reps are specialized agents who neither own nor take possession of the merchandise that they sell to wholesalers, distributors, businesses, or retail customers.

(5) Nonprofit and service distribution

Nonprofit programs and services are rarely sold from inventory, and extensive systems of warehouses and retail stores are not needed. Nonprofit programs are often sold through networks of branch offices. Sales offices may be owned and operated by the parent organization or franchised to local independent managers. Some temporaries help companies operate their branches on a franchise basis, whereas loan companies typically own their local units.

(6) Channel ownership

Companies can sell their goods and services through independent wholesalers and retailers, or they can acquire facilities to perform these activities by using their own employees. This method of distribution can improve efficiency by eliminating promotion and selling expenses that normally occur between the company and the wholesaler and between the wholesaler and the retailer. With a completely integrated channel, the main task for marketing executives is to increase demand among the final buyers and to coordinate the activities of different units in the channel.

(7) Franchise distribution

Franchising is a system of distribution whereby independent business managers are given the right to sell products or services in exchange for a fee or agreements on buying and merchandising policies. The main advantage of franchising is that it offers the parent organization a low-cost way to expand rapidly.

Summary of This Chapter
本章概要

1. 在整个国际商务活动中,营销是非常重要的环节。企业的生存,除了先进的科学管理之外,营销在某种程度上起决定性的作用。英语单词"marketing"翻译成汉语是"市场营销"。我们在此简称为营销。营销的基本含义是:在市场中进行交换的活动过程。营销是指企业发现、甄别并满足市场需要的一切活动。换言之,营销指与市场有关的整个企业活动,即在适当的时间和适合的地点,采用适当的方式,以适当的价格和适当的产品,提供给市场,以满足消费要求。国际营销涉及跨国的营销活动,是企业、公司把自己的产品或服务推销到国外以满足市场的需求,同时自己也获得相应的利润。国际营销可以分为狭义国际营销和广义国际营销。狭义国际营销主要指的是以销售商品为目的而进行的一切活动;广义的国际营销指的是国与国之间以交换关系为媒介的社会过程,它不仅指商品,而且指其他方面,如旅游、文化、体育等的交换过程。从社会角度来看,营销是个人和集体通过创造,提供出售,并与他人自由交换产品和价值,以获得其所需的一种社会和管理过程。营销被认为是推销产品的艺术。美国市场营销协会(American Marketing Association)对营销所下的定义是:营销(管理)是计划和执行关于商品、服务和创意的观念、定价、促销和分销,以创造符合个人和组织目标的交换的一种过程。

2. 营销理论早在19世纪末和20世纪初形成于美国。一百多年以来,市场营销学的发展主要在于营销理念方面。营销的观念不断改变、深化和趋于全面。营销对象的内涵、外延意义不断扩大。从传统的营销理念到新概念营销和战略营销,这一切的发展和变化,都伴随着社会经济的进步和发展。传统的营销理念重点放在生产产品上,新营销理念(产生于20世纪50年代)的重点放在顾客上,以顾客的需求为导向。实现企业目标最关键的一点就是:要确定目标市场的需要和欲望,并且能比竞争者更有效率和效能地、最大限度地满足顾客的需求和愿望。以顾客为中心的营销理念比起传统的营销理念是一次质的飞跃。营销理念的第二次质的飞跃发生在20世纪70—80年代,即战略营销。在新营销理念的基础上,战略营销从宏观的角度站在一个更高的层次来考虑营销活动,其考虑的问题更加全面、更有系统性,其理论体系也更丰富和完善。战略营销强调用战略管理的思想和方法对营销活动进行管理,创造竞争优势,不仅让顾客而且让所有的参与方(stakeholders)获得最大的利益。

3. 营销组合(Marketing mix)：营销组合指的是 4 个 P（4Ps），即以 4 个 P 开头的英语单词：Product，Price，Place，Promotion。营销组合理论最早由美国哈佛商学院内尔·博顿（Neil Borden）教授提出，后来另一位美国教授麦克·凯撒（E. Jerome MacCarthy）总结为 4Ps 理论。营销概念中的产品，不仅指产品本身，而且指与该产品有关的一切方面，如商标、包装、售后服务等；营销中的价格，不仅指商品上所表明的价格，还涉及该产品价格形成的诸多方面，如产品的定价策略、定价所涉及的生产成本等；营销中的地点，不仅指商品所出售的地点，更重要的是指销售渠道等促进商品销售的空间；营销中的促销，指的是一切能为产品的销售起促进作用的活动和手段，如做广告、举行产品展销会、进行市场调查等。此外，另外两个 P 也非常重要：权力（Power）和公共关系（Public Relations，PR）。权力指政权力量，即法律、政府职能部门及其他有影响的团体；公共关系是企业通过与其内部、外部公众之间，为了取得一定的相互理解、相互支持而产生的各种信息交流，以树立企业的信誉，建立起企业形象。

4. 市场的三个基本要素：顾客、购买欲和购买力。顾客通常指人，也可指某个公司，但是，公司是由人来操纵管理的。这三个基本要素，顾客最为重要，后两个要素都是与人有关的。国际营销人员必须熟悉这三大要素，了解客户购买产品的欲望及其相应的购买力。营销人员首先要考虑的是人的因素，他们必须具备与人打交道的基本能力。简单地说，营销是营销人员通过采取各种行之有效的手段，让顾客心甘情愿地、满意地购买商品。

5. SWOT 指的是：优势（Strengths）、劣势（Weaknesses）、机会（Opportunities）和挑战（Threats）。优势和劣势可以指公司本身或产品。机会是寻求发现市场机会，机会无时无地不在，关键是我们怎样能捕捉到机会。挑战可以理解为来自市场的竞争压力等问题。

6. PEST 分析是指宏观环境的分析。在分析一个企业集团所处的背景的时候，通常是通过这四个因素来进行分析企业集团所面临的状况。

（1）政治要素：指对组织经营活动具有实际与潜在影响的政治力量和有关的法律、法规等因素。当政治制度与体制、政府对组织所经营业务的态度发生变化时，当政府发布了对企业经营具有约束力的法律、法规时，企业的经营战略必须随之做出调整。

（2）经济要素：指一个国家的经济制度、经济结构、产业布局、资源状况、经济发展水平以及未来的经济走势等。构成经济环境的关键要素包括 GDP 的变化发展趋势、利率水平、通货膨胀程度及趋势、失业率、居民可支配收入水平、汇率水平、能源供给成本、市场机制的完善程度、市场需求状况等。由于企业是处于宏观大环境中的微观个体，经济环境决定和影响其自身战略的制定，经济全球化还带来了国家之间经济上的相互依赖性，企业在各种战略的决策过程中还需要关注、搜索、监测、预测和评估本国以外其他国家的经济状况。

（3）社会要素：指组织所在社会中成员的民族特征、文化传统、价值观念、宗教信仰、教育水平以及风俗习惯等因素。构成社会环境的要素包括人口规模、年龄结构、种族结构、收入分布、消费结构和水平、人口流动性等。其中人口规模直接影响着一个国家或地区市场的容量，年龄结构则决定着消费品的种类及推广方式。

（4）技术要素：技术要素不仅包括那些引起革命性变化的发明，还包括与企业生产有关的新技术、新工艺、新材料的出现和发展趋势以及应用前景。在过去的半个世纪里，最迅速的变化就发生在技术领域，像微软、惠普、通用电气等高技术公司的崛起改变着世界和人类的生活方式。同样,技术领先的医院、大学等非营利性组织,也比没有采用先进技术的同类组织具有更强的竞争力。

7. FABV 指的是:特征(Feature),亦即企业、产品的特点;优势(Advantage),亦即特点所带来的独特的优势;好处(Benefits),亦即所提供的技术的、社会的利益;价值(Value),亦即所提供的特别价值。

8. 市场细分(Market segmentation):市场细分指的是公司、企业将面向市场的范围加以适当的限定,将某个特定的大市场细分出若干个特定市场范围,以适合企业的营销管理,其目的是为了更好地运用自身的优势。细分的市场通常是可以识别的,符合企业的经营能力,而且细分后必须有一定效益。

9. 目标市场(Target market):目标市场指的是营销人员通过为之提供产品和服务满足其需要和欲望的细分市场。营销人员要在若干个划分出来的细分市场中选择最为适合的细分市场。选择目标市场的原因是:(1)将有限的能力服务于有限的市场;(2)由于市场的压力,企业不得不集中资源在有限的目标市场运作。

10. 市场调研(Market research):市场调研是把消费者、客户、公众和市场人员通过信息联系起来,营销者通过这些获得的信息去发现和锁定营销机会与营销问题,开展、改善、评估和监控营销活动,并加深对营销过程的认识。市场调研的主要目的是通过对市场的调研获得有效信息反馈,以供企业在制定策略时作为参考。市场调研可分为:(1)探索性调研,用于探询企业要研究的问题的一般性质;(2)描述性调研,通过细致的调查和分析,对市场营销活动的某个方面进行客观的描述,多数营销调研指的就是描述性调研;(3)因果性调研,找出关联现象或变量之间的因果关系,在描述性调研的基础上进一步分析问题的因果关系;(4)预测性调研,对未来市场的需求、前景进行估计。

11. 市场调研的内容包括:(1)对市场需求的调研;(2)对产品的调研;(3)对价格的调研;(4)对促销方式的调研;(5)对销售渠道的调研;(6)对竞争的调研;(7)对本国政府及有关的外国政府的政治、经济政策进行调研。

12. 市场调研的方法有:(1)观察法,其中包括直接观察法、亲身经历法、痕迹观察法、行为记录法;(2)询问法,其中包括面谈法、电话询问法、邮寄询问法、问卷法;(3)实验法,其中包括实验室实验、现场实验、模拟实验。

13. 差别化营销(Differentiation):差别化的含义是设计一系列有意义的差别,其目的是使本公司的产品与同行业者(竞争者)的产品区分开来。差别化由于行业的不同,其机会也不同。产品实行差别化可以从与产品有关的方面进行,如产品的形式、特色、性能、质量、包装等。此外,服务也能实行差别化,如提供方便的订货条件、及时的交货、安装调试、客户培训等有自己特色的服务。另外还可以实行其他方面的差别化,如分销渠道差别化、产品和企业形象差别化。

14. 品牌(Brand)与商标(Trade mark):品牌与商标是营销不变的主题。一般来说,成功的公司和企业都有自己成功的品牌。品牌是产品的牌子,是一个名称、一个符号或一个标记,用以区别其他企业的产品,使该产品与竞争者的产品相区别。商标是经过正式注册后的品牌,是一个企业特定的产品的标记。品牌和商标都是产品的标记,但是商标必须办理注册登记,并受有关法律的保护,而品牌无需办理注册也存在。商标是一种法律名称,是一个品牌或一个品牌中的某个部分。品牌营销是企业生产和销售产品的一个重要策略。建立品牌形象需要做出许多努力。一个品牌可包含以下一些意思:(1)属性;(2)利益;(3)价值;(4)文化;(5)个性;(6)使用者。品牌策略的选定可以是:(1)产品线扩展,即在现有品牌中加上新规格;(2)品牌延伸,即将品牌扩展到新产品目录中;(3)多品牌;(4)新品牌;(5)合作品牌,即两个或两个以上的著名品牌的组合。

15. 营销环境:从宏观的角度来看,影响营销的环境主要有以下几个方面。(1)人口环境,无论生产什么产品,都必须考虑到未来顾客群体的规模,对人口总量及其增长或减少的速度、人口收入水平、人口年龄分布、人口地理分布等能准确把握。(2)经济环境,营销者可以从不同的角度来考虑经济环境:世界性的、国家性的、产业性的及个人的等方面。经济环境的优劣直接影响营销效果。(3)科技环境,科学技术的发展水平对经济发展和人类的生存影响巨大。(4)政治环境,政治是经济的集中表现。政治与经济不可截然分开,政治环境对经济和科学技术的发展具有控制作用,稳定的、良好的、有利的政治环境可以带来好的经济政策,也可以使科技得以提高和发展。(5)社会文化环境,文化对营销的影响不可忽视。文化涉及价值观念、宗教信仰、伦理道德、风俗习惯等方面。国际营销者必须熟知有关国家的社会文化。文化环境也影响人们的消费习惯。

▶ New Words and Expressions

affluent *a.& n.* 丰富的;富裕的;富人

approach *n.& v.* (处理问题的)方式、方法;靠近;接近

attribute *n.& v.* (人物、职务等的)标志、象征;把……归因于

anchor *v.* 把……固定住;充当(新闻广播节目的)主持人

be geared to 适应于……

be tailored to 和……相适应

billboard *n.* 广告牌

bull's eye 靶心

census *n.* 人口调查;人口普查

commonalty *n.* [总称]平民百姓;法人团体(全体成员)

competitive edge 竞争优势

connote *v.* (事实等)暗示;表示

conspicuously *ad.* 显著地;显眼地

continuum *n.* (各部分有序紧密联系但首尾间差异很大的)连续体

coupon *n.* (债券等的)息票;(附在商品上

的)赠券;(黏在广告上的)订购单

demographic *a.* 人口的;人口统计的

differentiation *n.* 差别化(营销)

direct marketing 直接营销

disaggregate *v.* 分解

discrete *a.* 分离的;分别的

discretion *n.* 谨慎;慎重

disperse *v.& a.* 分散;散布;分散的

curve *n.* 曲线;曲线图

explicit *a.* (租金)须直接付款的;货币的;明晰的

FABV "发步"

focal *a.* 焦点的

fundamental *a.* 基础的;十分必要的

from this perspective 从这个角度看

generic *a.* 创始的;发生的

graphic *a.* 图的;图示的;书写的

incentive *n.& a.* 刺激;奖励;动机;刺激性的

in parallel with 与……平行

integrated marketing 整合营销

interpret *v.* 解释；说明

lobby *v.* 游说

loss-leader *n.* 为招揽顾客而亏本出售的商品

lucrative *a.* 挣钱的；生利的

market segmentation 市场细分

milk *v.* 榨取；套出（消息）

monopolistic *a.* 垄断的

monopoly *n.* 垄断；垄断权；专卖；垄断商品；专卖商品

motivate *v.* 使有动机；激发

necessitate *v.* 需要；使成为必需

negate *v.* 取消；使无效；否定

niche *n.* 专门市场；可赢利的市场；合适的职务

oligopoly *n.* 寡头卖主垄断

orientation *n.* 方向；倾向性；适应；熟悉

outweigh *v.* 在价值（或重要性等上）超过

parameter *n.* 参数；变量

perception *n.* 观念；认识；感觉

perishability *n.* 易腐烂性

personal selling 个人推销；上门推销

pitch *v.& n.* 竭力推销、叫卖；商贩摆摊处

pitfall *n.* 陷阱；圈套

plague *v.& n.* 折磨；烦恼

positioning *n.* 定位

publicity *n.* 广告宣传；宣传品；公众的注意

puffery *n.* 吹捧；吹捧的广告

rollout *n.* 新产品展览

saturate *v.& a.* 使饱和；饱和的

skim *v.* 为逃税而瞒报部分收入等；浏览

sophisticated *a.* 老练的；（机械产品等）高度发展的；尖端的

styrofoam *n.* 泡沫塑料

summative *a.* 累计的；累加的

take account of 考虑的；注意到

take… into account 将……考虑到/进去

total product 整形产品（不仅指产品本身，还包括与产品有关的东西，如商标、包装等）

ultimate *a.& n.* 最远的；最终的；基本的；基本原则

USP 差异化营销（独特的营销方式）

value-added *a.* 增值的

version *n.* 版本；产品型号

viability *n.* 生存性；生活力

view… as… 把……看作

vintage *n.* 酒；某一年代的生产或流行的东西

 Discussion Questions

1. What is international marketing?

2. What are the differences between marketing tangible products and marketing services?

3. What does "Marketing Mix" refer to?

4. Why is branding important in international marketing?

Chapter 7 | International Finance 国际金融

Objectives
学习目标

To understand what international finance is about.

理解国际金融的内涵意义。

To outline the function of international finance in international business.

概述国际金融在国际商务中的作用。

To have knowledge about foreign exchange, exchange rate and exchange market.

掌握外汇、汇率及外汇市场的基本知识。

7.1   The Role of Central Banks   中央银行的作用

Each country has a central bank responsible for the policies affecting the value of its currency. The People's Bank of China (PBOC) is the central bank of China. The PBOC is a ministerial-level agency directly under the State Council. It is responsible for:

(1) formulating and implementing monetary policies, and issuing yuan and managing its circulation;

(2) supervising financial institutions, regulating the financial industry and markets, and operating the state treasury;

(3) managing state gold and foreign exchange reserves, and safeguarding payment and clearing systems;

(4) monitoring government fund raising to ensure legality, reviewing institutional qualifications to issue bonds overseas, compiling financial statistics, conducting financial investigations and making forecasts.

Established in 1948, the PBOC became a de facto central bank in 1983. This status was legally confirmed in 1995, and the bank was modeled after the US Federal Reserve System. The PBOC replaced its provincial and municipal branches with regional branches to promote bank efficiency, limit local government interference in bank business and facilitate monetary policy implementation. In monitoring the commercial banks, the PBOC has replaced credit quotas with asset-liability ratio management. It uses market tools for macro-control, encourages commercial banks to improve services to attract customers and investment, and urges transparent accounting. The PBOC still requires state commercial banks to extend policy loans to state-owned enterprises (SOEs).

The central bank in the United States is the Federal Reserve System (the Fed). It is a system of 12 regional banks. The New York Fed, representing the Federal Reserve System and the US Treasury, is responsible for intervening in foreign exchange markets to achieve dollar exchange rate policy objectives and to counter disorderly conditions in foreign exchange markets. It makes such transactions in close coordination with the US Treasury and Board of Governors, and most often coordinates with the foreign exchange operations of other central banks.

In the European Union, the European Central Bank coordinates the activities of each member country's central bank to establish a common monetary policy in Europe, much as the Federal Reserve Bank does in the USA.

Central bank reserve assets are kept in three major forms: gold, foreign exchange, and IMF-related assets. The degree to which a central bank actively manages its reserves to earn a profit varies by country.

Central banks are concerned primarily with liquidity to ensure they have the cash and flexibility needed to protect their countries' currencies.

There are several ways that a central bank can intervene in currency markets. Central banks can do so by buying and selling currency to affect its price. Governments vary in their intervention policies by country and by administration.

7.2　International Monetary System (IMS)　国际货币体系

The international monetary system is an institutional arrangement among the central banks of the countries that belong to the International Monetary Fund (IMF). This overall monetary system includes different kinds of institutions, financial instruments, rules, and procedures within which foreign exchange markets function. This system is the framework within which countries borrow, lend, buy, sell and make payments across political frontiers. The framework determines how balance of payments disequilibrium is resolved and the consequences that the adjustment process will have on the countries involved.

The objective of this system is to create an international environment that is conducive to the free flow of goods, services, and capital among nations. Besides, this system also strives to create a stable foreign exchange market, to guarantee the convertibility of currencies, and to ensure adequate liquidity. The IMF is one of the primary organizations in this system.

7.2.1   Five Components of the IMS and Their Interaction   国际货币体系的五个组成部分及相互作用

The interaction of the five components of the IMS is illustrated in Figure 7.1. Each year a large volume of international financial transactions takes place. These transactions may be 100—150 times as large as total official reserves held by all countries participating in these transactions. This includes foreign trade and foreign investment transactions, payments for services (tourism, shipping, insurance), and remittances of income on foreign investments. These transactions are settled and cleared through the foreign exchange market. Private commercial banks that buy, sell, and hold foreign currency balances support the foreign exchange market in carrying out these financial operations (flow (1) in Figure 7.1).

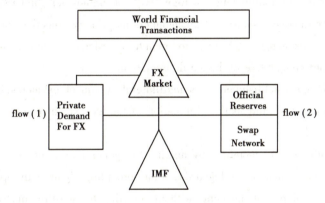

Figure 7.1   Components of International Monetary System

Discrepancies in any particular country's demand and supply for foreign exchange can be balanced off by that country drawing on (activating) its stock of official reserves. In cases of excess demand, the central bank can sell foreign exchange to its commercial banks from its official reserve holdings. This is shown in Figure 7.1, flow (2). Countries in the swap network can also draw on swap facilities with central banks in other countries. The IMF can provide short-term assistance (activate drawing facilities) for individual member countries in need of these financial resources.

7.2.2   The International Monetary Fund (IMF)   国际货币基金组织

The IMF is an international organisation of 188 member nations. It was established to promote international monetary co-operation, exchange stability and orderly exchange arrangements, to foster economic growth and high levels of employment, and to provide temporary financial assistance to countries to help ease balance of payments adjustment.

The IMF was founded in March 1946 and it started to operate in March of the following year. The headquarters of IMF are in Washington. The IMF operates with subscriptions paid by the members in acceptable currencies. The member countries pay subscriptions to the IMF according to their economic situations and status. The fund's sources are made available to applicant members through a system of quotas reviewed at five-year intervals. The quota allocated to each member is equal to the amount of its subscription. The member will use its own currency or other acceptable means (such as gold) to buy the amount taken in excess of quota, and strict conditions are imposed and designed to accomplish repurchase by the member of its own currency from the fund in the shortest possible time.

1. The Purposes of IMF

Article 1 of Agreement of the International Monetary Fund states the purposes of IMF as follows:

(1) To promote international monetary cooperation through a permanent institution which provides the machinery for consultation and collaboration on international monetary problems.

(2) To facilitate the expansion and balanced growth of international trade, and to contribute thereby to the promotion and maintenance of high levels of employment and real income and to the development of the productive resources of all members as primary objectives of economic policy.

(3) To promote exchange stability, to maintain orderly exchange arrangements among members, and to avoid competitive exchange depreciation.

(4) To assist in the establishment of a multilateral system of payments in respect of current transactions between members and in the elimination of foreign exchange restrictions which hamper the growth of world trade.

(5) To give confidence to members by making the general resources of the Fund temporarily available to them under adequate safeguards, thus providing them with opportunity to correct maladjustment in their balance of payments without resorting to measures destructive of national or international prosperity.

(6) In accordance with the above, to shorten the duration and lessen the degree of disequilibrium in the international balances of payments of members.

In other words, some of the IMF's chief responsibilities are listed as follows:

(1) To stabilize the exchange rates of its member country currencies.

(2) To extend loans to its member nations when they have a "temporary payments disequilibrium".

(3) To facilitate a relaxation in foreign exchange rate restrictions.

(4) To encourage trade financing for the countries involved in it.

(5) To promote the cooperation in terms of international currencies.

Since the IMF was established its purposes have remained unchanged but its operations—which involve surveillance, financial assistance, and technical assistance—have developed to meet the changing needs of its member countries in an evolving world economy.

2. IMF at Work

The work of the IMF is of three main types. Surveillance involves the monitoring of economic and financial developments, and the provision of policy advice, aimed especially at crisis-prevention. The IMF also lends to countries with balance of payments difficulties, to provide temporary financing and to support policies aimed at correcting the underlying problems; loans to low-income countries are also aimed especially at poverty reduction. Third, the IMF provides countries with technical assistance and training in its areas of expertise. Supporting all the three activities is IMF work in economic research and statistics.

One of the core responsibilities of the IMF is to maintain a dialogue with its member countries on the national and international consequences of their economic and financial policies. This process of monitoring and consultation is normally referred to as "surveillance", though there is nothing secret about it. Indeed, IMF surveillance has become increasingly open to public scrutiny in recent years.

A main function of the IMF is to provide loans to countries experiencing balance-of-payments problems so that they can restore conditions for sustainable economic growth. The financial assistance provided by the IMF enables countries to rebuild their international reserves, stabilize their currencies, and continue paying for imports without having to impose trade restrictions or capital controls. Unlike development banks, the IMF does not lend for specific projects.

The objective of IMF technical assistance, as described in its Articles of Agreement, "is to contribute to the development of the productive resources of member countries by enhancing the effectiveness of economic policy and financial policy". In practice, the IMF fulfils this objective by providing support to capacity building and policy design. It helps countries strengthen their human and institutional capacity, as a means to improve the quality of policy-making, and gives advice on how to design and implement effective macroeconomic and structural policies.

In recent years, as part of its efforts to strengthen the international financial system and to enhance its effectiveness at preventing and resolving crises, the IMF has applied both its surveillance and technical assistance work to the development of standards and codes of good practice in its areas of responsibility, and to the strengthening of financial sectors.

7.2.3　The European Monetary System　欧洲货币体系

The European Monetary System (EMS) has, since its inception in 1979, provided a fascinating example of policy coordination in practice. As concern about exchange-rate instability and global economic imbalances has grown, both academic researchers and policymakers have looked to the EMS for lessons about cooperation on a wider scale.

European Monetary System, arrangement by which most nations of the European Union (EU) linked their currencies to prevent large fluctuations relative to one another, was organized in 1979 to stabilize foreign exchange and counter inflation among members. Periodic adjustments raised the values of strong currencies and lowered those of weaker ones, but after 1986 changes in national interest rates were used to keep the currencies within a narrow range. In the early 1990s the European Monetary System was strained by the differing economic policies and conditions of its members, especially the reunified Germany, and Britain permanently withdrew from the system.

In 1994 the European Monetary Institute was created as a transitional step in establishing the European Central Bank (ECB) and a common currency. The ECB, which was established in 1998, is responsible for setting a single monetary policy and interest rate for the adopting nations, in conjunction with their national central banks. Later in 1998, Austria, Belgium, Finland, France, Germany, Ireland, Italy, Luxembourg, the Netherlands, Portugal, and Spain cut their interest rates to a nearly uniformly low level in an effort to promote growth and to prepare the way for a unified currency. At the beginning of 1999, the same EU members adopted a single currency, the euro, for foreign exchange and electronic payments. The introduction of the euro (worth about $1.17 at its inception) four decades after the beginning of the European Union was widely regarded as a major step toward European political unity. By creating a common economic policy, the nations acted to put a damper on excessive public spending, reduce debt, and make a strong attempt at taming inflation. The European Currency Unit (ECU), which was established in 1979, was the forerunner of the euro. Derived from a basket of varying amounts of the currencies of the EU nations, the ECU was a unit of accounting used to determine exchange rates among the national currencies.

When the EMS was created in 1979, it was given three objectives:

(1) To create a zone of monetary stability in Europe by reducing exchange rate volatility and converging national interest rates;

(2) To control inflation through the use of monetary discipline;

(3) To coordinate exchange rate policies versus non-EU currencies such as the US dollar and the Japanese yen.

7.2.4　The Bretton Woods System　布雷顿森林体系

The Bretton Woods System is commonly understood to refer to the international monetary regime that prevailed from the end of World War Ⅱ until the early 1970s. Taking its name from the site of the 1944 conference that created the International Monetary Fund (IMF) and World Bank, the Bretton Woods System was history's first example of a fully negotiated monetary order intended to govern currency relations among sovereign states. In principle, the regime was designed to combine binding legal obligations with multilateral decision-making conducted through an international organization, the IMF, endowed with limited supranational authority. In practice, the initial scheme, as well as its subsequent development and ultimate collapse, were directly dependent on the preferences and policies of its most powerful member, the United States.

The conference that gave birth to the system and was held in the American resort village of Bretton Woods, New Hampshire, was the culmination of some two and a half years of planning for postwar monetary reconstruction by the Treasuries of the United Kingdom and the United States. Although attended by all forty-four allied nations plus one neutral government (Argentina), conference discussion was dominated by two rival plans developed, respectively, by Harry Dexter White of the US Treasury and by John Maynard Keynes of Britain.

In fact, there was much common ground among all the participating governments at Bretton Woods. All agreed that the monetary chaos of the interwar period had yielded several valuable lessons. All were determined to avoid repeating what they perceived to be the errors of the past. Their consensus of judgment was reflected directly in the Articles of Agreement of the IMF.

7.2.5   The Managed Floating System   浮动汇率制度

Floating (flexible) exchange rate system means that the exchange rate is allowed to adjust freely to the supply and demand of one currency for another. The managed floating system originated in January 1976 when IMF members had a meeting in Jamaica and hammered out an agreement. The main elements of the agreement include：

(1) Floating rates were accepted and IMF members were allowed to enter the foreign exchange market to deal with any unwarranted speculative fluctuations；

(2) Gold was abandoned as a reserve asset；

(3) The amount of contributions made by IMF member countries was increased；

(4) Less developed countries were given greater access to these funds.

Major currencies were allowed to float in relation to each other. Consequently, during the period from 1976 to 1994, the US dollar, in the main, weakened against the other major world currencies, the German mark, and the Japanese yen. The US dollar, however, started to strengthen, especially against the yen, as the Japanese economy sank into an economic low period. This type of fluctuation of currency values made some people doubt whether a floating exchange rate was a good idea or whether there should be a return to fixed rates, which means that the price of the home currency in terms of another currency or commodity is fixed by the government；the gold standard and the gold exchange standard are two of the fixed rate system.

Because the Bretton Woods Agreement was based on a system of fixed exchange rates and par values, the IMF had to change its rules to accommodate floating exchange rates. The Jamaica Agreement of 1976 amended the original rules to eliminate the concept of par values in order to permit greater exchange rate flexibility. The move toward greater flexibility can occur on an individual-country basis as well as an overall system basis.

7.2.6   The World Bank Group   世界银行集团

The World Bank Group is made up of the World Bank, the International Development Association (IDA) and the International Finance Corporation (IFC). The Group's headquarters is located in Washington.

1. The World Bank

Another name for the World Bank is "International Bank for Reconstruction and Development". The World Bank was established in 1945 and began its operation in the following year. The World Bank is the biggest international lending organization in the world. The World Bank's Articles of Agreement specify its chief functions that are listed as follows：

(1) To promote private investment by means of guarantees and participation and, if necessary, to supplement this investment by providing finance for production purposes out of its own capital, funds raised by it, and other resources.

（2）To promote trade and balance of payments equilibrium by encouraging international investment for the development of productive resources.

（3）To ensure that priority projects are dealt with first.

（4）To conduct its operations with due regard to the effort of international investment on business conditions in its member territories.

In other words, the major functions of the World Bank are：

（1）to provide build-in export financing, where goods are imported for infrastructure projects；

（2）to finance the economic development requirements of member developing countries；

（3）to co-finance loans with government official credit agencies and commercial banks, covering imports of equipment needed in development projects such as power facilities.

The World Bank offers long-term lending facilities at a fixed interest rate to the member countries and helps the developing countries develop production and resources. The standard terms of the bank's loans are between 7 to 10 years grace and 25 years maturity, repayable in annuity form.

Funding of the World Bank comes from the subscriptions from the member countries based as in the case of IMF on their economic standing. The World Bank, to some extent, works like an ordinary investment bank. It borrows funds in the international capital markets, and lends the proceeds to developing countries. The World Bank has a lot of specialists to use in various areas. Those specialists act as advisors.

2. The International Development Association（IDA）

IDA provides low-interest, long-term loans to the poorest countries and participates in the co-financing of projects with government export credit agencies and private financial institutions similar to that of the World Bank. IDA's credit term is as long as 50 years including 10 years grace. The handling fee charged is very low：0.75%. The loans can be repaid in the currency of the borrower's country.

3. The International Financial Corporation（IFC）

IFC makes direct investments and loans to productive private enterprises in developing countries. These private businesses may use IFC financing for new ventures and resource exploration that stimulate international trade. There are three ways to make loans：

（1）To make loans directly to the private productive enterprises；

（2）To buy shares of private productive enterprises and become one of the shareholders and share the profits；

（3）The combination of the above two ways.

7.2.7 Special Drawing Rights（SDR） 特别提款权

Special drawing rights（ISO 4217 currency code XDR, also abbreviated SDR）are supplementary foreign exchange reserve assets defined and maintained by the International Monetary Fund（IMF）. The XDR is the unit of account for the IMF, and is not a currency per se. XDRs instead represent a claim to currency held by IMF member countries for which they may be exchanged. The XDR was created in 1969 to supplement a shortfall of preferred foreign exchange reserve assets, namely gold and the US dollar.

XDRs are allocated to countries by the IMF. Private parties do not hold or use them. The amount of XDRs in existence was around XDR 21.4 billion in August 2009. During the global financial crisis of 2009, an additional XDR 182.6 billion were allocated to "provide liquidity to the global economic system and supplement member countries' official reserves". By October 2014, the amount of XDRs in existence was XDR 204 billion.

The value of the XDR is based on a basket of key international currencies reviewed by IMF every five years. The weights assigned to each currency in the XDR basket are adjusted to take into account their current prominence in terms of international trade and national foreign exchange reserves. In the review conducted in November 2015, the IMF decided that the Renminbi (Chinese yuan) would be added to the basket effective October 1, 2016. From that date, the XDR basket will consist of the following five currencies: U.S. dollar 41.73%, Euro 30.93%, Chinese yuan 10.92%, Japanese yen 8.33%, British pound 8.09%.

7.3 Balance of Payments (BOP) 国际收支

The balance of payments (BOP) is an accounting of a country's international transactions over a certain period of time, typically a calendar quarter or year. It shows the sum of the transactions (purely financial ones, as well as those involving goods or services) between individuals, businesses, and government agencies in that country and those in the rest of the world.

Every international transaction results in a credit and a debit. Transactions that cause money to flow into a country are credits, and transactions that cause money to leave a country are debits. For instance, if someone in China buys a Japanese stereo, the purchase is a debit to the Chinese account and a credit to the Japanese account. If a Brazilian company sends an interest payment on a loan to a bank in the United States, the transaction represents a debit to the Brazilian BOP account and a credit to the United States BOP account.

A balance of payments is a situation achieved when the total sales of a country's goods and services to other nations exactly equal the total purchases it makes of goods and services from abroad; it has three elements: the balance of trade, the balance of invisibles, and the balance of capital items.

The balance of trade refers to the balance of visible trade in goods which are exported or imported or are the visible items that can actually be seen shipping from one country to another.

Suppose:

Country X exports 1,000 units of an item at $3.00 each.

Country X imports 700 units of another item at $4.00 each.

The value of exports is $1,000 \times \$3.00 = \$3,000$

The value of imports is $700 \times \$4.00 = \$2,800$

The Balance of Trade = Total exports—Total imports

= $\$3,000 - \$2,800$

= $\$200$ surplus

Hence, the balance of trade is favourable.

The invisibles refer to the services rendered to foreigners, or services received from foreigners. The most important invisible items are: insurance, banking, tourism, transport of goods, investment and overseas residents. The capital items chiefly consist of loans made by one country to another.

If we sell to a foreign country exactly as much as we want to buy from that country, then we have a very simple balance of payments with that country. But this situation hardly occurs. It is more likely that we will want more from a country in value than they want from us, or vice versa. In such cases, it is impossible to achieve a balance of payments.

Therefore, the balance of payments may result in a surplus or in a deficit in any year. By surplus, it is meant that we have sold more to foreigners than we have bought from them. By the same token, deficit means that we have bought more from foreigners than we have sold to them. In other words, in theory, the current account should balance with the capital plus the financial accounts. The sum of the balance of payments statements should be zero. For example, when China buys more goods and services than it sells (a current account deficit), it must finance the difference by borrowing, or by selling more capital assets than it buys (a capital account surplus). A country with a persistent current account deficit is, therefore, effectively exchanging capital assets for goods and services. Large trade deficits mean that the country is borrowing from abroad. In the balance of payments, this appears as an inflow of foreign capital. In reality, the accounts do not exactly offset each other, because of statistical discrepancies, accounting conventions, and exchange rate movements that change the recorded value of transactions.

In order to get over a deficit, a country must have reserves. Most nations keep a reserve of gold and foreign exchange just as a clever housewife keeps a reserve in a bank against a rainy day.

The balance of payments is made up of two primary sub-accounts: the Current Account and the Financial/Capital Account. Besides, the Official Reserves Account tracks government currency transactions, and a fourth statistical sub-account, the Net Errors and Omissio ns Account (Net Statistical Discrepancy), is produced to preserve the balance in the BOP. Please refer to Figure 7.2.

Balance of Payments Accounts

1. Current Account

   (1) Merchandise imports and exports

   (2) Services: Net goods and services balance

   (3) Unilateral transfers

      A. To abroad

      B. From abroad

      C. Net current account balance

Continued

---

2. Capital Account

　(1) Direct investment

　　　A. To abroad

　　　B. From abroad

　(2) Portfolio investment

　　　A. To abroad

　　　B. From abroad

　(3) Short-term capital

　　　A. To abroad

　　　B. From abroad

　　　C. Net capital account balance

3. Official Reserves Account

　(1) Gold export and import (net)

　(2) Increase or decrease in foreign exchange (net)

　(3) Increase or decrease in liabilities to foreign central banks (net). Net official reserves

4. Net Statistical Discrepancy

Figure 7.2　**Balance of Payments Accounts**

Generally speaking, the balance of payments is a double-entry system. It is like the system used in accounting. Every transaction is recorded in terms of both a debit and a credit. In international trade, debits record transactions such as the import of a good or service, an increase in assets, or a reduction in liabilities. On the other hand, credits record the export of a good or service, a decrease in assets, or an increase in liabilities.

The principal source of information on a country's external trading relations is the statement of its balance of payments, which is a summary record of all the transactions that occur between residents of that country and foreigners over a specified period of time. Therefore, the measurement of all international economic transactions between the residents of a country and foreign residents is also called "balance of payments". There are two types of business transactions that dominate the balance of payments.

(1) Real Assets: The exchange of goods and services for other goods and services (barter) or for the more common type of payment: money.

(2) Financial Assets: The exchange of financial claims (for example, stocks, bonds, loans, purchases or sales of companies) in exchange for other financial claims or money.

The Balance of Payments provides a systematic record of the value of a country's transactions in goods, services, income and transfers with the rest of the world, and the changes in the country's financial claims on (assets), and liabilities to, the rest of the world. This key economic indicator can be used to:

(1) formulate and evaluate economic policy;

(2) plan and make business decisions;

(3) monitor economic progress.

7.4 Foreign Exchange 外汇

Generally speaking, foreign exchange is the money denominated in the currency of another nation or group of nations. Foreign exchange can be of different forms. It can be in the form of cash, funds available on credit and debit cards, traveller's checks, bank deposits, or other short-term claims.

Foreign exchange is any financial instrument that carries out payment from one currency to another. The most common form of conducting foreign exchange payments between banks is the telephone transfer. Between companies is the draft. As to tourists it is the physical exchange of one currency for another.

7.4.1 Foreign Exchange Rate 汇率

So far as foreign exchange rate is concerned, it is the price of a currency or it is actually the number of units of one currency that buys one unit of another currency. This number of currency is likely to change every day. In other words, a foreign exchange rate is simply the value of one currency expressed in terms of another one. For example, one US dollar is equal to six point two of China's RMB yuan.

Foreign exchange rates bring an opportunity as well as a threat to international businesses. If Company X in country A sells its products to Company Y in country B in a foreign currency, Company X will lose money if that currency's value falls while Company Y earns more.

For example, a British importer buys goods from an American corporation. The British importer signs a contract with the American corporation to import goods worth US $60,000 and it is agreed by both parties that the importer should pay in US dollars. The foreign exchange rate at that time is £ 1 = US $1.5. The British importer is supposed to pay £ 40,000. But, to the joy of the importer, by the time the payment is due to be made, the exchange rate is £ 1 = US $1.55. In this way, the British importer only need to purchase £ 38,710 worth of US dollars in order to pay the seller. Thus, £ 1,290 is saved for the British importer.

It can then be seen that how important it is to be kept constantly informed of the foreign exchange rate. In addition, fluctuations in currency exchange rates will have a big impact on the financial viability of an international trade deal no matter how small the fluctuations may be.

7.4.2 Foreign Exchange Risk 外汇风险

International business involves foreign exchange risk since the value of transactions in different currencies will be sensitive to exchange rate changes. Although it is possible to manage a firm's foreign-currency-denominated assets and liabilities to avoid exposure to exchange rate changes, the benefit involved is not always worth the effort. Exchange risk is simple in concept: a potential gain or loss that occurs as a result of an exchange rate change. For example, if an individual owns a share in Hitachi, a Japanese company, he or she will lose if the value of the yen drops.

Yet from this simple question several more arise. First, whose gain or loss? Clearly not just those of a subsidiary, for they may be offset by positions taken elsewhere in the firm. And not just gains or losses on current transactions, for the firm's value consists of anticipated future cash flows as well as currently contracted ones. What counts, modern finance tells us, is shareholder value; yet the impact of any given currency change on shareholder value is difficult to assess, so proxies have to be used. The academic evidence linking exchange rate changes to stock prices is weak.

Moreover, the shareholder who has a diversified portfolio may find that the negative effect of exchange rate changes on one firm is offset by gains in other firms. Finally, risk is not risk if it is anticipated. In most currencies there are futures or forward exchange contracts whose prices give firms an indication of where the market expects currencies to go. And these contracts offer the ability to lock in the anticipated change. So perhaps a better concept of exchange risk is unanticipated exchange rate changes. A three-fold classification is applied to foreign exchange risks exposure.

(1) Translation exposure

Substantial movements in exchange rate may adversely (or favourably) affect the financial statements (i.e.the balance sheet or the income statement) of the MNE and this effect is known as translation exposure. This is also known as accounting exposure and is the difference between foreign-currency-denominated assets and foreign-currency-denominated liabilities.

In compiling consolidated financial statements the MNE needs to translate or restate the accounts of foreign subsidiaries and associated companies denominated in foreign currencies into the home reporting currency. Foreign currency translation is thus a process involving accounting restatements, not the monetary exchange of one currency for another.

As regards the exchange rate to be used, the choice is essentially between the historic rate (i.e. the rate applicable when the translation was initially recorded in the accounts), and the current rate (i.e. the market rate applicable to the period for which the financial statements are prepared).

(2) Transaction exposure

This is exposure resulting from the uncertain domestic currency value of a foreign-currency-denominated transaction to be completed at some future time. When a firm exports or imports goods, there will normally be a time lag between receiving/despatching foreign currency denominated invoices and the payment/receipt of cash. During this period, the firm has a transaction exposure, since the translated amount of foreign currency may fluctuate between the invoice date and the payment date. Foreign-currency-dominated short-term monetary assets and liabilities would constitute one possible measure of exposed assets.

(3) Economic exposure

This is exposure of the firm's value to changes in exchange rates. If the value of the firm is measured as the present value of future after-tax cash flows, then economic exposure is concerned with the sensitivity of the real domestic currency value of long-term cash flows to exchange rate changes. Or we may define economic exposure as the effects of exchange rate changes on the cash flows of the MNE. As such, transaction exposure is a subset of economic exposure, whereas translation exposure is an accounting rather than a cash-flow concept.

A change in exchange rates which has a competitive impact on the MNE is an example of economic exposure. For example, Asian MNEs relying mainly on exporting to serve the US market might be adversely affected by the strength of their local currencies (e.g. Japan's yen, China's yuan) against the US dollar, as it erodes their export competitiveness and may increase import penetration in their home market. It is this competitive impact that dominates discussions of economic exposure.

7.4.3 Purchasing Power Parity (PPP) Theory 购买力平价理论

Exchange rates, interest rates and inflation rates are linked to one another through a classical set of relationships which have import for the nature of corporate foreign exchange risk. These relationships are:

(1) the purchasing power parity theory, which describes the linkage between relative inflation rates and exchange rates;

(2) the international Fisher (Fisher Irving, 1867—1947, American mathematician and economist, professor of politics and economics at Yale University) effect, which ties interest rate differences to exchange rate expectations;

(3) the unbiased forward rate theory, which relates the forward exchange rate to exchange rate expectations.

The Purchasing Power Parity (PPP) theory can be stated in different ways, but the most common representation links the changes in exchange rates to those in relative price indices in two countries.

Rate of change of exchange rate = Difference in inflation rates

The relationship is derived from the basic idea that, in the absence of trade restrictions, changes in the exchange rate mirror changes in the relative price levels in the two countries. At the same time, under conditions of free trade, prices of similar commodities cannot differ between two countries, because arbitragers will take advantage of such situations until price differences are eliminated. This "Law of One Price" (the exchange rate between two currencies based on just one commodity or service) leads logically to the idea that what is true of one commodity should be true of the economy as a whole—the price level in two countries should be linked through the exchange rate—and hence to the notion that exchange rate changes are tied to inflation rate differences.

7.4.4 Foreign Exchange Convertibility 外汇兑换

A key aspect of exchanging one currency for another is its convertibility.

1. Hard Currency and Soft Currency

Generally speaking, hard currency, among other things, refers to the currency whose foreign exchange rate is relatively stable while soft currency refers to the currency whose foreign exchange rate is unstable.

To be more exact, a hard currency refers to the currency that is usually fully convertible and strong or relatively stable in value in comparison with other currencies such as the US dollar and Japanese yen. A soft (weak) currency is a currency that is not fully convertible. Soft currencies tend to be those of developing countries.

As the currency values fluctuations are always happening, the seller and the buyer are to be careful when choosing the currency. Hard currency is to the seller's advantage, as he receives the money. The seller of course does not want the currency he receives is worth 10 units today compared to the other currency but the next day the currency is greatly depreciated. On the other hand, the buyer prefers to choose soft currency which might be depreciated after he pays it to the seller. If so, the buyer loses nothing and, in some way, he earns some. Therefore, appreciation and depreciation of currencies should be paid attention to in conducting international business.

By depreciation, it is meant that the value of a currency is losing compared to another currency. Further, when a unit buys less of a currency it is said to have depreciated against that currency; and by the same token, the latter currency is said to have appreciated against the first currency. For instance:

US $1 = China RMB ¥ 8.2

But later the situation changes:

US $1 = China RMB ¥ 8.13

The dollar is then considered to have depreciated while the RMB appreciated.

As usual, the risk of loss through the depreciation of a currency actually starts from the time the buyer gets the seller's price lists unless these contain a rider to the effect that the prices are subject to confirmation when the orders are placed. But the risk of loss applies whatever currency is used. When the seller's home currency is at a time of high inflation when the currency is falling in value, there is a lot to be said for the seller to quote in a more stable currency which, when converted back to the seller's home currency, is going to produce a large reward to the seller. For that reason, the seller should care about the stability of the rate of foreign exchange and, of course, so should the buyer.

2. Control of Convertibility

Residents and non-residents of a country can exchange a convertible currency for other currencies. Some countries limit non-resident convertibility, though.

To conserve scarce foreign exchange by using import licensing, multiple exchange rates, import deposit requirements, and quantity controls, some governments impose exchange restrictions on companies or individuals who want to exchange money. Governmental license fixes the exchange rate by requiring all recipients, exporters, and others who receive foreign currency to sell it to its central bank at the official buying rate. An importer cannot purchase foreign exchange unless that importer has obtained an import license for the goods in question.

Besides, governments can control foreign exchange convertibility by establishing more than one exchange rate. This restrictive measure is known as a multiple exchange rate system.

Further, another form of foreign exchange convertibility control is the advance import deposit, namely, a deposit with the central bank is required before the release of foreign exchange.

In addition, by controlling quantity, governments can limit the amount of exchange, which often applies to tourism. The government sets a policy on how much money a tourist is allowed to take overseas. For example, for the moment, Chinese government specifies that each tourist to go abroad can only exchange RMB for US $2,000.

7.4.5 Foreign Exchange Market 外汇市场

The foreign exchange market is the framework of individuals, firms, banks and brokers who buy and sell foreign currencies. The foreign exchange market for any one currency, for example, the euro, consists of all the locations such as Paris, London, New York, Zurich, Frankfurt and so on, in which the euro is bought and sold for other currencies. Foreign exchange markets tend to be located in national financial centers near the local financial markets. The most important foreign exchange markets are found in London, New York, Tokyo, Frankfurt, Amsterdam, Paris, Zurich, Toronto, Brussels, Milan, Singapore and Hong Kong.

In the foreign exchange market, the currency of a nation is regarded as the commodity traded, and the currency of another nation is the active money ingredient. The foreign exchange market is the biggest financial market in the world. The foreign exchange market is usually operated by influential commercial banks that trade currencies they hold in the form of sight deposits in other banks. Sight deposits can be transferred or withdrawn while time deposits can only be withdrawn when the deposit matures.

The functions of the foreign exchange market are listed as follows:

(1) To transfer purchasing power from one country to another one.

(2) To offer a method of hedging open currency positions. (Forward exchange transactions perform this function.)

(3) To provide a clearing mechanism for international payments. On each trading day, the trading banks just buy and sell each currency that they trade with only a relatively small change in their net position by the end of the day.

(4) To provide a credit facility. Banks can buy time bills of exchange in foreign currency and hold the bills of exchange till they mature.

Foreign exchange market reflects disequilibrium by the frequency and intensity of exchange rate movements. There are four main types of transaction undertaken in the foreign exchange markets: spot transactions, forward deals, futures transactions and currency options.

7.4.6　Forecasting Foreign Exchange Rate Movements　汇率走向预测

Since future exchange rates are uncertain, participants in international financial markets can never know for sure what the spot rate will be one month or one year ahead. Therefore, forecasts must be made.

As far as international business is concerned, it is quite necessary for managers to be concerned with the timing, magnitude, and direction of a foreign exchange rate movement. The success of foreign exchange rate forecasting is dependent on the extent to which foreign exchange markets are efficient, and the related issue of the exchange rate regime. If exchange rates are floating freely and the market is fully efficient, then one would expect that the net benefit of utilizing a forecasting service would be nil. It is only if foreign exchange markets fail to reflect all available information, or if governments systematically intervene in the markets, that there may be benefits from the use of forecasts. It would appear that governments do often intervene to achieve a desired exchange rate, and therefore, MNEs will undertake forecasting or consult specialists in this area.

MNEs managers can forecast foreign exchange rates by using either of the two approaches: fundamental or technical. Fundamental forecasting uses trends in economic variables to predict future rates. The data can be plugged into an econometric model or evaluated on a more subjective basis. Technical forecasting uses past trends in exchange rates themselves to spot future trends in rates. Technical forecasters or chartists assume that if current exchange rates reflect all facts in the market, then under similar circumstances future rates will follow the same patterns.

However, it is hard to predict what will happen to currencies and to use those predictions to forecast profits and establish operation strategies.

For freely fluctuating currencies, the law of supply and demand determines market value. But the fact is that very few currencies in the world float freely without any government intervention. Most are managed to some extent, which implies that governments need to make political decisions about the value of their currencies. Manager can monitor the factors the governments follow so as to try to predict values. The key factors to monitor are: the institutional setting, fundamental analysis, confidence factors, and technical analysis.

7.4.7　Business Implications of Foreign Exchange Rate Changes　汇率变化的商务意义

To be always informed of the foreign exchange rate changes is very important for international businesses in making their strategies.

Marketing managers watch foreign exchange rates because they can affect demand for a company's products at home and abroad. Production decisions are also affected by foreign exchange rates. For example, a manufacturer in a country where wages and operating expenses are high might be tempted to locate production in a country with a currency that is rapidly losing value, because initial investment there is relatively cheap, and such a country is a good base for inexpensive exportation.

Besides, foreign exchange rates can affect the sourcing of financial resources, the cross-border remittance of funds, and the reporting of financial results.

7.4.8 How do Companies Use Foreign Exchange Market? 公司如何利用外汇市场?

There are a number of reasons for companies to use the foreign exchange markets.

First, companies use foreign exchange market just for import and export transactions. Besides, companies' personnel who travel on business abroad need deal in foreign exchange to pay for their local expenses.

Secondly, companies use the foreign exchange market for financial transactions, such as those in foreign direct investment.

Thirdly, companies sometimes (mostly traders and investors) deal in foreign exchange simply for profit. One type of profit-seeking activity is arbitrage, which is the purchase of foreign currency on one market for immediate resale on another market (in a different country) to get profit from a price discrepancy.

Investors can also use foreign exchange transactions to speculate for profit or to protect against risk. Speculation is the buying or selling of a commodity (here foreign currency) that has both an element of risk and the chance of great profit. As protection against risk, foreign exchange transactions can hedge against a potential loss due to an exchange rate change.

7.5 US Dollar, British Pound, the Euro, and RMB 美元、英镑、欧元和人民币

7.5.1 US Dollar 美元

US dollar has been dominating in the international trade payment since the end of the Second World War. It is the most important currency in the foreign exchange market. This is because US dollar comprises of 87 percent of all foreign currency transactions (buy or sell) all over the world. Besides, US dollar is the most widely used trade currency in the world and it is used as:

(1) an investment currency in a lot of capital markets;

(2) a reserve currency held by many central banks;

(3) a transaction currency in lots of international commodity markets;

(4) an invoice currency in many contracts;

(5) an intervention currency used by monetary authorities in market operations to influence their own exchange rates.

US dollar has become the most important type of foreign exchange held as international money. This is because the United States plays a very important role in international business.

The international monetary system evolved in a way that was not foreseen in the Articles of Agreement of IMF. During the 1950s the US emerged as the leading reserve country, and the dollar increasingly took over the function of gold as a major international reserve asset. The US was the dominant world power. Well over half of all international money transactions were financed in terms of dollar; the US produced more than half the world output.

Money normally serves three functions: it is a medium of exchange, a unit of account, and a store of value. International money does the same: it is used to settle international payments; it is used to fix prices, and it is held as a liquid asset for international transactions. An added dimension is provided by the distinction between private behaviour and the decisions of central banks.

The dollar is used as a medium of exchange in private transactions, or "vehicle", and is also bought and sold by central banks, thus making it an "intervention" currency. Trade contracts are sometimes dominated in dollars, making it an "invoice" currency, and the par values for exchange rates are sometimes stated in terms of the dollar, which makes it serve as a "peg". Finally, private agents hold liquid dollar-denominated assets—the "banking" role—and central banks hold the dollar as a reserve.

7.5.2　British Pound　英镑

British pound dominated in the international payment before World War Ⅱ. It was more often used in the international settlements. It is still in use but it has been replaced by the US dollar as the primary means of international payment.

Whether the UK should join the euro system remains an issue in the UK. It seems that the present British government will not decide to join the euro system too soon.

All of the non-Communist countries maintained a stable relationship between their currencies and the dollar either directly or indirectly through the British pound. Since the Great Britain halted gold convertibility of its currency, US dollar was the only currency directly convertible into gold for official purposes. Before World War I, the pound sterling performed a similar function, but the sterling area had shrunken to a small number of countries.

7.5.3　The Euro　欧元

The euro is the currency which is now being used in the euro-zone by twelve member nations of EU with the exception of UK, Denmark and Sweden. Here are the twelve nations:

Austria, Belgium, the Netherlands, Germany, Finland, France, Greece, Island, Italy, Luxemburg, Spain and Portugal.

Britain and Denmark have similar attitude toward the euro. It takes time for the two nations to adopt the euro. They might do so when the two governments think the economic conditions are proper enough. From the following, a brief development of the euro can be seen.

（1）1958, *Treaty of Rome* established the European Common Market with the aim of increasing co-operation and integration across Europe.

（2）1969, the Hague conference set out an objective to achieve economic and monetary union.

（3）1970, *Ten-year Plan* was published, outlining a three-stage approach for achieving EMU (European Economic and Monetary Union).

（4）1979, European Monetary System and the European Currency were introduced.

（5）1986, Single European Act set out the main aims of EMU.

（6）1988, Council of Hanover undertook to review what steps would be required to achieve EMU, leading to Delors plan recommending the creation of a single currency and the European Central Bank.

（7）1992, Treaty of Maastricht identified economic convergence criteria required for membership of EMU.

（8）1995, European Council in Madrid published a timetable for implementing the single currency.

（9）1996, European Council in Dublin set out the legal framework for monetary union.

（10）1997, European Council in Amsterdam signed the Stability and Growth Pact.

（11）1998, European Central Bank was introduced.

（12）1999, the euro was officially introduced as the European single currency.

（13）2002, ECB (European Central Bank) issued euro notes and coins for the first time as 12 legacy currencies were phased out.

On the 1st of July, 2002, the euro started to take the place of the currencies of the 12 EU member countries.

With the euro coming into being, the US dollar finds itself encountering a strong rival. It is quite likely that the euro could become a more important vehicle currency in the future and could replace the US dollars in some cases. Further, the euro is likely to carve up the market share of US dollars sooner or later.

7.5.4　Renminbi (RMB)　人民币

Chinese currency is the Renminbi (RMB). It is also known as "yuan". The sign of it is "￥", the same as that of Japanese currency. However, Japanese currency is called "yen". The Renminbi, China's legal tender, is issued and controlled solely by the People's Bank of China. The exchange rates of the Renminbi are decided by the People's Bank of China and issued by the State Administration of Exchange Control. China operates foreign exchange in a unified way, with the State Administration of Exchange Control exercising the functions and powers of exchange control.

Before 1994, the Chinese government managed the system as a dual-track foreign exchange system. The dual-track system provided for two government-approved exchange rates: one was the official exchange rate, the other was the swap-market rate. The State Administration of Exchange Control (SAEC) set the official exchange rate for the RMB based on China's balance of payments and the exchange rates of her major competitor countries, such as South Korea. In 1986, the SAEC first set the official rates at 3.72 RMB per dollar.

Primarily state-owned companies used the official exchange rate mostly to buy Foreign Exchange Certificates (FECs). FECs were a separate form of currency developed in 1980 for the foreigners to use when they paid for their expenses in China. But, in 1994, the People's Bank of China stopped to issue FECs and gradually withdrew them from circulation.

The swap market, the other half of the dual-market system, was created in Shenzhen in 1985 for foreign and local businesses that had received official approval to exchange RMB and hard currency. There were quite a lot of swap centers, the one in Shanghai being the largest. During that period, about 80% of the hard-currency transactions in this country took place in the swap market. The swap rate was 8.7 RMB per dollar.

The dual-track foreign exchange system was not favourable to China's international trade and affected China's application for joining the WTO. So in 1994 the Chinese government decided to close the swap centers. The swap center in Shanghai was replaced by the National Foreign Exchange Center, which is a national inter-bank center at which appointed banks can trade and settle foreign currencies.

After the beginning of the year 1994, companies in China could exchange RMB into foreign currency to buy imports controlled by quotas. It was also in the year 1994 that the Chinese government started to devalue the RMB, taking its value from about 5.8 yuan per dollar to just over 8.2 yuan per dollar, which was about the same as the old swap rate.

In 1996, the RMB could be fully changed on a current account (trade in goods and services) basis, but not on a capital account (investment and income flows) basis. On December 1, 1996, China formally accepted Article Eight of the *Agreement on International Currencies and Funds*, and realized the Renminbi's convertibility under the current account ahead of schedule. China included the foreign exchange business of the foreign-invested enterprises in the bank's exchange settlement system in 1996.

In 1997, when confronted with the Asian financial crisis, the Chinese government declared that the exchange rate of the Renminbi would remain stable, and the Renminbi would not be devalued. This earned China the praise of the international community.

In 2001, China's foreign exchange reserves reached US $212.2 billion. In addition, the variety of financial businesses has been increasing steadily, and China has opened an array of new businesses to become integrated into the various aspects of modern international financial business, such as consumer credit, securities investment funds and investments linked with insurance.

The exchange rate of the RMB has been stable in the past three years. The RMB Yuan trade to US $ is normally about 8.28 to 8.30 within a narrow change. China allows overseas financial institutions in Shanghai and Shenzhen to engage in Chinese Renminbi business since China has formally become a member of the World Trade Organization (WTO). Overseas financial institutions in Tianjin and Dalian are also allowed to apply to engage in Renminbi business starting.

China is willing to allow overseas financial institutions to provide foreign exchange services to all units and individuals within Chinese territory, on condition that the institutions accordingly increase their operating capital or minimum capital requirements, and change their operation licenses. Overseas non-banking financial institutions may apply for establishing companies in China specializing in car credit purchase services in accordance with regulations soon to be publicized by the PBOC.

The RMB, as the Chinese banking system is getting better and better, is quite promising and it is predicted by some that the RMB will become a dominating leader in the East of this world.

In 2003, Professor Robert Mundell, "Father of the euro", predicted that RMB might be converted freely by the year 2008. But the Chinese government cannot confirm the prediction. Besides, Professor Mundell thinks that the so-called "Asian currency" (Ya yuan) is likely to come into being in future. RMB and Japanese currency are two chief competitors. Further, he also emphasizes that it is not the proper time for RMB to appreciate.

In recent years, RMB has been appreciating. And it will continue to do so. The Chinese government will speed up the pace of RMB's appreciating, encouraging the outflow of capital. But it will not appreciate without any control.

RMB has become the fourth global currency in international business, the first three currencies being US dollars, the euro and Britishi sterling. RMB will be gradually internationalized as China further reforms and open her door wider to the outside world.

▶ 7.6 International Money Markets 国际货币市场

From the perspective of traditional way, money market is normally understood as a market for deposits, accounts, or securities that have maturity of one year or less. The international money markets are often termed the "Eurocurrency markets", which constitute an enormous financial market that is in many ways outside the jurisdiction and supervision of world financial and governmental authorities.

7.6.1 Eurocurrency Market 欧洲货币市场

Eurocurrencies are domestic currencies of one country on deposit in a second country. In other words, Eurocurrency refers to the currency deposited by companies and federal governments in banks outside their own country. It is usually a currency of a non-European country deposited in Europe.

The historical origin of the Eurocurrency markets may be traced to shortly after World War Ⅱ. At that time, the Soviet Union, the Eastern European countries and China chose to protect their dollar balances against "freezing orders" or other US governmental interference by transferring them from US banks to banks under their control in Western Europe.

Euromarkets refer to the markets in securities and futures denominated in Eurocurrencies and sold to investors based outside the country which is home to the currency used as the unit of payment and valuation for the instrument.

The Eurocurrency market is the market for deposits placed under a regulatory regime different than the regulations applied to deposits used to execute domestic transactions. The Eurocurrency market in Asia is sometimes referred to separately as the Asian dollar market. The primary function of banks in the Asian dollar market is to channel funds from depositors to borrowers.

The Eurocurrency market includes Eurosterling (British pounds deposited outside the United Kingdom), Euroeuros (euros on deposit outside the euro zone), Euroyen (Japanese yen deposited outside Japan), and Eurodollars.

Eurocurrency markets serve the following two valuable purposes.

(1) Eurocurrency deposits are an efficient and convenient money market device for holding excess corporate liquidity.

(2) The Eurocurrency market is a major source of short-term bank loans to finance corporate working capital needs, including the financing of imports and exports.

7.6.2 Eurobanks 欧洲银行

Banks in which Eurocurrencies are deposited are known as Eurobanks. A Eurobank is a financial intermediary that simultaneously bids for time deposits and makes loans in a currency other than that of the currency in which it is located. Eurobanks is a generic term used to name the banks that make transactions in the Eurocurrency market. For example, the London or Paris branch of a US bank engaged in the Eurodollar market is an Eurobank. In the same way, the Singapore branch of a Brazilian bank taking deposits in Euroyen can be called a Eurobank. Eurobanks cannot create money. Dollars are only created in the US, yen in Japan, etc. Eurobanks are financial intermediaries that take short-term deposits and make long-term loans. Large loans are made by syndicates of Eurobanks.

7.7 Eurobond Market 欧洲债券市场

Eurobond is a specific type of bond. A Eurobond is understood as a bond issued outside of the country in whose currency it is denominated. Eurobonds are usually denominated in one of the major Eurocurrencies or, in some cases, a virtual currency such as the European Currency Unit (ECU).

The main Eurobond features are as follows:

(1) Not issued on or into only a domestic market but marketed internationally.

(2) Sold to a wide range of investors through a multinational syndicate of underwriting firms and banks.

(3) Denominated in a currency that is not necessarily native to the investors or the syndicate members through whom the securities are sold. Therefore, investors in Eurobonds take both credit and foreign exchange risks.

(4) Generally bearer instruments to facilitate negotiability (high liquidity and, therefore, easy cash convertibility) and anonymity of the ultimate investors.

(5) Either issued with the benefit of a stock exchange listing, normally in London or

Luxembourg (although still placed with investors in various countries) and therefore, called a "public offering", or placed with such investors without a listing (private placement).

It is believed by some that in the Eurobond market the buyers of the bonds, in the first instance, are exclusively financial institutions (the syndicate). Usually, Eurobonds are not offered directly to the public, but are offered mostly to banks and other financial institutions for placing with central banks, insurance companies, investment funds, multinational corporations and private investors.

There are two types of international bonds.

(1) A foreign bond is issued by a borrower foreign to the country where the bond is placed.

(2) Eurobonds are sold in countries other than the country represented by the currency denominating them.

7.8　International Stock Markets　国际证券市场

MNEs can obtain funds by issuing stock in international markets, in addition to the local market. By having access to various markets, the stocks may be more easily digested, the image of the MNE may be enhanced, and the shareholder base may be diversified. The proportion of individual versus institutional ownership of shares varies across stock markets. The regulations are different, too. The locations of the MNEs' operations may affect the decision about where to place stock, in view of the cash flows needed to cover dividend payments in the future.

Stock issued in the US by non-US firms or governments are called Yankee stock offerings. Non-US firms can also issue American depository receipts (ADRs), which are certificates representing bundles of stock. The use of ADRs circumvents some disclosure requirements.

7.9　The Asian Development Bank (ADB)　亚洲开发银行

The Asian Development Bank (ADB) is a regional development bank established on 22 August 1966, which is headquartered in Metro Manila, Philippines, to facilitate economic development in Asia. The bank admits the members of the United Nations Economic and Social Commission for Asia and the Pacific (UNESCAP, formerly the Economic Commission for Asia and the Far East or ECAFE) and non-regional developed countries. From 31 members at its establishment, ADB has so far 67 members, of which 48 are from within Asia and the Pacific and 19 outside. The ADB was modeled closely on the World Bank, and has a similar weighted voting system where votes are distributed in proportion with members' capital subscriptions. Since 2014, ADB releases annual report of Creative Productivity Index and comparatively includes Finland and United States for the list of Asia-Pacific members.

The highest policy-making body of the Bank is the Board of Governors, composed of one representative from each member state. The Board of Governors, in turn, elect among themselves the twelve members of the Board and their deputy. Eight of the twelve members come from regional (Asia-Pacific) members while the others come from non-regional members.

The Board of Governors also elect the Bank's president, who is the chairperson of the Board of Directors and manages ADB. The president has a term of office lasting five years, and may be reelected. Traditionally, and because Japan is one of the largest shareholders of the bank, the president has always been Japanese.

The headquarters of the Bank is at 6 ADB Avenue, Mandaluyong, Metro Manila, Philippines, and it has representative offices around the world. The bank employs 3,051 people, of which 1,463 (48%) are from the Philippines.

The ADB offers "hard" loans from ordinary capital resources (OCR) on commercial terms, and the Asian Development Fund (ADF) affiliated with the ADB extends "soft" loans from special fund resources with concessional conditions. For OCR, members subscribe capital, including paid-in and callable elements, a 50% paid-in ratio for the initial subscription, 5% for the Third General Capital Increase (GCI) in 1983 and 2% for the Fourth General Capital Increase in 1994. The ADB borrows from international capital markets with its capital as guarantee.

7.10   The Asian Infrustructure Investment Bank (AIIB)　亚洲基础设施投资很行

The AIIB is a multilateral development bank that will finance infrastructure needs in the Asia Pacific region. There are two prominent multilateral development banks already working on development needs in the region: the Asian Development Bank (ADB) and the World Bank, with the ADB also investing the majority of its funds in infrastructure projects.

The AIIB was first proposed by Chinese President Xi Jinping at the October 2013 Asia Pacific Economic Cooperation (APEC) meeting in Indonesia as a means of leveraging Chinese financial capital and experience in infrastructure development to bridge the widely acknowledged "infrastructure gap" in Asia. Xi Jinping met President of the World Bank Jim Yong Kim at the Great Hall of the People in Beijing on July 9, 2014. Kim welcomed China's proposal of setting up the Asian Infrastructure Investment Bank (AIIB), underscoring that the two agencies should be complimentary partners other than competitors.

The bank was established by a Memorandum of Understanding (MOU) signed by 21 countries in October, 2014. The MOU specifies that it will have authorized capital of $100 billion, with initial subscribed capital of $50 billion.

The bank is part of a broader agenda being pursued by Beijing to create new regional and global economic institutions, including the New Silk Road infrastructure fund and the BRICS led New Development Bank. The AIIB is the most high profile and fleshed out initiative. These are seen as being separate from and potential challengers to the existing U.S.-led Bretton Woods institutions such as the World Bank and Asian Development Bank. China has indicated that it will be open to

Japanese and American membership in the Bank, though at this moment that appears unlikely.

China contributes 50 percent of the Bank's capital. This shows that China's determination to establish the bank. (Source: CSIS)

The global economy remains short of investment. Investment in infrastructure in Asia will expand demand and support global recovery. With the current Asian economy under mounting downward pressure, strong infrastructure spending will help to create demand, increase jobs and bring about a smoother and more effective production, circulation, and consumption environment for the overall economic operation. It will also contribute to an enhanced regional infrastructure connectivity, which will then facilitate regional economic cooperation and integration. Therefore, as the driver of sustainable growth and regional economic integration, infrastructure investment will empower economic expansion in Asia.

As a new comer, the Asian Infrastructure Investment Bank will complement and cooperate with the World Bank and the Asian Development Bank, with the latter two focusing on poverty alleviation, but infrastructure also helps alleviate poverty.

Summary of This Chapter
本章概要

1. 一般说来,国际金融包括4个主要部分:(1)国际收支与国际储备;(2)外汇;(3)国际金融市场与国际信贷;(4)国际金融组织与国际货币体系。

2. 国际收支(Balance of International Payments):国际收支是一个国家在一定时期内,同其他国家进行贸易往来和非贸易往来、资金借贷、单方面转移等经济交往,所发生的外汇收支总和。国际收支有狭义和广义之分。建立在现金基础上的狭义概念指一个国家在一定时期(一年、一个季度或一个月)内,由于各种对外交往而发生的、必须立即结清的、来自其他国家的外汇收入与付给其他国家的外汇支出总额的对比;建立在经济交易基础上的广义概念是由国际货币基金组织制定的,它指某一时期的统计。

3. 国际收支平衡表(Statements of the Balance of International Payments):一个国家的国际收支是由各种经济交易构成的。一定期间内一个国家的国际收支情况集中反映在这个国家的国际收支平衡表中。国际收支平衡表是系统地记录一定时期或一定时期的,所有对外政治、经济、科学文化教育、军事活动而引起的货币收支项目及金额的对比表。它能表示一个国家对外经济交易的全部情况,并有助于经济的分析研究。

4. 国际货币制度(International Monetary System):为适应国际贸易和协调国际经济关系,各国政府在国际收支调节、货币兑换、国际结算等金融财政政策方面所做的安排制定的原则,以及对此做出的安排而设立组织机构的总称,即为国际货币制度。它一般包括以下内容:(1)各国货币比价的确定对汇率变动的要求;(2)国际储备资产的确定以及储备资产的供应方式;(3)各国货币的兑换性以及各国对此做出的安排;(4)国际收支的调节方式,调节措施以及国家间如何彼此协调。

5. 布雷顿森林体系（Bretton Woods System）：主要内容有：（1）布雷顿森林体系下的汇率制度是以美元为中心的固定汇率制；（2）调节国际收支，弥补国际收支逆差，为会员国融通弥补逆差所需要的基金，是国际货币体系顺利运转的必要条件；（3）取消外汇管制，以保障国际结算与国际支付的自由；（4）建立永久性国际金融机构——国际货币基金组织。布雷顿森林体系的作用有：（1）确立了美元的霸权地位，各国货币必须与美元保持固定比价，不能随意变动，如变幅超过 10%，须经基金组织的批准，这可在一定程度上防止其他国家利用货币贬值与美国竞争；（2）有利于世界经济增长；（3）成为美国向其他国家传播通货膨胀的工具。布雷顿森林体系的崩溃：由于该体系的两大支柱的相继倒塌而崩溃；崩溃表现为：美元停兑黄金，固定汇率波幅扩大。固定汇率制倒台：1973 年 3 月，西方国家的货币实行浮动汇率制，至此，支撑布雷顿森林体系的另一支柱，即各国货币盯住美元，与美元保持固定比价的固定汇率制彻底崩溃。

6. 欧洲货币（Eurocurrency）：指欧洲英镑、欧元等，与欧洲美元性质相同。一国货币支付到国外后，经收款人存入西欧其他国家的商业银行而成为当地外币存款，叫欧洲货币。

7. 欧元（the euro）：1995 年，欧盟首脑会议决定欧洲未来统一货币的名称为欧元；1998 年 5 月，确定了 11 个欧元创始国和欧洲中央银行行长；1999 年 1 月 1 日，欧元正式启动；2002 年 1 月 1 日，发行欧元纸币和硬币，并与各国货币共同流通；2002 年 7 月 1 日，欧元完全取代各国货币。

8. 国际金融组织（International Financial Institutions）：国际金融组织可以分为 3 个种类：（1）全球性国际金融组织，如国际货币基金组织、世界银行、国际农业发展基金组织等；（2）洲际性国际金融组织，如亚洲开发银行、非洲开发银行、泛美开发银行等；（3）区域性国际金融组织，如欧洲投资银行、阿拉伯货币基金组织、加勒比开发银行等。

9. 国际货币基金组织（International Monetary Fund, IMF）：国际货币基金组织是根据 1944 年 7 月联合国货币金融会议通过的《国际货币基金协定》而建立的国际金融机构，其主要任务有：（1）作为各成员国在国际金融问题上进行协商与合作的常设机构；（2）促进国际贸易的扩大和各国经济的平衡增长；（3）促进国际汇兑的稳定，防止竞争性货币贬值；（4）协助成员国在经常项目交易中建立多边支付制度；（5）在成员国国际收支发生暂时不平衡时提供资助。

10. 世界银行集团（The World Bank Group）：世界银行集团指世界银行（The World Bank）及其两个附属机构：国际金融公司（The International Financial Corporation）和国际开发协会（The International Development Agency）。世界银行是"国际复兴开发银行"的通称。

11. 中央银行（Central Bank）：是国家银行，它是控制和调节本国宏观经济最重要的职能部门，也是制定本国对外汇率政策，协调国际经济关系的重要机构。中央银行的职责通常是：（1）发行银行，独占货币的发行权，决定货币投放量，制定信贷政策，控制宏观经济；（2）银行的银行，它集中存储商业银行的现金准备，是商业银行的最后贷款者；（3）国家的银行，执行国库职能，是国家的总账房，代理国库收付款项，代国家发行公债券；（4）外汇储备银行，掌管国家黄金外汇储备，制定对外汇率政策，稳定本币的外汇汇率。中央银行只和银行来往而不和工商企业打交道，不从事普通商业银行的业务活动。

12. 货币制度（Monetary System）：一个国家以法令规定的货币流通组织形式，使货币流通诸因素结合成一个统一体，其内容包括：（1）确定本位货币的币材，货币单位；（2）发行本位币和辅币的具体规定;(3)流通制度;(4)纸币的发行程序;(5)准备金制度。

13. 浮动汇率制度(Floating Foreign Exchange Rate System):在黄金与货币的固定关系脱钩的情况下,政府不再规定本国货币与外国货币的黄金原价,不规定汇率波动的上下限,中央银行也不承担维持汇率波动界限的义务,市场汇率根据外汇市场对某项外汇的供求情况,自行决定本国货币对外币的汇率。外国货币供过于求时,外国货币的价格就下跌,外币的汇率就下浮。

14. 亚洲美元(Asia-dollar):存放在亚洲及太平洋地区一些银行中的境外美元和其他可兑换货币的总称,主要是在新加坡大商业银行中的美元存款。广义上说,亚洲美元也属于欧洲美元的一部分。

15. 黄金储备(Gold Reserve):一国政府为维持货币信用,应付国际收支而储存的金块和金币总额。

16. 外汇储备(Foreign Exchange Reservcs):一国国际储备资产的一种形式,通常以国际贸易中最常用的货币作为外汇储备。储备的形式可以是在国外银行的存款或持有外国的有价证券,如国库券、公司债券、大额存单等。外汇储备主要用于保持本国国际收支平衡,或作为本国进口商品的备用金。

17. 外汇(Foreign Exchange):外汇的原意指以一种货币兑换成另外一种外国货币。一个国家对外支付时一般要把本国货币换成外国货币,所以"外汇"现用来指一个国家所持有的外国货币,以及以外币表示的可以用以进行国际结算的支付手段。通常包括以外币表示的信用工具、有价证券及其他可以取得外国货币的债权等。外汇汇率(Foreign Exchange Rate)是一国的货币折算成另一个国家的货币的比价、比率或价格。外汇市场(Foreign Exchange Market)一般无特定的固定场所。一个国家的中央银行为执行外汇政策,经常买卖外汇以影响外汇汇率。所有经营外汇买卖业务的商业银行、经纪人和商人都在经营各种现汇及期汇交易。这一切外汇业务的综合就体现为一国的外汇市场。国际商务从业者必须关注外汇市场,因为国际支付中的货币直接受到外汇市场的影响。

18. 特别提款权(Special Drawing Rights,SDR):国际货币基金组织为解决国际支付手段不足,于1969年9月创设的一种新的国际储备资产和记账单位,是在普通提款权之外赋予成员国一种特别使用资金的权利。特别提款权的分配原则是按成员国在基金组织所占的份额,分到的特别提款权可以通过基金组织换取外汇,可以作为外汇储备,平衡国际收支。

19. 国际支付货币(Vehicle Currency):国际贸易中最常用的支付货币。美元是目前使用最多的国际支付货币。

20. 货币政策(Monetary Policy):一个国家为调节宏观经济,而通过中央银行对贷款利率和货币供应量等方面采取的措施。货币政策包括:(1)提高或降低商业银行存款准备金的比率,以影响商业银行存贷款成本,使市场呈现紧缩或扩张;(2)提高或降低中央银行的再贴现率,从而影响市场利率水平;(3)通过公开市场活动,控制货币投放量,使市场信用规模发生变化。

21. 人民币升值(Appreciation of RMB):2005年7月21日正式升值,美元对人民币交易价格调为一比八点——(US $1:¥8.11 RMB),人民币对美元升值幅度为2%。这一调整幅度主要是根据我国贸易顺差程度和结构调整的需要来确定的,同时也考虑了国内企业进行结构调整的适应能力。此次小幅度升值在我国改革过程中恰到好处,有利于促进中国经济调整结构,不会对老百姓的生活带来大的影响。我国开始实行以市场供求为基础、参考一篮子货币进行调节、有管理的浮动汇率制度,汇率不再盯住单一美元,形成更富有弹性的人民币汇率机制。人民币已经为第四大全球支付货币,仅次于美元、欧元及英镑。而根据 SWIFT 提供的资料,2015 年 8 月全球的人民币支付额增加 9.13%,而所有货币支付额减少 8.3%。由此,人民币 8 月在全球支付市场占有率也达到创纪录的 2.79% 的高位,而 2014 年 1 月还仅为 1.39%。这是人民币国际化步伐加快的重要标志,也是中国对外开放步伐加快的充分体现。

22. 亚洲开发银行:简称"亚行"(Asian Development Bank , ADB),是一个致力于促进亚洲及太平洋地区发展中成员经济和社会发展的区域性政府间金融开发机构。自 1999 年以来,亚行特别强调扶贫为其首要战略目标。它不是联合国下属机构,但它是联合国亚洲及太平洋经济社会委员会(联合国亚太经社会)赞助建立的机构,同联合国及其区域和专门机构有密切的联系。

23. 亚洲基础设施投资银行:简称"亚投行"(Asian Infrastructure Investment Bank , AIIB),是一个政府间性质的亚洲区域多边开发机构,重点支持基础设施建设。"亚投行"宗旨:促进亚洲区域的建设互联互通化和经济一体化的进程,并加强中国与及其他亚洲国家和地区的合作。总部设在北京。

24. "一带一路":是"丝绸之路经济带"和"21 世纪海上丝绸之路"的简称。它将充分依靠中国与有关国家既有的双多边机制,借助既有的、行之有效的区域合作平台,"一带一路"旨在借用古代丝绸之路的历史符号,高举和平发展的旗帜,积极发展与沿线国家的经济合作伙伴关系,共同打造政治互信、经济融合、文化包容的利益共同体、命运共同体和责任共同体。

▶ New Words and Expressions

activate *v.* 使活动起来

anonymity *n.* 匿名

arbitrage *v.* 仲裁

balance of payments(BOP) 国际收支;国际收支平衡表

be subject to 取决于……;须经……的;受……的制约

benchmark *n.* 基准

call money 活期贷款,拆款(银行可以随时通知偿还的贷款总额)

chronic *a.* 长期的;慢性的

circumvent *v.* 围绕;回避

conductive *a.* 传导性的,传导的

consensus *n.* (意见等的)一致;合意

constraint *n.* 限制;制约;抑制

culminate *v.* 达到顶点;告终

culmination *n.* 达到顶点;顶点;告终

damper *n.* 抑制因素

de facto *a. & ad.* 实际的;事实上的;实际上

discrepancy *n.* 差异

dominate *v.* 在……占首要位置;统治

dual track 双轨(制)

ECB(European Central Bank) 欧洲中央银行

embed *v.* 把……嵌入

EMS(The European Monetary System) 欧洲货币体系

facelift *n.& v.* 整容;翻新

floating exchange rates 浮动汇率

greenback n. 美钞

hamper v. 妨碍；牵制

hedging n. 套头交易；对冲买卖；套期保值

IDA（The International Development Association）国际发展协会

IFC（The International Financial Corporation）国际金融公司

IMF（International Monetary Fund）国际货币基金组织

IMS（International Monetary System）国际货币体系

import n. 重要性

impose …on … 对……征收税款；把……强加于……

inception n. 开端；初期

indices n.（index 的复数）标志；指数

inherent a. 内在的；固有的

in respect of … 就……而言

legal tender 法定货币

leverage n. & v. 举债经营；力量；影响

maladjustment n. 失调；（人的）不适应环境

maneuver n. 策略；花招；使用策略/花招

municipal a. & n. 市的；市政的；市政公债（用复数）

nil n. 无；零

option n. 期权；购买选择权

par value 平价，票面价值（印在普通股、优先股和债券等票面上的价值）

peg v. 钉住；限定

phase out 逐步停止使用或生产和实行

PPP（Purchasing Power Parity）购买力平价，购买力平准（用于说明两种通货间适当汇率的原则或理论）

proxy n. 代理权；代理人

reserves n. 储备金；储备

resort to 凭借；求助于

rider n.（文件后面的）附文；附加条款

SDR（Special Drawing Right）特别提款权（国际货币基金组织成员国优先享有的权利，在暂时遇到国际收支逆差时，可以从基金所集中管理的储备金中购买有限数量的外币）

SOE（state-owned enterprise）国有企业

spot transaction 现货交易

spread n.（买价和卖价之间的）差额

strain v. & n. 使紧张；过度的使用；气质

subset n.（组成大套的）小套

supranational a. 超国家的,超民族的

surveillance n. 监视；监管

swap n. & v. 交易；交换

to the effect that … 以便……；目的是……

translation n. 折算；转换（把海外资产和债务转换成公司的本国货币）

under the auspices of … 在……的赞助或支持下

vice versa 反之亦然

vis-à-vis prep. 同……相比；关于

woe n. 悲苦；苦恼

yearn v. 怀念；想念；渴望

▶ Discussion Questions

1. What are the functions of the International Monetary Fund?

2. What are the characteristics of hard currency?

3. Is foreign currency the same as foreign exchange? If not, what are the differences between them?

4. Does Eurocurrency refer to the currency issued by European countries?

5. Is it possible that RMB will become a hard currency in the future? Why or why not?

Chapter 8

International Accounting, Auditing and Tax
国际会计、国际审计和国际税收

Objectives
学习目标

To outline how important the international accounting is to international business.

概述国际会计对国际商务的重要性。

To have knowledge about auditing and taxation in international business.

了解国际商务中的审计与税务。

To understand some accounting differences between countries.

了解财会在国家间的差异。

To get to know the relationship between accounting and auditing.

熟悉会计与审计的关系。

To have some knowledge about China's accounting and auditing in international business.

了解中国国际商务中的会计与审计。

▶ 8.1 General View of International Accounting 国际会计概述

International accounting and taxation are both important in international business strategies, as without the two good decisions cannot really be made. Managers of MNEs are of course not accounting specialists, but they should keep themselves regularly informed of the accounting and taxation data of the firms. Besides, managers of MNEs must also understand which data they need and the problems specialists face in gathering it from around the world. The accounting and finance functions of MNEs are closely related. Each relies on the other in fulfilling its own responsibilities. Accounting is defined as:

A service activity whose function is to provide quantitative information, primarily financial in nature, about economic entities that is intended to be useful in making economic decisions—in making reasoned choices among alternative course of action. (Daniels, 2001, p.667)

Accounting is a branch of applied economics that provides information about business and financial transactions for users of that information. Critical users of accounting information are investors, employees, lenders, suppliers and other trade creditors, customers, governments and their agencies, and the public. International accounting is distinct because the information is concerned with a multinational enterprise (MNE) with foreign operations and transactions, or the users of the information are in a different domicile from the reporting entity.

Accounting amounts may be quite different according to the principles that govern them. As international accounting is closely related to operations in foreign nations, there may appear differences in culture, business practice, political and regulatory structure, legal system, currency value, foreign exchange rate, local inflation rate, business risk, tax, and so on.

Accounting can be thought of as having three broad areas: measurement, disclosure, and auditing. Measurement is the process of identifying, categorizing, and quantifying economic activities or transactions. The aim of accounting measurements is to provide users with information that will be very useful for economic decisions. Disclosure is the process by which accounting measurements are transmitted to their users. This area is mainly concerned with such issues as what is to be disclosed, when, by what means, and to whom. Auditing is the process by which specialized accounting professionals (auditors) examine and verify the adequacy of a company's financial and control systems and the accuracy of its financial records.

As globalization of market is an overwhelming tendency of today's world, financial market is becoming more and more global. Therefore, it is quite necessary and important to understand international accounting and taxation. The key ideas to be discussed in the following are mainly based on those of Frederick D. S. Choi (2002) and Lee H. Radebaugh (2002).

8.2 International Accounting and International Business 国际会计与国际商务

Now that we are in the new millennium, we are closer than ever to having a uniform set of international accounting standards that firms can use as they list on stock exchanges all over the world.

International business activity is increasing dramatically through traditional exporting and importing of goods and services as well as foreign direct investment (FDI). Capital markets are opening up and becoming more transparent and capital is flowing freely around the world at a quicker speed. Stock markets are linking up with each other just as firms are doing to increase their global competitiveness, and accounting will be one of the key areas that will help determine how successful cross-border stock markets linkages become.

As the firm becomes more and more involved in trade, the international accounting activity increases. To meet the increasing demands of international business, special accounting systems and procedures must be established in controlling, reporting, and taxation areas.

A company may establish an operation of some kind abroad. For example, it may decide to license a foreign manufacturer to produce its product or some part of its products. This involves developing an accounting system to monitor contract performance and royalty and technical payments and to handle the foreign money that flows into the company's tax and financial statements.

Besides, the company may establish a wholly owned subsidiary in a foreign country. Accounting for the foreign subsidiary would include the following:

(1) Meeting the requirements of the foreign government, which would be based on procedures and practices different from those in the parent company's country;

(2) Establishing a management information system to monitor, control, and evaluate the foreign subsidiary;

(3) Developing a system to consolidate the foreign subsidiary's operating results with those of the parent company for financial and tax-reporting purposes.

The actual and potential flow of assets across national boundaries makes the finance and accounting functions more complicated. The MNE must learn to deal with different inflation rates, foreign exchange rate changes, currency controls, expropriation risks, customs duties, tax rates and methods of determining taxable income, backgrounds of local accounting personnel, and local as well as home-country reporting requirements. A company's controllership (accounting) function collects and analyses data for internal and external users. The controller of an international company must be concerned about different currencies and accounting systems.

8.3   The Field of International Accounting   国际会计的领域

Generally speaking, there are two major fields involved in international accounting study: descriptive (comparative) accounting and the accounting dimensions of international transactions (multi-national enterprises).

The first area is fascinating because it is truly fundamental to an understanding of the nature and uses of accounting. But it is impossible to study accounting for each country in the world in the same depth as one does for one's own country. Therefore, colonial ties and direct investment require a basic understanding of those countries and their accounting systems.

There are firms that are not considered multi-national enterprises. Those firms are involved in import and export transactions and special attention need to be paid to them. Multinational enterprises have some of these problems and a lot of others. Financial problems, translation of foreign currency, financial statements, information systems, budgets and performance evaluation, audits, and taxes are some of the major problems faced by these firms.

⊳ 8.4 Classifications of Accounting Systems 国际会计制度的分类

So far as the nature of international business is concerned, it is important to classify international accounting systems. Classification is fundamental to understanding and analysing why and how national accounting systems differ. We can also analyse whether these systems are converging or diverging. The goal of classification is to group countries according to the distinctive characteristics of their accounting systems. Classifications reveal fundamental structures that group members have in common and that distinguish the various groups from each other. Classification is a way of viewing the world. Classification has the following practical benefits (Choi, 2002).

(1) It is possible that the countries in a particular group can react to new circumstances in similar ways. Countries may benefit from the experiences of other countries in the same group. For example, standard setters in Australia, Canada, New Zealand, the UK, and the USA have found it both effective and efficient to cooperate and find common solutions to certain accounting issues.

(2) The differences among groups are barriers to the regional and worldwide harmonization efforts. For these efforts to succeed, the groups involved (such as the International Accounting Standards Board at the international level and the European Union at the regional level) must understand the differences to be overcome and whether the partners are changing over time.

(3) Developing countries often lack the resources to develop their own accounting standards. These countries may be able to pattern their own standards based on existing standards (as China and certain countries in Eastern Europe are now doing).

(4) Communication problems are likely to be severer when a company reports to that financial statement users who are unfamiliar with the company's home-country accounting standards. Therefore, the company may need to provide additional information to these users. There could be similar problems in internal communications in an MNE. Accountants communicating with counterparts in another country need to be careful to speak the same language.

Although accounting standards and practices are quite different in different countries, it is possible to group systems used in various countries according to their common characteristics. Figure 8.1 illustrates one approach to classifying international accounting systems.

⊳ 8.5 Principal Accounting Differences Between Countries 各国间会计的主要差别

Financial accounting systems vary from country to country. So managers in MNEs must realize the differences and know what information their accounting records really convey. Likewise, managers must be aware of the special circumstances and rules affecting the handling of international transactions and the parent company's consolidated statements reporting on the MNE's global

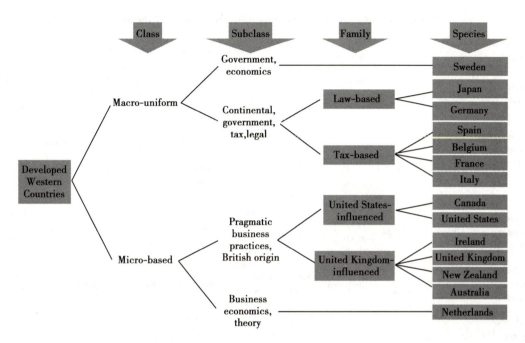

Figure 8.1 Classification of Accounting Systems of Developed Western Countries

situation. Financial accounting at the subsidiary and parent levels reflects not only traditional accounting practices but also laws and regulations regarding disclosure (with publicly held companies) and taxation. Variations in accounting practices and in exchange rates, which alter the unit of measurements, complicate the financial accounting systems of MNEs.

International accounting diversity is likely to result in any of the following problems in international business conducted with the use of financial statements:

(1) Poor and improper business decision making.

(2) Hindering the ability of a firm or enterprise to raise capital in different or foreign markets.

(3) Hindering or preventing a firm from monitoring competitive factors across firms, industries, and countries.

The financial statements of one country differ from those of another country in six major ways.

(1) Language.

(2) Currency.

(3) Type of statements (income statements, balance sheet, etc.)

(4) Financial statement format.

(5) Extent of footnote disclosure.

(6) Underlying GAAP on which the financial statements are based.

A company wishing to provide financial information for investors throughout the world need to deal with the above six issues.

Figure 8.2 illustrates principal accounting differences around the world.

Summary of Principal Accounting Differences Around the World

Accounting Principle	United States	Japan	United Kingdom	France	Germany	Netherlands	Switzerland	Canada	Italy	Brazil
1. Capitalization of R&D costs	Not allowed	Allowed in certain cases	Allowed in certain cases	Allowed in certain cases	Not allowed	Allowed in certain cases	Allowed in certain cases	Allowed in certain cases	Allowed in certain cases	Allowed in certain cases
2. Fixed asset revaluations state at amount in excess of cost	Not allowed	Not allowed	Allowed	Allowed	Not allowed	Allowed in certain cases	Not allowed	Not allowed	Allowed in certain cases	Allowed
3. Inventory valuation using LIFO	Allowed	Allowed	Allowed but rarely done	Not allowed	Allowed in certain cases	Allowed	Allowed	Allowed	Allowed	Allowed but rarely done
4. Finance leases capitalized	Required	Allowed in certain cases	Required	Not allowed	Allowed in certain cases	Required	Allowed	Required	Not allowed	Not allowed
5. Pension expense accrued during period of service	Required	Allowed	Required	Allowed	Required	Required	Allowed	Required	Allowed	Allowed
6. Book and tax timing differences on balance sheet as deferred tax	Required	Allowed in certain cases	Allowed	Allowed in certain cases	Allowed but rarely done	Required	Allowed	Allowed	Allowed but rarely done	Allowed
7. Current rate method of currency translation	Required	Allowed in certain cases	Required	Allowed	Allowed	Required	Required	Allowed but rarely done	Required	Required
8. Pooling method used for mergers	Required in certain cases	Allowed in certain cases	Allowed in certain cases	Not allowed	Allowed in certain cases	Allowed but rarely done	Allowed but rarely done	Allowed but rarely done	Not allowed	Allowed but rarely done
9. Equity method used for 20%—50% ownership	Required	Required	Required	Allowed in certain cases	Allowed	Required	Required	Required	Allowed	Required

Figure 8.2　Summary of Principal Accounting Differences Around the World

8.6　International Accounting Harmonization　国际会计协调

"Harmonization" is a process of increasing the compatibility of accounting practices by setting limits on how much they vary. Harmonized standards are free of logical conflicts, and should improve the comparability of financial information from different countries.

Efforts to harmonize accounting standards began even before the establishment of the

International Accounting Standards Committee (IASC) in 1973. International accounting harmonization now is one of the most important issues facing securities regulators, stock exchanges, and those who prepare or use financial statements.

Harmonization and standardization are sometimes used interchangeably. But there is still a difference between them. Standardization normally means the imposition of a rigid and narrow set of rules, and may even apply a single standard or rule to all situations. Besides, standardization does not accommodate national differences and, therefore, is more difficult to implement internationally, whereas harmonization is much more flexible and open. It does not take a one-size-fits-all approach, but accommodates national differences and has made a great progress internationally in recent years. However, within accounting, these two words have almost become technical terms, and one cannot rely on the normal difference in their meanings. "Harmonization" is a word that tends to be associated with the transnational legislation originating from the European Union while "standardization" is a word that is often associated with the International Accounting Standard Committee.

8.7　The International Accounting Standards Board (IASB, formerly IASC)　国际会计标准委员会

The International Accounting Standards Board (IASB), formerly the International Accounting Standards Committee (IASC), is an independent private sector standards-setting body founded in 1973 by professional accounting organizations in nine countries and restructured in 2001. Before the restructuring, the IASC issued 41 International Accounting Standards (IAS) and a Framework for the Preparation and Presentation of Financial Statements.

The International Accounting Standards Board has been working for the last 30 years to develop a comprehensive set of high-quality accounting standards that can be used to bring uniformity in financial reporting around the world. These standards are already officially accepted in many countries, and are used by a growing number of major global corporations. The European Commission has proposed that by 2005, all EU companies listed on a regulated market should be required to prepare consolidated accounts in accordance with IAS. Furthermore, other international organizations such as the Basle Committee, the G7, the World Bank, the World Trade Organization, and the International Monetary Fund have expressed support for international accounting harmonization, and for the work of the IASB.

However, the adoption of IAS is producing a profound impact on the financial reporting practices of organizations around the world, and will continue to do so as new standards are developed.

Publication of an exposure draft, standard or interpretation requires approval by eight of the fourteen members of the Board. Other matters require a simple majority of those present, subject to 60% attendance either in person or by telecommunication link. The IASB's objectives are as follows:

(1) To develop, in the public interest, a single set of high quality, understandable and enforceable global accounting standards that require high quality, transparent and comparable information in financial statements and other financial reporting to help participants in the world's capital markets and other users make economic decisions.

(2) To promote the use and rigorous application of those standards.

(3) To bring about convergence of national accounting standards and International Accounting Standards to high quality solutions. (Please refer to the IASB Web site: http://www.iasb.org.uk)

The restructured IASB met for the first time in April, 2001.

The IASB represents over 120 accounting organizations from 91 countries. With a remarkably broad base of support, IASB is the driving force in international accounting standard setting.

▶ 8.8 International Accounting Transparency and Disclosure 国际会计透明与公开

There is growing pressure around the world to promote greater "transparency" and disclosure consistent with the importance of cross-border capital raisings and the growth of world trade and investment. Disclosure regulation varies internationally and there is often a lack of transparency, especially in the emerging economies.

Although many MNEs tend to be willing to disclose additional information, a growing number of major MNEs are more enlightened and often perceive it to be in their own interests to make voluntary disclosures likely to be relevant to external stakeholders, particularly investors. However, the nature of the disclosures would seem to depend not only on international capital market factors but also on local national concerns and traditions. The IASB is trying its best to raise the standard of disclosure globally. One of the most important areas concerns segmental disclosure where the latest IAS endeavours to reveal the returns and risks of MNE operations on a more strategic and hence a more insightful basis.

8.8.1 The Pressures for Information Disclosure 信息公开的压力

It is understandable that MNEs are concerned about the manner in which apparently ever-increasing requirements for information disclosure are determined by regulatory bodies and standard-setting agencies at both governmental and professional levels.

The acceleration in the demand for information for investments purposes might well appear to be unsustainable and hence must eventually decline. However, the increasing internationalisation of financial markets and share ownership diversity of accounting principles and practices in different countries, has fueled the demand for additional information disclosures to increase both the quality and comparability of MNE reports.

In addition, the increased supply of information appears in some respects to have actually increased, rather than reduced, the demand for additional information. If the demand for information were fixed, corporations could include this as one of the benefits to be matched against the costs of information disclosure. However, this is clearly not possible in the current dynamic context of information demand.

8.8.2　The Importance of Information Disclosures　信息公开的重要性

MNEs increasingly realize the importance of information disclosed in financial statements and accompanying reports. This information provides an important input to the financial analysis process of evaluating the quality of earnings and financial position, both current and prospective. A particularly important motivation for voluntary information disclosures by MNEs is that the annual report provides the opportunity to communicate more policy and future-oriented information about the corporation. This may better inform or influence investors in the increasingly globalized securities market. For example, more than 400 of the Fortune Global 500 firms now provide financial and other corporate information on the Internet. This is a trend that is likely to have an increasing impact on the disclosure practices of stock exchange-listed companies around the world.

In particular, the need for MNEs to maintain business confidentiality in sensitive areas and to avoid jeopardizing their competitive position should be taken into account. At the same time, this need must be weighed against the interests of analysts, investors, and the public in the transparency of multinational business operations.

In practice, it appears that the more specific and the more future-oriented and especially the more quantitative the information proposed for disclosure, the more sensitive becomes the attitude of MNEs toward its provision.

8.8.3　Reporting and Disclosure　报告与公开

There is a concern about what companies around the world actually disclose in their annual reports. Annual report disclosure practices reflect managers' responses to regulatory disclosure requirements and their incentives to provide information to financial statement users voluntarily.

In many parts of the world, disclosure rules mean little and monitoring and enforcement are largely absent. Insofar as disclosure rules are not enforced, the required disclosures are (in practice) voluntary, because corporate managers will not comply with disclosure rules if compliance is more costly than the expected costs of noncompliance.

➤ 8.9 Foreign Currency Translation 外币换算

Foreign currency translation is the process of restating financial statement information from one currency to another. A company with operations in more than one country need prepare consolidated (or group) financial statements that combine financial accounts denominated in one national currency with accounts denominated in another (i.e., the parent country's) currency. To put it simply, the process of restating foreign-currency financial statements into Chinese RMB is translation. And the combination of all of these translated financial statements into one is consolidation.

Foreign currency translation is necessary due to fluctuating currency markets and the globalization of business and the world's securities markets.

8.9.1 Reasons for Translation 换算的原因

Companies with significant overseas operations cannot prepare consolidated financial statements unless their accounts and those of their subsidiaries are expressed in a single currency. For example, we cannot add up Chinese RMB, Japanese yen, Swiss francs, and New Zealand dollars and obtain meaningful results. The single currency traditionally is the reporting currency of the parent company. Other reasons for foreign currency translation are:

(1) recording foreign currency transactions;

(2) reporting international branches and subsidiaries;

(3) reporting the results of independent operations abroad.

Just as with consolidation procedures, foreign currency transactions, such as the purchase of merchandise from China by a Canadian importer, must be translated because financial statements cannot be prepared from accounts that are expressed in more than one currency.

8.9.2 Foreign Currency Translation Methods 外币换算的方法

In the process of translation, all foreign currency balance sheet and income statement accounts are related in terms of the reporting currency by multiplying the foreign currency amount by the appropriate exchange rate. There are four major translation methods.

1. Current/Non-current Method

Under the current/non-current method, current assets and liabilities are translated at current exchange rates, while non-current assets, liabilities and stockholders' equity are translated at historical exchange rates.

The current/non-current method is based on the assumption that accounts should be grouped according to maturity. Anything due to mature in one year or less or within the normal business cycle should be translated at the current rate, whereas everything else should be carried at the rate in effect when the translation was originally recorded.

2. Monetary/Non-monetary Method

Accounts are considered as either monetary or non-monetary rather than current or non-current. Under this method, monetary assets and liabilities are translated at the current rate, while non-money assets and liabilities and stockholders' equity are translated at historical rates. This method was a radical departure from the current/non-current method widely used in the areas of inventory, long-term receivables and long-term payables.

3. Temporal Method

According to the temporal method, cash, receivables, and payables (both current and non-current) are translated at the current rate. Other assets and liabilities may be translated at current or historical rates, depending on their characteristics. Assets and liabilities carried at past exchange prices are translated at historical rates.

4. Current Rate Method

Under the current rate method, all assets and liabilities are required to be translated at the current exchange rate. Therefore, it is an easier method to use than the others because a company would not have to keep track of various historical exchange rates. The current rate method results in translated statements that retain the same ratios and relationships that exist in the local currency.

Having discussed the foreign currency translation methods, an example is provided to further illustrate the methods.

When a multinational corporation based in the US owns more than 50 percent of the voting stock of a foreign company, a parent-subsidiary relationship exists. The parent company is usually required to prepare consolidated financial statements. Before this can be done, the financial statements of the foreign subsidiary must be recast using US generally accepted accounting principles (GAAP). Next, the foreign accounts must be re-measured (translated) from the foreign currency into US dollars. To make the translation, the first step is to identify three currencies:

(1) Currency of books and records (CBR)—the CBR is the currency in which the foreign financial statements are denominated;

(2) Functional currency (FC)—the FC is the one in which the subsidiary generally buys, sells, borrows, repays, etc.;

(3) The reporting currency (RC)—the RC is the one in which the consolidated financial statements are denominated.

The following three rules are used to determine the method of translation.

Rule 1: If the FC is hyper-inflationary (i.e., 100% cumulative inflation within three years), then ignore the FC and re-measure the CBR into the RC using the temporal rate method.

Rule 2: If the CBR is different from the FC, re-measure the CBR into the FC using the temporal rate method.

Rule 3: Translate from the FC into the RC using the current rate method.

The rules must be applied in sequence, stopping when the subsidiary's financial statements have been converted into the parent's reporting currency (RC). For example, when the functional currency (FC) is hyper-inflationary, Rule 1 applies; that is, the financial statements which are denominated in the CBR are translated into the RC using the temporal rate method, and Rules 2 and 3 aren't used.

A second example is as follows: If the CBR is British pounds, the FC is Dutch guilders (not hyper-inflationary), and the RC is US dollars. Rule 1 is to be skipped and Rule 2 is to be used, translating the CBR (pounds) into the FC (guilders) using the temporal rate method. Since the FC (guilders) is not the RC (dollars), Rule 3 would be applied to translate the FC (guilders) into the RC (dollars) using the current rate method. A third example is as follows: when the CBR is the same as the FC, then Rule 3 is directly to be used.

Using the current rate method, all assets and liabilities are translated at the current rate (i.e., exchange rate on the balance sheet date). Owners' equity and dividends are translated at historical rates (exchange rate at the time the asset was acquired, liability incurred, or element of paid-in capital was issued or reacquired). Income statement items can be translated by using the average exchange rate (the average of the exchange rate at the beginning of the accounting period and the current rate).

Under the temporal rate method, the objective is to measure each subsidiary transaction as though the transaction had been made by the parent. Monetary items (e.g. cash, receivables, inventories carried at market, payables, and long-term debt) are remeasured using the current exchange rate. Other items (e.g. prepaid expenses, inventories carried at cost, fixed assets, and stock) are remeasured using historical exchange rates.

▶ 8.10 Accounting for Changing Prices 变化价格会计

Accounting is closely related to price changing. Fluctuating currency values and changes in money prices of goods and services today are integral features of international business.

Price movements must be paid close attention to in international accounting. Price movements can be understood in two ways: a general and a specific price movements. A general price level change occurs when, on average, the prices of all goods and services in an economy change. The monetary unit gains or loses purchasing power. An overall increase in prices is called inflation; a decrease, deflation. A specific price change, on the other hand, refers to a change in the price of specific goods or services caused by changes in demand and supply. Therefore, the annual rate of inflation in a country may rise by 50% during the same period.

While changing prices occur all over the world, their business and financial standard effects vary from country to country. For example, Europe and North America have had relatively modest general price level increases while Eastern Europe and Latin America have had much higher inflation rates.

Local inflation affects exchange rates used to translate foreign currency balances to their domestic currency equivalents. It is hard to separate foreign currency translation from inflation when accounting for foreign operations.

8.10.1 Impact of Inflation on the Corporation 通货膨胀对公司的影响

The effect of inflation on the financial position and performance of a corporation can result in inefficient operating decisions by managers who do not understand its impact. In terms of financial position, financial assets such as cash lose value during inflation because their purchasing power diminishes. For example, if a company holds financial assets such as cash during a period when inflation rises by 10%, that cash has 10% less purchasing power at the end of the period than at the beginning.

The effect of inflation on nonmonetary assets is reflected in both the income statement and the balance sheet. During a period of rising prices, current sales revenues are matched against inventory that may have been purchased several months earlier and against depreciation computed on the historical cost of property, plant, and equipment that may have been purchased several years ago, despite the fact that replacing inventory and fixed assets have become more expensive.

The income statement and balance sheet effects could lead the corporation into liquidity problems as the cash generated from revenues is consumed by the ever-increasing replacement cost of assets.

8.10.2 General Purchasing Power (GPP) Accounting 综合购买力会计

The general philosophy supporting general purchasing power accounting is to report assets, liabilities, revenues, and expenses in units of the same purchasing power. The approach here is that the monetary unit of measure should be uniform while retaining the basis of measurement used in the financial statements (e.g. historical cost). In most countries, financial statements are prepared on a historical cost-nominal currency basis. This means that the statements are not adjusted for changes in the general price level. Under GPP accounting, the non-financial items in the financial statements (inventory, plant, and equipment) are restated to reflect a common purchasing power, normally at the ending balance sheet date.

For example, suppose Joansong Company purchased a machine on January 1st, 2003, for $10,000 and that the general price level, as measured by the consumer price index, increased by 15% during the year. On December 31, the machine would appear on the balance sheet at $11,500 ($10,000+[$10,000×0.15]) from which depreciation would be deducted, adjusted in GPP terms, to be charged against income. This implies that it would take $ 11,500 of end-of-year purchasing power to buy what 10,000 bought on January 1.

8.10.3 Current Value Accounting 现行价值会计

Current value accounting is concerned with the rise or fall in the cost or value of specific assets, not with the overall loss of purchasing power of a currency. Under this concept, income is not considered to be earned until the corporation has maintained its capital in current value terms.

There are two major approaches to current value accounting: current cost (or replacement cost) and current exit price (selling price or net realizable value).

Current cost accounting is the most widely accepted method and is used for most classes of nonmonetary assets. Under this approach, assets are valued at what it would cost to replace them.

Current exit price accounting, on the other hand, values asset, especially finished goods inventory, at what they could be sold for, less costs to complete and sell the items.

Current value accounting results in holding gains and losses when nonmonetary assets are revalued. This is the gain or loss during the period the asset is held by the corporation. The gains and losses involved can either be taken into the income statement or reflected on the balance sheet as a capital adjustment account.

8.11 International Financial Statement Analysis 国际财务报表分析

Investors, equity research analysts, bankers, and other financial statement users have a growing need to read and analyze non-domestic financial statements and make cross-border financial comparisons. The need to understand and use non-domestic financial statements has also increased as merger and acquisition activities have become more international. Besides, as business becomes more global, financial statements become more important than ever as a basis for competitive analysis, credit decisions and business negotiations.

8.11.1 International Business Strategy Analysis 国际商务战略分析

Business strategy analysis is a first necessary step in financial statement analysis. It provides a qualitative understanding of a company, its competitors, and its economic environment which ensures that quantitative analysis is based on reality. By identifying key profit drivers and business risks, business strategy analysis helps the analysts make realistic forecasts.

However, business strategy analysis is often complex and difficult in an international setting, because the environmental factors in different countries are quite different (please refer to Chapter 4 about international business environment).

8.11.2 Accounting Analysis 会计分析

Accounting analysis is about assessing the extent to which a firm's accounting amounts reflect economic reality. The analyst need to evaluate the firm's accounting policies and estimates, and assess the nature and extent of a firm's accounting flexibility. To reach reliable conclusions, the analyst must adjust reported accounting amounts to remove distortions caused by the use of accounting methods which the analyst may judge to be inappropriate.

In carrying out accounting analysis, it is suggested by some people to adopt the following sequence for evaluating a firm's accounting quality.

(1) To identify key accounting policies.

(2) To assess accounting flexibility.

(3) To evaluate accounting strategy.

(4) To evaluate the quality of disclosure.

(5) To identify potential red flags (e.g.unusually large asset write-offs, unexplained transactions that boost profits, or an increasing gap between a company's reported income and its cash flow from operations).

(6) To adjust for accounting distortions.

8.11.3   International Financial Analysis   国际财务分析

The aim of financial analysis is to evaluate a firm's current and past performance, and to judge whether its performance can be sustained. Ratio analysis and cash flow analysis are important tools in financial analysis.

Ratio analysis involves comparison of ratios between one firm and other firms in the same industry, comparison of a firm's ratios across years or other fiscal periods, and/or comparison of ratios to some absolute benchmark. It provides insights into the comparative and relative significance of financial statement items.

Cash flow analysis focuses on disclosures about periodic non-cash investing and financing activities, and on cash flow statement which provides information about a firm's cash inflows and outflows classified among operating, investing, and financing activities.

8.12   International Auditing   国际审计

Auditing, like accounting, has a long history. Anthropologists have found records of auditing activities dating back to early Babylonian time (around 3,000 BC). There were also auditing activity in ancient China, Greece and Rome. The practice of modern auditing dates back to the beginning of the modern corporation at the dawn of the Industrial Revolution.

Auditing refers to the examination of financial statements primarily of business organizations by an independent, qualified auditor for the purpose of expressing an opinion on how well the financial statements meet certain established criteria, often called "accounting standards" or "principles". This function is normally referred to as the "attest function". The users of financial statements may rely on the representations in the statements if they are accompanied by a positive or unqualified opinion from the qualified auditor. This relationship between the auditor and the financial statements lends credibility to the statements and makes possible much of the flow of capital throughout the world.

The overall objective of an audit of financial statements is to enable the auditor to express an opinion whether the financial statements are prepared, in all material respects, in accordance with an identified financial reporting framework. The following discussion is mainly based on the ideas of Rick Hayes (1999).

8.12.1　The Auditor, Corporations and Financial Information　审计员、公司及财务信息

The Latin meaning of the word "auditor" was a "hearer" or "listener" because in Rome auditors heard taxpayers.

By the audit process, the auditor enhances the usefulness and the value of the financial statements, but he also increases the credibility of other non-audited information released by management. The current importance of the auditor is easily seen when judged against the rapid growth in the size and the number of major corporations, whose debt and equity securities constitute such an important part of the invested savings in the economy. The capital markets simply could not operate without the confidence that the work of the auditor adds.

The following questions are all concerns of the auditor.

(1) Is the company a going concern?

(2) Is it free of fraud?

(3) Is it managed properly?

(4) Is there integrity in its database?

(5) Do directors have proper and adequate information to make decisions?

(6) Are there adequate controls?

(7) What effect do the company's products and by-products have on the environment?

(8) Can an unfortunate mistake bring this company to its knees?

The above questions are also concerns of a company. They are matters of corporate governance as well as reporting.

The external auditors are not part of the company team, but the chairmen (members of a corporate board of directors) have a direct interest in assuring themselves of the effectiveness of the audit approach within their companies. The relationship between auditors and managers should be one where the auditors work with the appropriate people in the company, but do so on a strictly objective and professional basis, never losing sight of the fact that they are there on the shareholders' behalf. Chairmen need auditors who will stand up to management when necessary and who will unhesitatingly raise any doubts about the people or procedures with the audit committee. Weak auditors expose chairmen to hazards.

Considerable expertise is needed to perform the auditing function, since the auditor must not only be at least as competent in financial accounting as the most competent of his clients, but must also be an expert in deciding what evidence is necessary to satisfy the assertions of the financial statements. The new auditing environment will demand new skills of auditors if they are to be reporters and assessors of governance and measurements.

8.12.2   The Audit Process Model   审计过程模式

The financial audit is a systematic process which begins with a client's request for an audit of financial statements and culminates in an auditor's opinion in the form of a report. The audit process is made up of a series of tasks. These audit tasks are more efficiently completed if the auditor uses a plan for conducting the tasks based on a model of the process.

According to Rick Hayes (1999), a four-phase standard audit process model is used, based on the scientific empirical cycle. The four phases are as follows:

(1) Client acceptance (pre-planning);

(2) Planning and design of an audit approach;

(3) Tests for evidence;

(4) Completion of the audit and issuance of an audit report.

1. Phase 1—Client Acceptance

(1) Objective: Determine both acceptance of a client and acceptance by a client. Decide on acquiring a new client or continuation of relationship with an existing one and the type and amount of staff required.

(2) Procedures:

A. Evaluate the client's background and reasons for the audit;

B. Communicate with predecessor auditors;

C. Determine need for other professionals;

D. Prepare client proposal;

E. Obtain an engagement letter;

F. Select staff to perform the audit.

2. Phase 2—Planning

(1) Objective: Determine the amount and type of evidence and review required to give the auditor assurance that there is no material misstatement of the financial statements.

(2) Procedures:

A. Obtain company and industry background information;

B. Investigate legal information;

C. Perform initial analytical procedures;

D. Perform procedures to obtain an understanding of internal control;

E. Based on the evidence, assess risk and set materiality;

F. Prepare the audit program.

3. Phase 3—Testing and Evidence

(1) Objective: Test for evidence supporting internal controls and the fairness of the financial statements.

(2) Procedures:

A. Tests of controls;

B. Substantive tests of transactions;

C. Analytical procedures;

D. Tests of details of balances;

E. Obtain legal letters;

F. Obtain management representative's letter;

G. Final evidence accumulation and search for unrecorded liabilities.

4. Phase 4—Evaluation and Judgement

(1) Objective: Complete the audit procedures and issue an opinion.

(2) Procedures:

A. Perform overall review;

B. Perform procedures to identify subsequent events;

C. Review financial statements and other report materials;

D. Perform wrap-up procedures;

E. Prepare Matters of Attention for Partners;

F. Report to the Board of Directors;

G. Prepare Audit Report.

8.12.3 Internal Auditing   内部审计

Internal auditing and external auditing perform two separate but related functions. The two audit functions share a common objective: to determine reliability of accounting information.

Internal auditing is defined as an objective of operations and control systems of an organization to determine whether its policies and procedures are being followed and also whether its resources are safeguarded and used efficiently to achieve organizational objectives. The objectives of internal auditing, based on the above definition, are to determine whether:

(1) management and accounting controls are in place and are effective;

(2) assets are safeguarded and used efficiently.

The importance and practice of internal auditing are increasing worldwide. This is especially the case in North America, Japan, Western Europe, India, and so on. In many countries internal auditing is required by law.

Internal audit is an integral part of an internal control system. It provides feedback and may result in changing the goals of the parent company, or the expected level of performance from the international operation. It would be erroneous to assume, therefore, that the corrective action always takes place at the local level. We must know that when central or regional staff is involved in the internal audit, it is a common practice for them to report both to the central headquarters and to the managers of local operations. By reporting to the local managers, they make it possible for the local managers to take corrective action without any unnecessary delay. It also fosters a more cooperative attitude on the part of the local managers towards central or regional internal audit staff. The central or regional staff need to have excellent interpersonal skills, and should display sensitivity toward local managers to avoid conflicts.

In the international business setting, internal auditing involves some factors which internal auditing of domestic operation does not have. Such factors are:

(1) geographic distance makes it impossible to oversee distant operations through physical observation and visual inspection;

(2) knowledge of local laws is essential to ensure their compliance;

(3) business practices are different in different countries;

(4) each country has its monetary unit;

(5) local records are kept in the local language and create translation problem;

(6) lack of availability of skilled internal auditors may be a problem in some countries.

Although international operations add certain complexities to internal auditing, some of those complexities are decreasing. This is because the ever-increasing magnitude and importance of international business have resulted in greater uniformity in business practices all over the world, and because advancements in technology such as computers, faxes, bar-coding, and scanners have alleviated many problems posed by geographic distance or lack of well-developed infrastructure within a country.

8.12.4 External Auditing 外部审计

External audits are performed by the public accountants. The basic objective of the external audit is similar in all countries: to determine whether the financial statements are properly prepared. The external auditors audit financial statements and supporting evidence by applying the auditing standards. Nevertheless, external audits are performed differently in different countries because accounting standards and auditing standards differ from country to country.

In the course of audit, external auditors perform some necessary audit procedures to the financial statements and to support evidence to determine whether the financial statements are in conformity with applicable standards. If the auditor's opinion states that the statements conform to the standards, it lends credibility to the representations contained in the financial statements.

The opinion of the external auditor is especially important for the parent company, investors, and creditors. The parent company can rely on the financial statements of international operations for preparation of consolidated financial statements and for decision making. The investors and creditors

（4）have accounting experience, since a large part of daily tax administration includes decisions about whether specific transactions are tax deductible or whether a particular transfer price can be defended as an arm's length transaction.

8.14.1 Tax Types 税收种类

A company operating in a foreign country meets a variety of taxes. Taxes are classified on the basis of whether they are applied directly to income, called "direct taxes", or to some other measurable performance characteristic of the firm, called "indirect taxes". Direct taxes, such as income tax, are easy to recognize and normally are disclosed on companies' financial statements. Other indirect taxes, such as consumption tax, are not so clearly recognized or as frequently disclosed.

1. Income Tax

Many governments rely on income taxes, both personal and corporate, for their primary revenue source. Corporate income taxes are widely used today. Corporate income tax rates vary over a relatively wide range, rising as high as 55% in Kuwait and falling as low as 16.5% in Hong Kong. Since the mid-1980s, the international trend has been to lower income tax rates. Fueling this trend is the recognition that reduced tax rates increase the global competitiveness of a country's business enterprises and create an attractive environment for international business.

2. Withholding Tax

The taxes that are imposed by governments on dividend, interest, and royalty payments to foreign investors are called "withholding taxes". The reason for the institution of withholding taxes is that governments recognize that most international investors will not file a tax return in each country in which they invest, and the government therefore wishes to ensure that it receives a minimum tax payment. For example, a Chinese purchaser of Italian bonds receives only 90% of the interest paid by the bonds because Italy has a 10% withholding tax on interest payments. Withholding taxes may hinder the international flow of long-term investment capital, so they are often modified by bilateral tax treaties and generally range between 0% and 25%.

3. Value-added Tax

The basic concept behind the value-added tax (VAT) is that a tax is applied at each stage of the production process for the value added by the firm to goods purchased from the outside, which have been subject to the VAT. The tax is charged by businesses on the value of their sales, but the tax burden eventually falls on the consumer because a company that pays VAT on its own expenses can reclaim that tax already paid. This tax applies to total sales less purchases from any intermediate sales unit. For example, a Norwegian merchant buys 500,000 krone of merchandise from a Norwegian wholesaler and then sells it for 600,000 krone, the value added is 100,000 krone and a tax is assessed just on this amount. Companies that pay the tax in their own costs can reclaim them later from the tax authorities. It is the consumers who ultimately bear the cost of the VAT.

VAT can be further divided into consumption VAT, income VAT and gross product VAT. With consumption VAT, the VAT credit on purchases includes both purchases of goods and capital assets. Under income-type VAT, the VAT credit on purchases includes both the purchases of goods and the amortization value of the capital assets for the year. It is labelled as income-type VAT because the economic base of VAT is net national income. Under gross product VAT, the VAT credit on purchases includes only the purchases of goods and does not include any credit for capital assets (in total or in part). It is called the gross product type because the economic base is the open national product, which is equivalent to consumption plus investment.

4. Border Tax

Border taxes refer to such taxes as customs or import duties. They generally aim at keeping domestic goods price competitive with imports. Accordingly, taxes assessed on imports typically parallel excise and other indirect taxes paid by domestic producers of similar goods.

5. Transfer Tax

Transfer tax is another indirect tax. This tax is imposed on the transfer of items between taxpayers and can have important effects on business decisions such as the structure of acquisitions.

6. Turnover Tax

Turnover taxes are indirect taxes which may be assessed at one or more stages in the production process, including sales. Therefore, they can be assessed when production is completed, when the products are wholesaled, when the products are retailed, or even at all of these stages. This tax obviously creates a premise for firms to integrate vertically in order to reduce payments, whether or not this integration is desirable from an economic or social point of view.

8.14.2 Foreign Tax Incentives 对外征税优惠

Countries eager to speed up their economic development should be keenly aware of the benefits of international business. Many countries offer tax incentives to attract foreign investment. Tax incentives are one of the most effective ways to attract foreign investment and to support exports.

Incentives may include tax-free cash grants applied toward the cost of fixed assets of new industrial undertakings or relief from paying taxes for certain time periods (tax holidays). Foreign investors are exempt from taxes for the holiday period if they fulfil certain conditions, such as investing in a specific industry or employing some quota of native workers. Tax incentives to encourage exports take many forms. Countries may exempt exported goods from paying taxes such as VAT, or give favourable tax treatment to income earned from exporting goods and services. Other forms of temporary tax relief include reduced income tax rates, tax deferrals, and reduction or elimination of various indirect taxes.

8.14.3   Foreign Tax Credit   外国纳税抵免

In an increasingly global economy, the chances are that if you invest in a large corporation or mutual fund, you may find that you have received income from a foreign source, and paid income taxes to a foreign government.

Under the worldwide principle of taxation, the foreign earnings of a domestic company are subject to full levies of both its host and home countries. The foreign branches and subsidiaries of MNEs are therefore subject to a variety of taxes, both direct and indirect, in the countries where they operate. The problem is that the income earned in the foreign country may be subject to income taxes twice: MNEs' income is taxed in the country where the income is earned and again, the income might be taxed in the parent country. This could result in double taxation.

A foreign tax credit is a means to avoid double taxation of foreign source income. A parent company's domicile (country of residence) can elect to treat foreign taxes paid as a credit against the parent's domestic tax liability or as a deduction from taxable income. Companies generally choose the credit, as it yields a one-for-one reduction of domestic taxes payable (limited to the amount of income taxes actually paid), whereas a deduction is only worth the product of the foreign tax expense and the domestic marginal tax rate.

Foreign tax credits may be calculated as a straightforward credit against income taxes paid on branch or subsidiary earnings and any taxes withheld at the source, such as dividends, interests, and royalties remitted to a domestic investor. The tax credit can also be estimated when the amount of foreign income tax paid is not evident (e.g. when a foreign subsidiary remits a fraction of its foreign source earnings to its domestic parent). Here, reported dividends on the parent company's tax return would be grossed up to include the amount of the tax (deemed paid) plus any applicable foreign withholding taxes. It is as if the domestic parent received a dividend including the tax due to the foreign government and then paid the tax.

For example, in the USA credit is given for foreign income taxes paid by foreign subsidiaries. When a USA subsidiary in China pays withholding taxes on dividends distributed to its US parent company, its USA parent company is allowed a tax credit equal to the withholding tax paid in China.

8.14.4   Tax Havens   避税天堂(低税国)

A tax haven is a phenomenon that has emerged from the philosophy that foreign source income should not be taxed at all or should be taxed only when a dividend is declared. Tax havens offer a variety of benefits, including low taxes or no taxes on certain classes of income. A tax haven may be defined as "a place where foreigners may receive income or own assets without paying higher rates of taxes upon them". In fact, tax havens can be classified in various categories:

(1) Traditional tax havens with virtually no taxes at all;

(2) Tax havens which impose a relatively low rate;

（3）Tax havens which tax income from domestic sources but exempt all income from foreign sources;

（4）Tax havens which allow special privileges.

To take advantage of a tax haven, a company would ordinarily set up a subsidiary in the tax haven country through which different forms of income would pass. The aim is to shift income from high tax to tax haven countries. This is normally accomplished by using the tax haven subsidiary as an intermediary. Actually many countries are naturally concerned about minimizing the opportunities for using tax havens where they are likely to be disadvantaged.

8.14.5　Tax Treaties　税约

To create a favourable climate to foreign trade and foreign investment, and to avoid or relieve double taxation of profits, countries sign bilateral or multilateral agreements known as tax treaties. These treaties basically define, in general, the way joint income should be allocated between national taxing jurisdictions and are intended, in particular, to limit taxation by the source country.

The most important provision of these treaties focuses on the term "permanent establishment". The individual bilateral jurisdiction as specified through tax treaties is particularly important for firms that are primarily exporting to another country rather than doing business there through a "permanent establishment". The latter would be the case for manufacturing operations. A firm that only exports would not want any of its other worldwide income taxed by the importing country.

Besides the concept of permanent establishment, most treaties have provisions limiting the amount of withholding tax on various items, such as interests, dividends, and royalties.

In the area of double taxation, treaties can specify that certain classes of income would not be subject to tax, can reduce the rate on income and/or withholding taxes, and can specifically deal with the issue of tax credit.

As mentioned previously, tax treaties typically result in reduced withholding tax rates between the two signatory countries, the negotiation of the treaty itself serving as a forum for opening and expanding business relationships between the two countries. This practice is important both to MNEs operating through foreign subsidiaries, earning active income, and to individual portfolio investors who are simply receiving passive income in the form of dividends, interests, or royalties.

Summary of This Chapter
本章概要

1. 会计是公司、企业的交流工具。国际会计是跨国公司向出资者和政府传达其财务状况的手段。通过会计可以评价公司的业绩，反映公司的营运状况。会计是由企业经营所处的环境形成的。每个国家有自己的会计体制。影响一个国家会计制度的因素主要有：（1）企业与投资者之间的关系；(2)与外国的政治、经济联系；(3)通货膨胀状况；(4)一个国际的经济发展水平；(5)一个国家的文化氛围。

2. 会计是"企业的语言"，它是以损益表、资产负债表、预算、投资分析和税务分析来表述的。国际会计比国内会计更复杂，首先是语言的障碍，然后是货币的差异，这给做账带来了难度。国与国之间的会计制度差异也给国际会计带来问题。不同的国家有不同的政治体制，不同的政治体制会有不同的会计制度。每个国家的会计体制的发展都顺应了对会计信息的需求。

3. 正是由于各个国家的会计制度有所不同，国际社会一直努力推行公认的会计规范来协调各国的会计准则。许多国家使用不同的销货计价方法，不同的资产收益评估法，不同的计算利润法。国际会计准则委员会(IASC)倡导国际会计的统一标准。国际会计准则委员会是在英国、美国和加拿大的推动下于1973年成立的。1977年成立了国际会计师联合会。国际会计准则委员会及其制定的会计准则被越来越多的国家所接受。迄今，国际会计准则委员会逐渐被认为在制定全球公认的会计准则方面有一定权威性。

4. 外汇换算(Translation)：跨国公司的子公司一般以东道国的货币来做会计账目。当跨国公司编制合并账户时，它必须把所有的财务报表转换成其母国的货币。一般说来，公司可以使用现行汇率法和时限法这两种主要的方法，来确定应该使用什么汇率来换算财务报表中的货币。(1)现行汇率法：使用编制资产负债表时的汇率，把国外子公司的财务报表换算成跨国公司母国的货币；(2)时限法：采用购入资产时的汇率将外汇计价的资产换算成母国的货币。

5. 中国的会计制度以前一直沿用苏联的会计体制。按照这种体制，很少涉及利润。中国改革开放以来，会计制度不断地进行改革以适应国家对外经济贸易的需要。中国目前需要真正合格的会计师、审计师，尤其是需要有市场经验和国际会计工作经历的人。不过，中国政府在财务会计方面的改革正在加大步伐，以适应加入世界贸易组织后的要求，在会计制度方面尽快与国际接轨。

6. 审计(Audit)是由独立的、有资格的人员(审计师)对某一组织的年度账户进行的正式审查和核实，以便确保账户准确地反映其真实的财务状况，没有舞弊行为，没有假账。审计师完成了审计后，应该提交一份审计报告。一般说来，股份有限公司在每年的股东大会上需任命一名审计师，其任期到下次股东大会为止。审计报告(Auditor's Report)是由某组织正式任命的、稽查账户的审计师提交的报告。该报告通常写在或附在资产负债表上。根据有关法律，该报告必须说明：他是否已获得所有必需的信息和说明，会计账簿是否记录正确，资产负债表和损益账户是否与会计账簿相一致，他是否认为损益账户正确、清晰地反映了财务年度末的损益情况，资产负债表是否正确、清晰地反映了财务年度末的状况，账目总体上是否符合公司法的规定。

7. 财务审计是一个系统过程，首先由客户提出申请，然后审计师开始做准备工作，之后写出审计报告。一般说来，审计过程包括以下程序：(1)接受客户申请(前期准备工作)，其程序通常为：评估客户的背景及审计原因，与前任审计师联系获取有关信息，确定是否需要与其他从业者联系，准备客户建议书，挑选员工进行审计；(2)计划设计审计方法：获取公司和行业背景信息，调查法律信息，进行初步分析，了解该公司内部操作营运系统，根据所获得信息评估风险并确定重点信息，准备审计计划；(3)检验证据(查账)：测试、检查公司控制系统及交易账务检查,对信息分析研究,测试检查账目细节,获得被审计单位代表证明函以证明其企业财务信息真实无误,最后收集及搜取未录账债务;(4)完成审计报告:进行评估与判断,进行全面核实,确定程序以辩明事后事宜,检查财务报表及其他财务信息,开始总结性程序,准备给合作伙伴的注意事项,向董事会汇报,准备审计报告。

8. 审计分内部审计(Internal Auditing)和外部审计(External Auditing),它们是两个不同的审计,但是彼此又有关联。这两种审计的目的相同,即确定财务信息的可靠性,换言之,就是对公司、企业账务的真实性进行检测以辨明其真伪。内部审计是内部控制系统的不可分割的一部分。外部审计由公共会计师执行。外部审计的基本目的是:根据审计标准来确定,被审计的公司企业的财务报表是否正确并与事实是否相符。外部审计师的结论对母公司和投资者及有关方面十分重要。必须指出,由于每个国家的会计标准和审计标准不同,外部审计的操作程序会有所不同。

9. 审计报告一般包括以下内容:(1)标题;(2)地址;(3)开篇语;(4)审计范围;(5)审计结论;(6)撰写日期;(7)审计师地址;(8)审计师签字。

10. 税务计划对企业至关重要,因为税务计划很大程度上影响利润和现金流量,国际公司更是如此。税务因素对以下几个方面的决策有很大影响:(1)投资方向;(2)营运方式,如:是选择进出口还是海外投资或进行许可证贸易;(3)新企业的形式,如:是分支机构还是子公司等;(4)确定转换价格方法。

11. 避税天堂(Tax Haven):避税天堂也被称为低税国、避税地,指的是对外国企业提供低税率和其他特殊优惠待遇以吸引外资的国家或地区。

12. 非课税期(Tax Holiday):也被称为免税期。在某些国家里,免税期是为期数年的一段规定的时期。在此期间,一个建立新的企业单位或扩大其现有生产单位以增加出口的生产者,享有对其部分或全部利润免征税收的好处。这种免税是为了吸引新工业或鼓励现有工业出口更多商品。

13. 税收抵免(Tax Credit):每个国家都有权对在其境内经营的企业纳税。跨国公司这样就面临被双层纳税:首先,它需向东道国纳税,然后在母国又被要求纳税。有的国家,如美国,对这种情况采取措施,实行纳税积分制。美国的跨国公司就其在国外所纳的税获得积分,根据该积分,对其在美国国内的纳税实行优惠,抵免一定的税款。

14. 增值税(Value-added Tax):增值税是一种间接税,是普通销售税的一种形式,是按照一件物品或商品的销售价的某一百分比课税的。它是以企业的增值额为征税依据的税种。在产销的每一个阶段,应纳税人员必须向政府上报产出税,但是允许抵消投入税,即他的供应商向他索取的税额。

▶ New Words and Expressions

abide by 遵守;信守
acceleration n. 加速;促进
accommodate v. 调整;对……给予考虑;
  提供

adhere v. 遵守;坚持
advocate v. & n. 拥护;主张;(法国、苏格兰
  等地的)律师
alleviate v. 减轻;缓和

anthropologist *n.* 人类学者

appraisal *n.* 估价;估计;评价

arm's length 近处

attest *v.* 证实;证明;表明

audit *n. & v.* 审计;查账

boost *v. & n.* 提高;增强;增加;广告;宣传

bureaux *n.* bureau 局(复数)

carry-forward *n.* (下年度应税损益的)冲转(额)

codify *v.* 把法律编集成典;编纂

collateral *a. & n.* 抵押担保的;附属的;抵押担保品

compatibility *n.* 融洽;和睦;适合

consolidate *v.* 巩固;加强;(集装箱运输中)把(零担货物)拼装成箱;合并

constituency *n.* (某一机构、企业等的)相关人员,赞助人员

converge *v.* (为共同利益或目的而)汇合

couple *v.* 连接;结合;联想

de-harmonization *n.* 反对趋同化

dichotomy *n.* 对分;二分(法)

disclosure *n.* 公开

distortion *n.* 歪曲;曲解

diverge *v.* (意见等的)分歧

domicile *n. & v.* 住处;[法律]原籍;户籍;期票支付场所;指定(期票)在某地支付

empirical *a.* 以经验为依据的

endeavor *v. & n.* 努力;尝试;事业;活动

enlighten *v.* 启发;开导

ethics *n.* 人种学

excise *v. & n.* 向(某人)强征货物税;(对某货物)课以货物税;国内消费税;货物税

expropriation *n.* 没收;征用;征购

fees-for-tax *n.* 费转税

flat *a. & ad.* (市场的)萧条的;(价格等的)无涨落的,一律的;完全地

format *n.* 格式;安排;计划

foster *v.* 培养;促进

fuel *v. & n.* 支持;刺激;燃料

futile *a.* 无效的,无益的;没有出息的

GAAP (Generally Accepted Accounting Principles) 普遍接受会计原则

GPP (General Purchasing Power) 普遍购买力

governance *n.* 统治;管理

gross up 使……增长至付税前最高值

guilder *n.* (荷兰货币)盾

harmonization *n.* 协调;统一(在会计业务中意思与 standardization 类似)

hurdle *n. & v.* 障碍;克服障碍

IAASB (The International Auditing and Assurance Standard Board) 国际审计与保险标准委员会

IAS (The International Accounting Standards) 国际会计标准

IASB (The International Accounting Standard Board) 国际会计标准委员会(前身为 IASC, The International Accounting Standard Committee)

IFAC (The International Federation of Accounts) 国际会计委员会

indifferent *a.* 不关心的;中庸的

interpose *v.* 使干预;提出;行使权力等

jeopardize *v.* 危害

jurisdiction *n.* 司法;司法权;管辖权

loophole *n.* (条文等的)漏洞

magnitude *n.* 巨大;庞大;重大

mandate *n. & v.* (上级法院给下级法院的)指令,执行令;授权于;指令

material *a.* 重要的;实质性的

modify *v.* 缓和;减轻;更改;修改

neutrality *n.* 中立(地位)

OECD (The Organization for Economic Cooperation and Development) 经济合作与发展组织

one-size-fits-all *a.* 全面适合的

outreach *v. & n. & a.* 超出……的范围;服务(或活动等)范围的扩大;扩大范围的

out-salary income 薪水之外的收入

parallel *v.* & *a.* 使平行;比得上;与……相当;平行的;相对应的

preferential tax regime 优惠税制

proliferation *n.* 增加;激增

promulgate *v.* 颁布

pronouncement *n.* 声明;公告

recharacterize *v.* 再定格

royalty *n.* (专利权)使用费;特许使用费;版税

skip *v.* 跳过;略过

speak out 读懂;研究出

stand up to 经得起……;勇敢面对

succumb *v.* 屈服;屈从

tax haven 避税天堂(区域)

tax holiday 免税期

threshold *n.* 门槛;入门;开端

translation *n.* (货币的)折算,转换

transparency *n.* 透明(度)

unremitting *a.* 不松懈的;持续的

unsustainable *a.* 无法支撑/维持的

withholding tax 预扣税

write-off *n.* 注销;冲销

▶ Discussion Questions

1. What does "harmonization" mean in international accounting?

2. What are the reasons for the foreign currency translation?

3. How many phases does auditing normally involve?

4. Why does a host country offer tax incentives to foreign investors? Please give some examples of incentives.

Chapter 9 Multinational Enterprises 跨国企业

Objectives
学习目标

To understand the reasons why enterprises tend to become multinational.

理解公司成为跨国企业的原因。

To have knowledge about the benefits and problems of multinational enterprises.

了解跨国企业的益处和问题。

To get to know the situations and functions of multinational enterprises in the developing countries.

熟悉发展中国家的跨国企业的作用及现状。

To have some knowledge about China's multinational enterprises.

初步了解中国跨国企业的情况。

9.1 The Nature of Multinational Enterprises（MNEs） 跨国企业的性质

Multinational enterprises now play an important part in the economies of countries such as China and in international economic relations. Through international direct investment, such enterprises can bring substantial benefits to home and host countries by contributing to the efficient utilisation of capital, technology and human resources between countries and can thus fulfil an important role in the promotion of economic and social welfare.

On the other hand, the advances made by multinational enterprises in organizing their operations beyond the national framework may lead to abuse of concentrations of economic power and to conflicts with national policy objectives. In addition, the complexity of these multinational enterprises and the difficulty of clearly perceiving their diverse structures, operations and policies sometimes give rise to concern.

Multinational companies are becoming stronger. Generally, these international corporations are immune from the democratic controls which often limit the actions of national governments. The UN has noted that more than half of world trade is produced by multinational companies and more than one third of world trade is composed of goods transferred within different branches of the same multinational corporations. Two thirds of all international transactions in goods and services combined are dependent on multinational company operations.

The increasingly free movement of capital allows corporations to transfer production to wherever costs are low with no regard to national boundaries. Often production is outsourced or subcontracted to ever smaller units of production. Some of the largest and most powerful corporations have very few direct employees but they are able to maintain the required quantity and quality of production by franchise or subcontract arrangements around the world. It is at this level that the worst employment practices are found.

A multinational enterprise, which is sometimes known as a transnational enterprise, is an enterprise that engages in foreign direct investment (FDI) and owns or controls value-adding activities in more than one country. In other words, a multinational enterprise can be defined as an enterprise that controls and manages production establishments (plants) located in at least two countries. It is just one subspecies of multiplant firm. "Enterprise" is used here instead of "company" for the reason that attention is directed to coordination in the hierarchy of business decisions; a company, itself multinational, may be the controlled subsidiary of another firm.

The multinational enterprise is the principle agent for the international transfer of economic resources (technology, management skills, marketing know-how and so on). A number of alternative terminologies exist, such as the transnational corporation (TNC) and the multinational corporation (MNC). But the term "multinational enterprise" is now most frequently used.

There are a number of criteria for assessing the degree of an enterprise's transnationality.

(1) The number and size of foreign subsidiaries or associate companies it owns or controls.

(2) The number of countries where it engages in value-adding activities such as mines, plantations, factories, selling branches, banks, offices and hotels.

(3) The proportion of its global assets, revenue, income or employment accounted for by its foreign affiliates.

(4) The degree to which its management or stock ownership is internationalized.

(5) The extent to which its higher value activities, for example, research and development, are internationalized.

(6) The extent and pattern of the systemic advantages arising from its governance of, and influence over, a network of economic activities in different countries.

MNEs have come to account for a large percentage of the world's total output. Basically, they are large in size. Practically, all the 500 of the biggest enterprises in the world show great business interests in the form of operating units located abroad. MNEs normally undertake nearly every type of international business practice.

There are more than 60,000 MNEs worldwide. The largest 500 account for 80% of all the foreign direct investment. Of the 500 MNEs, 430 are from the Triad, of which 185 from the USA,

141 from the EU and 104 from Japan. So it can be said that the Triad is the basic unit of analysis for MNE strategy.

Firms that have developed a multinational structure tend to be engaged in certain kinds of business activities. It is found out that more MNEs are engaged in manufacturing than in mining, agriculture or banking. Besides, MNEs have rapidly been acquiring dominant positions in the service industries. They have proved especially prominent in financial services, hotels, fast food, accounting, engineering and large-scale construction, and management consulting. Attention should be paid to the fact that firms in certain developing countries have been particularly successful in establishing overseas activities that provide engineering and construction service.

Managers of MNEs must realize that operating in foreign countries is quite different from operating at home. They need to be aware of and sensitive to:

(1) differences between countries in culture, taste, political system, economic system, legal system and level of development. Despite the hype about the global village and the globalization of markets and production, many differences between countries are profound and enduring.

(2) international transactions, by their nature, involve converting funds into different currencies. International companies need to adopt appropriate financial strategies to minimize their exposure to exchange rate risk.

(3) the role of host country and supra-national governments and institutions (e.g. the World Trade Organisation, WTO) that can, and often do, intervene to affect and regulate cross-border trade and investment.

(4) greater complexity in the business decision making process. Besides issues arising from differences in countries, managers need to decide on which foreign market to enter (or to avoid) in order to minimize cost and maximize value added. Managers must also choose the appropriate entry mode to enter the selected market successfully.

9.2 Characteristics of an MNE 跨国企业的特点

Generally speaking, an MNE has the following three characteristics.

The first characteristic of an MNE is that its affiliates must be responsive to a number of important environment forces, including competitors, customers, suppliers, financial institutions and the government.

The second one is that it draws on a common pool of resources, including assets, trademarks, information, patents, information and systems, money and credit and human resources. The affiliates are all part of the same company, so they have access to assets that are often not available to outsiders. In other words, all affiliates share the same sources.

The third one is that it links together the affiliates and business partners with a common strategic vision. Simply put, all of the firms with whom the MNE works fit into the company's overall plan of what it wants to do and how it intends to go about implementing this strategy. In other words, the affiliates respond to a common strategy, aiming at increasing the profit and reducing the risk of the enterprise as a whole.

9.3 The Reasons for Companies' Becoming Multinational Enterprises 公司转型为跨国企业之原因

Today, more and more companies want to enlarge their markets abroad so that they can take up more market shares and can become more competitive. As the world economy is tending to become internationalized and globalized, companies have stronger motivations to become multinational enterprises. The reasons are listed as follows:

(1) To diversify themselves in order to avoid risks and uncertainties of the domestic business cycle. After establishing overseas operations, they can often reduce the negative effects of domestic economic fluctuations.

(2) To develop the growing world market for goods and services, which is part of the process of growth in an integrated world market (globalization) to satisfy a demand for a unique product or service from a foreign market, and to increase global market share.

(3) To become stronger in foreign competition, to maintain their home market share, to generate greater profits by reducing costs or acquiring resources, and to reduce risks by diversifying sources of sales and inputs.

(4) To reduce costs. Setting up operations closer to the foreign customer can eliminate transportation expenses and avoid expenses involved in the middlemen's services. In addition, being closer to the customer, they can meet the customer's needs better and take advantage of the local resources.

(5) To overcome protective devices such as tariff and non-tariff barriers by serving a foreign market from within. The EU is a good example. Companies of the EU member nations are not subject to tariffs on goods transported from one EU country to another.

(6) To take advantage of technological expertise by producing goods directly rather than allowing others to do it under a license, and to take advantage of tax benefits.

(7) To yield greater economies of scale, and to satisfy managerial targets, ambitions and commitment.

Besides, there are some other reasons:

(1) Competitive pressures in the domestic market;

(2) Declining domestic sales;

(3) Increasing costs at home;

(4) A saturated domestic market;

(5) Unused managerial or production capacity at home;

(6) Over production at home (to sell excess stock);

(7) To prolong the lifecycle of products aging at home.

9.4   Using the OECD Guidelines for Multinational Enterprises 将经济合作与发展组织的准则应用于跨国企业

The Organization for Economic Cooperation and Development (OECD), set up in 1961, has a stated aim of building strong economies in its member countries, improving efficiency and market systems, expanding free trade and contributing to development in industrialized and developing countries. In 1976 the OECD adopted a set of voluntary guidelines for companies. These guidelines are basically a set of recommendations on standards for responsible corporate behavior. They have been reviewed periodically (most recently in 2000) and cover a broad range of issues (e. g. employment and industrial relations, the environment, bribery, taxation, consumer interests). The governments of the 30 OECD member countries are supposed to encourage companies in their countries to observe this code of conduct, officially known as the "OECD Guidelines for Multinational Enterprises", wherever they operate.

Each member country is supposed to set up a "national contact point" (a government official, a government office, a body that includes representatives of several government agencies or even a body that includes representatives of employee organizations, the business community and other interested parties) to make the Guidelines more effective. Any "interested party" can file a complaint regarding alleged violations of the OECD Guidelines with the national contact points. Who should file the complaint and with which contact point depend on the specific circumstances of the case.

9.5   The Impact of Multinational Enterprises   跨国企业的影响

A multinational enterprise is a firm that has productive capacity in a number of countries. The profit and income flows that they generate are part of the foreign capital flows moving between countries.

As countries adopt more open outward-oriented approaches to economic growth and development, the role of multinational enterprises or transnational corporations become more important. As local markets throughout the world are being deregulated and liberalized, foreign firms are looking to locate part of the production process in other countries where there are cost advantages. These might be cheaper sources of labour, raw materials and components or preferential government regulations. Although the least developed countries (LDCs) may present high levels of risk, they also present the potential for higher levels of profit. Many LDCs with growing economies and increasing incomes may provide future growth markets.

Many economists are concerned with the role of the MNEs in low income countries and identify a number of problems associated with foreign direct investment. Equally, other economists and politicians argue that MNEs' activities can drive growth and development. The true answer is that probably the arguments put by both sides are applicable in certain countries with certain MNEs at certain times.

9.5.1　The Benefits of MNEs　跨国企业的益处

There exist some benefits of MNEs. Let us consider the arguments from both sides. Firstly, from those who maintain the importance of foreign direct investment as part of the engine necessary for growth.

(1) An MNE investing in an area may result in a significant injection into the local economy. This may provide jobs directly or through the growth of local ancillary businesses such as banks and insurance. It might initiate a multiplier process generating more income as newly employed workers spend their wages on consumption.

(2) MNEs may provide training and education for employees thus creating a higher skilled labour force. These skills may be transferred to other areas of the host country. Often management and entrepreneurial skills learned from MNEs are an important source of human capital.

(3) MNEs will contribute tax revenue to the government and other revenues if they purchase existing national assets.

9.5.2　The Problems of MNEs　跨国企业引起的问题

There are some problems concerning MNEs.

(1) MNEs may employ largely expatriate managers ensuring that incomes generated are maintained within a relatively small group of people. The attraction for the MNE may be the large supply of cheap manual labour. This may contribute to a widening of the income distribution. It will also not lead to the transfer of management skills.

(2) MNEs investment in LDCs often involves the use of capital-intensive production methods. Given that many LDCs are often endowed with potentially large low wage labour forces and have high level of unemployment, this might be considered inappropriate technology. More labour-intensive production methods might be a more appropriate option for alleviating poverty and aiding development. Any resulting growth might be considered anti-developmental.

(3) MNEs engage in transfer pricing where they shift production between countries so as to benefit from lower tax arrangements in certain countries. By doing this, they can minimize their tax burden and the tax revenue of national governments.

(4) As many MNEs are very large and have considerable power, they can exert influence on governments to gain preferential tax concessions, subsidies and grants.

Outward-oriented economists maintain that the cycles of poverty will not be broken from within the domestic economy. The level of investment needed to raise productivity and income is not possible to achieve. Thus foreign direct investment through the MNE activity is essential.

By investing in areas and utilizing the factors of production where the LDCs have an absolute and comparative advantage, MNEs will lead to a more efficient allocation of the worlds' resources. However, if this leads to overspecialization and overdependence in certain sectors of the economy then the host country will be vulnerable especially if the MNE decides for commercial reasons to leave the country in the future.

9.6 Multinational Enterprises and Trade Theory   跨国企业与贸易理论

International trade theory and the theory of multinational enterprise have historically been developed and researched quite separately. Trade theory has taken a general equilibrium path based on the twin assumptions of constant returns to scale and perfect competition. Multinational firms are excluded from such a framework because there is no support for their existence in equilibrium. In current trade theory models, a firm is generally synonymous with a plant or production facility, or an independent organization that manufactures one product in one location. Hence, multi-plant and multi-product considerations are generally excluded from the analyses.

Industries characterized by scale economies and imperfect competition are often dominated by multinational firms. Substantial foreign ownership of domestic production facilities radically alters policy implications for the industry and businesses in question. Trade theory cannot afford to ignore multinationals given their tremendous importance in international economic activity. Firms and industries that are dominated by multinationals have the following characteristics:

(1) Multinationals are associated with high ratios of research and development budgets relative to sales.

(2) Multinationals employ large numbers of scientific, technical, and other white-collar workers.

(3) Multinationals have high-value intangible assets.

(4) Multinationals are associated with new and/or technically complex products.

(5) Multinationals are associated with product-differentiation variables, like high advertising to sales ratios.

(6) A minimum level of firm size seems to be important for a firm to be a multinational.

(7) Multinationals tend to be older, more established firms.

These characteristics of multinational firms coincide with the following typical characteristics of host countries.

(1) High-income and developed countries are not only major sources of direct investment, but also major recipients.

(2) High volumes of direct investment are associated with similarities among countries in terms of relative factor endowments and per capita incomes.

(3) High volume of outward direct investment is positively related to a country's endowment of skilled labor and insignificantly related to physical capital endowments.

(4) There is little supporting evidence that direct investment is motivated primarily to avoid trade barriers.

（5）Direct investment stocks among high-income countries have grown significantly faster than trade flows over the last two decades.

（6）There is mixed evidence that tax avoidance and/or risk diversification are important motives for direct investment.

（7）Infrastructure, skill levels, minimum threshold level of per capita income are important determinants of direct investment.

（8）Agglomeration effects are important in direct investment.

It has been conclusively observed that direct investment is concentrated among the high-income countries where skilled labor is an important determinant of outward direct investment. Additionally, taxes and trade barriers do not seem to be of first importance, but good infrastructure and agglomeration economies are significant factors.

The purpose here is to draw the connection between the host country characteristics and the firm characteristics listed above. So, it must be recognized that three conditions are necessary for a firm to consider foreign direct investment.

The first condition is ownership. Ownership refers to a firm's possession of a patented product or production process that would confer valuable market power abroad, enough to outweigh the cost and pitfalls of doing business abroad. The second one is location advantage. This simply refers to the potential profitability of producing a product in a foreign country rather than producing it domestically and exporting it. The third one is called the internalization advantage where a firm has an interest in maintaining control of a product, otherwise it would license a foreign firm to produce the product. This behavior indicates that the process is exploited internally within the firm rather than at arm's length through markets affording the firm more control of the overall process of production.

Multinationals reflect high ratios of intangible firm assets to their total market value. These knowledge-based, firm specific assets refer to human capital of the employees, patents, and other exclusive knowledge. These types of knowledge-based assets are more likely to give rise to direct foreign investment than physical-capital assets for two reasons. Primarily, knowledge-based assets can be transferred easily back and forth at low cost, i.e., at lower cost than capital assets. Secondly, knowledge has such a joint-input characteristic that it can be supplied to additional production facilities at very low cost. Essentially, this makes multinational firms exporters of ideas rather than goods. Of course, these ideas do take various forms such as management practices, engineering techniques, marketing plans, etc.

9.7 The Role and Place of Multinational Enterprises in Export Processing Zones（EPZs） 跨国企业在出口加工区的作用与地位

Most EPZs were originally set up to promote export and employment and little attention was given at the time to the social problems posed by EPZs, to the role played by MNEs or to the backward linkages of EPZs with the local economy.

The economic and social importance of EPZs varies considerably from country to country. The critical yardstick in this respect is the share of total manufacturing employment accounted for by EPZ industries. The greater the share of EPZ employment, the more sensitive the host country will tend to be to the role played by MNEs and the social conditions in EPZs.

Contrary to a widely held belief, MNEs are not necessarily the largest or the only investors in EPZs. Fully-owned foreign subsidiaries represent in fact a minority of the enterprises in EPZs, and joint ventures a small majority. The emergence of investors from Third World countries is one of the major characteristics of EPZs. The export performance of EPZ industries varies considerably from country to country. The yardstick of export performance is not total exports, but net exports (i.e. total exports minus imports).

(1) The employment effects

In the leading EPZ countries and areas, the zones have accounted for a very significant share of new manufacturing employment. Since 1970, over 60 per cent of all new manufacturing jobs in Malaysia and Singapore have been created in EPZs. For the Dominican Republic, the corresponding figure is above 30 per cent, and for Mexico around 20 per cent. In Mauritius, the near totality of new manufacturing jobs is attributable to EPZ industries.

The two most important EPZ industries are electronics, and textiles and garments. In the industrialized countries, these industries employ a very high proportion of women, and the same is true in EPZ industries.

Between 1975 and 1986, some 200,000 new jobs have been created in the textile and garments industries of EPZs in developing countries, which is considerably less than the approximately 400,000 jobs lost in these industries in the OECD countries. Of these 200,000 new jobs, around 130,000 have been created by MNEs, and could represent jobs relocated from the industrialized countries.

EPZs also generate jobs indirectly through the local expenditure of the wages and salaries paid to EPZ workers. Very tentative estimates indicate that these indirect employment effects are slightly higher than the direct employment effects.

(2) Labour conditions and industrial relations

Evaluating the social performance of enterprises in EPZs is particularly difficult, because of the lack of data, the absence of mutually acceptable points of comparison and the sensitive nature of such issues as union rights, length of working time or quality of labour relations.

Workers in EPZs usually work much longer than workers in the highly industrialized countries, but the length of their working week is generally rather similar to that found in other industries. In the Republic of Korea, however, the working week is much longer for everyone, including EPZ workers, than in all other countries. Only in the Philippines would it appear that EPZ workers have a much longer working week than in other industries.

The evidence on this point is, however, very sketchy and there is a clear need for much better internationally comparable data on working hours in EPZs.

A firm or a country which condones the employment of women on the night shift could enjoy a production cost advantage of up to 30 per cent. A firm's decision to invest in an EPZ is not determined solely by the cost of labour, but also by such factors as the overall quality of the labour force and the political stability of the country and the region in which the EPZ is located.

The data on wage levels in EPZ are rather sketchy and unreliable, but the evidence points to the fact that in many countries, these wages are extraordinarily low by international standards. Wage levels reflect to a large extent the overall level of the development of a country, but when industries trade most of their output on the world market, wage levels become an extremely important element in the competitiveness of EPZ host countries relative to one another.

Because they combine the low wages of the host country with the organizational and technological advantages of the MNE, EPZ industries tend to be extremely competitive internationally, and the central issue is whether this competitiveness is not further enhanced by the non-compliance with certain basic rules and principles about the length of working time, safety, health and night work for women.

The non-ratification by certain countries with important EPZ industries of a number of international labour conventions could be an indication that their EPZ enterprises are in fact enjoying an unfair competitive advantage over the countries and enterprises that comply with these international standards.

It is a generally accepted view that unionization rates in EPZ industries are very low. Evidence assembled by one major international trade union suggests that it is far from true. Unionization rates are very high in some countries, and very low in others, but generally much higher than conventionally assumed.

From the little available evidence, it does not appear that union activities are significantly more difficult in EPZ industries than in other industries. In most countries, the rules and regulations concerning union activities are the same for EPZs as for any other industry.

Only in the Philippines is there an express prohibition against strikes in EPZs. In other countries, restrictions on the right to strike in EPZs are essentially a reflection of more general restrictions on this right throughout the industrial sector.

(3) The process of technology transfer

Some EPZs have been much more successful than others. In most cases, success cannot be attributed to a single cause (wage levels, political stability of host country, quality of workforce, etc.).

One of the keys to success for an EPZ is its exclusive preoccupation with exports and employment promotion; a simultaneous focus on regional development, social policy or the promotion of technological development is likely to detract from its main task and hamper its development.

As a physical, economic and even social enclave in the host country, the EPZ is perhaps the most achieved mechanism for preventing the development of technological linkages between the foreign firms in the EPZ and the enterprises in the host country. This is first of all because of the

EPZs export orientation: since EPZ firms are legally bound to export all their output (with a few minor exceptions), they do not compete with local enterprises, and therefore cannot have the technologically stimulating effects usually associated with MNE subsidiaries.

Since EPZ firms tend to import all their inputs—and are in fact actively encouraged to do so by the EPZs regulatory system—they do not have the motivation to build up relations with local suppliers of raw materials, machinery, components or semi-finished goods.

These backward linkages with local suppliers are known to be a potentially very important channel of technology transfer from foreign to domestic firms, as well as a major instrument for building up and developing the technological competence of domestic enterprises.

A further element which discourages the development of linkages between EPZ firms and domestic enterprises is the typical product range of EPZ industries. In the great majority of cases, this product range, and more generally the EPZ's industrial composition, has nothing to do with the host country's market requirements, its industrial and technological traditions or its pre-existing technological competence.

Very substantial amounts of technology are transferred internationally from parent companies to their subsidiaries located in EPZs. The technology thus transferred is essentially production technology of a fairly simple nature. EPZ firms also invest in the training of production workers. This training, however, is usually rather short (a few days to a few weeks at the most). Because of the fairly short-term nature of employment in EPZ industries, firms do not have an incentive to make substantial investments in training and professional development.

A very large number of firms in EPZs are joint ventures between MNEs and domestically owned enterprises. Within these joint ventures, a lot of technology is transferred from one partner to the other, and notably from the MNE to the domestically owned firm.

There are good reasons to believe that quite a lot of know-how and information are transferred informally between unrelated firms in an EPZ. This transfer is facilitated by the geographical proximity of EPZ enterprises. As time goes by, backward linkages between EPZ enterprises and local industries tend to develop, but this is usually the result of individual initiatives of enterprises rather than the result of government policies to this effect.

In most countries, EPZs are under the authority of a public or semi-public EPZ authority which has a great degree of administrative and political autonomy, and whose central priority is to attract new firms in order to provide new employment and amortize the heavy development costs of the EPZ. This administrative autonomy, coupled with the EPZ authority's preoccupation with employment and with load factors in the EPZ, probably makes the typical EPZ authority a rather inadequate institution for fostering the development of technological linkages between EPZ enterprises and the host country.

(4) The costs and benefits of Export Processing Zones

The most successful EPZs have generated large amounts of new employment. Data show that the countries where EPZs account for the largest percentage of manufacturing employment have increased their share in world manufacturing value added twice as rapidly as the countries where EPZs account for a small share of manufacturing employment.

EPZs have probably played a significant role through their demonstration effects on other local industries and the industrial labour force, and these demonstration effects could well represent the most important macro-economic contribution to the host country's economy.

All countries offer a wide range of special subsidies, incentives and advantages to prospective investors in EPZs, in addition to the usual customs advantages and infrastructural facilities of EPZs. These special subsidies and advantages are very difficult to compare on an international basis, and do not appear to play a major part in the investment decision of foreign firms. For the firm which eventually settles in the EPZ, they represent a welcome bonus, but their total cost to the host country can be quite considerable.

Economic success depends also on keeping total infrastructural investment costs within reasonable limits. An EPZ can be evaluated on the basis of total cost per job. This cost includes both the infrastructural investments in the EPZ itself and the investments made by the EPZ enterprises. This cost per job should bear some relationship with the total per capita income and the average wages paid to EPZ workers.

Wage levels are known to be one of the centrally important factors in the world-wide competition between EPZ sites. Another important but largely neglected factor is the rental cost of factory space, which indirectly reflects total investment costs in the EPZ.

EPZ sites have in effect become internationally traded goods. This, however, is not reflected in the economic calculations made in the feasibility studies of new EPZs. These calculations are based essentially on the costs and benefits to the host country, and not on the relative international price of the facilities offered by a new EPZ. Because of this, it would appear that quite a few EPZs are set up without giving enough attention to this problem of international competitiveness, and ultimately, cannot achieve the minimum occupancy rates to justify such investments.

(5) The future of Export Processing Zones

An innovation never develops quite along the lines originally envisaged by its originators and in this respect the EPZ is no different from any other type of innovation. All EPZs tend to go through the same type of life cycle. In the first few years, one major industry rapidly comes to be the dominant industry and its relative importance declines rather slowly as the years go by.

One can measure the performance of EPZs in terms of employment creation, export promotion or technology transfer, but there is no way of assessing what might have happened in the absence of an EPZ, or whether a country might have developed better or more rapidly without such an EPZ. In effect, there is no way of verifying the alternative situation hypothesis. One should nevertheless ask whether the special benefits accorded to foreign firms investing in an EPZ might not have had equally positive effects on domestic enterprises, if the latter had benefited from these same benefits and incentives. The question here is one of equity and economic democracy.

9.8   MNEs in Developing Countries   发展中国家的跨国企业

Foreign subsidiaries' operations in the least developed countries (LDCs) tend to fall sharply into three categories. First of all, the exporters of natural resources and resource-based products need no explanation: they go where the resources are, if conditions in the sector call for vertical integration. The second class is made up of exporters of manufactured goods or components. The third class comprises producers largely engaged in servicing the LDC's domestic market. An important point of fact is the sharpness of the distinction between the second and the third groups. The theory of MNEs' locational choices indicates that, given scale economies and the very small domestic markets of most LDCs, a foreign subsidiary will locate there either to serve the market or to export extensively.

The forces explaining MNEs' presence in the domestic markets of LDCs are almost the same as those explaining their presence in industrial countries. Foreign investment in the LDCs by various industrial source countries depends on the prevalence in the source countries of industrial congenial to foreign investment. Besides, MNEs respond to LDCs' tariff incentive in industries where proprietary assets are important.

9.9   China's Multinational Enterprises   中国的跨国企业

At the very beginning of China's reform and opening to the outside world, Chinese government tried its best to attract foreign MNEs to invest China. Those MNEs have facilitated China's economy. Almost forty years have passed since the reform. China's economy has been greatly enhanced and has become an economic giant in the world. China has been encouraging its enterprises to invest abroad. By the end of the year 2012, there had been more than twenty thousand of China's MNEs investing abroad, covering over 70% of the countries and regions of the world.

Now, Chinapossesses thousands of its own MNEs. According to the Summit Forum of China's 500 Top Companies of the Year 2014, there were 100 big MNEs in China in 2014. They all have investments in different parts of the world. It is believed that China's MNEs will grow bigger and stronger in the following years.

Summary of This Chapter
本章概要

1.跨国企业通常指从事对外直接投资的企业,它在国外拥有自己的子公司或控股公司。跨国企业占全世界产量的很大比例。世界500强企业在国外都有分支机构。世界500强企业约占全球对外直接投资的80%。世界500强企业中,有绝大多数企业来自欧盟各国、美国和日本等发达国家。

2. 跨国企业的业务范围广泛,相比之下,许多跨国企业从事制造业。跨国企业也涉足服务业,如银行业、宾馆业、餐饮业、信息咨询等。

3. 建立出口加工区的目的是促进出口及增加就业。出口加工区就业率越高,东道国对出口加工区的作用及其社会条件就越敏感。跨国企业不一定是出口加工区最大的或唯一的投资者,独资企业实际上在出口加工区所占的比例很小,合资企业所占的比例更大。第三世界国家投资商的出现是出口加工区的一大特点。

4. 自改革开放以来,中国在吸引对外投资方面取得了举世瞩目的成绩,尤其是中国加入世界贸易组织以来,越来越多的跨国企业看好中国市场;另一方面,中国的企业增加了对外直接投资,中国政府一直鼓励国内企业向国外市场投资。但是,无论在数量还是质量上,中国的跨国公司与西方的巨型跨国公司相比都存在着很大的差距。从发展趋势来看,随着世界巨型跨国公司的飞速发展,中国的跨国公司必将以强劲的势头跟进,利用有利的国际经济环境和自身的发展优势,大展宏图,在未来的国际经济舞台上发挥应有的作用。

▶ New Words and Expressions

abuse *v. & n.* 滥用

account for... 占……比例;补偿;作出解释

affiliate *v. & n.* 使隶属;接纳为分支机构;关系企业;附属公司;联营公司

agglomeration *n.* 凝聚

amortize *v.* 摊销;摊还;分期偿还(债务等)

ancillary *a. & n.* 附属的;助手;附属物

associate company 联营公司(其股票至少有20%但不到50%或51%掌握在别的一家或一组公司手中)

attach importance to 重视……

be associated with 与……有联系/关系

be bound to 有义务做……;一定会……

bolster *v. & n.* 支撑;支持;垫子

brain drain 人才流失

catastrophe *n.* 灾难

coincide *v.* 相一致;相符

concession *n.* 让步;承认;(政府对采矿权、土地使用权等的)特许;租地营业(权)

condone *v.* 宽恕;(行为)抵消(过失等)

confer *v.* 授予;赐给

congenial *a.* 意气相投的;(职位等)合意的;好交际的

controversy *n.* 争吵;论战

coordinate *v.* 使协调;调整

delete *v.* 删除

deregulate *v.* 撤销对……的管制规定

destiny *n.* 命运;天命

detract *v.* 转移;使分心;减损

developmental *a.* 发展的

enclave *n.* 在一国境内的外国领土;孤立的小块地区

endow *v.* 捐赠;资助

entrepreneurial *a.* 企业的

envisage *v. & n.* 想象;设想

expatriate *n. & a. & v.* 移居国外的人;被派往国外工作的人;移居国外的;使移居国外

fit into... 符合;适合

footloose *a.* 无牵累的;自由自在的

give rise to... 引起

given that... 考虑到……;鉴于……

grant *v. & n.* 同意;转让(财产等);准许;转让证书

hedge *v. & n.* 以保值措施避免投资损失;套期保值

hierarchy *n.* 统治集团；等级制度

hype *n.* 瞎吹的广告；欺骗

ideological *a.* 思想上的；意识形态的；思想坚定的

immune from 豁免于……

initiate *v.* 创始；发起

interplay *v. & n.* 互为影响；相互作用

LDC（**least developed country**）最不发达国家

map out 详细制定；筹划

national *n. & a.* （侨居国外的）国民；国有的

nationalistic *a.* 民族主义的；国家主义的

nurture *v. & n.* 培养；教养

outsource *v.* 外购（指从外国供应商等获得货物或服务）；外包（工程）

pay regard to 重视；注意

perceive *v.* 意识到；理解；把……认为……

peripheral *a.* 次要的；外表面的

ration *n. & v.* （粮食等）定量；应得的一份；配给

red tape 拖拉的公司程序

repatriation *n.* 派遣回国

ride on 随……而定；依靠

setup *n.* 机构；装置；计划；方案

skepticism *n.* 怀疑态度

sketchy *a.* 粗略的；肤浅的

sober-minded *a.* 头脑清醒的

stem from 起源于……

subcontract *v. & n.* 转包；分包（合同）

subsidy *n.* 补贴；津贴

supra-national *a.* 超国家的

synonymous *a.* 同义的

terminology *n.* 术语

to this effect 大致这样的意思

ultimately *ad.* 最后地；最终地

unfetter *v.* 使自由

verdict *n.* （陪审团的）裁定；定论

viable *a.* 能独立生存或发展的；可望成功的

vulnerable *a.* 易受……的；脆弱的

yardstick *n.* 码尺；衡量标准

❯ Discussion Questions

1. Why do companies want to become multinational?

2. What are the benefits and problems of multinational enterprises?

3. What are the functions of multinational enterprises in Export Processing Zones?

4. Why are multinational enterprises criticized?

Chapter 10 | Foreign Direct Investment (FDI) 对外直接投资

Objectives
学习目标

To understand what foreign direct investment is about.

理解对外直接投资的内容。

To understand the reasons for foreign direct investment.

理解对外直接投资的原因。

To know the advantages and disadvantages of foreign direct investment.

了解对外直接投资的利弊。

To learn the modes of foreign direct investment.

了解对外直接投资的形式。

To know the present situation of foreign direct investment in China.

了解中国境内对外投资的现状。

One of the most visible indications of the increasing global integration of the world economy over the past decade or so has been the phenomenal growth of foreign direct investment flows and the expansion of cross-border activities of multinational enterprises. FDI inflows are considered channels of entrepreneurship, technology, management skills, and of resources that are scarce in developing countries. Hence, they could help their host countries in their industrialisation. Besides, they could assist developing countries' manufactured exports expansion by providing access to their marketing networks and by locating export-platform production facilities in the host countries. However, FDI inflows have been distributed across countries in a highly asymmetric manner and the poorest countries have been neglected in their distribution.

Foreign direct investment has come to be widely recognized over the past decade as a major potential contributor to growth and development. It can bring capital, technology, management know-how and access to new markets. In comparison with other forms of capital flows, it is also more stable, with a longer-term commitment to the host economy.

10.1   The Nature of FDI   对外直接投资的性质

FDI occurs when a firm invests directly in new facilities to produce and/or market a product in a foreign country. Once a firm undertakes FDI it becomes a multinational enterprise (MNE). In other words, FDI can be a company controlled through ownership by a foreign company or foreign individuals.

Foreign direct investment is defined by some as an investment involving a long-term relationship and reflecting a lasting interest and control of a resident entity in one economy (foreign direct investor or parent enterprise) other than that of the foreign direct investor enterprise or affiliate enterprise or foreign affiliate. FDI implies that the investor exerts a significant degree of influence on the management of the enterprise resident in the other economy. Such investment involves both the initial transaction between the two entities and all subsequent transactions between them and among foreign affiliates, both incorporated and unincorporated. FDI may be undertaken by individuals as well as business entities.

Flows of FDI comprise capital provided (either directly or through other related enterprises) by a foreign direct investor to an FDI enterprise, or capital received from an FDI enterprise by a foreign direct investor. There are three components in FDI: equity capital, reinvested earnings and intra-company loans.

(1) Equity capital is the foreign direct investor's purchase of shares of an enterprise in a country other than its own.

(2) Reinvested earnings comprise the direct investor's share (in proportion to direct equity participation) of earnings not distributed as dividends by affiliates or earnings not remitted to the direct investor. Such retained profits by affiliates are reinvested.

(3) Intra-company loans or intra-company debt transactions refer to short-or long-term borrowing and lending of funds between direct investors (parent enterprises) and affiliate enterprises.

FDI stock is the value of the share of their capital and reserves (including retained profits) attributable to the parent enterprise, plus the net indebtedness of affiliates to the parent enterprise.

Foreign direct investors may also obtain an effective voice in the management of another business entity through means other than acquiring an equity stake. These are non-equity forms of FDI, and they include subcontracting, management contracts, turnkey arrangements, franchising, licensing and product sharing. Data on transnational corporate activity through these forms are usually not separately identified in balance-of-payments statistics. These statistics, however, usually present data on royalties and licensing fees, defined as "receipts and payments of residents and non-residents for: 1) the authorized use of intangible non-produced, non-financial assets and proprietary rights such as trademarks, copyrights, patents, processes, techniques, designs, manufacturing rights, franchises, etc., and 2) the use, through licensing agreements, of produced originals or prototypes, such as manuscripts, films, etc."

In fact, it is not so easy to define FDI. Some define it in terms of its international characteristics and contrast it with portfolio investment; others express it in terms of the activities of MNEs. Most definitions, however, seem to have two common elements. One is that FDI involves at least two countries. This criterion relates to the multinational character of FDI. The other is the issue of ownership and control, which distinguishes FDI from portfolio investment. Foreign portfolio investment is just a simple transfer of financial capital—equity or loan—from one country to another, whereas FDI involves the ownership and control of production activities abroad.

In exchange for ownership, the investing company normally transfers some of its financial, managerial, technical, trademark, and other resources to the foreign country. The foreign company may be created as a new venture by the investor, or it may be acquired from an existing owner. A company can view this kind of investment just as it views domestic investment, but in this case the project is located in a foreign country. So it involves more problems in the investments, such as laws, regulations and rules, customs, cultures, and so on.

Some investors bring in substantial funding with them; others borrow locally to finance their new affiliates, and still others do both. Some investors transfer many people to work in the new affiliate, while others just employ local people.

The main concept behind FDI is the control of assets in another country. That is, foreign direct investment is generally undertaken by a firm that seeks to serve a new market for its products or service or seeks to obtain additional supplies for its existing markets.

Many see both trade and foreign investment as being all about markets. A local market can be serviced by local investment, production and sales, or by imports. A foreign market can be serviced either by investing and producing domestically and then exporting or by investing, or by producing and selling directly into that foreign market. In actual business practice, international firms use different combinations of these two possibilities. Thus trade and FDI are sometimes competing and sometimes complementary ways of servicing a foreign market.

To some extent, we may say that FDI is now more important than trade as a vehicle for international business because production facilities abroad comprise a large and increasingly important part of international companies' activities and strategies.

10.2 Reasons for FDI 对外直接投资的原因

Comparing three options of serving foreign markets: export, direct investment and licensing, we find that direct investment is much more likely to occur between large countries with similar levels of investment. We have seen that the internal transfer of assets is usually chosen when knowledge capital can be a joint input to a number of plants.

In many situations, however, host countries lack sufficient capital, technology or management resources to realise the potential comparative advantage in international trade. Therefore, FDI is effective in supplementing these factors of production, thus making the industry internationally competitive. If FDI is undertaken along the line of comparative advantage, it contributes harmoniously both to the steady industrialisation and economic development of the host country on the one hand, and to a lower-cost foreign supply for the investing country on the other. Thus FDI works to complement, instead of substituting for, international trade, and both will grow in step with each other. This may result in prosperity of the international economy.

The other reasons for FDI may be as follows:

(1) The increase in world trade and the opening up of new markets in recent decades.

(2) The development of new technologies that can be transplanted between countries.

(3) Liberalization of the economies of nations throughout the world, including removal of exchange controls and controls on the repatriation of profits.

(4) Establishment of common markets and other regional trading blocs with common external tariffs.

Figure 10.1   further illustrates the motivations of FDI.

Marketing Factors:

1. Size of market and market growth.

2. Desire to maintain share of market, to follow customers, and to follow competition.

3. Need to advance exports of parent company, and to maintain close customer contact.

4. Dissatisfaction with existing market arrangements.

5. Export base.

Barriers to Trade:

1. Government-erected barriers to trade.

2. Preference of local customers for local products.

Cost Factors:

1. Desire to be near source of supply.

2. Availability of raw materials, capital/technology and labour.

3. Lower labour costs, other production costs, and transport costs.

4. Financial (and other) inducements by government.

5. More favourable cost levels.

Investment Climate:

1. General attitude toward foreign investment.

2. Political stability, and stability of foreign exchange.

3. Limitation on ownership.

4. Currency exchange regulations.

5. Tax structure.

6. Familiarity with country.

General:

1. Expected higher profits.

2. Others.

Figure 10.1   Major Determinants of Foreign Direct Investment

10.3　Theories of FDI　对外直接投资理论

Any practice is actually concerned with some kind of theory which might be or might not be felt. Theory and practice interplay. Theory is used to direct the practice, while repeated practice might generate theory.

FDI, a kind of international practice, occurs under a certain theory which the practitioners may not realize. In practice, those practitioners, following their own ideas, just focus on possibilities of the returns of their investment. While scholars focus on the study of those practices. There are a number of theories which are the interest of economists, such as the Neoclassical Theory, the Industrial Organization Theory and so on.

10.4　Advantages of FDI　对外直接投资的利益

Companies invest directly only if they think that they hold some supremacy over similar companies in countries of interest. The advantage results from a foreign company's ownership of some resources—patents, product differentiation, management skills, access to markets—unavailable at the same price or terms to the local company. This is known as monopoly advantages before direct investment. The cost of transferring resources abroad is increasing and there is perceived greater risk of operating in a foreign country. Therefore, a company will not undertake FDI if it does not see a higher return than it can get at home country and if it does not think it can outperform local firms. Companies from certain countries may enjoy a monopoly advantage if they borrow capital at a lower interest rate than companies from other countries. In recent years, capital markets have become international, so it is possible for companies to borrow abroad more easily if interest rates are lower there.

Another advantage occurs when the foreign company's currency has high buying power. Currency values, however, do not provide a strong explanation for FDI patterns. The currency-strength scenario only partially explains direct investment flows.

More internationally oriented companies can get advantages from spreading out some of the costs of product differentiation, R&D, and advertising compared to less internationally oriented companies. Among industry groups and groups of companies of similar size that spent comparable amounts on advertising and R&D, the more internationally oriented companies can earn more in almost every case.

On the other hand, local companies can enjoy the advanced technology which they lack. Besides, with inflow of equipment, the skills of local workers can be improved. New management know-how can also be introduced to the local companies to improve their administration.

From the perspective of a nation, FDI may bring some benefits.

FDI can make a positive contribution to a host economy by supplying capital, technology, and management resources that would otherwise not be available. The provision of these skills by an MNE (through FDI) may boost that country's economic growth rate. Besides, new advanced technology can be introduced to the host country. Technology is a catalyst that can stimulate a country's economic growth and industrialization. Technology can take two forms, both of which are valuable. It can be incorporated in a production process (e.g. the technology for discovering, extracting, and refining oil). However, many countries lack the research and development resources and skills required to develop their local product and process technology. This is particularly true of the less developed countries (LDCs). Such countries need rely on advanced industrialized nations for much of the technology required to stimulate economic growth, and FDI can provide it.

Foreign management skills provided through FDI may also produce important benefits for the host countries. Beneficial spinoff effects arise when local personnel who are trained to occupy managerial, financial, and technical posts in the subsidiaries of a foreign MNE subsequently leave the firm and help to establish local firms. Likewise, benefits may arise if the superior management skills of a foreign MNE stimulate local suppliers, distributors, and competitors to improve their own management skills.

Besides, FDI may bring employment effects to the host countries. Direct effects arise when a foreign MNE directly employs a number of host country citizens. Indirect effects arise when jobs are created in local suppliers as a result of the investment and when jobs are created because of the increased spending in the local economy resulting from employees of the MNE.

Further, the effect of FDI on a country's balance-of-payments accounts is an important issue for most host governments. When the FDI is a substitute for imports of goods or services, it can improve the current account of the host country's balance of payments. For example, much of the FDI by Japanese automobile companies in the USA and the UK can be seen as substituting for imports from Japan. Thus, the current account of the USA balance of payments has improved somewhat because many Japanese companies are now supplying the USA market with production facilities in the USA, as opposed to facilities in Japan. When the MNE uses a foreign subsidiary to export goods and services to other countries, another potential benefit arises.

10.5   Strategies for FDI   对外直接投资战略

Strategies for FDI may be categorized as product-driven, market-driven, or technology-driven.

Product-driven strategies arise when a firm's welfare depends critically on the properties, capabilities or composition of a specific product. For example, an international oil company cannot survive unless it continually explores for fresh reserves of crude oil and arranges for its processing and distribution. Hence it needs to invest in oil refineries, pipeline networks and so on in order to serve chosen markets. Many natural-resource-related industries pursue product-driven investment strategies, as do pharmaceutical companies, and other businesses that are locked into a specific type of product.

Market-driven strategies relate to the quest for new markets, served by foreign-owned local manufacturing plants and distribution systems. This type of FDI typically arises when a firm's existing markets cannot absorb its potential output.

Technology-driven strategies are found among enterprises that rely on the application of state-of-the-art technologies for their competitive advantage. Such firms invest in order to undercut the prices of foreign local competitors using out-of-date production methods, or to introduce completely new products to foreign markets.

FDI may involve vertical or horizontal integration, or the conscious diversification of the scope of a firm's activities.

Vertical integration means mergers or takeovers among firms in the same industry but at different stages in the chain of production or distribution, e.g. by taking over distributors or suppliers of raw materials. It enables the linking up of technically-related processes and remove the profit margins and transactions costs associated with contracts between different companies. The firm might obtain total control over sources of supply, sales outlets, etc., and may acquire the ability to deprive competitors of low-cost inputs or convenient distribution systems.

Horizontal integration, on the other hand, is the combination of firms operating in the same industry and at the same stage of the production/distribution chain. Growth through horizontal integration has the following advantages.

(1) It enables a firm with a just-so-so performance record to improve its market position.

(2) Economies of scale might become available (e.g. bulk purchasing discounts, integration of production processes, extensive application of the division of labour, etc.).

(3) The business develops a "critical mass" which might arise from the process.

(4) Opportunities for diversification might arise from the process.

But, the problem with both vertical and horizontal integration is that the business becomes locked into a specific market which, if it collapses, leaves the company in a dangerous position.

▶ 10.6 Costs of FDI 对外直接投资的成本

Although FDI can bring benefits to both host country and home country, there are some costs to both countries.

10.6.1 Costs to Host Country 东道国承担的成本

Generally speaking, there are three main costs of inward FDI related to host countries: the possible adverse effects of FDI on competition within the host nation, adverse effects on the balance of payments, and the perceived loss of national sovereignty.

(1) Adverse effects on competition

While introducing FDI, host governments may occasionally worry about the subsidiaries of foreign MNEs operating in their countries. The MNEs are more competitive because they are much stronger in terms of finance and technology. Besides, the foreign MNE may be able to draw on funds generated elsewhere to subsidize its costs in the host market, which could drive local companies out of business and allow the firm to monopolize the market. Once the market is monopolized by the foreign MNE, the host country's economic welfare will be seriously affected.

Further, the infant industry of the host country might be more easily affected because it is not competitive. If a country with a potential comparative advantage in a particular industry allows FDI in that industry, host country's local firms can hardly have a chance to develop.

(2) Adverse effects of the balance of payments

Outflow of capital occurs when MNEs repatriate earnings to their parent companies. Such outflows show up a debit on the capital account of the balance of payments (the capital account records transactions involving the purchase and sale of assets). Net outflows of capital can result in a fall in the value of a country's currency on the foreign exchange markets. In addition, when an MNE imports a substantial number of its inputs from abroad, another debit occurs on the current account of the host country's balance of payments.

(3) National sovereignty and autonomy

Many host country governments worry that FDI is accompanied by some loss of economic independence. The concern is that key decisions that can affect the host country's economy will be made by a foreign parent company that has no real commitment to the host country, and over which the host country's government has no real control.

10.6.2 Costs to Home Country   母国承担的成本

The most important concerns are about the balance-of-payments and employment effects of outward FDI. The home country's trade position (its current account) may deteriorate if the purpose of the foreign investment is to serve the home market from a low-cost production location. For example, when a USA textile company closes its plants in South Carolina and moves production to Central America, imports into the USA rise and the trade position deteriorates. The current account of the balance of payments also suffers if the FDI is a substitute for direct exports.

Besides, the most serious concerns about employment arise when FDI is seen as a substitute for domestic production. For example, Nissan's investment resulted in the home country's decrease in employment.

10.7   Diversification   多元化经营

Diversification is a concern of an MNE. It is quite likely that an MNE may turn to other lines of work for some reasons. Diversification can involve the supply of completely new products, entering fresh market segments (possibly using modified versions of existing brands), or imitating the products of other firms. There are a number of reasons for diversification (Bennett, 1999).

（1）Attempts to strengthen a hold on a market by controlling diverse activities connected with it, e.g. a paper manufacturer diversifying into carton making, wallpaper production, gift wrapping manufacture, etc.. This is an example of "concentric" diversification, i.e. diversification involving a common technological base and market outlets.

（2）Loss of traditional products or markets.

（3）Large seasonal variations in demand for a firm's existing product.

（4）Overdependence on a handful of customers.

（5）Successful research and technical development activities resulting in new products and applications.

（6）Existing products reaching the ends of their life-cycles.

（7）Increased competition within existing markets.

（8）Potential for the joint marketing of a wide range of goods.

（9）Spare capacity within the firm that can be utilized via the supply of fresh products.

10.8　FDI Decision Making　对外直接投资决策

Before discussing FDI decision making, let's study the following figure.

Suppose a firm plans to exploit its competitive advantage by assessing foreign market as illustrated in Figure 10.2.

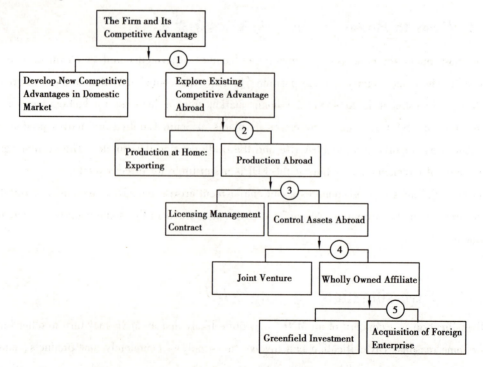

Figure 10.2　FDI Decision Sequence

The first problem is to decide whether to exploit the existing competitive advantage in new foreign markets or to just focus on resources in the development of new competitive advantages in the home markets. Some firms may choose to do both if resources allow. But it is found out that more and more firms are choosing to go international as at least part of their expansion strategies.

The second problem is about whether the firm should produce at home and export to the foreign markets or produce abroad. Normally, the firm will choose the path that will allow it to access the resources and markets it needs to exploit its existing competitive advantage. That is the minimum requirement. Besides, it also should consider two additional dimensions of each foreign investment decision.

(1) The degree of control over assets, technology, information, and operations.

(2) The magnitude of capital that the firm must risk.

Either of the two decisions increases the firm's control at the cost of increasing capital outlays.

The firm may decide to produce abroad. There are a number of ways to produce abroad. The distinctions among different kinds of FDI (branch 3 and downward in Figure 10.2) vary by degrees of ownership. The licensing management contract is by far the simplest and cheapest way to produce abroad; another firm is actually doing the production, but with your firm's technology and know-how. The question for most firms is whether the reduced capital investment of simply licensing the product to another manufacturer is worth the risk of the loss of control over the product and technology.

The firm that wants direct control over the production process next determines the degree of equity control, to wholly own the firm or as a joint investment with another firm.

Trade-offs with shared ownership continue the debate over control of assets and other sources of the firm's original competitive advantage. Many countries try to ensure the continued growth of local firms and investors, and those countries require that foreign firms operate jointly with local firms.

The final decision branch between a "greenfield investment" (building a firm from the ground up) and the purchase of an existing firm is often a question of cost. A greenfield investment is normally the most expensive of all foreign investment methods. The acquisition of an existing firm is often lower in initial cost but may also contain a number of customizing and adjustment costs that are not apparent at the initial purchase. The purchase of a going concern may also have substantial benefits if the existing business possesses substantial customer and supplier relationships that can be used by the new owner in the pursuit of its own business line.

10.8.1　Franchising　专营

1. Nature of Franchising

International franchising is undergoing a period of rapid growth in the global economy. It is a mode of expansion that offers large company advantages, such as economies of scale in marketing and production for the franchiser, and in the case of independent franchising a low-risk means of starting a business for the franchisee.

Franchising is a form of licensing whereby the franchisee adopts the parent company's entire business format: its name, trademarks, business methods, layout of premises, etc. The franchiser provides (in return for a royalty and lump sum fee) a variety of supplementary management services: training, technical advice, stock control system, and even financial loans. Hence it retains complete control over how the product is marketed. The franchisee carries the risks of failure and the franchiser's capital commitment is typically low.

Accordingly, international franchising allows companies to expand rapidly from a limited capital base. It combines the technical experience of the franchiser with the intimate local knowledge of the franchisee. Franchisees are self-employed, not employees of the parent company, and rarely possess rights against a parent organization in the event of the collapse of either the entire systems or just an individual outlet.

Usually, franchisees must follow standardized business techniques and layouts of premises, and are subject to some control by the franchiser. Franchisees are sheltered under a protective umbrella of specialist skills, resources and experiences already possessed by the parent organization. They obtain a well-known name and a set of activities with a proven reputation. Franchisees are required to protect the franchiser's good name through maintenance of minimum quality standards, adoption of a uniform appearance, adherence to standard opening hours, and so on. If the franchiser is a manufacturer, the franchisee is normally required to purchase supplies (for example, meat for hamburgers, spare parts, ingredients for alcoholic or soft drinks) from the franchiser at prices predetermined by the parent firm (which buys raw materials in bulk at big discounts).

Franchising began when investors of new machines, processes or business methods were forced by lack of finance or inadequate knowledge of the business world into allowing other parties the right to manufacture or otherwise adopt new inventions in exchange for a license fee.

Today, franchisers impose levies on franchisees to cover national advertising and servicing costs. The cost of local advertising is borne by franchisees. Successful franchising requires that the product or service involved have a distinct and unique image which is conceptually dissimilar to competing lines. Besides, demand for the franchised product should be really international, and expected to continue in the long term. Franchising is not suitable for fashion products with short lives.

2. Types of Franchising

Franchising started to boom in the 1950s. At that time it became apparent that there were several types of franchising:

(1) Franchises between manufacturers and retailers (as in the motor industry);

(2) Franchises between manufacturers and wholesalers (as in the soft drink industry);

（3）Franchises between wholesalers and retailers（as when retailers form wholesaling companies）;

（4）Trademark and trade name franchising, the commonest form.

The first three types, supply dealerships, are known as first generation franchising. In an international setting, first-generation franchising can be regarded as a variant of the licenses entry mode found in manufacturing. Trademark franchising is known as second-generation franchising or business franchising. Most of the global growth in franchising since the 1950s is due to second-generation franchising. This type can be further divided into job, investment, business, management, executive, retail shop and sales/distribution franchises. This type offers a far more comprehensive package than first generation franchising. However, the last has become increasingly sophisticated, so there is no longer a clear distinction between first and second generation franchising.

3. Advantages and Disadvantages of Direct International Franchising

（1）Advantages

1）Low risk, low entry mode.

2）Offer of the ability to develop new and unfamiliar markets relatively quickly and on a larger scale than otherwise possible.

3）Use of highly motivated partners with local market knowledge and experience.

4）Creation of additional turnover with relatively low levels of investment in personnel, capital outlay, production and distribution.

5）A way to test the market before committing to direct investment.

6）Establishment of standardized, global company profile and brand image, generating marketing economies of scale.

（2）Disadvantages

1）Lack of full control over operations, resulting in problems with cooperation, communications quality control.

2）Limits on franchiser's profit.

3）Costs of creating and marketing the franchised package.

4）Costs of protecting goodwill and brand names.

5）Problems with local legislation, including transfers of fees and government restrictions on franchise agreements.

6）Disclosure of trade secrets may create a future competitor.

7）Risk to the franchiser's reputation if some franchisees underperform.

4. Franchising vs. Licensing

Franchising is often regarded as a form of licensing. But as a matter of fact, the only common feature of the two modes is that they both involve the transfer of intellectual property rights. But there are a number of differences between the two modes.

First, a licence agreement normally embraces a range of intellectual property embodied in patents, trademarks, trade secrets and know-how. Franchising, however, is normally limited to trademarks.

Second, the licensee receives just a small part of the licensor's business format, but the franchisee receives a complete business package, which includes all the elements the franchisee needs to operate successfully.

Third, unlike the franchiser, the licensor has limited control over the way the licensee conducts business. Franchisees are start-up businesses that take on the "image" of the franchiser; licensees are normally well-established businesses with their own identity. Figure 10.3 further illustrates the differences between the two modes.

Licensing	Franchising
Regarded as a low to zero-equity organization form.	Can involve substantial equity investment in the host country.
Only part of a business package is transferred to the other party.	Most of the entrant's business format is transferred.
Usually concerns specific products.	Franchiser passes on new elements of the business format.
Simple direct relationship between the parties.	Intermediaries can exist between the market entrant and local entities.
Entrant has limited control over daily activities of licensees.	Entrant exerts considerable control over licensees' daily activities.
Licensees tend to be self-selecting.	Franchisees are selected by the franchise.
Limited common characteristics between licensor and licensees.	Established chains of commonly owned entities.
Licensees are normally established businesses.	Franchised chains of commonly owned entities.
Substantial fee negotiations take place.	Standard fee structure.
Licensor's earnings based on royalties.	Franchiser earns from royalties+fees+sale of inputs.

Figure 10.3   Differences Between International Franchising and Licensing

10.8.2 Licensing 特许

Licensing is appropriate where the firm has legal control over its intellectual property (via registered patents and/or trademarks), where transport costs or the cost of establishing local manufacturing facilities would be prohibitive, or where rapid installation of a manufacturing capability in a particular market is necessary in order to beat the competitors.

Besides, licensing may occur on the following occasions.

(1) Images of locally produced items will improve sales.

(2) The licensee will have to purchase input components or materials from the licensor.

（3）The licensor is already exporting directly to more markets than it can conveniently handle.

（4）It is not technically feasible to establish a permanent presence in a particular country.

（5）The foreign market is small and does not justify the expense attached to alternative forms of market entry.

（6）The licensor is a small company with limited resources.

（7）There are possibilities for " technology feedback" from the licensee.

（8）The technology transferred under licence is " perishable" so that the licensor has considerable bargaining power through its ability to supply new technology in the future.

（9）Licensing can be a means for testing and developing a product in a foreign market, perhaps with a view to subsequent FDI.

（10）Auxiliary processes rather than a core technology can be licensed.

1. Types of Licensing

Licenses can take many forms, ranging from a permit to exploit an existing patent, to extensive and complicated arrangements on industrial cooperation. There are several types of licensing agreement.

（1）Assignment: For example, a firm hands over all its intellectual property rights in relation to a particular patent, trademark, design or whatever, to a licensee.

（2）Sole license: The firm that issues a sole license retains rights but agrees not to extend licenses to anyone other than a single licensee during the period of the agreement.

（3）Exclusive license: This type of license requires the licensor not to use their patents, trademarks, etc., for its own business while licensing contract is still in force.

（4）Know-how licensing: Know-how licensing means the licensing of confidential but non-patented technical knowledge.

2. Advantages and Disadvantages of Licensing

（1）Advantages

1）No capital investment is necessary.

2）Licensees avoid research and development costs, while acquiring experience of manufacturing the item.

3）The licensor has complete legal control over its intellectual property.

4）A manufacturing capability can be quickly established in an unfamiliar market.

5）Licensees carry some of the risk of failure.

6）The nucleus of the parent organization can remain small, have low overheads, yet control extensive operations.

（2）Disadvantages

1）Sacrifice of profits through allowing other firms to make the parent company's goods.

2）The risk of a licensee company setting up in competition once it has learned all the licensor's production methods and trade secrets and the license period has expired.

3）Possible ambiguities and interpretation difficulties in relation to minimum and/or maximum output levels, territory covered, basis of royalty payments (including the frequency of payment and the currency to be used) and the circumstances under which the agreement may be terminated.

4）Deciding how to control the licensee in relation to quality standards, declaration of production levels, and methods of marketing the product.

5）Problems arising if the licensee turns out to be less competent than first expected.

6）Possible failure of the licensee to exploit fully the local market.

7）Acquisition by the licensee of the licensor's technical knowledge.

8）The need for complex contractual arrangements in certain circumstances.

9）The numerous opportunities that arise for disagreements and misunderstandings.

10.8.3 Joint Ventures 合资企业

Joint ventures and wholly owned subsidiaries are the main forms of FDI.

A joint venture entails establishment of a firm that is jointly owned by two or more otherwise independent firms. An international joint venture is a partnership of two or more independent firms that share resources when at least one partner's headquarters are located outside the venture's country of operation or when the venture operates outside all the partners' home countries. Equity joint ventures and contractual joint ventures are the basic forms of joint venture found in international business.

In the equity joint ventures, the partners provide an agreed portion of the equity, which may take the form of funds or capital equipment, premises and management know-how.

Unlike equity joint ventures, contractual joint ventures have no separate legal entity. Rather, they involve the supply of technology, marketing and production know-how or management skills by one partner to the other on a contractual basis. This may turn contractual joint ventures into equity joint ventures if the long-term interests of the partners are best served and equity joint ventures commonly lead to mergers or acquisition by one of the partners.

1. Advantages of Joint Venture

There are a number of advantages of joint ventures.

First, a firm can benefit from a local partner's knowledge of the host country's competitive conditions, culture, language, political systems, and business systems.

Second, when the development costs and/or risks of opening a foreign market are high, a firm might gain by sharing these costs and/or risks with a local partner.

Third, in many countries, political considerations make joint ventures the only feasible entry mode.

· Fourth, multinational firms may require a partner in order to obtain knowledge of new and unfamiliar host country environment.

Besides, it is found out that joint ventures with local partners face a low risk of being subject to nationalization or other forms of government interference.

2. Disadvantages of Joint Venture

There are two main disadvantages with joint ventures.

First, just as with licensing, a firm that enters into a joint venture risks giving control of its technology to its partner.

Second, a joint venture does not give a firm the tight control over subsidiaries that it might need to realize experience curve or location economies. Nor does it give a firm the tight control over a foreign subsidiary that it might need for engaging in coordinated global attacks against it rivals.

Besides, another disadvantage of joint venture is that the shared ownership arrangement can lead to conflicts and battles for control between the investing firms if their goals and objectives change over time, or if they take different views as to what the venture's strategy should be.

3. Traditional International Joint Ventures and New International Strategic Alliance

Traditional international joint ventures were typically alliances between Western firms and firms or public sector entities in developing countries. Historically, traditional international joint ventures have demonstrated short lives and high failure rates—between 30 and 60 per cent, depending on the criteria used to measure success.

In recent years, although the traditional joint venture continues to dominate cooperative international agreements, many international alliances have begun to be formed that focus more on strategy and strategic intent.

An international strategic alliance is a collaborative agreement in which partner firms of different nationalities have a presence in the same international or global markets and where at least one partner regards that alliance as a means to safeguard or enhance its competitive position. These strategic alliances seek to create added value through exploiting the core competencies or comparative advantage of the respective partners. This strategic exchange of core competencies perceives the firm as being a portfolio of competencies rather than products. The main features of these new strategic alliances, in contrast to traditional international joint ventures, are their targeting of global industries and high technology industries, their domination by firms from the Triad countries of North America, Western Europe and Japan, and their strategic intent—each partner seeking capabilities it has not yet possessed. Often, partners are competitors in the other markets but also in the alliance market.

In traditional joint ventures partners seek to exploit their existing competencies in new markets while partners in strategic alliances are seeking to gain new capabilities to be exploited on an international, and even global scale. Thus, technology transfer, R&D collaboration, production and market sharing agreements account for most strategic alliances.

10.8.4   Wholly Owned Subsidiaries   独资企业

A wholly owned subsidiary operation is defined as 100% ownership and control by a parent company headquartered, normally but not exclusively, in a foreign country. Establishing a wholly owned subsidiary in a foreign market can be done in two ways: the firm can either set up a new operation in that country or it can acquire an established firm and use that firm to promote its products in the country's market.

In most cases, choosing the wholly owned subsidiary operation as an entry method into a foreign country by a multinational firm amounts to a vote of confidence in the host country given the level of commitment and capital investment that is required for such an alternative. In other cases, a company with a broad policy of complete internationalization may insist on wholly owned subsidiary. Therefore, the decision concerning ownership and control of subsidiaries in host countries has to be viewed within the context of two primary determinants: economic considerations and internationalization policy.

1. Advantages of Wholly Owned Subsidiaries

There are normally three advantages of wholly owned subsidiaries.

First, when a firm's competitive advantage is based on technological competence, a wholly owned subsidiary will often be the preferred entry mode, since it reduces the risk of losing control over that competence. For this reason, many high-tech firms prefer this entry mode for overseas expansion.

Second, a wholly owned subsidiary gives a firm the tight control over operations in different countries that is necessary for engaging in global strategic coordination, that is to say, profits from one country are used to support competitive attacks in another.

Third, a wholly owned subsidiary may be required if a firm is trying to realize location and experience curve economies (as firms pursuing global and transnational strategies try to do).

Besides, there are some other advantages.

First, by establishing a wholly owned subsidiary, secrecy surrounding proprietary technology can be maintained.

Second, establishing a wholly owned subsidiary eliminates problems such as those associated with joint ventures.

Third, wholly owned subsidiary operation ensures consistency of policy, strategy, product quality and marketing programme between the subsidiary and headquarters.

2. Disadvantages of Wholly Owned Subsidiaries

Some of the disadvantages of wholly owned subsidiaries are as follows:

Generally speaking, establishing a wholly owned subsidiary is the most costly method of serving a foreign market. Firms doing this must bear the full costs and risks of setting up overseas operations. The risks associated with learning to do business in a new culture are less if the firms acquire an established host country enterprise. However, acquisitions raise a whole set of additional problems, including those associated with trying to marry divergent corporate cultures. These problems may more than offset any benefits derived by acquiring an established operation.

Besides, the operation of wholly owned subsidiaries is normally subject to close scrutiny by governments. Consequently, even legitimate activities such as repatriation of profits and other assets can be a sensitive issue and may lead to accusation of exploitation.

10.8.5   Turnkey Project   交钥匙工程

A turnkey project refers to a project in which a firm agrees to set up an operating plant for a foreign client and hand over the "key" when the plant is fully in operation.

Firms that specialize in the design, construction, and start-up of turnkey plants are common in some industries. In a turnkey project, the contractor agrees to handle every detail of the project for a foreign client, including the training of operating personnel. At completion of the contract, the foreign client is handed the "key" to a plant that is ready for full operation—hence the term "turnkey". This is actually a means of exporting process technology to other countries. In a sense it is just a very specialized kind of exporting.

Turnkey projects are most common in the chemical, pharmaceutical, petroleum refining, and metal refining industries, all of which use complex, expensive production-process technologies.

1. Advantages of Turnkey Projects

The advantages of turnkey projects are as follows:

First, turnkey projects are a way of earning great economic returns from that asset. The strategy is particularly useful in cases where FDI is limited by host government regulations. For example, the governments of many oil-rich countries have set out to build their own petroleum refining industries and, as a step toward that goal, have restricted FDI in their oil and refining sectors. Many of these countries lacked petroleum refining technology, so they had to gain it by entering into turnkey projects with foreign firms that had the technology.

Second, a turnkey strategy, as opposed to a more conventional type of FDI, may make sense in a country where the political and economic environment is such that a long-term investment might expose the firm to unacceptable political and/or economic risks.

Third, there exists the opportunity to sell both components and other intangible assets.

Fourth, host government patronage ensures that payments are made promptly and may also lead to mutually beneficial relationship in other areas.

And finally, the host country gets the opportunity to build complexes and train local personnel.

2. Disadvantages of Turnkey Projects

Disadvantages of turnkey projects are as follows:

First, by building an industrial complex in a host country, the possibility of exporting to or making other forms of investment in the market is effectively lost.

Second, turnkey contracts may result in the purchase of inappropriate technology.

Third, designing and building complex and advanced industrial facilities in a host country may require the permanent attention of the suppliers, thus perpetuating management and other contractual arrangements to the harm of the owner/purchaser.

Fourth, by definition, the firm that enters into a turnkey deal will have no long-term interest in the foreign country. And the firm that enters into a turnkey project with a foreign enterprise may create a competitor. For example, many of the western firms that sold oil refining technology to firms in Saudi Arabia, Kuwait, and other Gulf states now find themselves competing head to head with these firms in the world oil market.

Finally, and related to the fourth point, if the firms' process technology is a source of competitive advantage, then selling this technology through a turnkey project is also selling competitive advantage to potential competitors.

10.8.6　BOT 基础设施建营特许权

A Build-Operate-Transfer (BOT) project is a concession contract in which a Principal grants a concession to a Concessionaire who is responsible for the construction and operation of a facility over the period of the concession before finally transferring the facility, at no cost to the Principal, as a fully operational facility.

The build-operate-transfer (BOT) / design-build-operate-maintain (DBOM) model is an integrated partnership that combines the design and construction responsibilities of design-build procurements with operations and maintenance. These integrated PPPs transfer design, construction, and operation of a single facility or group of assets to a private sector partner. This project delivery approach is practiced by several governments around the world and is known by a number of different names, including "turnkey" procurement, BOT, and DBOM. BOT is usually concerned with the construction of high ways, power plants, subways, bridges, quays, channels, heating, and other infrastrucrue facilities.

BOT normally experience the following phases:
(1) making decision on BOT;
(2) making preparations for BOT project;
(3) inviting tenders;
(4) negotiating the terms and conditions of the contract;
(5) carrying out the project (normally in the form of turnkey project);
(6) operating the finished facility;
(7) transferring the facility to the government.

BOT developed rather fast in the 1980s in the world. In China, since the reforming and opening the door to the outsideworld, BOT projects have been performed successfully, especially in the eastern coastal provinces and cities. For example, Shenzhen Power Plant and Changsha Power Plant were built up this way.

It is believed that it is urgent to let private investors enter the industry. Chinese government encourages private investmentin the Build-Operation-Transfer and Transter-Operation-Transfer models, and will provide favorable policies in taxation, land, electricity, and credit guarantee.

10. 9   FDI Inside and Outside China   中国境内外直接投资

China's absorption of foreign investment is an important part of China's fundamental principle of opening up to the outside world, and is one of the great practices of building up socialist economy with Chinese characteristics. The Third Session of the Eleventh Central Committee of the Party in 1978 confirmed over again the ideological line of emancipating the mind and seeking truth from facts, and realized the historical transformation of key work for the entire Party. It also established the basic line of focusing on the central task of economic construction, and made the great decision of reform and opening up to the outside world. The Law of the People's Republic of China on Chinese-Foreign Equity Joint Ventures was promulgated by the National People's Congress in 1979, then the work of utilizing foreign capital as an important content of opening up to the outside world initiated as China's fundamental principle. After almost forty years of great efforts, the scale of absorbing foreign capital increasingly expanded and the level was increasingly upgraded when China's law and managerial system on foreign investment have been gradually perfected. The achievements won the whole world's attention, which effectively promoted the continuous, fast and healthy development of national economy.

10.9.1   FDI inflows into China from 1984 to 2014

During the early period (1949—1976), China spurned foreign investment and paid back all its foreign loans (mostly to the Soviet Union) by 1965. After taking up economic policy at the end of 1978, China started to open its door to foreign trade and investment and in the early 1980s the first Special Economic Zones were set up to absorb direct investment from Hong Kong and elsewhere.

During the 1980s, FDI inflows grew steadily but remained relatively low, confined largely to joint ventures with Chinese state-owned enterprises. In late 1980s, western and Japanese companies withheld investment in China, but the momentum was maintained, partly by a new influx of capital from Taiwan.

From early 1992, Chinese government started to encourage a further and much more massive wave of foreign direct investment, increasingly in the form of wholly-owned subsidiaries of foreign companies, which contributed towards an acceleration in GDP growth and inflation. FDI inflows peaked at over US $ 45bn a year in 1997—1998.

A further surge in FDI preceded and accompanied China's accession to the World Trade Organisation (WTO) in December 2001, promoting China to top position as an FDI destination in 2003.

In the early 1990s, contracted FDI exceeded actually used FDI by a large margin. This gap narrowed in the second half of the decade as the authorities became more realistic in registered inflows and as the pace of increase slowed, but it has widened again sharply in recent years. By 2003 contracted FDI was more than double utilised FDI.

In the first decade of the century, doubts emerged as to the usefulness of FDI, especially as

China's own corporations had developed to the stage where they were encountering competition from foreign multinationals and economic development needed to shift away from dependence on fixed investment.

Nevertheless, FDI inflows continued to rise in line with economic growth, reaching nearly USD 120 billion in 2014. (Source: Ministry of Commerce of the People's Republic of China. Latest update: 12 November 2015.)

10.9.2　The Basic Means of China's Absorption of Foreign Investments

FDI in China is promising and increasing and contributes a lot to the development of China's economy. (The following discussion concerned with China is mainly based on the sources from the Internet. The writer of this book feels much obliged to the contributors of the sources.)

The foreign investments are basically divided into direct investment and other means of investment. The direct investment, which is widely adopted, includes Sino-foreign joint ventures, joint exploitation and exclusively foreign-owned enterprises, foreign-funded share-holding companies and joint development. The other means of investment includes compensation trade and processing and assembling.

(1) Sino-foreign joint ventures

Sino-foreign joint ventures are also known as share-holding corporations. They are formed in China with joint capitals by foreign companies, enterprises, other economic organizations and individuals with Chinese companies enterprises, other economic organizations and individuals. The main feature is that the joint parties invest together, operate together, take risk according to the ratio of their capitals and take responsibility of losses and profits. The capitals from different parties are translated into the ratios of capitals, and in general the capital from foreign party should not be lower than 25%.

The Sino-foreign joint ventures are among the first forms of China's absorption of foreign direct investment and they account for the biggest part.

(2) Cooperative businesses

Cooperative business is also called contractual cooperation businesses. They are formed in China with joint capitals or terms of cooperation by foreign companies, enterprises, other economic organizations and individuals with Chinese companies, enterprises, other economic organizations and individuals. The rights and obligations of different parties are embedded in the contract. To establish a cooperative business, the foreign party, generally speaking, supplies all or most of the capital while Chinese party supplies land, factory buildings, and useful facilities, and also some supply a certain amount of capital, too.

(3) Exclusively foreign-owned enterprises

Exclusively foreign-owned enterprises, which are totally invested by foreign party in China by foreign companies, enterprises, other economic organizations and individuals in accordance with laws of China. According to the law of foreign-funded enterprises, the establishment of foreign enterprises should benefit the development of China's national economy and agree with at least one of the following criteria: the enterprises must adopt international advanced technology and facility; all or most of the products must be export-oriented. The foreign funded enterprises often take the form of limited liability.

(4) Joint exploitation

Joint exploitation is the abbreviation of maritime and overland oil joint exploitation. It is a widely adopted measure of economic cooperation in the international natural resources field. The striking features are high risk, high investment and high reward. The joint development is often divided into three steps: exploitation, development and production. Compared with the other three means mentioned above, joint cooperation accounts for a small ratio.

(5) Foreign-funded share-holding companies

Foreign companies, enterprises, and other economic organizations and individuals can form foreign funded share-holding companies in China with Chinese companies, enterprises, and other economic organizations. The total capital of the share-holding company is formed by equal shares, and shareholders will take due responsibilities for the company according to shares purchased; the company will take responsibilities for all its debts through all its assets and the Chinese and foreign shareholders will hold the shares of the company. Among them, the shares purchased and held by foreign investors account for more than 25% of the total registered capital of the company. Limited company can be founded either by means of starting-up or raising fund, and the limited liability company invested by the foreigners can also apply to turn into share-holding companies. The qualified enterprises can also apply to issue A & B shares and list abroad.

(6) New types of foreign investment

While expanding areas and opening-up domestic market, China is also exploring and expanding actively its new types of utilizing foreign investment such as BOT, investment company and so on. Since multinational merger and acquisition has become the major type of international direct investment, Chinese government is now researching and enacting related policies so as to facilitate foreigners to invest in China by means of merger and acquisition.

10.9.3   China's Policy Direction of Absorption of Foreign Investment

We should center on the principles and policies of our nation's economic and social development determined at the 16th National Congress of the Communist Party of China, adapt to the new situation of world economic development, stick to the principles of active and reasonable utilization of foreign capital, combine foreign capital absorption with economic structure adjustment and industrial upgrading promotion, the improvement of socialist market economy system, the reinforcement of enterprise competitiveness, the expansion of export and development of open economy, the vigorous exploitation of China's western area, and promotion of regional economies' harmonious development. Measures should be taken to further improve the soft environment for foreign investment, explore actively new methods for absorbing foreign capital, put emphasis on absorbing advanced technologies, modern management and special talents, and actively absorb foreign capital to invest in industries of new and advanced technologies, encourage multinational to set up district headquarters, research and procurement centers; speed up the development of supporting industries and push on the service trade field to open up to foreign countries step by step.

(1) To energetically improve the political and legal environment for foreign investment, and to enhance legal administration level. According to our commitments for joining WTO and the requirement for our opening-up process, we will further improve the legal system of absorbing foreign investment, keep on the steadiness, consistency, predictability and feasibility of the policies and laws of foreign investment laws, try to create a united, steady, transparent and predictable environment for foreign investment. We will further simplify the examination and approval procedures for foreign investment and adopt a standardized examination and approval system; reinforce our sense of legality, try to be open, just and transparent, and establish an incorruptible, industrious, pragmatic and effective government, creating a good administrative environment for foreign investment.

(2) To maintain and improve an open and fair market environment. We should combine this with the current work of rectifying and standardizing the order of market economy, prohibit firmly the improper collecting fees from foreign companies as well as improper inspection and fine of them. Measures should be taken to destroy local protectionism and industrial monopoly. We should also enhance the lawful measures to protect the intellectual property right and take strong actions against illegal piracy, therefore, establish an open, unified and fair market environment, further perfect the complaining mechanism of foreign-funded and protect the legal rights of foreign merchants.

(3) To further open the field of service industry. In accordance with China's self-development and Commitment to the WTO, we will open this field vigorously and steadily and systematically, perfect rules and regulations for service industry and formulate a united and standard system for accession into the market of foreign investment in service. We will encourage the import of modern service concepts and advanced management experience, technologies and modes of modern market operation and improve structure of service industry in China.

(4) To encourage foreign businessmen to invest in the new high-tech industry, the basic industry, and supporting industry. The ability of technology innovation and sustainable development directly reflect the competitiveness advantages of a country. We will continue to encourage foreign investors to introduce, develop and innovate technology and to invest in technology-intensive project, and projects with advanced technology and to guide in enterprise registered capital proportion limitation and funding condition. The relevant stipulations of setting pioneering investment enterprise should also be consummated in order to facilitate the conditions of setting up and developing high-tech corporations. We should attract foreigners to invest in supporting industry and encourage the localization of new materials, push domestic small and medium-sized enterprises to enforce cooperation with foreign companies and introduce the advanced and applicable technology to match the large foreign-funded enterprises, thus to enter the production and sales network of multinational companies.

（5）To attract actively more multinational companies to invest in China. Multinational companies are regarded as the leading force of today's world economy. We will try to improve the relevant policies to attract multinationals to invest in China, establish the local headquarters and set up cross-country procurement centers, using the experience and methods of merger and acquisition of other countries and taking the economical system with China's characteristics and realities of into consideration. We should speed up the step to draft and improve the practical policy and stipulations of investment through merger and acquisition, further revise the relevant stipulations of the foreign-invested share-holding companies, push the formulation and perfecting of BOT.

（6）To further promote foreign investment in the central and western regions. Vast areas in these regions are rich in resources for farming and stock raising, mineral resources and tourist resources. With a large population and a market of great potential labor forces, other key elements for production are relatively inexpensive, and with the steady progress and western development strategy, such facilities as transportation, communication and construction have impressively improved. Because of the improvement of investment environment and ecological development and emergence of potential for the development of specialty economy, foreign businessmen who invest in these regions are facing brand-new opportunities and great development space. (Source: CHINA. ORG.CN, Ministry of Commerce)

▶ 10.10　China's Outbound FDI　中国的对外直接投资

China's outbound investment is expected to continue to increase and could soon exceed foreign direct investment (FDI) in China. From January to August of 2104, FDI, which excludes investment in the financial sector, stood at $ 78.34 billion, down 1.8 percent from the same period of the previous year. In contrast, China's outbound direct investment by non-financial firms surged 15.3 percent to $ 65.17 billion in the same period. The outbound investment in the first eight months of the previous year was greatly boosted by CNOOC's $ 15.1 billion acquisition of Canada's oil and gas company Nexen. China's outbound investment will continue growing rapidly, and the long-term growth trend will not change. By the end of 2014, China had become the second largest FDI country. And it is predicted that by 2022 China may become the largest FDI country with its outbound direct investment volume reaching 367.3 billion US dollars. The non-state-owned businesses are the key outbound investors abroad. As the government is carrying out "One Belt, One Road" strategy, more Chinese enterprises will invest in the countries in the "Belt" and on the "Road".

Summary of This Chapter
本章概要

1. 当一国的个人或企业/组织，或附属机构从其国外的商务活动中获得了 10% 或更多的利润时，就意味着产生了对外直接投资。从事对外直接投资的企业就成了跨国公司。一个国家的企业若在外国购买一家现有的企业，这也是一种对外直接投资。企业可在外国投资于与国内经营范围相同的行业（水平对外直接投资），也可以在国外投资于能为国内经营提供投入的行业（垂直对外直接投资）。

2. 对外直接投资与组合投资相对，但不同于组合投资，它对生产性资产拥有控制权和所有权。至于持多少股份才有控制权，视情况而定。如果股权多但份额小，那么持有10%或20%的股份就可能享有对企业的控制权。如果只有两家股东，持有51%的股份的一方才有控制权。

3. 对外直接投资对国际商务的宏观环境与企业微观环境的改进起到一定促进作用。在宏观上，对外直接投资给接受国带来利益：(1)传播了新的科学技术；(2)促进当地企业国际化发展进程；(3)增加了当地的就业机会；(4)促进新思想的涌现；(5)激发竞争，促进当地技术的革新，提高了生产效率。

4. 一般来说，对外直接投资都是由发达国家的企业向其他国家市场进行投资。不过，发展中国家的对外投资量也在逐步增加，中国尤是如此。中国的中、小企业对许多国家进行直接投资。

5. 中国的对外投资形势看好。自改革开放以来，中国吸引了大量的外国投资，尤其是中国正式加入世界贸易组织后，外国投资在中国呈快速增长趋势。中国政府采取了一系列措施吸引外国投资，实行了许多宏观经济政策，维护稳定的经济增长，保持低通胀和强而稳定的通货。中国实行"走出去"策略，鼓励企业到国外投资。从2010年开始，尤其是2012年6月国家发改委、商务部、外交部等八部委联合发布《关于鼓励和引导民营企业积极开展境外投资的实施意见》之后，民营企业对外投资在数量和金额方面突飞猛进，日益成为对外投资的主力军。《中国企业全球化报告（2015）》指出，2014年中国对外投资流量首超日本，成为世界第二大对外投资国。

6. 对外直接投资包括以下主要形式。(1)交钥匙工程(turnkey project)：交钥匙工程是引进成套设备的一种方式，它是由承包工程的企业或企业集团按照承包合同内容，承担建造某项工程，在项目完工时，交给买方一个能正常运行的完整的生产工厂或生产车间，并向买方提供工厂的设计和运行的全套技术资料，最后向买方提供技术服务，以保证在试生产中能制造出完全符合合同要求的产品。(2)特许经营（franchising)：特许经营是最近几十年迅速发展起来的一种新型商业技术转让。特许经营合同是指已经取得成功经验的商业企业，将其商标、商号、服务标志、专利、专有技术及经营管理方法或经验转让给另一家商业企业的技术转让合同。(3)许可证贸易(licensing)：许可证贸易是目前技术贸易的主要方式。许可证贸易指，技术引进方从技术转让方通过许可证协议取得制造某种产品（或技术）的权利，并得到相应的专有技术，按此生产和销售此产品，其核心就是技术使用权、产品制造权和产品销售权的许可转让。(4)合资企业(joint venture)：合资企业指一个国家的企业在东道国按照东道国的法律、政策等与东道国企业合资经营的企业。一个国家为了扩大国际经济合作和技术交流，吸引外资和获得作为投资的技术和设备，建立合资经营企业。(5)合作经营企业(cooperative enterprise)：合作经营企业也称契约式合营。合作经营企业是按照东道国的有关法律和政策组建的、并非独立的法人实体的合作形式，一般不在东道国单独登记注册，而由合营各方分别以法人身份在东道国登记注册。合作经营是合作各方按照所签订的协议确定其权利和义务的一种经济合作关系。(6)独资企业(wholly foreign owned enterprise):指依照东道国有关法律和政策在东道国境内设立的、全部由外国投资者投资的企业,但不包括外国企业和其他的经济组织在东道国境内的分支机构。(7)BOT(Build—Operation—Transfer)意思是"基础设施建营特许",它指政府通过契约授予外国私营企业以一定期限的特许专营权,许可其融资建设和经营特定的公用基础设施,并准许其通过向用户收取费用或出售产品以清偿贷款,回收投资并赚取利润;特许权期限届满时,该基础设施无偿移交给政府。其特征是:向私营企业给予许可,使其取得通常由政府部门承担的建设和经营特定基础设施的专营权(由招标方式进行);由获专营权的私营企业在特许权期限内负责项目的经营、建设、管理,并用取得的收益偿还贷款;特许权期限届满时,项目公司须无偿将该基础设施移交给政府。

▶ New Words and Expressions

account for 占……比例;是……的理由

acquisition *n.* 获得;买到;收购,并购

affiliate *v. & n.* 接纳为……的分支机构;分支机构

agroeconomic *a.* 农业经济的

apparel *n.* 衣服;服饰;船具(如索具、锚等)

arbitrage *n. & v.* 套利;套汇

asymmetric *a.* 不对称的

backdrop *n.* 背景

beggar-thy-neighbour *n. & a.* 损人利己(的)

biodiversity *n.* 生物多样性

catalyst *n.* 催化剂

close out 清仓出售;出让;(盘出)商店

concentric *a.* 同一中心的

consecutive *a.* 按时间顺序的;连续的

consensus *n.* (意见等的)一致

contract *v.* 使收缩;缩小;承包

curb *v. & n.* 抑制;控制

cyclical *a.* 周期的;循环的

debit *n. & v.* 借方;借项;将……记入借方

deforestation *n.* 砍伐树林

degradation *n.* 降级;(价值等的)低落

deprive *v.* 剥夺

divergent *a.* 有分歧的

diversification *n.* 经营多样化

ecosystem *n.* 生态系统

entrepreneurship *n.* 中小企业开发

exacerbate *v.* 使加剧/恶化

exert *v.* 发挥;产生影响;行使(职权等)

far-fetched *a.* 牵强的

franchise *n. & v.* 特许权;特许经营权;给予……特许经营权

geopolitical *a.* 地理政治学的

glibly *ad.* 流利地;能说会道地

goodwill *n.* (企业或商店等的)信誉

greenfield construction 未开发地域建设

haven *n.* 港口;避难所

hypothesis *n.* 假说;假定

impede *v.* 阻碍;妨碍

incompatible *a.* 不能和谐相处的;不一致的

indebtedness *n.* 感激;感谢

intercept *v.* 截取(情报等)

internationalisation *n.* 国际化

intra-industry *a.* 行业内的

irreversible *a.* 不可逆的

isotope *n.* 同位素

levy *v. & n.* 征收;税款;扣押财产

lump sum 一次性付清的钱

macroeconomic *a.* 宏观经济学的

magnitude *n.* 巨大;重大

mandatory *a. & n.* 强制的;义务的

monopolistic *a.* 垄断的,垄断者的

multilateral *a.* 多边的

neoclassical theory 新古典主义理论

offshore *a.* 国外的

outlaw *v. & n.* 取缔

outright *a.* 不分批(或分期付款)的

patronage *n.* 庇护人;赞助;[总称]顾客

perpetuate *v.* 使永久

portfolio *n.* (皮制的)公文包;组合投资

primary industry 第一产业

privatization *n.* 私有化

propensity *n.* (性格上的)倾向;习性

prototype *n.* 原型;样品

rebound *v. & n.* 反弹,回升

reciprocity *n.* 相互关系;相关性;交换

repatriate *v.* 把……遣还回国

repatriation *n.* 派遣回国

royalty *n.* 版税;专利权使用费

scenario *n.* 方案;设想

scrutiny *n.* 详细调查;研究

seminal *a.* 有潜在发展可能性的;创新的

spin-off *n.* 资产分派(指公司以特定的资产分派给股东,尤指其他公司的股票);资产分派产生的新公司;副产品;派生产品

supremacy *n.* 最高权力/地位

tantamount *v. & n.* (与……)相等;相当(于……)的 (to)

tertiary industry 第三产业

toll road 收费路

transparency *n.* 透明度

under-estimate *v.* 低估

under-invoice *v.* 发票金额少开

undermine *v.* 强调;预告

vocal *a.* 口述的

voice *n. & v.* 投票权;表达

whop *v. & n.* 彻底打败

▶ Discussion Questions

1. Why do companies engage in foreign direct investment?

2. What are the disadvantages of foreign direct investment for the host country?

3. What are the differences between franchising and licensing?

4. How did China manage to become the largest recipient of foreign direct investment?

5. Will China become the largest outbound investing country in the future? Why or why not?

Chapter 11 Human Resource Management 人力资源管理

Objectives
学习目标

To have knowledge on how human resource management functions.

了解人力资源管理的功能。

To understand the importance of global staffing policies and strategy.

了解全球性人力资源配备策略的重要性。

To outline the contents of compensation in international human resource management.

概述国际人力资源管理外派补贴的内容。

To understand how a multinational enterprise is organized.

了解跨国公司的组织结构。

To understand why expatriates meet culture shock.

了解外派人员受到文化冲击的原因。

> 11.1 General View of Human Resource Management（HRM）
人力资源管理概述

In a way, of all the factors in international business, human beings are the most important, as they play the key role in all matters.

In international business management, the management of human resources is a key to the other aspects of management. This is because all the other aspects of management are based on human beings' efforts and influences. As a matter of fact, any type of problem in international business is either created by people or must be solved by people. Hence, having the right people in the right place at the right time emerges as the key to a company's international growth. If we want to solve that problem, first we have to solve the problem of managing human resources.

The important role of human resource management in the process of organizational development cannot be overstated. Human resources are the most valuable asset of any organization. All competitions are less important than competition in managing human resources.

Human resources are regarded as having a central role in determining the success of global and transnational strategy. People have a crucial role to play in devising and implementing strategy, in strategic decision-making and in making strategy successful. Human resources are important mainly for the following reasons.

(1) They play a unique part in organizational learning and competence building.

(2) Their management poses particular questions in a global context.

(3) They are crucial in converting strategies into action.

The management of human resources is a complex and challenging task which extends beyond the traditional role of personnel management (recruitment and selection, performance appraisal, pay bargaining, training and development). It involves the integration of people management issues into the strategic planning process.

HRM carries the promise that, if people are regarded and managed as strategic resources, it can help the firm to obtain a competitive advantage and superior performance. The implementation of effective managerial and labour strategies within global businesses is complicated by variations in culture, value systems, language, business environment and industrial relations systems between countries.

11.2　What Is International HRM?　何谓国际人力资源管理?

HRM involves all management decisions and actions that affect the nature of the relationship between the organization and its employees—its human resources. HRM can also be defined as a strategic and coherent approach to the management of an organization's most valued assets: the people working there who individually and collectively contribute to the achievement of its objectives for sustainable competitive advantage. It can therefore be seen that HRM is concerned with making the most effective use of people in determining and operationalizing strategy. International HRM is the process of selecting, training, developing, and compensating personnel in overseas positions.

Typically, HRM refers to those activities undertaken by an organization effectively to utilize its human resources. These activities would include at least the following:

(1) Human resources planning;

(2) Staffing;

(3) Performance management;

(4) Training and development;

(5) Compensation and benefits;

(6) Labour relations.

Now we can consider the question of which activities change when HRM goes international. Please study the following Figure.

The Figure illustrates the model of international HRM, which is made up of three dimensions.

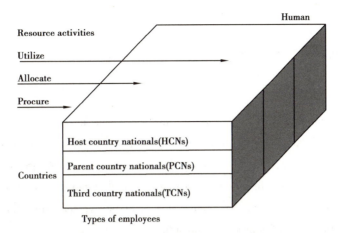

Figure 11.1   Model of International HRM in Multinational Enterprises

(1) The three broad human resource activities: procurement, allocation and utilisation. The three broad activities can be further divided into the 6 HR activities just listed above.

(2) The three national or country categories involved in international HRM activities:

A. The host country where a subsidiary may be located.

B. The home country where the headquarters are located.

C. "Other" countries that may be the source of labour or finance.

(3) There are three types of employees of an international firm:

A. Host country nationals (HCNs).

B. Parent country nationals (PCNs).

C. Third country nationals (TCNs).

For example, IBM employs Chinese citizens (HCNs) in its Chinese operations, and often sends US citizens (PCNs) to Asia-Pacific countries on assignment and may send some of its Singapore employees on an assignment to its Japanese operations (TCNs).

International HRM is considered the interplay among these three dimensions: human resource activities, types of employee and countries of operation. We can see that in broad terms international HRM involves the same activities as domestic HRM. But international HRM is more complex than domestic HRM. This complexity results from the following factors:

(1) More HR activities.

(2) Need for a broader perspective.

(3) More involvement in employees' personal lives.

(4) Changes in emphasis as the workforce mix of expatriates and locals varies.

(5) Risk exposure.

(6) More external influences.

(7) Cultural differences.

11.3　Country Nationals　国民

11.3.1　Parent Country Nationals（PCNs）　母国国民

Parent country nationals（PCNs）refer to employees who are citizens from the country that headquarters the firm. "Parent" refers to the headquarters of the company; "country" refers to the location of the headquarters, and "nationals" refer to the citizenship of the employee. In international business, PCNs are normally managers, technicians, trouble-shooters, subsidiary heads, and experts who travel from the home office to assist overseas subsidiaries and operations. They normally take the key positions of the subsidiary.

There are some advantages of sending PCNs overseas to staff foreign subsidiaries.

First, PCNs are very much familiar with the parent company's operations. They know what the headquarters wants, and thus they can pass on this knowledge to local workers.

Second, PCNs can learn in an intimate way how foreign markets operate, and how foreign consumers and clients react to the products or services the company offers.

Third, PCNs, being in the overseas operations, can gain skills in cross-culture management.

Fourth, PCNs enhance parent company control and co-ordination of overseas operations. Sending TCNs can provide the parent company with a pool of managers with international experience as well as increase the international orientation of the parent firm.

Fifth, PCNs assist the parent company in transferring its best business practices and customs to subsidiaries.

If the subsidiary is located in a country where the political situation is not stable, PCNs are normally assigned there so that they can take top positions of the subsidiary and can pass on true and reliable information, provide advice, control what is going on in the subsidiary, and provide inputs to headquarters about strategy and political considerations.

Besides, PCNs tend to be sent to countries that have significantly different cultural values, business systems, and social norms than those of the home country.

On the other hand, there are some disadvantages of sending PCNs overseas.

First, it is very expensive to send PCNs overseas. In addition to increasing domestic salaries, companies must pick up the cost of relocation, cost-of-living allowances, family benefit packages（such as housing and school）, and costs of protection against terrorism. It has been estimated that a PCN manager costs the company three times the amount a local manager would cost for the same position.

Second, PCNs have cultural problems that may result in additional costs. PCNs have to spend much time adjusting themselves to the local situation. They have to learn nuances, intricacies, and norms of working in a foreign business culture. The time they spend on this cultural problem may have otherwise produced much efficiency and effectiveness in their work.

Third, it is just because PCNs are not familiar with a foreign business world that costs the company money in terms of real business: lost contracts, poor community relations, personal offences to key government officials, poor relations with customers and suppliers, and poor moral at the office.

11.3.2　Host Country Nationals (HCNs)　东道国国民

"Host country nationals" refer to employees of the organization who work in an overseas subsidiary and are natives of the country in which the subsidiary is located. "Host country" refers to the country that hosts the subsidiary, and "national" refers to the citizenship of the workers. For example, An HCN would be a Chinese who works in a Shanghai subsidiary of an American company. Sometimes HCNs are just called "host nationals".

There are advantages of employing HCNs.

HCNs are very much familiar with local business norms and practices. They have no language or culture problem in practice. They can even speak the local dialect. So they may be more adept at motivating and managing workers from the host culture. Therefore, to employ HCNs do not cost as much as it does to employ PCNs.

HCNs can reduce the need for establishing expatriate policies designed to reduce the problems involved in foreign assignments as well as meeting host government regulation.

There are also disadvantages of employing HCNs.

They may not be aware of headquarters' needs since they have never worked at the home office. Besides, they tend to take a local rather than global view of how the subsidiary should operate, and may have cultural problems when communicating and interacting with executives from the parent company.

In addition, it may be difficult to train and develop managers in third world countries where views about achievement, equity, the work ethic, and productivity can differ greatly from western views.

Employing a totally HCN work force may or may not make sense, depending on the culture and industry of the subsidiary. Some think that HCN managers are not as well trained or skilful as PCN managers. But, many countries have a large pool of well-educated and highly motivated HCNs to choose from. In China, HCNs working for foreign companies are normally well-educated. A lot of HCN managers have master degrees or doctorates. Furthermore, some governments require a certain percentage of HCNs to make up the managerial staff of foreign firms operating within their borders.

11.3.3　Third Country Nationals (TCNs)　第三国国民

Third country nationals refer to employees of an organization that work outside of their own country and outside of the country where the parent company is headquartered. For example, a Chinese manager who works for the Singapore subsidiary of an American MNE is a TCN. The reason to transfer or hire TCNs is that they have the necessary expertise or that they are able to work more cheaply than either PCNs or HCNs.

However, the use of TCNs runs the risk of combining the disadvantages associated with both using PCNs and HCNs. TCNs will be unfamiliar with both the local environment and with the business practices of the parent company. In addition, it is possible that the employment of TCNs is very expensive in terms of training, language orientation and compensation complications.

In Europe it is common to meet professionals who have skills that firms eagerly want and who move round the world following their company's (or another firm's) next lucrative offer. Some of these TCNs in Europe are being called "Euro-Managers", because they regard the European continent as their domain, not just their home country.

11.4 Global Staffing Policies and Strategy 全球员工配备政策与策略

Staffing policy is concerned with the selection of employees for particular jobs. At one level, this involves selecting individuals who have the skills required to do particular jobs. At another level, staffing policy can be a tool for developing and promoting corporate culture (the organization's norm and value system).

Basically, there are three types of staffing policies in international businesses: the ethnocentric approach, the polycentric approach, and the geocentric approach. The three aspects of staffing policies are concerned with the three kinds of nationals discussed just above.

11.4.1 The Ethnocentric Approach 以一国为中心

An ethnocentric staffing policy is one in which all key management positions are filled by parent country nationals. This practice was very widespread at one time. But the ethnocentric staffing policy is now on the wane in most international businesses for two reasons.

(1) An ethnocentric staffing policy limits advancement opportunities for host country nationals. As a result, it may lead to resentment, lower productivity, and so on.

(2) An ethnocentric policy can lead to "cultural myopia", the firm's failure to understand host country cultural differences that require different approaches to marketing and management. The adaptation of expatriate managers can take a long time, during which they may make major mistakes.

11.4.2 The Polycentric Approach 以多国为中心

A polycentric staffing policy requires host country nationals to be recruited to manage subsidiaries, while parent country nationals occupy key positions at corporate headquarters. In many respects, a polycentric approach is a response to the shortcomings of an ethnocentric approach. The advantage of adopting a polycentric approach is that the firm is less likely to suffer from cultural myopia. Host country managers are very much familiar with the host country's culture and are less likely to make mistakes due to lack of knowledge about the host country's culture. Another advantage of adopting this approach is that a polycentric approach may be less expensive to implement. Expatriate managers can be very expensive to maintain.

On the other hand, a polycentric approach also has its disadvantages. Host country nationals have limited opportunities to gain experience outside their own country and their views of management are thus limited.

11.4.3　The Geocentric Approach　以全球为中心

A geocentric staffing policy seeks the best people for key positions throughout the organization, regardless of nationality. The advantages of this approach are as follows:

(1) It enables the firm to make the best use of its human resources.

(2) It enables the firm to build a cadre of international executives who feel at home working in a number of countries.

(3) Firms using a geocentric staffing policy may be better able to create value from the pursuit of experience curve and location economies and from the multinational transfer of core competencies than firms using other staffing policies.

(4) The multinational composition of the management team that results from geocentric staffing tends to reduce cultural myopia and to enhance local responsiveness. Therefore, if other things were equal, a geocentric staffing policy would seem the most attractive.

Nevertheless, there are some problems with geocentric approach. Many countries want to hire their citizens. Then there may be some regulations concerning this matter. Besides, a geocentric staffing policy can be very expensive to implement, as there are increased training costs, relocation costs and so on.

11.4.4　Staffing Strategy　员工配备战略

The staffing policies adopted by global business organizations will be influenced mainly by several factors.

(1) The characteristics of both parent and subsidiary.

(2) Characteristics of the host country.

(3) The relative costs of the alternatives.

Besides, there are some other factors that need to be considered in international staffing (Kahal, 1994).

(1) The nature and characteristics of the firm, such as type of ownership of the foreign subsidiary, whether wholly owned, minority-owned or a joint venture.

(2) The time span or duration of the foreign operation of the firm: whether it is long-term, short-term or permanent.

(3) Method of establishing the overseas subsidiary: Whether it is a take-over, merger or acquisition, or foreign direct investment.

(4) International organizational structure: Whether the firm has a geographic, product,

functional or matrix structure.

(5) The type of industry and product line: Whether it is in the manufacturing or service industries.

(6) The market: If, for example, the product is manufactured locally and only for the local market, there will be less need for expatriates, in contrast with global brands, where global managers are needed to ensure the application of standardized global techniques in worldwide markets.

(7) The external environment of the host country, such as the host government's attitude towards FDI, the political system, the sociocultural environment, attitudes towards women, and geographical location.

Therefore, the availability of local management talent in the host country and government restrictions on the employment of expatriates will obviously be important in the choice of home, host or third country nationals. Likewise, differences in salary levels, expatriate transfer costs and failure costs will also be important. The employment of home country nationals is generally greater in new subsidiaries (especially in the start-up phase), greenfield entrants as opposed to acquisition, poor performances, and large subsidiaries.

Although there exist such factors, the dominant influences on global organization staffing policies are likely to be related to the strategic predispositions and value systems of the parent company and its global corporate strategy. In this respect, there is a clear link between staffing policies and the broader strategy of the organization.

It was thought by some that exchange and transfer of personnel within an international business occured for the following three main reasons.

(1) Transfers for staffing: whereby headquarters executives are temporarily transferred abroad to fill key management positions at the overseas subsidiary.

(2) Transfers for management development, which involves a two-way flow of personnel from parent company to foreign subsidiary for management training and development.

(3) Transfers for organizational development, which involves the creation of a pool of international-experienced and trained executives through frequent foreign assignments, and the development of an informal network of interpersonal communications within the organization.

Both the number of international transfers and their direction (parent to subsidiary and vice versa) will vary with the underlying philosophy of the organization. As discussed just above, in ethnocentric businesses, transfers of staff will be normally one-way only: from parent to subsidiary for staffing purposes. Career opportunities for host and third country nationals in ethnocentric companies will be confined to their own countries.

On the other hand, in polycentric businesses, host and third country nationals will spend time at the parent company as part of their management development. The international exchange and transfer of personnel will normally be most frequent in geocentric businesses. This will involve a three-way flow between parent, regional HQs and local subsidiary for staffing, management and organizational development purposes. This can also be regarded as the most "global" of the approaches and is likely to support a corporate strategy which is both global and transnational.

11.5　Training and Development　培训与发展

Training is the process of changing employee behaviour and attitudes in a way that increases the probability of goal attainment (Rugman, 2003). Training programs are designed to provide individuals who are going overseas with information and experience related to local customs, cultures, and work habits and thus help these managers to interact and work more effectively and efficiently with the local workforce in foreign cultures.

Managerial development is the process by which managers obtain the necessary skills, experiences, and attitudes that they need to become or remain successful leaders. Besides, development is typically used to help managers improve their overall effectiveness, and maintain high job satisfactions.

The training of expatriates in preparation for an overseas assignment is important and necessary before, during and after sending the expatriate abroad. These aspects are commonly known as pre-departure training, on-site orientation, and repatriation programs. The training of employees can take place either within the firm or outside.

Training programs seek to prepare potential expatriates for the situations and problems unique to an overseas assignment. For this reason, such programs are country-specific and are quite often tailored to individual needs and time constrains. Among the topics typically are a cultural orientation, the social and religious setting, political and social issues, language training, home country-host country relations, and the legal environment.

11.5.1　Pre-departure Training　赴任前培训

Pre-departure training programs include language studies, documentary and practical information, sensitivity training and field experience. This program normally involves two phases: one for the executive and one for the executive's family.

Documentary information about the subsidiary and its operations in the country is also essential to the clarification of the relationship between the role of the subsidiary and head office (HO). It is important for expatriates to understand clearly the extent to which the subsidiary's operation relates to the overall company's goals and objectives. Besides, documentary information should also include details of the company's relationship with the host country, and the government's policies in terms of job creation, localization, industrial relations, labour structure, labour laws and so on.

Cultural sensitivity training is crucial to the success of expatriates in handling foreign assignments effectively, and in acquiring the ability to interact with people who may have different life styles, habits and viewpoints. There are normally three stages in cultural sensitivity training.

(1) Cultural awareness and self-awareness: Focusing on the cultural differences.

（2）Simulation exercises and role playing：Focusing on actual practice situations.

（3）Field trips to the country of assignment：Focusing on direct contact with foreign environment.

An expatriate's spouse and immediate family members also need to be trained in order that they may more quickly get accustomed to the foreign environment. This cannot be neglected, as the trouble with the expatriate's family in foreign environment will directly affect the expatriate's work effectiveness.

11.5.2　The Orientation Program　适应环境培训计划

The orientation program should include documentary material on daily living, advice from other foreign nationals, information on such things as doing shopping, finding recreation centres, restaurants, schools and university requirements and so on.

For the employees a one-week induction is essential. A guide tour of the facilities, and a month or two coaching from the manager whom the expatriate will replace are essential. Besides, repatriation programs should also be developed by the company to solve the considerable problems expatriate might meet upon returning home.

11.5.3　Repatriation　外派人员归国

A largely overlooked but critically important issue in the training and development of expatriate managers is to prepare them for re-entry into their home country organization. Repatriation should be seen as the final link in an integrated, circular process that connects good selection and cross-cultural training of expatriate managers with completion of their term abroad and reintegration into their national organization. However, instead of having employees come home to share their knowledge and encourage other high-performing managers to take the same international career track, expatriates often face a different scenario.

When starting to work in the home company, the expatriates have to, as they did when going overseas to work, receive some kind of training for the purpose of getting accustomed to working back in the domestic company. There might be some repatriation problems concerning expatriates.

Repatriation refers to the process of returning home at the end of an overseas assignment. In other words, repatriation means that when expatriates return to their home country, planning and preparing for this event are important for expatriates and the home office alike.

The whole process of adjusting to one's home culture after having lived abroad is complex. Dealing with disappointments in the return job is just one aspect of the process. There are normally four major variables that affect repatriation adjustment：individual, job, organization, and non-work. Under each of these classifications are a subset of issues that can positively or negatively influence repatriation adjustment. The return job issue is generally viewed by researchers in the field as being the most significant indicator of level of repatriation adjustment；however, the other factors may play important roles in repatriation adjustment as well.

Returning home may evoke mixed feelings on the part of the expatriate and the family. Their concerns are both professional and personal. Even in two years, dramatic changes may have occurred not only at home but also in the way the individual and the family perceive the foreign environment. At worst, reverse culture shock may emerge.

1. Reasons for Repatriation

Managers are repatriated for several reasons. The most common one is that the predetermined time assignment is completed. Another is the desire to have their children educated in the home country. The expatriates do not want their children to forget their own culture. The expatriate may be unhappy overseas, and the company may feel there is more to be gained by bringing the person back than in trying to persuade the individual to stay on. Finally, as in any position, if the manager has performed poorly, the MNE may decide to put someone else to replace the position.

2. Readjusting

Expatriates coming back from abroad after working for a long time find it hard to adjust themselves to the "new surroundings" back in the domestic company. This may be for the reasons as follows:

First, the home office job lacks the high degree of authority and responsibility that expatriates had in their overseas job.

Second, expatriates feel the company does not value international experience and the time spent overseas seems to have been wasted in terms of career progress.

Some companies do not have plans for handling returning managers. If these individuals are assigned jobs at random, they can find their career progress jeopardized.

It is found out that the longer people work in a foreign country, the more problems they are likely to have been reabsorbed into the operations back home. In addition to the factors mentioned just above, some factors make repatriation after longer periods difficult.

(1) Expatriates may no longer be well known among people at headquarters.

(2) Their old job may have been eliminated or drastically changed.

(3) Technological advances at headquarters may have rendered their existing skills and knowledge obsolete.

3. Adjustment Strategies

It is necessary and also very important to help expatriates to adjust themselves to the domestic company surroundings for the sake of the expatriate and the company as well. The management of the headquarters need have plans to achieve this aim.

It is found out that in recent years some MNEs have begun to tackle adjustment problems faced by returning expatriates. Some organizations have now developed transition strategies that are designed to help smooth the move from foreign to domestic assignments.

Basically, the adjustment strategies that can be helpful are as follows (Rugman, 2003):

(1) Repatriation agreement: It stipulates clearly how long the person will be posted overseas

and sets forth the type of job that will be given to the person upon his returning. The agreement typically does not stipulate a particular position or salary, but it promises a job that is at least equal in authority and compensation to the one the person held overseas. This agreement relieves much of the anxiety that expatriates encounter.

(2) To rent or maintain the expatriate's home while he works overseas. It can help the expatriate to reduce financial burden to some extent.

(3) To assign a senior executive as a sponsor for each manager who is posted abroad. In this way, there is someone looking after each expatriate and ensuring that his or her performance, compensation, and career path are on track. When the person is scheduled to return home, the sponsor will begin working internally to ensure that there is a suitable position for the expatriate.

(4) To maintain ongoing communications with expatriate managers, thereby ensuring that they are aware of what is happening in the home office.

11.5.4　Types of Training　培训类型

The aim of training is to ensure that the adjustment to the new environment is quick and smooth. The methods range from relatively superficial country briefings to in-depth environmental experiences. The type of appropriate training depends on the candidate's previous experience and the degree of similarity or dissimilarity between the home country and the host country, as well as the length of stay, type of position, and the required degree of integration into the community.

The cost of extensive, in-depth training is high; therefore, the company wants to use this type of training effectively.

It is found out that the appropriate training of expatriates and their families improves their success rate. Given the costs associated with an expatriate's failure, it seems that international companies should consider training as an integral part of the expatriation process. The aim of cross-cultural training program is to increase individuals' sensitivity to their own and other cultures, to promote acceptance of cultural differences, and to provide understanding of a specific culture.

Training and development programs can be divided into two general categories: standardized and tailor-made.

Standardized training programs are generic and can be used with managers anywhere in the world. Examples include programs for improving quantitative analysis or technical skills that can be used universally. It is found out that behavioral-oriented concepts can also be handled with a standardized program (although follow-on program must be tailor-made to meet the specific needs of the country).

Tailor-made training programs are designed to meet the specific needs of the participants and typically include a large amount of culturally based input. These programs are more commonly developed by large MNEs and by multinationals that need working knowledge of the local country's beliefs, norms, attitudes, and work values.

Research shows that the following six types of programs are most popular (Rugman, 2003).

(1) Environmental briefings used to provide information about such things as geography, climate, housing, and schools.

(2) Cultural orientation designed to familiarize the individual with cultural institutions and value systems of the host country.

(3) Cultural assimilators using programmed learning approaches designed to provide the participants with intercultural encounters.

(4) Language training.

(5) Sensitivity training designed to develop attitudinal flexibility.

(6) Field experience, which sends the participant to the country of assignment to undergo some of the emotional stress of living and working with people from a different culture.

In international business practice, MNEs tend to use a combination of the above programs, tailoring the package to meet their specific needs.

It is suggested that training for the manager should focus on job-related issues, including:

(1) economic, political, and legal environments;

(2) government policies and regulations;

(3) management practices (including labour relations, hiring and firing, religious holidays, and so on);

(4) relationship between the subsidiary and the rest of the company;

(5) specifics of the job (including reporting relationships, time frames, objectives, and so on).

On the other hand, training for the manager and his family should focus on relationship issues, including:

(1) language training (at least an elementary knowledge of the local language to allow some basic communication on arrival);

(2) area training (including history, religion, culture, and so forth);

(3) practical training (including currency, food, dress, climate, specific customs, and so on).

From a different perspective of this issue we can divide training into the following.

(1) Environmental briefing: It consists of a short briefing by someone with knowledge of the foreign environment. This normally includes readings, films, lectures, and discussion. This training approach is specific to one location and gives general information.

(2) Cultural sensitive training: It consists of a variety of interactions with people of other cultures. The aim is to increase individuals' sensitivity to cultural differences by allowing them to develop a better understanding of why people behave in different ways. This training approach is not location-specific and focuses on relationships rather than specific information. A particular form of this training approach is the cultural simulation, in which real or imagined cultures are simulated and participants interact with people who exhibit different cultural behaviors.

(3) Critical incidents and cases: They consist of a variety of simulated real-life episodes that are location-specific and involve interactions between people of different cultural backgrounds. The trainee assesses and responds to different situations, and these responses are evaluated and

discussed. The aim is to increase sensitivity to locational differences and to focus on specific issues that may arise in a particular location. This approach can focus on location-specifics as well as general cultural sensitivity.

▶ 11.6   Expatriates   外派人员

Parent company nationals, third-country nationals assigned to subsidiaries, and foreign nationals assigned to parent companies are typically referred to as expatriates. Expatriates are generally found in technical and managerial assignments, and their numbers have historically been significant.

11.6.1   Selection of Expatriates   外派人员的挑选

No matter what general staffing policy a company has adopted, it normally has at least some PCNs who serve in foreign positions, generally at the managerial level. The success of these expatriate managers is often very important to the company's overall success. And the careful selection contributes to the overall success of the company.

The selection process involves evaluating all the job applications received, conducting initial interviews, testing skills or ability to learn on the job, gathering references, checking the truthfulness of applicants' resumes, conducting physical examinations, and finally making the job offer, specifying the salary and benefit packages.

Recruitment and selection are much more complex at the international level. A candidate's technical expertise, education, local experience and past record of achievement are good indicators for his or her suitability and potential success in a domestic market, but do not automatically guarantee successful performance in foreign markets.

An effective expatriate manager must have special abilities and traits if he or she is to avoid blundering. The most important characteristics include the following.

(1) An ability to get along well with people.

(2) An awareness of cultural differences.

(3) Open-mindedness.

(4) Tolerance of foreign cultures.

(5) Adaptability to new cultures, ideas, and challenges.

(6) An ability to adjust quickly to new conditions.

(7) An interest in facts, not blind assumptions.

(8) Previous business experience, and previous experience with foreign language.

(9) An ability to learn foreign languages.

Therefore, when selecting candidates to work overseas, the above should be carefully considered. Candidates who have an interest in serving in foreign locations are identified and assessed in terms of their general suitability for foreign assignments. This general assessment considers each candidate's apparent adaptability, flexibility, openness to other cultures, and reasons for applying for a position in a foreign country. A candidate who appears to be generally suitable is considered in more detail as specific opportunities arise. The candidates judged to be less suitable receive suggestions for improvement.

In addition, the family of a successful candidate should also be considered. If the family of the potential expatriate support and are very much interested in this assignment, the expatriate may work more effectively.

11.6.2　Reasons for Using Expatriates　使用外派人员的原因

Only those who are the most qualified may be expatriates. Although expatriate managers comprise a minority of total managers within MNEs, companies employ expatriates because of their competence to fill positions, their need to gain foreign experience, and their ability to control operations according to headquarters' preference. There are a number of reasons why companies use expatriate managers.

First, when companies cannot find qualified local candidates, expatriate managers are used. This is partly determined by a country's level of development. Normally there are more expatriate managers in developing countries. This is determined by the need to transfer technologies abroad.

Second, to transfer people to overseas subsidiaries is to attempt to understand the overall corporate system. In companies with specialized activities only in certain countries (such as extraction separated from manufacturing or basic R&D separated from applied R&D), long-term foreign assignments may be the only means of developing a manager's breadth.

Third, home-country expatriates are used to control foreign operation because they are used to doing things in the headquarters' way. People transferred from headquarters are more likely to know corporate policies.

In addition, expatriates can pass on true information about subsidiaries to the headquarters and they will work fully for the sake of the headquarters.

11.6.3　The Expatriate Adaptation Process　外派人员的适应过程

Generally speaking there are four phases in the expatriate adaptation process.

(1) The initial phase: When the expatriate transfers to the foreign assignment, the newness of the culture creates a great deal of excitement for him or her.

(2) The disillusionment phase: After about two months, the novelty of the new culture wears out, and day-to-day inconveniences caused, for example, by different practices in the local culture and not being able to communicate effectively create disillusionment for the expatriate.

(3) The cultural shock phase: After about two months of the day-to-day confusions the expatriate faces a cultural shock. By now the expatriate is ready to go back to his or her old, familiar environment.

(4) The positive adjustment phase: If the expatriate remains, at about Month Four of the

assignment, he or she begins to adapt, and by Month Six he or she feels more positive about the foreign environment; he or she, however, does not attain the "high" of the first two months, but not the "low" of the next two months.

Expatriates need time to adjust themselves to the new environment. It is thought by some that expatriates should be exempted from active management activities in the first six months after arriving in the foreign market. This is because they need time for adjustment. Normally they will undergo the above four phases in the course of adapting themselves to the new culture. But it should be noted that this model of four phases is just general, and that some people are not able to pull out of the culture shock phase.

11.6.4   Women as Sources of Expatriates   女性外派人力资源

The option of using women expatriates is underutilized by some MNEs. The underutilization of women for foreign assignments may derive from the presumption that male managers in foreign countries culturally do not accept women as business partners and equals. Cultural biases against women in some host countries (especially in the Middle East, Japan, and Latin America) may deter the acceptance of women as managers. Subordinates in such host-country subsidiaries may interpret the assignment of a woman executive to mean that the headquarters has low regard for its business with that subsidiary. They may also worry that a woman will have less autonomy in local negotiations, and will thus be less able to represent the subsidiary in local transactions. Besides, not many women in the home office were at a level at which they would be eligible for most foreign assignments. Further, many companies believe that it would be difficult for women to undergo some of the hardships associated with foreign assignments.

However, more women are now in eligible positions, and pressure for equality in the workplace, including in foreign assignments, is increasing, particularly when foreign assignments are seen as a stepping stone to top-level position. Women want access to these assignments. More and more women have the sense of independence and competition with men. They are willing to undergo the hardships associated with foreign assignments and believe that they are equally capable of undertaking them. Research reveals that women are good expatriate managers and that foreign women are accepted as managers, even in countries in which local women do not hold such positions—they are seen, in a sense, as a third sex. Besides, male managers in many countries do make a distinction between foreign women professionals and local women—many male managers may not accept local females in managerial roles but will accept foreign females.

It is suggested that it is necessary to explore the possibilities of utilizing female expatriates more than in the past. Many expatriates fail because of a shortage of relational skills. These skills are abilities generally ascribed to female managers. It has been found out that women managers, compared with their male counterparts, experienced significantly lower levels of boundary-spanning stress; that is, women were more adept in coping with the pressures and strains resulting from the foreign environment. It has also been found out that women sometimes are more sensitive to cultural difference than their male counterparts, that they may be treated with deference in some locations, and that they can sometimes gain access to locals when men cannot.

There emerges a new issue in recent years: dual-career couple. The dual-career issue becomes particularly important when considering women expatriates because these women normally have spouses with careers of their own. North American society has encouraged equality in the workplace between women and men, but in general it is still more difficult socially for men to accept the subordinate work role or the homemaker role. Such roles are very often necessary when a man accompanies his wife on an expatriate assignment. International companies need to give careful thought to this if they want to make the best use of their human resources in international assignments.

11.7　Compensation　报酬

In recent years compensation has become a primary aspect of international human resource management. In addition to the complex process of selecting the right individuals for foreign positions, training those individuals and their families, and implementing systems designed to ensure their success, the company should design an acceptable compensation package for the expatriates. Ineffective expatriate compensation can lead to expatriate failures. Therefore, international companies need to establish policy for effective management of expatriate compensation. To arrive at this goal, it is necessary to obtain knowledge of the foreign country's laws, customs, environment, employment practices, and the effects of currency exchange fluctuations and inflation on compensation. Besides, within the context of changing political, economic, and social conditions, it is also necessary to understand why certain allowances are essential and must be provided. For example, an assignment in a hostile or undesirable environment would require greater compensation than an assignment in a friendly, desirable environment.

The compensation of the manager overseas can be divided into two general categories: first, base salary and salary-related allowances; second, nonsalary-related allowances. Although incentives to leave home are justifiable in both categories, they create administrative complications for the personnel department in tying them to packages at home and elsewhere. As the number of transfers increases, firms develop general policies for compensating the manager rather than negotiate individually on every aspect of the arrangement.

11.7.1　Objectives of Compensation　报酬的目标

A firm's international compensation program has to be effective in the following aspects.

(1) Providing an incentive to leave the home country on a foreign assignment.

(2) Maintaining a given standard of living.

(3) Taking into consideration career and family needs.

(4) Facilitating reentry into the home country.

To achieve the above objectives, firms normally pay a high premium beyond base salaries to include managers to accept overseas assignments.

Generally speaking, the main objectives of expatriate compensation policies are as follows (Rodrigues, 1996):

(1) The policy should be consistent and fair in its treatment of all categories of expatriate employees.

(2) The policy must work to attract and retain expatriates in the areas where the corporation has the greatest need.

(3) The policy should facilitate the transfer of expatriates in the most cost-effective manner.

(4) The policy should be consistent with the overall strategy and structure of the organization.

(5) The compensation should serve to motivate employees.

When designing the policy, a decision must be made about whether to establish an overall policy for all employees or to distinguish between home country nationals (expatriates) and host-country and third-country nationals. Currently, it is common for international companies to distinguish between them.

11.7.2　Common Elements in an International Compensation Package　外派人员报酬的常见形式

People performing relatively similar jobs in different countries may receive different amounts and forms of compensation. Designing an adequate compensation package for expatriates is crucial to the attraction and retaining of managers in overseas assignments. However, developing an equitable plan is not easy. This is especially true when a company operates in more than one country.

Typically, international compensation package elements include base salary, benefits, and allowances. Besides, the issue of tax protection and/or tax equalization is also involved in most such packages.

1. Base Salary

A manager's base salary depends on qualifications, responsibilities, and duties, just as it would for a domestic position. Besides, criteria applying to merit increases, promotions, and other increases are administered as they are domestically. Equity and comparability with domestic positions are important, especially in ensuring that repatriation will not cause cuts in base pay. For administrative and control purposes, the compensation and benefits function in MNEs is most often centralized.

Generally speaking, salaries paid to expatriates assigned to different foreign countries vary significantly according to local competitive conditions, cost of living, taxes, life style, currency fluctuation, hardship factors, difference in cost of housing, education, recreation, food and so on.

Base salary is the amount of cash compensation that an individual receives in the home country. This salary is typically the benchmark against which bonuses and benefits are calculated. Basically, the salaries of expatriates are tied to their home country. This salary is normally paid in either home currency, local currency, or a combination of the two.

Besides, as mentioned just above, the base salary for the expatriates is normally determined by comparing the overseas position with comparable domestic positions in the parent company. Because the expatriate is normally moving to an overseas position that is a promotion from his or her current position, the base salary often is, in essence, a pay raise. The purpose of the base salary is to allow the expatriate to maintain the same personal purchasing power while overseas. Further, the base salary normally covers the costs of goods and services, saving, and income taxes.

2. Benefits

Benefits make up a large portion of the compensation package. Benefits may include medical coverage, social security, retirement package and so on. In addition, MNEs also provide vacation and special leave to expatriates. This often includes company-paid air fare back home for the manager and family on an annual basis, as well as emergency leave and expense payments in case of death or illness in the family.

3. Allowances

Allowances are another major portion of some expatriate compensation packages. One of the most common is the cost-of-living allowance. There are a number of allowances that are stated as follows:

(1) Cost-of-living allowance (COLA). COLA is to help expatriates maintain their domestic standard of living while overseas. It is a payment to compensate for differences in expenditures between the home country and the foreign location. This allowance is designed to provide the employee with the same standard of living that he or she enjoyed in the home country. COLA is basically a salary adjustment because it is virtually impossible to find living conditions overseas that perfectly reflect the expatriate's domestic conditions and costs. The COLA is a buffer that makes sure that the expatriate has enough spendable income to take care of food, clothing, entertainment, and other daily expenses. The COLA changes are based upon exchange rate fluctuations and cost-of-living index fluctuations.

(2) Hardship or site allowance. It is payment given to expatriates who relocate to a country that is designated as a "hardship" country. Many companies consider some countries as being more difficult to live in and adjust to than others. As a reward for accepting an assignment in such countries, companies sometimes give lump sum payments as bonuses.

(3) Housing allowance. It is the most significant aspect of the compensation package next to the base salary. Housing allowances cover a wide range. Some firms will provide the manager with a residence while overseas and pay all expenses associated with running the house. Other firms will give the individual a predetermined amount of money each month and the manager can make the housing choice by himself or herself. Some MNEs will also help the individual to sell his or her house back home or to rent it until the manager returns. The company normally pays expenses associated with these activities. But some companies may encourage their people to retain ownership of their

home by paying all rental management fees and reimbursing the employee for up to six months' rent if the house remains unoccupied.

（4）Foreign service premium. Foreign service premium is actually a bridge to encourage a manager to leave familiar conditions and adapt to new surroundings. Although the methods of paying the premium vary, as do its percentages, most firms pay it as a percentage of the base salary. The percentage normally ranges from 10 to 30 percent of base salary. Foreign service premium is in fact extra pay that companies provide to expatriates for working outside the home country. It is a kind of compensation for the inconveniences of having to live in a new environment isolated from family and friends, for difficulty in language and cultural barriers, for greater responsibility and reduced access to home-office resources, and for the effort of dealing with different work habits.

（5）Education allowance. Education allowances for the expatriate's children are an integral part of most compensation packages. These expenses cover such things as tuition, enrolment fees, books, supplies, transportation, room, board, and school uniforms. In some cases attendance at post-secondary schools is also provided.

（6）Tax protection and tax-equalization. One of the major determinants of the manager's life style abroad is taxes. MNEs normally provide tax protection and/or tax equalization for expatriates. Companies usually handle taxation of expatriates in two ways. Because expatriates must pay taxes both to their home country and to the host country, companies either make up the difference in the expatriates' net pay (called " tax protection"), or the company pays the expatriate's foreign taxes that are in excess of the expatriate's home-country tax (called " tax equalization").

11.7.3　Current Compensation Trends　当前报酬政策的趋势

It has been the practice of international compensation for the expatriates that MNEs try to find out most cost-effective ways in this respect. In terms of compensation, the MNE's objective is normally to ensure that the expatriate does not have to pay any additional expenses as a result of living abroad. Experience is accumulated through the practice. Nowadays, there seem to be some trends in international compensation.

First, there is a trend towards not sending expatriates to overseas positions unless it is quite necessary for some specific services.

Second, MNEs are increasingly replacing permanent relocation and long-term assignment with short trips that typically last less than a year.

Third, MNEs tend to create special incentive system designed to keep expatriates motivated. In the process, a growing number of MNEs are now dropping bonuses or premiums for overseas assignments and replacing them with lump-sum premiums. This method produces two benefits: expatriates realize that they will be given this payment just once; the costs to the company are less because there is only one payment and no future financial commitment.

Finally, a new trend is that many companies are beginning to phase out incentive premium. Instead, they are focusing on creating a cadre of expats who are motivated by non-financial incentives.

🔵 11.8　Labour Relations　劳资关系

MNEs always face the problems of labour relations. In each country where an MNE operates, it must deal with a group of workers whose approach will be affected by the socio-political environment of the country.

National differences in economic, political, and legal systems create a variety of labour relations systems, and the strategy that is effective in one country or region might not be useful in another country.

Relationships with other employees in different cultural environments are crucial to the success of MNEs. This is especially the case in globally-integrated organizations, where industrial relations problem at one subsidiary may have wider effects on the global network. The effective management of labour and industrial relations within transnational companies is also much more difficult than in purely domestic companies due to variations in culture, attitudes towards work, working practices, industrial relations systems and the legal environment governing labour and management relations. Such variations cause two major difficulties for the business.

(1) The extent to which labour and industrial relations decisions-making should be centralized at the level of the parent company.

(2) The extent to which the business should transfer its country of origin HR and industrial relations practices abroad.

The modern approach to the management of employee relations is to emphasize co-operation rather than conflict and to integrate employee relations policies into the overall corporate strategy of the firm. Therefore, the management of the business must recognize the critical importance of harmonious relations with its workforce in various countries, and relate its employee relations policies to the achievement of increased competitiveness in the international field. Major decisions that have to be taken when formulating an employee relations strategy include the following (Bennett, 1999):

(1) whether to recognize trade unions.

(2) managerial approaches to personnel policies and procedures that affect employee relations (recruitment and promotion; appraisal; selection of workers for training, redundancy, etc.).

(3) whether management is prepared to use external bodies to arbitrate and help resolve disputes.

(4) the basic formula to be applied to the division of the firm's profit between the owners of the business and workers.

(5) the methods to be used for communicating with employees.

(6) the degree to which employee representatives are to be involved in management decision-making.

In managing labour relations, most MNEs use a combination of centralization and decentralization with some decisions being made at headquarters and others being handled by managers on-site. It is found out that US MNEs tend to exercise more centralized control in contrast to European MNEs such as the British.

In reality, there are striking international differences in how labour and management view each other. When there is little mobility between the two groups (children of labourers become labourers, and children of managers become managers), a marked class difference exists, and companies may face considerable labour disputes. Labour may regard itself in a class struggle, even though it may have been closing wage gaps for some time. In such countries as Brazil, Switzerland, and the USA, labour demands are largely met through an adversarial process between the directly affected management and labour.

In the USA, unions negligibly influence members' vote in political elections. In contrast, labour groups in many other countries vote the way their labour leaders instruct them, so their demands are met primarily through national legislation rather than collective bargaining with management.

11.9　The Role of Union　工会的作用

The role of trade unions is different in different countries. This may be due to local traditions in management-labour relations. The differences include the extent of union power in negotiation and the activities of unions in general. In Europe, especially in the Northern European countries, collective bargaining takes place between an employer's association and an umbrella organization of union, on either a national or a regional basis, establishing the conditions for an entire industry.

Another striking difference emerges in terms of the objectives of union and the means by which they attempt to attain them. For instance, in the United Kingdom, union activity is more politics-orientated; while in the USA, they focus more on improving workers' overall quality of life. Companies in a given country may deal with one or more unions. A union itself may represent workers in many industries, in many companies within the same industry, or in only one company. If it represents only one company, the union may represent all plants or just one plant. Although there are diversities within countries, one type of relationship is most prevalent within most countries. For example, unions in the USA tend to be national, as mentioned previously, representing certain types of workers (for instance, airline pilots, coal miners, truck drivers, or university professors). So a company may deal with several different national unions. Each collective-bargaining process normally is characterized by a single company on one side rather than an association of different companies that deal with one of the unions representing a certain type of workers in all the plants of the companies.

11.10　Organization Structure of the MNE　跨国企业组织结构

A manager of an MNE must keep a clear picture of the organization structure in mind. In this way he can know how the company is organized, the functions of the divisions, to whom he is responsible, and to whom he is entitled to give directions.

Figure 11.2 is a simple function structure.

Figure 11.2　A Simple Function Structure

An organizational structure is the arrangement and interrelationship of the component parts and positions of a company. It clearly shows the division of work activities and functions within the firm, and their relationships. Besides, it also indicates the level of specification for each function, the hierarchy and authority structure, and how decision-making takes place.

An organizational structure is neither predetermined nor permanently fixed. It should follow and reflect the growth of the firm. Many factors influence the design of organizational structure, such as corporate goals and objectives, management styles and philosophy, staffing and capital needs, product and production line, as well as factors in the external environment.

Organizational structure may differ from one company to another and from one country to another, depending on the nature of the business activities, environmental requirements and the assets employed. Consequently, there is no " best" or " universally" valid organizational structure suitable for international business operations.

Organizational structure is fundamental to its ability to achieve its goals effectively; thus the structure provides a framework for control of the firm. The structure of the organization ensures that the work to be performed is identified and broken into manageable units, that these units are meaningfully related to each other, and that desired communication among these units can take place.

Organizations need a defined structure in order to accomplish their chosen strategy. Designing the formal structure of an organization is like designing the structure of a building. The nature and design of the structure of an organization is largely determined by its size. The following Figure 11.3 and Figure 11.4 are samples of organization charts.

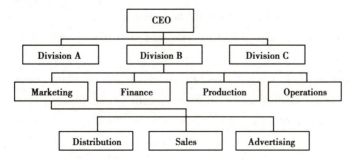

Figure 11.3　A Divisionalized Structure

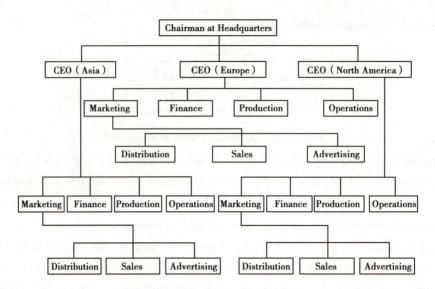

Figure 11.4   A Multinational Structure

11.11   Culture Shock   文化冲击

The term, culture shock, was introduced for the first time in 1958 to describe the anxiety produced when a person moves to a completely new environment. This term expresses the lack of direction, the feeling of not knowing what to do or how to do things in a new environment, and not knowing what is appropriate or inappropriate. The feeling of culture shock generally sets in after the first few weeks of coming to a new place.

We can describe culture shock as the physical and emotional discomfort one suffers when coming to live in another country or a place different from the place of origin. Often, the way that we lived before is not accepted as or considered normal in the new place. Everything is different, for example, not speaking the language, not knowing how to use banking machines, not knowing how to use the telephone and so forth.

Starting to work in a new culture, managers will face the problem of culture shock. Culture shock follows the general pattern of a U-shaped curve. The cycle of culture shock is divided into four stages: honeymoon, culture shock, adjustment, and mastery.

During the honeymoon stage, the expatriate is fascinated by the host country's culture. Everything is new and exciting.

During the culture shock stage the expatriate changes from being infatuated with the host country's culture to being disillusioned, frustrated, confused, or unhappy with living and working overseas. They will run into problems resulting from cultural differences, which make it hard for him to perform his management duties. Some expatriates can never get out of the culture shock stage. They either return home early from their assignments or simply " gut it out" and complete their assignments but are never completely effective in their assignment or happy about living in the host culture.

The adjustment stage occurs when the expatriate begins to learn the norm and ways of getting things done in the new culture and in the job. In other words, they are getting used to the new culture while tolerating some hardships from the cultural differences. This stage is a gradual adaptation. This gradual learning of the host country's culture requires intensive effort on the part of expatriates—it does not occur naturally.

As time goes by, the expatriate may enter the mastery stage when he or she can function effectively in and enjoy the nuances of the host country's culture and its institutions, norms, traditions, and activities. At this stage, expatriates are almost accustomed to the new culture although they may not completely accept the new culture.

Not all expatriates go through this cycle of four stages, though there is evidence that expatriates do generally go through each phase of the cycle.

Summary of This Chapter
本章概要

1. 国际人力资源管理主要指某个组织(公司、企业等)有效地管理、运用其人力资源的活动。这些活动涉及公司的人力资源策略制定、人员配备、任务和责任限定、业绩评估、工作酬劳、劳工关系等方面。国际人力资源管理涉及不同国家的种种因素,如文化、政治制度、宗教、法律制度、经济状况等。所以,国际人力资源管理比起本国人力资源管理要复杂得多。人力资源管理的好坏直接影响公司的生存,因为人是决定一切事物的主要因素。

2. 人员配备通常指委派适当的人选担任特定的工作。科学、合理地配备公司员工是发展、促进企业文化的一个重要方面。跨国公司通常有 3 种人员配备策略。(1)以一国为中心(ethnocentric approach):公司的重要职位由母国公司所派的人担任,其利是能较好地贯彻母公司的经营策略;其弊是将限制东道国员工的发展机会,从而引起负面作用。(2)以多国为中心(polycentric approach):子公司的管理人员由东道国雇员担任,但是公司总部的关键职位由母国所派人员担任。其利是避免了以一国为中心的策略的缺点,并且还避免了文化隔膜,此外,这种策略能降低成本;其弊是东道国雇员不能透彻地理解、贯彻母公司的经营策略,并且很可能与母国公司的经理产生隔阂。(3)以全球为中心(geocentric approach):从科学、合理的人力资源管理出发,不侧重人员的国籍,重点在于人力资源的优化组合。其利是能更合理地使用人力资源,并能因此为公司建立起一支强健的国际管理层,以适应在不同的文化背景下运作;其弊是成本较高,国际间转移管理人员需要增加培训费和再安置费。另外,由于公司的报酬结构通常需要采用国际标准,其结果是:这些管理人员的高报酬会引起公司其他管理人员的不满。

3. 外派人员:以一国为中心和以全球为中心的策略需要使用外派经理。挑选外派人员进入公司管理层必须慎重。外派人员必须具备以下几个方面的条件:(1)拥有自尊、自信及敢于迎接挑战的心态;(2)拥有较高的情商,善于与人打交道,较好地掌握了东道国的语言,以便和东道国员工沟通;(3)具有较好的异国文化适应能力,能较快地走出文化隔膜期,顺利有效地开展工作。外派人员任职期满归国后的问题也应该引起注意。人力资源管理必须为外派人员回国后尽快适应母国公司的工作、生活,而作出合理的安排。

4. 培训指外派人员的培训。(1)文化培训:派往国外的管理人员必须熟悉所去国家的文化、历史、政治、经济、宗教,以便顺利地开展工作;(2)语言培训:外派管理人员最好能懂一些东道国语言,这样便于和本土的员工沟通及相处;(3)实践培训:外派人员需要接受培训以尽快适应东道主国家的日常生活。此外,外派人员的配偶也需要接受培训,因为如果配偶不能适应国外的生活,势必会影响外派人员的工作。

5. 外派人员的待遇:外派人员的报酬通常包括基本工资、国外服务奖金、补贴、纳税及其他有关福利。基本工资与在国内工作时的基本工资水平相同。国外服务奖金是一种鼓励员工接受外派的手段。补贴一般包括辛苦补贴、住房补贴、生活成本补贴和教育补贴。纳税通常指公司为外派人员支付东道国的所得税。福利指诸如医疗、养老金等福利。

6. 国际劳工关系:人力资源管理的一个主要职能就是促进企业与劳工组织之间的和谐,减少二者之间的矛盾与冲突。国际劳工关系的关键问题是劳工组织所能限制国际企业的程度。劳动工会的行动会极大地限制企业追求跨国或全球战略的能力。工会的作用不容忽视。工会在处理劳资关系时能发挥重要的作用。

New Words and Expressions

adversarial *a.* 敌对的;对抗的

appraisal *n.* 估价;评价;估计

ascribe *v.* 把……归因(或归属)于

blunder *v. & n.* 犯大错误;大错

buffer *v. & n.* 缓冲,缓和;缓冲器

compensation *n.* 补贴

deference *n.* 听从;敬重

deter *v.* 使不敢;阻止

eligible *a. & n.* 合格的 (人)

ethnocentric *a.* 种族中心主义的

exempt *v.* 免除;豁免

expat(=**expatriate**) *n.* 外派人员

geocentric *a.* 以全球为中心的

gut it out 坚持到底

incentive *a. & n.* 刺激性的;鼓励(性)的; 刺激;鼓励;奖励;动机

infatuate *v.* 使冲昏头脑;使着迷

motivate *v.* 使有动机;推动;激发

negligibly *ad.* 忽略地

novelty *n.* 新颖;新奇

polycentric *a.* 多中心的

redundancy *n.* 裁员;解雇;累赘

subordinate *n. & v. & a.* 下级;下属;控制;下级的; 从属的

trait *n.* 品质; 特性;少许

wear out 穿破;用旧;(使)疲乏;经受住

Discussion Questions

1. What does international human resource management mean?

2. Why should expatriates receive training before going to work overseas?

3. Women are not welcomed as expatriates, are they? Why or why not?

4. Does trade union have the same function in different countries? Why or why not?

Chapter 12 International Logistics 国际物流

Objectives
学习目标

To understand the nature of international logistics.

了解国际物流的性质。

To understand the position of international logistics in international business.

了解国际物流在国际商务中的地位。

To understand the functions of international logistics.

了解国际物流的功能。

12.1 Nature of Logistics 国际物流的性质

The term "logistics" has become much more widely recognized by the general public in the last thirty years. Transportation companies, especially trucking companies, frequently refer to their organizations as logistics companies and paint it on the side of their trailers. Another factor contributing to the recognition of logistics has been the increasing sensitivity to not only product quality but also the associated service quality.

Logistics is often seen as just the transportation of goods from one place to another. In fact, this view is too narrow and does not reflect the more complex and comprehensive nature of the function. Logistics is really about managing every aspect of a company's business, from sourcing raw materials to production, warehousing, marketing, pricing, sales and ultimately the transportation of the finished goods to the buyer.

Logistics is big business. Its consumption of land, labour, capital, and information—coupled with its impact on the world's standard of living—is enormous. Logistics and the closely related concept of supply chain management are necessary cornerstones of competitive strategy, increased market share, and shareholder value for most organizations.

Even with the increased recognition of the term "logistics", however, there is still confusion about the definition of logistics or what it really means.

Logistics is actually a word closely associated with the military, where it has come to stand for all of the activities associated with the wartime deployment and ongoing support of a nation's armed forces. Logistics concept began to appear in the business-related literature in the 1960s under the label of "physical distribution", which had a focus on the outbound side of the logistics system. Business logistics is a relatively new field of integrated management study in comparison with the traditional fields of finance, marketing, and production.

Logistics is normally defined as: the process of planning, implementing, and controlling the efficient, cost-effective flow and storage of raw materials, in-process inventory, finished goods and related information from point of origin to point of consumption for the purpose of conforming to customer requirements. (Ballou, 1999)

From the above definition we can see that logistics not only concerns goods but also the services involved in it. The mission of logistics is to get the right goods or services to the right place, at the right time, and in the desired condition, while making the greatest contribution to the firm.

In international business, international firms are beginning to regard logistics as a competitive tool. Managers become aware of the fact that competition is the name of the game in global business and that distribution is key to making and keeping customers. Those managers have also realized that future sales growth in the international market will come mainly from the development of wider and better logistics systems.

From the perspective of international business, logistics can be usually defined as the designing and managing of a system that controls the flow of materials into, through, and out of the international corporations, and as the whole process of sending goods from the point of origin and providing services involved in the process to the overseas end-users to meet their needs.

The following Figure 12.1 illustrates the logistics system.

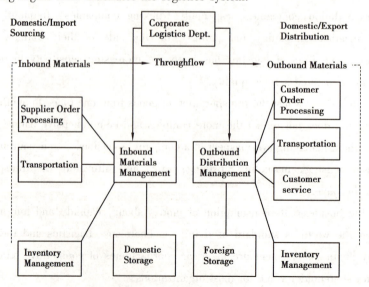

Figure 12.1　Logistics System

Two major phases in the movement of materials are important. The first phase is inbound materials management which means the timely movement of raw materials, parts, and suppliers into and through the firm. The second phase is outbound distributions, which involves the movement of the firm's finished product to its customers. Stationary periods (storage and inventory) are included. The basic aim of logistics management is the effective coordination of both inbound and outbound phases to achieve a given level of customer service at the lowest total cost.

The logistics function begins with an understanding of the requirements of the design and development teams and is used to source components and raw materials quickly and cheaply, either domestically or from around the world. The logistics department needs to understand how the product is manufactured in order to take into account any special requirements for packaging, marking and labelling as well as any warehousing considerations.

The logistics department must then appreciate how the goods have been priced for sale and which delivery terms (Incoterms) or other contractually binding clauses have been specified that might have a bearing on transportation. Finally, the logistics manager should be fully briefed on where the goods are to be shipped so that the most appropriate method of transport can be identified and arranged.

Logistics is a vital piece of the international trade jigsaw. It is in the company's best interest to make effective use of the process and to ensure that costs are kept to minimum wherever possible.

12.2　New Concept of 21st Century Logistics　21 世纪国际物流新概念

The business or commercial sector approach to logistics developed into inbound logistics and outbound logistics during the 1970s and 1980s. Then in the 1990s, the business or commercial sector began to view logistics in the context of a supply or demand chain that linked all of the organizations from the sellers' seller to the customer's customer. The supply chain management requires a collaborative, coordinated flow of materials and goods through the logistics systems of all the organizations in the network.

Now that we are already in the 21st century, with the fast development of science and technology, especially information technology, logistics should be regarded as a part of management and has four subdivisions (Coyle, 2003).

(1) Business logistics: This involves the part of the supply chain process that plans, implements, and controls the efficient, effective flow and storage of goods, services, and related information from point of origin to point of use or consumption in order to meet customer requirements.

(2) Military logistics: The sign and integration of all aspects of support for the operational capability of the military forces (developed or in garrison) and their equipment to ensure readiness, reliability, and efficiency.

（3）Event logistics：The network of activities, facilities, and personnel required to organize, schedule, and deploy the resources for an event to take place and to efficiently withdraw after event.

（4）Service logistics：The acquisition, scheduling, and management of the facilities/assets, personnel, and materials to support and sustain a service operation or business.

All the above four subdivisions have some common features and requirements such as forecasting, scheduling, and transportation, but they also have some differences in terms of their primary purposes. Therefore, based on the above four points, logistics could be understood as the following (Coyle, 2003)：

Logistics is the process of anticipating customer needs and wants, acquiring the capital, material, people, technologies,and information necessary to meet those needs and wants, optimizing the goods—or service—producing network to fulfil customer requests, and utilizing the network to fulfil customer requests in a timely way.

12.3   Components of a Logistics System   物流系统的组成部分

According to Gourdin (2001), components of a logistics system may include a number of functional activities, some of which are listed as follows：

（1）Customer service. It is a multi-dimensional and very important part of any organization's logistics effort. In a broad sense, it is the output of the entire logistics effort; that is, customer service and some resulting level of satisfaction are what the logistics system ultimately provides the buyer.

（2）Inventory management. It deals with balancing the cost of maintaining additional products on hand against the risk of not having those items when the customer wants them (i.e. the cost of lost sales). This task has become more complex as firms have gradually lowered inventory levels. For inventories of raw materials and components, the customer is the firm's own production line; for finished goods the customer is the final user of the product. Both "customers" have different needs which must be assessed in formulating an appropriate inventory policy that balances the cost of maintaining stocks on the one hand with costs that could result from not having requisite items (i.e. production line stoppages, lost sales) on the other hand.

（3）Transportation. It refers to physical movement of goods from a point of origin to a point of consumption and can involve raw materials being brought into the production process and/or finished goods being shipped out to the customer. Transportation has assumed a greater role in many logistics systems.

（4）Storage and material handling. They involve the physical requirements of holding inventory. Storage includes the tasks necessary to manage whatever space is needed; materials handling is concerned with the movement of goods within that space. Storage is mainly concerned with warehouse number, size, layout, and design. Material handling is mainly concerned with moving goods into, through, and out of each facility.

（5）Packaging. It is mainly concerned with protecting the product in the course of being shipped and stored.

（6）Information processing. It is what links all areas of the logistics system together. The growth of reasonably priced computers and software has put sophisticated management information systems within the reach of even the smallest organization.

（7）Demand forecasting. It involves the need for accurate information on future customer needs so that the logistics system can ensure the right products and/or services are available to meet those requirements.

（8）Production planning. It can be included under logistics because manufacturing needs components and raw materials in order to make finished goods that are, in turn, demanded by a customer. So production planning is arguably at the centre of the entire logistics process, yet it is often viewed as a stand-alone entity with its own objectives and agenda.

（9）Purchasing. It deals with the buying of goods and services that keep the organization functioning. This activity is vital to the overall success of the logistics effort.

（10）Facility location. It involves the strategic placement of warehouses, plants, and transportation resources to achieve customer service objectives and minimize cost.

（11）Other activities. Other activities for a specific organization could include tasks such as after-sales parts and service support, maintenance functions, return goods handling, and recycling operations.

Attention should be paid to the fact that no organization is likely to require the accomplishment of all these specific tasks. Some of the activities have traditionally had a well-defined stand-alone role within a company, such as purchasing, production, information processing, and so on. Others have generally been more closely associated with logistics, such as transportation, warehousing, packaging, and so on. Figure 12.2 shows the key parts of the logistics system.

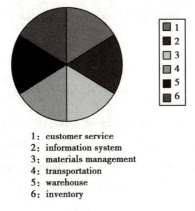

1: customer service
2: information system
3: materials management
4: transportation
5: warehouse
6: inventory

Figure 12.2　The Key Components of The Logistics System

12.4 The Role of Logistics in the Economy 物流在经济中的作用

Logistics plays a very important role in the economy of a country.

First, logistics is one of the major expenditures for businesses, thereby affecting and being affected by other economic activities. Logistics is an important component of a country's GDP. By improving the efficiency of logistics operations, logistics makes an important contribution to the economy as a whole.

Second, Logistics supports the movement and flow of many economic transactions; it is an important activity in facilitating the sale of virtually all goods and services. To understand this role from a system perspective, we should know that if all goods do not arrive on time, customers cannot buy them. If goods do not arrive at the proper place, or in the proper condition, no sale can be made. Thus, all economic activities throughout the supply chain will suffer.

On the other hand, logistics adds value by creating time and place utility. The key way that logistics adds value is by creating utility. From an economic standpoint, utility represents the value or usefulness that an item or service has in fulfilling a want or need. Generally speaking, there are four types of utility.

(1) Form utility: It is the process of creating the goods or service, or putting it in the proper form for the customer to use.

(2) Possession utility: It is the value added to a product or service because the customer is able to take actual possession. This is made possible by credit arrangements, loans, and so on.

(3) Time utility: It is the value added by having an item when it is needed. This could occur within the organization, as in having all the materials and parts that are needed for manufacturing, so that the production line does not have to shut down.

(4) Place utility: It means having the item or service available where it is needed. If a product desired by consumers is in transit, in a warehouse, or in another store, it does not create any place utility for them.

12.5 Logistics in the Organization 企业中的物流

In recent years, effective logistics management has been recognized as a key opportunity to improve both the profitability and competitive performance of firms. By the late 1980s and early 1990s, customer service took centre stage in many organizations. Even organizations that had previously adhered to the marketing concept were re-examining what it meant to be customer-drive. The trend toward strong customer focus continues today.

As business management has become main interest of firms, logistics management for a firm to engage in international business is of vital importance. Logistics, which focuses on the management of materials flow and movement of finished goods, is considered a whole in the management system of a company. This is because every part of the management chain is interrelated and interacted.

Therefore, logistics holds an important position in a business.

As the world's markets become more and more open, managers are finding that new ways of doing business are necessary both to fully exploit the opportunities available as well as to guard against emerging threats to corporate success. Global organizations normally look at the whole world as one potential market—sourcing, manufacturing, researching, raising capital, and selling wherever the job can be done best. Logistics is a particularly powerful management tool in a global organization because it is an approach to doing business that works anywhere. It is very clear that to fulfil customer needs in the USA or Europe requires different skills and resources from those used to satisfy buyers in India or China. The aim is the same, though. By understanding the basics of logistics management and how to put together a logistics system responsive to customer requirements, managers will be better able to deal with the unique challengers inherent in doing business outside the confines of their own country.

The growth of world trade is made possible by the planning of logistics companies all over the world. Countries are becoming closer and closer because of the success in logistics. In an organization, the smooth, effective and efficient movement of logistics will contribute a great deal to the success of the organization. An organization's success first relies on the business orders; then on the whole chain of the business management, the management of materials and the movement of the goods are critically important, as the faster the goods reach the end-user, the better. The whole world is becoming more and more competitive due to the growth in logistics activity. A firm will produce anywhere in the world where it is feasible and leave the transportation from one country to another to the logistics professionals.

▶ 12.6 Domestic Logistics and International Logistics　国内物流与国际物流

In essence, domestic logistics and international logistics are the same. The obvious difference between the two is the country borders across which international logistics will move. In other words, international logistics is concerned with more than one country, so the differences between countries in terms of law, customs, regulations, policies, business practices, and so on can be found in international logistics.

In the domestic environment, logistics decisions are guided by the experience of the manager, possible industry comparison, an intimate knowledge of trends and rules of thumb. The logistics manager in the international firm, on the other hand, often has to depend on educated guesses to determine the steps required to obtain a desired service level. Variation in location means variations in environment. The long-term survival of international activities depends on an understanding of the differences inherent in the international logistics.

Basic differences in international logistics emerge because the company is active in more than one country, as mentioned above.

First, the distance is different. Global business activities often require goods to be shipped farther to reach final customers. These distances in turn result in longer lead time, more opportunities for things to go wrong, more inventories, in short, greater complexity or risks.

Second, currency variation is another difference. There is foreign exchange rate risk involved in international logistics, while domestic logistics does not run this kind of risk at all. The companies must adjust its planning to incorporate the existence of different currencies and change in exchange rates.

Third, due to different regulations in different countries, international logistics deals with customs, while domestic logistics needn't. Therefore, additional intermediaries participate in the international logistics. They include freight forwarders, customs agencies, customs brokers, banks, and other financial intermediaries.

Finally, the transportation modes are different in some way. In domestic logistics, goods are more often transported by land (by water and sometimes by air). But in international logistics, goods are normally transported by water and by multi-mode transportation means.

In reality, in each country, the multinational companies face specific logistics attributes that may be quite different from those experienced at home. Transportation system might differ a great deal. Packaging and labelling may also be quite different. So management of an international firm must consider the differences to develop an efficient international logistics operation.

12.7 Key Logistics Activities 物流的主要内容

Communication is of great importance in doing anything. Excellent communications within a system can be a key source of competitive advantage. For example, part of Wal-Mart's success can be attributed to the advanced communication systems which link their suppliers to their actual customer sales on a regular basis, so that the suppliers can plan according to up-to-date demand information, and provide timely and adequate replenishment to Wal-Mart stores.

The key activities required to facilitate the flow of a product from point of origin to point of consumption are as follows (arranged alphabetically):

(1) Customer service: Customer service is the output of the logistics system. It involves getting the right product to the right customer at the right place, in the right condition and at the right time, at the lowest total cost possible. Excellent customer service is the basis of international logistics. Good customer service supports customer satisfaction.

(2) Demand forecasting/planning: Forecasting is a complex issue, with many interactions among functions and forecast variables. There are many types of demand forecasts. For example, marketing forecasts customer demand based on promotions, pricing, competition, etc. Manufacturing forecasts production requirements based on marketing's sales demand forecasts and current inventory levels.

(3) Inventory management: It involves trading off the level of inventory held to achieve high

customer service levels with the cost of holding inventory, including capital tied up in inventory, variable storage costs, and obsolescence.

(4) Logistics communications: They are becoming increasingly automated, complex, and rapid. Logistics interfaces with a wide array of functions and organizations in its communication processes. According to Lamber (1998), communication must occur between:

A. the organization and its suppliers and customers;

B. the major functions within the organization, such as logistics, engineering, accounting, marketing, and production;

C. the various logistics activities listed here;

D. the various aspects of each logistics activity, such as coordinating warehousing of material, work in process, and finished goods;

E. various members of the supply chain, such as intermediaries and secondary customers or suppliers who may not be directly linked to the firm;

(5) Material handling: It is a broad area that involves virtually all aspects of all movements of raw materials, work in process, or finished goods within a plant or warehouse. By carefully analysing material flows, materials management can save the organization great amounts of money.

(6) Order processing: It entails the systems that an organization has for getting orders from customers, checking on the status of orders and communicating to customers about them, and actually filling the order and making it available to the customers. Part of the order processing includes checking inventory status, customer credit, invoicing, and accounts receivable. So order processing is a broad, highly automated area.

(7) Packaging: It is a form of advertising/marketing and for protection and storage from a logistical perspective. Logistically, packaging provides protection during storage and transportation. Besides, packaging can ease movement and storage by being properly designed for the warehouse configuration and materials handling equipment.

(8) Parts and service support: In addition to supporting production through the movement of materials, work in process, and finished goods, logistics is also responsible for providing after-sale service support. This may include delivery of repair parts to dealers, stocking adequate spares, picking up defective or malfunctioning products from customers, and responding quickly to demand for repairs.

(9) Plant and warehouse site selection: This is very important in corporate strategies. Determining the location of the company's plant(s) and warehouse(s) is a strategic decision that affects not only the costs of transporting raw materials inbound and finished goods outbound, but also customer service levels and speed of response.

(10) Procurement: It refers to the purchase of materials and services from outside organizations to support the firm's operations from production to marketing, sale, and logistics. Besides, it also refers to purchasing, supply management, and comes by a number of other names. It includes such activities as supplier selection, negotiation of price, terms and quantities, and supplier quality

assessment.

(11) Return goods handling: It is complex because it involves moving small quantities of goods back from the customer rather than to the customer as the company is accustomed to. Many logistics systems have a difficult time dealing with this type of movement.

(12) Reverse logistics: Logistics is also involved in removal and disposal of waste materials left over from the production, distribution, or packaging processes. There could be temporary storage followed by transportation to the disposal, reuse, reprocessing, or recycling location.

(13) Traffic and transportation: A key logistics activity is to actually provide for the movement of materials and goods from point of origin to point of consumption, and perhaps to its ultimate point of disposal as well. Transportation involves selection of the mode, such as air, rail, water, truck, or even pipeline. Besides, it also involves the routing of the shipment, assuring of compliance with regulations in the region of the country where shipment is occurring, and selection of the carrier. It is often the largest single cost among logistics activities.

(14) Warehouse and storage: Warehousing supports time and place utility by allowing an item to be produced and held for later consumption. It can be held near the location where it will be needed, or transported later. Warehousing and storage activities relate to warehouse layout, design, ownership, automation, training of employees, and related issues.

12.8　When Does International Logistics Occur?　什么情况下会出现国际物流?

International logistics, the movement of goods across national boundaries, occurs in the following situations.

(1) A company exports a portion of a product made or grown to a foreign country's organization.

(2) A company imports raw materials or finished products.

(3) Goods are partially assembled in one country and then shipped to another where they are further assembled or processed.

(4) Products are assembled in a foreign country for distribution in that and other foreign countries and in the company's home country.

12.9　International Sourcing, Third Party Logistics (TPL) and Fourth Party Logistics(FPL)　国际采购与第三方物流和第四方物流

12.9.1　International Sourcing　国际采购

The term "international sourcing" applies to buying components and inputs anywhere in the world. It means that the manufacturer, rather than relying solely on its local Yellow Pages, casts out a much wider net in search of sources. Some companies are really international in stature and try to develop products that can be manufactured and sold in many parts of the world.

As international sourcing has become more prevalent, companies have incorporated into their new supply chains the most recent inventory-control methodologies.

The availability of cheap and efficient labour and transportation services has made it economical for companies to source parts, components, and finished goods from every corner of the rest of the world.

12.9.2   Third Party Logistics   第三方物流

The globalization of businesses and the competitive pressures of the business arena have led to the growing strategic importance of the logistics function within the organization. In fact, the logistics function has often been referred to as the last frontier for the development of strategic competitive advantages. Increasingly therefore, many organizations are looking to their logistics operations, seeking to manage them strategically so that significant competitive advantages may be made available for the business as a whole.

The TPL concept is used in different contexts and with different degrees of precision. A definition representative of the established view of TPL is the following:

"Third party logistics involves the use of external companies to perform logistics functions that have traditionally been performed within an organization. The functions performed by the third party can encompass the entire logistics process or selected activities within that process."

According to this definition there is a focus on the functions performed and the party that is responsible for carrying out the functions. Most definitions are quite loose when it comes to which activities are included. Thus, determined from a functional perspective, TPL is defined as a situation "where a third party takes responsibility for primarily transport and warehousing activities, but also related services such as consolidation, order administration and simple assembly".[1]

A very influential definition defines TPL as "the services offered by a middleman in the logistics channel that has specialized in providing, by contract, for a given time period, all or a considerable number of logistics activities for other firms".

These are important characteristics, which may limit the number of TPL relationships to rather few:

(1) Outsourcing of transportation and/or warehousing and some value-added services;

(2) Inter-organizational features are related to TPL;

(3) TPL consists of a long-term (not less than 2—3 years) relationship between two parties that regard each other as partners;

---

[1]   Andersson, Sjöholm. "Third Party Logistics-a new research area or a buzzword". The paper was presented at the Third NOFOMA Conference in 1991 in Linköping.

（4）The logistics solution is also a tailor-made solution, which is worked out in co-operation specifically for each shipper;

（5）Solution developed based on mutual orientation. Both parties are contributing to the solution;

（6）The goal for the relationship should be to develop into strategic alliances with win-win relationship for both parties. The two parties should consider themselves as strategic partners.

Another way of defining TPL is by using the stage model to describe different levels of TPL arrangements, spanning from simple arm's length relationships encompassing few, and very standardized logistics activities to advanced logistics solutions.

On the one hand, TPL is suggested consisting of four stages:

- Outsourcing strategy
- Internal planning
- Joint planning
- Operations and Auditing.

On the other hand, TPL is considered as comprising four different levels:

- Market exchanges
- Customized logistics solutions
- Joint logistics solutions
- In-house logistics solutions.

12.9.3　Fourth Party Logistics　第四方物流

Fourth Party Logistics (4PL) is the evolution of supply chain outsourcing. The convergence of technology and the rapid acceleration of e-capabilities have heightened the need for an over-arching integrator for supply chain-spanning activities. Fourth Party Logistics is the shared sourcing of supply chain spanning activity with a client and selected teaming partner, under the direction of a 4PL integrator.

As conceptually illustrated and discussed in the book, "Strategic Supply Chain Alignment" by John Gattorna, an evolution has occurred in supply chain management, with organizations moving from insourcing to outsourcing to 4PL arrangements. According to Gattorna, "While outsourcing third-party logistics is now accepted business practice, Fourth Party Logistics is emerging as a breakthrough solution to modern supply chain challenges to provide maximum overall benefit."

Central to the 4PLs' success is the "best of breed" approach to providing services to a client. The development of 4PL solutions leverages the capabilities of 3PLs, technology service providers, and business process managers to provide the client organization with greater cross-functional integration and broader operational autonomy.

Two key distinctions make the concept of 4PL unique and set it apart from other supply chain outsourcing options available to the market today:

（1）A 4PL delivers a comprehensive supply chain solution; and,

(2) A 4PL delivers value through the ability to have an impact on the entire supply chain.

Fourth Party Logistics is the next generation of supply chain outsourcing. Supply chain activities are information-rich, complex and increasingly global. At the same time, technology and e-enabled capabilities are racing ahead.

▶ 12.10   Managing Materials Flow   材料流动管理

As defined previously, logistics is concerned with the efficient flow of raw materials, in-process inventory, and finished goods from point of origin to point of consumption. Materials management is an integral part of the logistics management process. Materials management involves the administration of raw materials, subassemblies, manufactured parts, packing materials, and in-process inventory.

Material management is very important to the total logistics process. Although materials management does not directly concern the end-user, decisions made in its portion of the logistics process will directly affect the level of customer service offered, the ability of the firm to compete with other companies, and the level of sales and profits the firm is able to achieve in the marketplace. Without efficient and effective management of inbound materials flow, the manufacturing process cannot produce products at the desired price and at the time they are required for distribution to the firm's customers. Therefore, it is quite important to understand the importance of materials management in the logistics process.

Materials management is typically made up of the following four activities:

(1) Anticipating materials requirements.

(2) Sourcing and obtaining materials.

(3) Introducing materials into the organization.

(4) Monitoring the status of materials as a current asset.

The Aims of materials management are to solve materials problem from a total company viewpoint (optimize) by coordinating performance of the various materials functions, providing a communications network, and controlling materials flow. The following Figure 12.3 further illustrates materials management:

Figure 12.3 highlights the major aims of materials management: low costs, high levels of service, quality assurance, low level of tied-up capital, and support of other functions.

Each aim is linked to overall corporate goals and objectives. Thus trade-offs among the aims must be made using a broad perspective of materials flow throughout the total system, from source of supply to the final end-user.

Integrated aspects of materials management include purchasing and procurement, production control, inbound traffic and transportation, warehousing and storage, management information system (MIS) control, inventory planning and control, and salvage and scrap disposal.

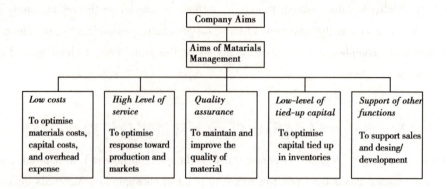

Figure 12.3　The Aims of Integrated Materials Management

12.11　Inventory　存货

Inventory management has received much attention in recent years, primarily from the point of view of eliminating as much inventory as possible. Inventory is a large and costly investment. Better corporate inventories can improve cash flow and return on investment. Therefore, it is very important to improve inventory management.

12.11.1　Purposes of Inventory　存货的目的

Inventory can serve some useful purposes within an organization.

(1) Facilitates economies of scale: Management may decide, for example, to purchase large quantities of an item in order to qualify for a discount. Or lower transportation costs may be realized by shipping large quantities at one time. Likewise, a long production run may significantly reduce manufacturing costs. In every case, inventory is being used as a way to obtain savings in other parts of the logistics system.

(2) Offers a means of balancing supply and demand: Some firms can only sell their products at certain times of the year. In order to use their fixed investment in building and equipment and maintain a skilled labour force, management may decide to produce all year and store the finished goods until the selling season arrives.

(3) Provides protection from uncertain demand: Despite management's best forecasting efforts, demand can never be known with absolute certainty. Likewise, transport vehicles may break down, raw materials may suddenly be unavailable, and manufacturing lines may stop. For all of these reasons, inventory is used to ensure that customer needs are met even when the production process itself is interrupted.

12.11.2　Types of Inventory　存货的类型

Inventories can be classified based on the reasons for which they are accumulated. Generally speaking, inventories can be categorized into the following sorts.

(1) Cycle stock: Cycle stock is inventory that results from replenishment of inventory sold or used in production. It is required in order to meet demand under conditions of certainty, that is, when the firm can predict demand and replenishment times (lead time). Cycle inventory is also known as "normal inventory" or "batching economies". Cycle stock normally arises from three sources: acquisition, production, and/or transportation. Scale economies, often associated with all the three, can result in the accumulation of stock that will not be used or sold immediately, which means there will be cycle stock or inventory that will be used up or sold over some period of time.

(2) Safety stock: Safety stock is held in addition to cycle inventory to cover uncertainty in demand and lead time. Its purpose is to protect the firm and the customer against stock-outs, as all businesses are normally faced with uncertainty, which can arise from a variety of sources. On the demand or customer side, there is normally uncertainty about how much customers will buy and when. On the supply side, there may be uncertainty about obtaining what is needed from vendors or suppliers and about how long it will take for fulfilment of the order. Uncertainty can arise from transportation in terms of getting reliable delivery. Safety stock is also known as "uncertainty stock" or "buffer stock".

(3) In-transit inventory: In-transit inventory is en route from one location to another. In other words, in-transit inventories are items that are en route from one location to another. It may belong to the shipper or the customer depending upon the terms of sale. In-transit inventory may be regarded as part of cycle stock even though it is not available for sale or shipment until it arrives at the destination.

(4) Speculative stock: Speculative stock is held for reasons other than meeting current demand needs. Management may fear the price of a needed raw material will rise in the future or that availability may be limited for some reason and elects to buy a large quantity in anticipation of either eventuality. Alternatively, a vendor may offer an especially low price if a large quantity is purchased at one time. Speculative inventory is also known as "anticipatory stock", as this inventory occurs when companies anticipate some unusual events, such as strike, significant price increase, a major shortage of supply due to weather or political unrest and so on.

(5) Seasonal inventory: Seasonal inventory is a form of speculative stock that involves the accumulation of inventory before a season period begins. This often occurs with agricultural products and seasonal items. In addition, the fashion industry is also subject to seasonality with new fashion coming out many times a year. Seasonal inventory provides management the ability to stabilize production and maintain a long-term labour force even when the majority of sales occur during a relatively small part of the year.

12.11.3 Improving Inventory Management 改进存货管理

Since inventory management is so important in a firm's business administration system, attention should always be paid to improving inventory management so that the firm is always active in the chain of logistics management. According to Gourdin (2001), the following aspects need be paid attention to.

(1) Top management commitment: Key management support is essential if inventory is to be managed effectively. Because lower inventories have an impact on many different parts of the logistics system, senior leadership must ensure that all of those activities are working together to meet customer needs without the luxury of excess stock.

(2) ABC analysis of all inventory items: Management must first understand which goods in inventory are the most important in terms of their contribution to the objectives of the organization. Those few items that generate the most profits, for example, or those that are deemed mission-essential by the firm's most important customers would be designated "A" items and perhaps maintained at virtually 100 percent availability.

(3) Improved performance of other logistics activities: Managers should ensure that the rest of the logistics system is functioning effectively.

(4) Improved demand forecasting: Demand forecasting is also a way of reducing variability, this time in terms of expected versus actual sales. Better forecasting techniques can be utilized to more accurately predict actual sales.

(5) Inventory management software: Software is currently available for virtually any type of inventory management situation and allows managers to track sales by items, costs, length of time in inventory, etc. Many of the more comprehensive packages are structured around some variation of material requirements planning (MRP) or distribution requirements planning (DRP) depending on the nature of the inventory concerned.

12.11.4 Just-In-Time (JIT) Inventory Management 零库存(及时交货)存货管理

Originating from Japanese company Toyota Motor Manufacturing in the early 1970s, Just-In-Time (JIT) is an inventory management philosophy aimed at reducing waste and redundant inventory by delivering products, components, or materials just when an organization needs them. JIT has profound implication of logistics systems. JIT requires close coordination of demand needs among logistics, carriers, suppliers, and manufacturing. JIT also represents a tremendous opportunity for the logistics function to contribute to the organization's success by reducing inventory while simultaneously maintaining or improving customer service levels. JIT represents an important trend in inventory management. In addition, JIT represents a move away from holding large quantities of inventory.

1. Basic Principles of JIT

A successful JIT system is based on the following key concepts (Gourdin, 2001):

(1) Quality: With JIT, the customer must receive high quality goods. One of the historical roles of inventory has been to protect the customer against defective items. With a JIT system, poor quality means the production line stops or the external customer gets a defective item. There are no "extra" items to replace the poor ones.

（2）Vendors as partners: Basically, firms using JIT rely on fewer vendors rather than more. Purchases are concentrated with a limited number of suppliers in order to give the buyer leverage with respect to quality and service. Purchasers include vendors in the planning process, sharing information regarding sales and production forecasts so that vendors then have a clear idea of what their customers need.

（3）Vendor co-location with customer: Ideally, suppliers should be located as near as possible to their customers. This is because when the distance between vendors and buyers increases, so does the opportunities for system disruption and stock-outs. In order to minimize this risk, customers often demand that vendor facilities be co-located on the same site or at least in the same geographical area as their own.

2. Advantages of JIT

Basically, JIT has the following advantages.

（1）More inventory turns: Because there is less on hand, the inventory that is maintained stays for a shorter period of time.

（2）Better quality: As was mentioned previously, high quality products must be received with a JIT system or else the entire benefit production process collapses. Customers concentrate their purchases on a small number of vendors in exchange for receiving high quality items and requisite service.

（3）Less warehouse space needed: When there is less inventory, fewer and/or smaller warehouses are needed.

3. Disadvantages of JIT

Although JIT has a number of advantages, it also has some disadvantages.

First, there is a risk of stock-outs. When firms eliminate inventory, the risk of stocking out can rise.

Second, there are increasing transportation costs involved. Since JIT requires frequent shipments of small quantities, transportation costs almost always rise. In fact, those expenses can rise very quickly because motor carriage and air are the modes best suited to provide the necessary levels of service. When these costs exceed offset by the inventory saving, it is advantageous for the organization; otherwise, it is disadvantageous for the organization.

Third, there are increasing costs. Purchasing discounts are generally associated with buying large quantities at one time. Theoretically, JIT means foregoing those price-breaks in favour of obtaining smaller amounts more frequently. In actuality, there are ways to take advantage of volume discounts while enjoying the benefits of JIT. Managers must make sure that purchasing costs are not rising more than inventory costs are falling.

Finally, small channel members may suffer. JIT is sometimes criticized as a system that allows strong organizations to unload their inventory on smaller firms in the channel.

Additionally, there are environmental issues about JIT. In a macro sense, JIT can result in higher levels of traffic congestion and air pollution because additional transportation is often required to maintain customer service levels in the absence of inventory.

12.12 Warehousing 仓储

Warehousing is often referred to as the storage of goods. Broadly interpreted, this definition includes a wide range of facilities and locations that provide warehousing, including the storage of iron ore in open fields, the storage of finished goods in the production facility, and the storage of raw materials, industrial goods, and finished goods while they are in transit. It also includes highly specialized storage facilities such as bean and grain elevators, tobacco warehouses, potato cellars, and refrigeration facilities. Every product manufactured, grown, or caught is warehoused at least once during its life cycle (from creation to consumption). Therefore, it can be seen that how important warehousing is in the whole chain of logistics.

With JIT coming into logistics field and with logistics chain philosophies' appearance, the warehouse has taken on a strategic role of attaining the logistics goals of shorter times, lower inventories, lower costs, and better customer service. The warehouse of today is not a long-term storage facility; the activity level in the facility is fast paced. It is found out that many companies' products are in the warehouse for just a few days or even a few hours, making full use of facilities.

In order to satisfy customer's demand for shorter cycle times and lower prices, logistics managers are examining the warehouse process for productivity and cost improvements. Warehouses are being redesigned and automated to achieve order-processing and cost goals and are being relocated to achieve overall-supply-chain customer service goals.

12.12.1 Objectives of Warehousing 仓储的目的

Warehousing has traditionally provided storage of products (referred to as inventory) in the course of all phases of the logistics process. The warehousing of products has occurred for one or more of the following objectives.

(1) To achieve transportation economies.

(2) To achieve production economies.

(3) To take advantage of quantity purchase discounts and forward buys.

(4) To maintain a source of supply.

(5) To support the firm's customer service policies.

(6) To meet changing market conditions such as seasonality, demand fluctuations, competitions, etc.

(7) To overcome the time and space differentials that exist between producers and consumers.

(8) To accomplish least-total-cost logistics commensurate with a desired level of customer service.

(9) To support the JIT programs of suppliers and customers.

(10) To provide customers with a mix of products instead of a single product on each order.

(11) To provide temporary storage of materials to be disposed of or recycled (i.e. reverse

logistics).

12.12.2   Functions of Warehousing   仓储的功能

Warehousing plays an important role in a company's logistics system. Together with other activities, it provides the company's customers with an acceptable level of service. The obvious role of warehousing is to store products, but warehousing also provides break-bulk, consolidation, and information services. These activities emphasize product flow rather than storage.

Basically, warehousing has three functions: movement, storage, and information transfer. In recent years, organizations pay much more attention to the movement function, as organizations focus on improving inventory turns and speeding orders from manufacturing to final delivery. The movement functions can be further divided into a number of activities, including the following.

(1) Receiving: The receiving activity includes the actual unloading of products from the transportation carrier, the updating of warehouse inventory records, inspection for damage, and verification of the merchandise count against orders and shipping records.

(2) Transfer or put-away: Transfer or put-away involves the physical movement of the product into the warehouse for storage, movement to areas for specialized services such as consolidation, and movement to outbound shipment.

(3) Order picking/selection: Customer order selection or order picking is the major movement activity and involves regrouping products into the assortments customers desire. Packing slips are made up at this point.

(4) Cross-docking: Cross-docking bypasses the storage activity by transferring items directly from the receiving dock to the shipping dock. A pure cross-docking operation would avoid put-away, storage, and order picking. Information transfer would become very important because shipments require close cooperation. Further, cross-docking has become commonplace in warehousing because of its impact on costs and customer service.

(5) Shipping: Shipping consists of product staging and physically moving the assembled orders onto carrier equipment, adjusting inventory records, and checking orders to be shipped. It can consist of sortation and packaging of items that are placed on pallets or shrinkwrapped (the process of wrapping products in a plastic film), and are marked with information necessary for shipment, such as origin, destination, shipper, consignee, and package contents.

12.12.3   Bonded Warehousing   保税仓储

There is an increasing demand for bonded warehousing in international business.

Bonded warehousing and storage services and warehouses are located in free trade zones.

The importers could store cargo and effect partial releases thereby deferring duty payment to Customs, and at the same time releasing the international (ISO) container in which the cargo is imported.

Bonded warehousing offers a dual advantage to the importer. For one thing, it allows the deferral to duty payment, and for another, it allows cargo to be stored under the relatively cheaper option of warehouse storage as opposed to holding on to an ISO container for which dollar lease rentals accrue on the importer.

In bonded warehousing, the user is normally interested in delaying the payment of taxes or tariffs, or even avoiding their payment altogether. Because taxes are relatively high on certain items such as cigarettes and liquor, the seller, who is liable for the taxes, may want to postpone paying them until the goods are immediately ready for sale. The same may be true of imported items that a seller needs to hold in inventory before sale. If a public warehouse holds the items in bonded custody, the seller does not have to pay the tax or duty until the warehouse releases the items.

12.12.4 Basic Warehouse Operations 仓储基本运作

The basic warehouse operations consist of movement and storage, with storage most obvious. The movement function characterizes a distribution and cross-docking warehouse for finished goods.

As mentioned above, product movement occurs at four key operations: receiving, put-away, order picking, and shipping, which is further shown in Figure 12.4.

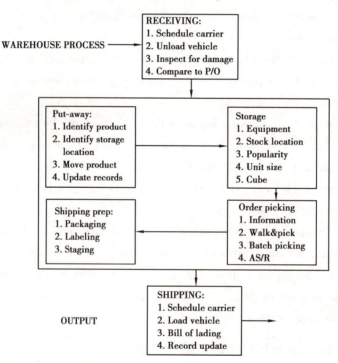

Figure 12.4 Basic Warehouse Operations

Here are some explanations about the operations.

(1) Receiving: At the receiving operation, the inbound carrier is scheduled to deliver the goods at a specific time in order to improve warehouse labour productivity and unloading efficiency. The goods are physically moved to the transport vehicle to the receiving dock.

(2) The put-away operation physically moves the items from the receiving dock to the storage

area of the warehouse.

(3) The order-picking process, as discussed previously, requires warehouse personnel to select from the storage area the items ordered by the customer or manufacturing operation. The order information is given to the warehouse personnel on a pick slip.

(4) Batch picking: In the batch picking process, the total number of units of a given product on all orders are picked at one time and sent to the shipment preparation area.

(5) AS/R: The AS/R process is an automated storage and retrieval material-handling system that will do the picking process (for instance, the picking of ice cream from a frozen foods warehouse).

(6) Shipping operation: Shipping operation is the last movement process. After the outbound carrier arrives at the loading dock, the goods are moved from the staging area to the loading dock and into the carrier's vehicle. The carrier indicating receipt of the goods from the shipper signs a bill of lading. In the end, the warehouse information system is updated to reflect removal of the item from the warehouse inventory and shipment of the goods to the customer.

12.12.5　Warehousing Alternatives　仓储的选择

1. Private Warehousing

Private warehousing is owned and operated by the company whose goods are stored in the building. The major advantage of it is that the facility can be designed to meet the organization's needs. Owning the facility also permits the management to have total control over the warehousing function and its integration into the overall logistics system.

2. Public Warehousing

A public warehouse is operated by a third party that stores goods for multiple shippers/owners.

The public warehousing companies can provide cost-effective public warehousing services such as trans-loading, cross docking, pick and pack operations, labelling, packaging, inventory control, just-in-time inventory management, pallet exchange services, local trucking and local drayage, stretch and shrink wrapping, quality control, lot number control, import and export handling, containerization and pool distribution.

The benefits of using the services of a public warehouse are stated as follows:

First, the management only use (and pay for) the space they need. If their storage needs should change during the year, they can rent more or less space as required. Second, there is no capital outlay required to erect a building. Third, the upkeep of the facility is the responsibility of the warehouse owner, not the user. Fourth, there is the benefit of knowing exactly what storage costs are being incurred each month in the sense that a bill is received from the warehousing company.

On the other hand, there are some disadvantages of using a public warehouse:

First, there is relinquishing control of the warehousing operation to the service provider. Second, merely leasing space in a public warehouse may imply an impermanence some customers might find disturbing. Third, operating costs tend to be higher owing to the inclusion of profit and overhead components in the warehouse operator's monthly charge. Fourth, the building design may not be very suitable for the user's products or needs. Finally, administering the warehousing function may be more complicated by virtue of having to work with a third party.

In a word, public warehousing is a simple process and its pricing is based on the usage factor. You only pay for what you use for space and labour. The risks are fully absorbed by the warehouse company and therefore the costs of public warehousing are higher than contract warehousing.

3. Contract Warehousing

A contract warehouse is operated by a third party that dedicates resources to the company owning the goods in storage.

The contract warehousing is similar to public warehousing other than that the owner of the goods absorbs some of the cost risks by making a commitment to pay fees whether or not the space is utilized. That the risks are shared by both the owner of the goods and the warehouse company means the costs will be less than public warehousing costs.

Although similar to public facilities, contract providers offer their customers specialized services that typically cannot be obtained at a public warehouse. For example, they may be equipped to handle specialized types of products, perform various functions such as packaging, labelling, or billing, and dedicate personnel to support a given customer's needs. In exchange for such tailored support, the customer contractually commits to use these services for a specified period of time. In essence, a contract warehouse offers the customer benefits like those found in a private facility, but at a lower cost.

The contract warehousing companies can provide cost-effective contract warehousing services such as trans-loading, cross docking, pick and pack operations, labelling, packaging, inventory control, just-in-time inventory management, pallet exchange services, local trucking and local drayage, stretch and shrink wrapping, quality control, lot number control, import and export handling, containerization, and pool distribution.

It is necessary to draw attention to the trend that the line between private, contract, and public is becoming increasingly blurred. For instance, public warehousing companies, rather than serving merely as storage areas, are offering more and diverse services to attract customers.

12.12.6 International Dimensions of Warehousing 仓储的国际尺寸

Products must be stored at some point before being transported to their final consumption. Depending on the particular conditions in effect in each foreign market, products may be stored at different points within the channel of distribution.

If distributors or other intermediaries are used, inventories will have to be stored or warehoused at other locations within the channel. The ability of the manufacturer or supplier to push the inventory down the channel of distribution varies from market to market, depending on the size of the channel intermediaries, customer service levels necessary to serve each market.

When an international company needs warehousing facilities in a foreign market, it may find a lot of sophisticated, modern warehouses in some industrial nations. But, even in developed markets, there exist warehousing concerns. For example, the attractiveness of warehousing automation differs widely across Europe. Costs of labour and land, as well as social legislation (for instance, rules affecting working hours) vary greatly from country to country. On the other hand, in many developing countries, storage facilities may not be found or may be limited in availability or sophistication. In those developing countries, perhaps, the product package or shipping container may have to serve the warehousing purpose.

Like all logistics activities, the warehousing and storage activity must be administered differently in each foreign market. The logistics executive is responsible for recognizing how the storage activity differs and adjusting the company's strategy accordingly.

12.13　Transportation in Logistics　物流环节中的运输

The transportation system is the physical link connecting a company's customers, raw material suppliers, plants, warehouses, and channel members—the fixed points in a logistics supply chain. The fixed points in the logistics system are where some activity temporarily halts the flow of goods in the logistics pipeline.

12.13.1　The Role of Transportation in Logistics　运输在物流中的作用

Logistics system is quite closely related to transportation, as in logistics the movement of goods is a key part. Transportation plays a key role in the logistics system. The functions of transportation are stated as follows:

(1) Bridge over the buyer-seller gap. A firm's logistics supply chain is a series of fixed points where the goods come to rest and transportation links. The transportation link makes it possible for goods to flow between the various fixed points, and bridges the buyer-seller gap.

(2) Value added. Transportation adds value to the firm by creating time and place utility. The value added is the physical movement of goods to the place desired and at the time desired.

(3) Global impact. As supply chains become increasingly longer in our global economy, the transportation function is connecting buyers and sellers that may be at the far end of the globe. This wide gap results in greater transportation costs. Besides, much more time is needed in international transportation. This results in higher inventories and higher storage costs.

(4) Importance in economy. The transportation has great impact on the nation's economy. The total expenditure involved in transportation of a country may be comparatively very high in its economy.

(5) Importance in company. In a company, the total expenditure includes warehousing and transportation. A company has to spend money on physical distribution (outbound only), customer service, warehousing, administration, inventory carrying, and so on.

(6) Cost-service trade-off. For example, if a company switches from rail to air transportation to move raw materials from a vendor to the plant, the air carrier's increased speed, or lower transit time, permits the company to hold lower inventories to meet demand during transit time and to use less warehousing space and less stringent product packaging; but the company realizes these advantages at the expense of higher transportation costs. Thus, a firm cannot make the transportation decision in a vacuum. Applying the total cost or systems approach requires a company to consider how the transport decision will affect other elements of the logistics system.

12.13.2　The Role and Essentials of a Transport System　运输系统的作用及要素

Transport is an essential facility for the development of economic resources on a national or international scale. Articles or materials are transported from areas of low utility to areas of high utility. In this way, value is added to the product. Transport makes it possible for the economic resources to develop to the full. It also makes possible specialization in economic development no matter whether it may be mining, car manufacturing or farming. Transport is considered a kind of product that is consumed the moment it is produced. Hence it is not possible to store it.

The essentials of a transport system include three elements: the way route, the vehicle (including motive power unit), and the terminal.

The way route may be naturally occurring such as the sea or river, or artificially made by man such as the railway, canal or motorway. It is possible to have a combination of these two circumstances. The transport unit may either be of the integral type embracing the carrying and motive power unit, such as an aircraft or ship, or have an independent motive power unit, such as a railway locomotive.

The terminal must be made by man, and be well designed to ensure the most efficient operation/utilization of the transport unit using it. Basically, the terminal is the link in the transport chain and merges at an interchange point involving one or more forms of transport, to offer through transit such as airport or seaport.

The three essential elements must be so designed as to produce an efficient system.

Summary of This Chapter
本章概要

1. 物流是 21 世纪最具有发展潜力的行业之一。随着经济全球一体化进程的加快及信息技术的迅猛发展,物流作为一种先进的组织方式和管理技术,被认为是企业的第三利润源泉。物流起源于美国。目前对于物流还没有一个统一的定义。美国物流协会对其的定义是:"物流是供应链过程的一部分,是以满足客户需要为目的的,为提高产品、服务和相关信息从起始点到消费点的流动储存效率和效益而对其进行计划、执行和控制的过程。"中国对物流的定义是："物品从供应地向接收地的实体流动过程,根据实际需要,将运输、储存、装卸、搬运、包装、配送、流通加工、信息处理等基本功能实现有机结合。"

2. 国际物流与国内物流概念基本相同,只不过国际物流涉及跨国界货物的仓储、运输等环节。国际物流是国际商务的重要组成部分。一方面,国际商务促进物流国际化。物流是国际贸易的必要条件,没有物流,国际贸易货物买卖便不可能成为现实。另一方面,国际物流与国内物流又有所不同。首先,完成周期不同,国际物流比国内物流周期要长,有时长很多;其次,国际物流运输量大,仓储较复杂;再次,整个国际物流作业过程涉及更多、更复杂的单证;最后,从系统一体化角度来说,国际物流在作业上的差异要求企业加强整个系统一体化的作业协调。此外,在联盟方面,国际物流比起国内物流更加重要。

3. (1)第三方物流(Third Party Logistics):指由物流劳务的供方、需方之外的第三方完成物流服务的物流运作方式。所谓第三方,其实指的就是提供物流交易双方的部分或全部物流功能的外部服务提供者。换言之,第三方指本身并不拥有货物,而是为物流交易双方的物流作业提供管理、控制和专业化作业服务的企业。必须指出,我们不能把一个纯粹的货物运输公司等同于第三方物流公司。第三方物流的特点:①仓储、运输及物资配送是主要部分;②信息化、科技化;③多功能、全方位物流服务(包括仓储、运输、EDI 信息交换、订货履行、自动补货、包装、进出口代理等)。现代意义上的第三方物流是一个约有 10 到 15 年历史的行业。(2)第四方物流(4PL):第四方物流指一个供应链的集成商,它对公司内部和具有互补性的服务供应商所拥有的不同资源、能力和技术进行整合和管理,提供一整套供应链解决方案,又称为"总承包商"或"领衔物流服务商",它实际上是一种虚拟物流,是依靠业内最优秀的第三方物流供应商、技术供应商、管理咨询顾问和其他增值服务商,整合社会资源,为用户提供独特的和广泛的供应链解决方案。随着企业从自营物流到第三方物流,再到第四方物流的逐步转变,供应链革命的时代已到来了。第四方物流能向客户提供一个全面的供应链解决方案,使其获得价值最大化的服务,并通过对整个供应链产生影响力来增加客户服务的价值。

4. 零库存 (JIT)系统 :在原材料向产品转换的过程中,用以整合与控制生产过程的工具,其过程包括供应商与供应源的选择、运输、储存和检验、制造和质量控制。零库存源自日本丰田汽车公司,所以也被称为丰田生产系统,它指的是零部件、原材料在工厂生产过程中需要时再供应。这样可以减少库存成本、提高产品质量。零库存的优点是:(1)提高了原材料、在制品库存的周转率;(2)生产准备时间可以减少75%;(3)减少了装配线脱节的几率;(4)减少了在制品库存的成本;(5)减少了顾客对产品缺陷和担保的索赔。

5. 库存(inventory):库存策略与整个物流有密切关系。库存的目的主要有:(1)平衡供求关系;(2)实现公司的规模经济;(3)使生产专业化;(4)解决需求与订货周期出现的不稳定性;(5)在分销渠道中发挥缓冲作用。

6. 仓储 (warehousing):仓储是物流的必然组成部分。仓储是用于物流系统所有环节之间的货物储存。储存是保护、管理和储藏物品。仓储的物品有两类:一是原材料和零部件(物料供应);二是产成品(实物分销)。此外,还有在制品库存,不过,通常在制品库存只占公司库存的一小部分。仓储有三大功能:位移、储存和信息传递。

7. 运输:运输与仓储是物流的两个主要功能要素。国际货物运输是指国家与国家、国家与地区之间的货物运输。国际货物运输包括国际贸易货物运输和国际非贸易物资(如展览品、援外物资、个人行李、办公用品等)运输。国际物流运输方式主要是海运。国际贸易中的货物绝大多数是通过海运,此外还有航空运输、公路运输、铁路运输、管道运输。

▶ New Words and Expressions

accrue *v.* (权利或要求)能实施,产生;积累;积攒;(利息)积累而成

adhere *v.* 遵守;坚持;依附

arm's length 一臂之遥的

as opposed to 与……对照之下;而非

blur *v. & n.* 弄脏;变模糊;污迹

break-bulk *a.* (货物)分装的;分件的;非集装箱化的

brief *v. & a. & n.* (尤指事前)向……介绍基本情况;向……下达命令;聘请(律师);概要;传票;简短的;简洁的

bypass *v.* 绕过;忽略

by virtue of 依靠……;借助

coaster *n.* 滑坡的车(或橇);沿海船

commensurate *a.* 相称的;相当的

configuration *n.* 配置;构造

confine *v. & n.* 限制;界限;范围

conform *v.* 使一致;符合

congestion *n.* 密集;拥挤

consolidation *n.* 巩固;合并;(股票等交易的)盘整期

consummate *a. & v.* 完全无缺的;绝顶的;完成

cost-effective *a.* 有成本效益的;有利可图的

culmination *n.* 顶点;高潮

deadweight *n.* (车)自重;(船)载重量

deferral *n.* 延期

deployment *n.* 施展;调动部署

drayage *n.* 大车运输(费)

encompass *vt.* 包含;包括;完成

garrison *n.* 驻地;要塞

gauge *n. & v.* 标准尺寸;容量;手段;测量;估计

implement *v. & n.* 贯彻;执行;弥补;使生效;工具;装备

inbound *a.* 归航的;回程的;入境的

inherent *a.* 内在的;生来就有的

integrate *v.* 使结合/合并

inventory *n.* 存货;财产清单

jigsaw *v. & n.* 使互相交错搭接;线锯

lash *v. & n.* 讽刺;煽动

lead time 订货与交货间的时间;产品设计与实际投产的时间

leverage *v. & n.* (使)举债经营;举债经营;力量;影响

lighter *n. & v.* 驳船;驳运

logistics *n.* 物流

malfunction *v. & n.* 失灵;故障

obsolescence *n.* 淘汰;过时

organically *ad.* 不可分割地

outbound *a.* 向外去的

peculiarity *n.* 特质;特性

proactive *a.* 前摄的;积极主动的

profound *a.* 深奥的;渊博的

put-away *n.* 储存

relinquish *v.* 放弃,撤离

rules of thumb 经验工作法;毛估计

shareholder *n.* 股东

simultaneously *ad.* 同时发生地;同步地

source *v. & n.* 向……提供消息;根源

stand-alone *a.* 独立的

suffice *v.* 足够;能满足……的要求

trade-off *n.* 协调,平衡;(平等)交换

unravel *v.* 解开;澄清

Discussion Questions

1. What does international logistics refer to?

2. What is the difference between international logistics and domestic logistics?

3. What are the two key parts of international logistics?

4. Why is just-in-time inventory management popular? And what are the advantages of it?

5. What is the difference between third party logistics and fourth party logistics?

Chapter 13 | Electronic Commerce 电子商务

Objectives
学习目标

To understand what Electronic Commerce(E-commerce) is about.

理解电子商务的内涵。

To know the importance of E-commerce.

知晓电子商务的重要性。

To get to know the prospect of Electronic Commerce.

了解电子商务的前景。

To get to know the development of M-commerce.

了解移动电子商务的发展

We are now already in the second millennium which is said to be an era of information. It is quite true to say so as we have been experiencing one of the most important changes in our lives—the move to an Internet-based society. Almost everything will be changed at home, in school, at work, in the government and in our leisure activities as well. One of the most significant changes is in the manner we conduct business, especially in how we manage the marketplace and commerce.

E-commerce (EC) is an epoch-making concept of operational revolution. It has its great impact on the development of our respective business lines.

13.1 What Is Electronic Commerce (E-commerce, EC)？ 何谓电子商务？

13.1.1 Definition of EC 电子商务的定义

EC describes the manner in which transactions take place over networks, mostly the Internet. It is the process of electronically buying and selling goods, services, and information. Certain EC applications, such as buying and selling stocks or books on the Internet, are growing at a rate of several hundred percent every year. EC could have an impact on almost every aspect of our life.

EC is a merging concept concerning the process of buying and selling or exchanging of products, services, and information via computer networks including the Internet. EC can be defined from the following different perspectives.

(1) From a communications perspective: EC is the delivery of information, products/services, or payments over telephone lines, computer networks, or any other electronic means.

(2) From a business process perspective: EC is the application of technology toward the automation of business transactions and work flow.

(3) From a service perspective: EC is a tool that addresses the desire of firms, consumers, and management to cut service costs while improving the quality of goods and increasing the speed of service delivery.

(4) From an online perspective: EC provides the capability of buying and selling products and information on the Internet and other online services.

13.1.2 Significance of EC 电子商务的重要意义

EC is a direct product of Internet's explosive development. It is a brand-new development for the appliance of network technology. With Internet's intrinsic characteristics of its openness, low cost and high efficiency, EC will not only change an enterprise's activities of production, operation and management itself, but also affect the economic operation and structure of the whole society. From the perspective of companies, EC, on the surface, is the complete process of commercial activities between two or more parties over computer networks. It involves commercial activities between enterprises, enterprises' on-line promotion towards customers, and the digitized process of business flow inside an enterprise. Besides, EC has promoted a deep earth-shaking revolution on enterprises all over the world, from operational philosophy to marketing strategy, from internal management to organizational culture. E-commerce has brought about a global operational revolution.

Currently, there sweeps a forceful, brand-new hurricane of operational revolution throughout the globe. That is E-commerce. It does bring substantial benefit to our business and various social circles.

(1) E-commerce digitizes traditional commercial process by an electronic vehicle. On the one hand, it replaces material flow with electronic flow, which can substantially reduce manpower, material resources and cost. On the other hand, it surmounts the restriction on time and place so that a deal may be conducted in any place at any time, which would improve business efficiency a great deal.

(2) E-commerce's open and global strong points have created more trade opportunities for enterprises.

(3) E-commerce allows enterprises to enter global digital market with similar cost, which makes it possible for small-and medium-sized enterprises to have the same information as large enterprises and to increase their competitive power.

（4）E-commerce has redefined traditional circulation module and reduced intermediate links and made it possible for producers and customers to make a direct transaction, changing the whole society's way of economic operation to some extent.

（5）Breaking time and space barriers on the one hand, E-commerce has on the other hand provided true information resources. Therefore, more possibilities are given to the realignment of various social elements and it affects the society's economic distribution and structure.

13.1.3　E-commerce, E-business（EB）and E-marketing（EM）　电子商务、电子业务和电子营销

It seems that the term "commerce" will be considered transactions conducted between business partners. For the same reason, "electronic commerce" may make people associate it with transactions between businesses by electronic means.

E-commerce is commonly thought to include e-tailing, online banking and shopping. It involves transactions where buyers actually buy and shoppers actually shop. Others think that e-commerce is any transaction such as a support enquiry or an online catalogue search. In fact, EC is often used interchangeably with EB.

E-business is often used to refer to a broader sense of EC. EB refers to not only buying and selling but also servicing customers and collaborating with business partners, and conducting electronic transactions within an organization. It involves the automation of all the business processes in the value chain—from procurement or purchasing of raw materials, to production, to stock holding, distribution and logistics, to sales and marketing, after-sales, invoicing, debt collection and so on. Generally speaking, EB includes EC and E-marketing（EM）which will be discussed later in this chapter. Here is IBM's definition about EB:

The transformation of key business processes through the use of Internet technologies.

E-marketing is at the heart of EB. EM adds value to products, widens distribution channels and boosts sales and after-sales service, while getting closer to customers and understanding them better. The following Figure 13.1 shows the relationships between EB, EC and EM.

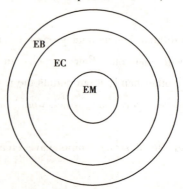

Figure 13.1　Relationships Between EB, EC and EM

As EC is often used interchangeably with EB, in this book EC is used in the same way as EB.

13.2   A Brief History of EC   电子商务历史概述

The initial development of EC started in the 1960s and 1970s when banks began to transfer money to each other in electronic way, using electronic funds transfer (EFT), and when large firms began sharing transaction information electronically with their suppliers and customers via electronic data interchange (EDI).

Using EDI, companies exchange information electronically with their suppliers and customers, called trading partners, including information traditionally submitted on paper forms such as invoices, purchase orders, quotes, and bills of lading. These transmissions generally occur over private telecommunications networks called value-added networks (VANs). Now companies are beginning to use the Internet, which is a less expensive network alternative to VANs for the exchange of information, products, services, and payments.

With the commercialization of the Internet in the early 1990s and its rapid growth to millions of potential customers, the term "electronic commerce" was born. And EC applications expanded quickly. From 1995 to 1999, people have witnessed many innovation applications ranging from advertisements to auctions and virtual reality experiences.

Use of the Internet as a business tool has increased dramatically since 1996, particularly with the development of the World Wide Web (WWW) and its intuitive and user-friendly graphical user interface. Worldwide business access to the web is predicted to grow from 1.3 million at the end of 1997 to 8 million by 2001, with much of this growth occurring in the Pacific Rim and Europe. Common applications of such information exchange tools include marketing and advertising, publishing, the exchange and dissemination of information on a global scale and, more recently, commercial transactions.

EC has penetrated into almost every aspect of our life. It is developing faster and faster and its application will involve many aspects of our business and our life as well.

13.3   Classification of the EC Field by the Nature of the Transactions 基于交易性质的电子商务分类

According to the nature of the EC field, we can divide it into the following types.

(1) Business-to-business (B2B): Most EC today is of this type, which includes the IOS (inter-organizational information system) transactions and electronic market transactions between organizations;

(2) Business-to-consumer (B2C);

(3) Consumer-to-consumer (C2C);

(4) Consumer-to-business (C2B);

(5) Non-business EC;

（6）Intra-business（organizational）EC.

13.4　EC Applications　电子商务应用

Many people think EC is just having a Web site, but EC is much more than that. There are a number of applications of EC such as home banking, shopping in online stores and malls, buying stocks, finding a job, conducting an auction, and collaborating electronically on research and development projects.

To execute these applications, it is necessary to have supporting information and organizational infrastructure and systems. Figure 13.2 shows the applications fields of EC.

Figure 13. 2 shows that the EC applications are supported by infrastructures, and their implementation is dependent on four major areas（shown as supporting pillars）：people, public policy, technical standards and protocols, and other organizations. It also shows that the EC management coordinates the applications, infrastructures, and pillars. On the other hand, we can view the applications from a different perspective：buy-side applications, sell-side applications and in-side applications.

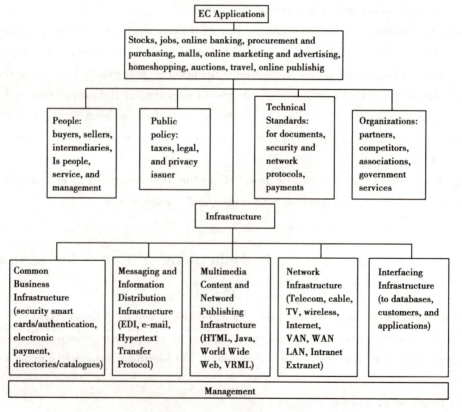

Figure 13.2　EC Applications

13.4.1　Buy-side Applications　买方应用

Internet technology can be used to open up the purchasing, in-bound logistics, stock management and re-ordering system to an exclusive audience of carefully selected suppliers who gain direct access to the company's back-office systems via the exclusive external internet—the company's extranet. In this way, the company can get to trade with suppliers, manufacturers and/or distributors more accurately, more swiftly and more easily as troublesome paperwork processes are abandoned and faster, easier, smarter systems are opened up to supply partners.

13.4.2　Sell-side Applications　卖方应用

The sell-side involves processes and applications that help to both sell and service customers whether directly or indirectly.

Sell-side applications include transactional E-commerce sites, E-commerce selling chain management applications and E-CRM applications.

13.4.3　In-side Applications　内部应用

In-side applications use intranets to share knowledge among staff while avoiding problems of information overload.

The internal Internet—the intranet—can change the way people work together. Cumbersome paper-based systems can be replaced, information overload can be reduced, "responsive knowledge workers" can be created, and better decisions can be made by using collaboration and knowledge management tools.

13.5　Advantages and Disadvantages of EC　电子商务的利弊

It is easy to understand that EC is so useful to us and without EC we could not imagine how we could deal with our business. EC brings us a lot of benefits though some limitations exist in the meantime. Sellers are finding tremendous advantages in doing E-commerce. Buyers, on the other hand, are enjoying greater access to markets.

13.5.1　Advantages of EC for the Sellers　电子商务对卖方的好处

(1) Increasing sales opportunities.

(2) Decreasing transaction costs.

(3) Operating 24 hours a day, 7 days a week from one virtual market-space.

(4) Reaching narrow market segments that may be widely distributed geographically.

(5) Increasing speed and accuracy of information exchange.

(6) Bringing multiple buyers and sellers together in one virtual marketplace.

13.5.2　Advantages of EC for the Buyers　电子商务对买方的好处

（1）Wider product availability.

（2）Customized and personalized information and buying options.

（3）Shopping 24 hours a day, 7 days a week.

（4）Easy comparison shopping and one-stop shopping for business buyers.

（5）Access to global markets.

（6）Quick delivery of digital products; quicker delivery of information.

（7）Participating in auctions, reverse auctions, knowledge exchanges.

13.5.3　Disadvantages of EC for the Sellers　电子商务对卖方的不利之处

（1）Rapidly changing technology.

（2）Insufficient telecommunications capacity or bandwidth.

（3）Difficulty in integrating existing systems with e-commerce software.

（4）Problemsin maintaining system security and reliability.

（5）Global market issues: language, political environment, currency conversions.

（6）Conflicted legal environment.

（7）Shortage of skilled technical employees.

13.5.4　Disadvantages of EC for the Buyers　电子商务对买方的不利之处

（1）Concern over transaction security and privacy.

（2）Lack of trust when dealing with unfamiliar sellers.

（3）Desire to touch and feel products before purchase.

（4）Resistance to unfamiliar buying process, paperless transactions, and electronic money.

Although there are some disadvantages, EC is still progressing fast. With the fast development of computer science, disadvantages may be gradually overcome.

13.6　The Internet, the Intranet, the Extranet, and the World Wide Web　因特网、内联网、外联网及万维网

13.6.1　The Internet　因特网

To understand the Internet, we have to understand networks. A network is just a group of two or more computers linked by cable or telephone lines. The group of linked computers includes special computers called "servers" that provide users with access to shared resources such as files, programs, and printers. Please refer to Figure 13.3.

It can be said that the Internet is a public worldwide network of networks, connecting many small private networks. Computers on the Internet use a common set of rules, called protocols, for

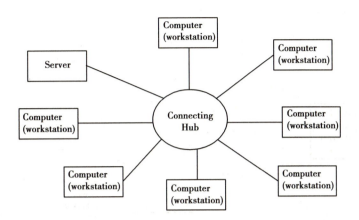

Figure 13.3　Computer Network

communication. The private Internet protocol is called TCP/IP (Transmission Control Protocol/Internet Protocol). In other words, the Internet is a public and global communication network that provides direct connectivity to anyone over a local area network (LAN) or Internet Service Provider (ISP). The Internet is a public network that is connected and routed over gateways.

13.6.2　The Intranet　内联网

An intranet is a corporate LAN or wide area network (WAN) that uses Internet technology and is secured behind company's firewalls (a kind of access control server). The intranet links various servers, clients, databases, and application programs like Enterprise Resource Planning (ERP).

Intranets operate as a private network with limited access. Only authorized employees are able to use it. Besides, intranets are limited to information pertinent to the company and contain exclusive and often proprietary and sensitive information. The intranet can be used to enhance the communication and collaboration among authorized employees, customers, suppliers, and other business partners. Since the intranet allows access through the Internet, it does not require any additional implementation of leased networks. This open and flexible connectivity is a major capability and advantage of intranets. Please refer to Figure 13.4 about the architecture of intranet.

13.6.3　The Extranet　外联网

An extranet, or "extended intranet", uses the TCP/IP protocol networks of the Internet to link intranets in different locations.

Extra-transmissions are normally conducted over the Internet, which offers little privacy or transmission security. Therefore, when using an extranet, it is necessary to improve the security of the connecting portions of the Internet. This is done by creating tunnels of secured data flows, using cryptography and authorization algorithms. The Internet with tunnelling technology is known as a virtually private network (VPN).

Extranets provide secured connectivity between a corporation's intranets and the intranets of its

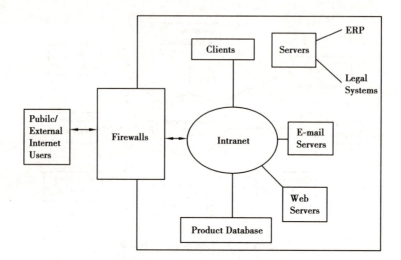

Figure 13.4 Architecture of the Intranet

business partners, material suppliers, financial services, government and customers.

Since an extranet allows connectivity between businesses through the Internet, it is an open and flexible platform suitable for supply chain management. Figure 13.5 shows the contrast of the Internet, Intranet and Extranet.

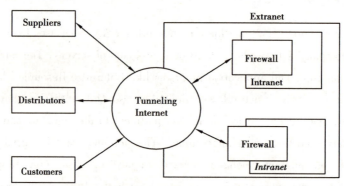

Figure 13.5 Diagrammatic Contrast of the Internet, Intranet, and Extranet

13.6.4   The World Wide Web (WWW)　万维网

The Internet, intranet, and extranet are considered enabling tools in the emerging digital economy. The three communication systems and most of the use of information technology are finding a way onto the public information highway, the World Wide Web (WWW).

The World Wide Web, which is called Web, is a sunset of the Internet where computers called Web servers store documents that are linked together by hypertext links, called hyperlinks. A hyperlink can be a text or a picture that is associated with the location (path and filename) of another document. The documents, called Web pages, can contain text, graphics, video, and audio as well as hyperlinks. A Web site is a collection of related Web pages. A Web browser is a software application used to access and view Web pages stored on a Web server.

Among the most recent advances is the use of the World Wide Web for business-to-business (B2B) and business-to-consumer (B2C) transactions. Much of the recent research signalled the huge potential of the online transactions market with a number of key development making the World Wide Web a better place to conduct B2B and B2C transactions.

▶ 13.7　Electronic Data Interchange (EDI) and the Internet　电子数据交换与因特网

Electronic Data Interchange (EDI) has been defined as "the application to application exchange of computer held information in a structural format via a telecommunications network". With EDI, data pass from an application on one computer into an application on another computer without printing or manual manipulation. It requires structured data—normally in a neutral data standard—to allow further processing. Basically, it permits paperless trading with no boundaries or time zones.

EDI is not a new technique and, in some markets, it has become the way to exchange commercial information. EDI is concerned with the regular electronic exchange of commercial information in a standard format and between established trading partners.

Businesspeople show great interest in the potential of exchanging EDI messages over the Internet because of the costs of traditional EDI via dedicated Value Added Networks (VANs). By comparison the Internet is easy to connect to, on a global basis, with relatively low charges, significantly undercutting some of the traditional VANs.

The development of "simpler" EDI techniques such as web-based EDI forms or "Lite EDI" is also likely to impact on the purchasing function. These initiatives involve the user accessing the website of a particular trading partner, selecting products from a catalogue or product and price list and completing an online order form. The information on the completed form is then translated into an EDI standard format and sent to a trading partner who processes the EDI message in the normal way.

The development of extranets in providing a secure trading environment, with the benefits of common TCP/IP communication standards and web browser interfaces, offers great potential to expanding not only electronic commerce transactions over the web, but also the spread of information which is of benefit to customers, suppliers and other interested parties.

EDI is very useful for familiar business trading partners to exchange large volumes of commercial information on a regular basis. Besides, EDI is ideal for some purchasing scenarios. EDI, the Internet, and web-based solutions respectively have different advantages over each other and a likely future scenario involves a merging of all three.

13.8 Types of Inter-organizational Systems 组织内部系统的种类

Inter-organizational systems (IOS) describe a variety of business activities, some of which are used in non-EC-related activities. The most prominent types of IOS are stated as follows:

(1) Electronic data interchange (EDI), which provides secured B2B connection over value-added networks (VANs).

(2) Electronic funds transfer.

(3) Electronic forms.

(4) Integrated messaging—delivery of e-mail and fax documents through a single electronic transmission system that can combine EDI, e-mail, and electronic forms.

(5) Shared databases—information stored in repositories are shared between trading partners and are accessible to all. Such databases are often used to reduce elapsed time in communicating information between parties as well as arranging cooperative activities. The sharing is mainly done over extranets.

(6) Supply chain management—cooperation between a company and its suppliers and/or customers regarding demand forecasting, inventory management, and orders fulfilment can reduce inventories, speed shipments, and enable just-in-time manufacturing.

13.9 E-commerce in the International Trade Arena 国际贸易环境中的电子商务

EC is quite important in doing international trade, as many procedures and processes are performed in an electronic way. By so doing, a lot of time is saved, which agrees with the well-known saying in doing business "Time means money". Besides, with EC, much paperwork is saved and it brings much convenience to the company staff in their work. Further, EC facilitates and improves communications between staff of a company or between the staffs of different companies. From the perspective of international trade, EC is applied in almost every aspect of it.

13.9.1 EDI—in Relation to Some Parties of International Trade 电子数据交换与国际贸易的某些当事方

EDI is applied regularly in doing international trade. We will discuss the application of EDI in EC in relation to some parties in the process of doing international trade.

1. The Exporter

Many documentary credits are incorrect on first presentation, which causes lost orders, costly delays and lower profits for exporters. EDI helps exporters to eliminate these frustrating and expensive errors. Standard documents for exporters and other shippers serving domestic markets can be created more accurately, amendments made more rapidly and the data transmitted quickly and reliably. Orders can be fulfilled faster and more cost-effectively.

2. The Importer

EDI has grown rapidly on a bilateral basis where buyer and seller agree to exchange standard data electronically between their respective computers. The messages can easily be created from data already stored on a company's existing computer system. These developments benefit both importers and exporters. The importer can make payments with the help of EDI. EDI facilities can also help importers with schedule information, consignment progress tracking and customs clearance routines.

3. The Freight Forwarder

Much of the information needed by the freight forwarder may already exist in the customer's computer. Currently forwarders must re-input the information on to their own computer, print out the documents and then despatch them. The creation of additional documents involves re-inputting much of the data that already exists. Furthermore, errors often require documents to be re-created adding to the waste of time and money.

EDI reduces paperwork, expensive telephone calls and wasteful communications costs. Forwarders can receive the essential data from their customers as an electronic message is directed to their computers via a certain network.

4. The Carrier

Many of the large carriers may use their own EDI system for the transmission of data internally and for "paperless trading" relationships with their customers. The problem with most customer-based systems is that they require the carrier's dedicated terminals to be installed in the offices of the shipper or forwarder. Many of the carriers have recognized the difficulties involved for all parties in this approach. But a certain network may give carriers the ability to send and receive messages to and from all their customers and suppliers of services rapidly and easily. It also enables the carriers to use the vital data without re-keying.

13.9.2   Paperless Documentation   无纸单证

As mentioned previously, reducing paperwork is one of the chief features of EC. With the fast development of EC, paperless documentation in doing international trade has become a trend, as dealing with documentation via networks is much faster and more efficient.

It is well-known that international trade cannot be done without documents. International businesspeople have to deal with numberless paper documents. As EC is growing, some documents can be made and transferred via networks. EC greatly promotes the realization of paperless documentation.

The EDI system plays a special role in this aspect. It is a computerized system using standardized electronic versions of common business documents. These include bills of lading, freight bills, purchase orders and so on. In addition, shippers despatching shipping instructions that are despatched in an EDI environment can reduce the risks of any error, wrong billing and delays in the documentation process.

Besides, small shippers can use the Web to prepare documents, and volume shippers can apply a system interface. The transportation company has all documents. These documents can be transmitted to the appropriate destination in advance, enabling easy document retention and recovery, if necessary. The shipper coordinates all activities with import and export personnel in advance of the shipment, coordinates receiving schedules, and works with inbound materials to stage receipts. In this way, dealing with lots of documents in international shipments is made much simpler and easier. As a result, efficiency is greatly improved.

Further, in company's daily administration, documents that need distributing within the organization need not be made in the form of paper. Instead, they can be made in the computer and can be distributed through the company's network. Besides, order form, enquiries, and quotations may be made in the computer and transferred through networks.

What's more, paperless documentation is especially important in international payments. Most documents in the documentary credit process can be effectively transmitted by EDI, except for the bill of lading, as the document of title function requires an original document to operate effectively. Messages and some documents concerning payments are sent via networks.

13.9.3　Business Administration　商务管理

Modern administration of business largely relies on EC. A lot of things are done electronically.

First of all, office automation is concerned with computer science. Nowadays, no businesses can operate without computers. With the help of computers and networks, the staff of a company communicate conveniently and quickly. Much paper work is reduced. On the other hand, messages from overseas trading partners or customers can be transmitted quickly through e-mail or fax.

Information is stored in the hardware of the computer or soft discs. It is easy to file the documents instead of many filing cabinets and/or organizers. In this way, it is easy to revise or to copy documents. Thus, efficiency in business administration is greatly improved.

As most of the goods in international trade are carried by sea, ocean shipping plays a very important role in international trade. EC facilitates ocean shipping and improves its efficiency.

13.10　E-marketing（EM）　电子营销

E-marketing is the most important part of EC and is the focus of EC. It is not about building a web site, but about building a web business. It harmonizes the power of customers.

EM impacts all aspects of marketing from strategy and planning through the marketing mix, marketing communications, buyer behaviour to marketing research. Besides, EM also impacts all organizations.

EM is best considered how e-tools such as web sites, CRM systems and databases can be used to get closer to customers—to be able to identify, anticipate and satisfy their needs efficiently and effectively.

13.10.1　The Objectives of EM—5 Ss　电子营销目的：5 Ss

Generally speaking, EM is intended to grow sales, add value, get closer to customers, save costs, and extend the brand online and reinforce brand values in a totally new medium. The objectives can be summarized as the 5 Ss: Sell, Service, Speak, Save and Sizzle (PR Smith, 2002).

（1）Sell—using the Internet as a sales tool

Just as anything can be sold offline, most things can be sold online. But some products and services are partly bought online.

The clearest benefit of EM is the capability to sell from an online presence. Although this may not be practical for all products, an online presence is still important in supporting the buying decision leading to sales through traditional channels. An online presence also offers opportunities to sell new markets and reach particular segments.

（2）Serve—using the Internet as a customer-service tool

A web presence can be used to add value to customers at different stages of the buying process, whether pre-sales, during the sale or post-sales support.

（3）Speak—using the Internet as a communications tool

A web site can be used as a new communications channel to increase awareness, build brand, shape customer opinion and communicate special offers. As good as speaking to customers, the Internet provides a tool to talk with, and listen to customers—get closer to them. E-marketers can enjoy direct access to customers, their attitudes, their interests and their buying patterns through the following ways.

1）Chat rooms. Chat rooms offer a new approach to focus groups—small groups of customers who discuss your product, pack, advertisements and so on.

2）Questionnaires. Questionnaires, on the other hand, are more structured and guide the respondent through specific questions.

3）Web logs. Web logs present the opportunity of seeing what are the most popular pages and how long they spend on specific pages. Web logs, or web stats, also track customers as they search on site so that the e-marketer can see how visitors' minds work.

4）Database. The database behind the web is a warehouse full of valuable information about customers and their patterns of purchasing, responses to promotions and much more.

（4）Save—using the Internet for cost-reduction

Saving means saving money, time and effort.

（5）Sizzle—using the Internet as a brand-building tool

The Internet offers new opportunities to build and strengthen the brand, to add some "sizzle" to the brand, to add extra value, to extend the experience and enhance the image. Without doubt, e-marketing can help to build the brand.

13.10.2　E-marketing Mix—7 Ps　电子营销组合：7 Ps

As early as 1949, marketing mix was first referred to at an American Marketing Association conference. But it rose to prominence in the early 1960s. Just around the beginning of the 1960s, Jerome McCarthy coined the term the "4 Ps": Product, Price, Place, Promotion.

As the 4 Ps worked for products rather than services, in 1981, American academics, Booms and Bitner then developed the 7 Ps, sometimes known as the service mix. They added three Ps to the 4 Ps: people, processes and physical evidence. From the perspective of EM, the marketing mix refers to the 7 Ps.

（1）Product

Products can be extended online by offering new information-based services and interaction with the brand to create new brand experience.

（2）Price

Reduction in market prices is caused by online price transparency through purchasing methods such as reverse auction, price comparison and shopping bots. B2B exchanges and hubs will become significant for routine purchase of commoditized products. Marketers will have to continually monitor prices to remain competitive.

（3）Place

Changes in the place of promotion, purchase, distribution and usage of products are taken into account when specifying the Place element of mix. Disintermediation and reintermediation are major marketplace changes which must be responded to.

（4）Promotion

Online options for all elements of the promotional mix from advertising, selling, sales promotion, PR, sponsorship, direct mail, exhibitions, merchandising, packaging to word-of-mouth should be reviewed for the promotion part of the mix. Key issues in devising the promotional mix are integration, creativity, globalization and resourcing.

（5）People

People are a significant contributor to the mix since service quality is a key differentiator online or offline. Organizations need to decide the best balance of automated online customer service and traditional human service to provide customers with service quality and choice while at the same time minimizing service costs.

（6）Physical Evidence

The quality of the site is the physical evidence online, so it is important to reassure customers buying intangible services through a site that meets acceptable standards of speed and ease of use. This can be supplemented by certification by independent organizations.

（7）Process

All processes impact on customers in terms of product and service quality. In the online context, it is particularly important to revise processes by integrating front- and back-office systems to provide efficient response to customer support requests and fulfilment.

Figure 13.6 further illustrates the relationships between the 7 Ps.

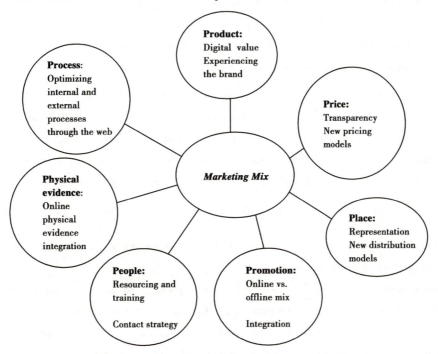

Figure 13.6   Key Aspects of the 7 Ps of the EM Mix

13.10.3   E-tools in EM   电子营销中的电子工具

EM involves not only the web access through PCs, but also other tools which are discussed as follows:

1. Interactive Digital TV

Compared with PCs, there are many more TVs involved. So we can see how interactive digital TVs have huge potential. Interactive TV converts sound and pictures into computerized digits, which are transmitted through the air by transmitters. It offers a large and rapid growing audience interactive tools which help engagement and generate a response. Marketing approaches include new programme sponsorship, product placement and advertising opportunities abound in interactive TV.

2. Interactive Radio

There are two kinds of interactive radios: web radio and digital radio. Both are interactive. The future of radio is in digital and web radio where interaction is possible by responding to on-screen prompts such as voting or e-mail.

3. Mobile Devices

Smart phones and bluetooth technology, text messaging, location-based marketing, voice portals and browserphones have come into the world. They can help the market achieve all 5 Ss but with the usual caveat.

4. Interactive Kiosks

Interactive kiosks come in all shapes and sizes. Compact and robust, they can be placed anywhere that attracts footfall of customers. This makes them ideal not only for sales and marketing, but also for public information purposes and corporate communications.

5. CD-ROMs and Interactive Business Cards

CD cards add impact to your message, communications and distinction to your brand. They work just like regular CDs and CD-ROMs and can contain all the same information on them, such as text, audio, images, animations, video clips, software, and so on. There are all types and shapes of interactive business cards, which can be used as sales force business cards, invitations to events, exhibitions and trade show, direct mail shots, and product launch press packs.

13.10.4 E-CRM 电子客户关系管理

E-CRM stands for Electronic Customer Relations Management, in other words, customer relations managed in an electronic way.

Customer Relations are well established as an approach to acquiring customers and then retaining them to develop a higher lifetime value for each customer. Managing CRM online and integrating it with offline CRM activities introduces new challenges. It is necessary for us to think about how to use online tools to have a more dynamic dialogue with the customer, answering their questions, understanding their needs, profiling them and then delivering appropriate services and communications.

13.10.5 Advertisement 广告

Doing advertising is a key part in marketing strategy and is a very important way to promote sales of goods and services. Even world-famous companies keep on advertising their world-famous brands in order to enlarge their sales.

1. EC Advertisement Advantages and Methods

Traditional marketing concerns many respects such as doing market research, pricing, giving presentations. Not all the activities of marketing can be carried out in an electronic way. Some of them can be performed through the network, though.

Advertisements can be made on the net. Advertising is an important promotion way in marketing strategy. Advertising is an attempt to pass information in order to effect a buyer-seller transaction. Traditional ways of doing advertisements may be more expensive, but the Internet has enabled consumers to interact directly with advertisers and advertisements. In interactive marketing, a consumer can click with his mouse on an ad. for more information or send an e-mail to ask a question.

Compared with traditional media of advertising, the Internet advertisement has the following advantages.

（1）Internet advertisements are accessed on demand 24 hours a day, and all the year round. Costs are the same regardless of audience location.

（2）Opportunity to create one-to-one direct marketing relationship with consumer.

（3）Multimedia will increasingly create more attractive and compelling ads.

（4）Distribution costs are low（just technology costs）, so the millions of consumers reached cost the same as one.

（5）Advertising and contents can be updated, supplemented, or changed at any time, and are therefore always up-to-date. Response（click-through rate）and results（page views）of advertising are immediately measurable.

（6）Ease of logical navigation—you click when and where you want, and spend as much time as desired there.

Some of the chief methods used for advertisements in EC are as follows:

（1）Banners

Banner advertising is the most commonly used form of advertising on the Internet. As you surf your way through the information superhighway, banners are here and there.

Typically, a banner contains a short text or graphical message to promote a product. Advertisers try their best to design a banner that catches consumers' attention. We can even find banners with video clips and sound. Banners contain links like that, when clicked on, transfer the customer to the advertiser's home page. There are two types of banners: key banner and random banner.

（2）Splash screen

A splash screen is an initial Web site page used to capture the user's attention for a short time as a promotion or lead-in to the site home page or to tell the user what kind of browser and other software they need to view the site.

（3）URL（Universal Resource Locators）

The major advantage of using URL as an advertising tool is that it is free. Anyone can submit its URL to a search engine and be listed. By using URL the target audience can be locked and the unwanted viewers can be filtered because of the keyword function.

（4）E-mail

A very useful way to advertise on the Internet is to purchase e-mail addresses and send the company information to those on the list. The advantages of this way are its low cost and the ability to reach a wide variety of target audience. Quite a lot of companies develop a customer database to whom they send e-mails.

E-mails are emerging as a marketing channel that affords cost-effective implementation and better, quicker response rates than other advertising channels.

（5）Chat rooms

Electronic chat refers to an arrangement where participants exchange messages in real time. Since many customer-supplier relationships have to be sustained without face-to-face meetings, online communities are increasingly being used to serve business interests, including advertising.

A vendor may sponsor a chat room (look for logo). Chat capabilities can be added to a business site for free by letting software chat vendors host your session on their site. You just put a chat link on your site and the chat vendor does the rest, including the advertising that pays for the session.

(6) Other forms

Online advertising can be done in several other ways, such as advertisements in newsgroups, advertisement on Internet radio, and even advertising on Internet TV is coming.

2. Online Catalogs

Distributing literature such as price list, product catalogue, instruction of products or introduction to the company is one of the best efficient ways to promote sales and improve the corporate image. An important factor of EC is the manner in which products or services are presented to the users. This is normally done via online catalogues. Normally, in order to market products or services, a company may send out or distribute its catalogues as well as other literature. Printed paper has been used as the medium of advertisement catalogues for a long time. But with EC coming into being, electronic catalogs on CD-ROM and on the Web are becoming popular. Electronic catalogs can be searched quickly with the help of software agents. Besides, comparisons involving catalogs' products can be made very effectively.

Electronic catalogues are made up of product database, directory and search capability, and a presentation function. On the Web-based e-malls, Web browser, along with Java and sometimes virtual reality, plays the role of presenting static and dynamic information.

Originally, online catalogs were online replication of text and pictures of the printed catalogs. Now online catalogs have evolved to be more dynamic, customized, and integrated with selling and buying procedures. As the online catalog is integrated with order taking and payment, the tools for building online catalogs are being integrated with merchant sites.

Traditional paper catalogs have the following features.

(1) Easy to create a catalog without high technology.

(2) Reader is able to look at the catalog without computer system.

(3) More portable than electronic catalog.

Compared with paper catalogs, online catalogs have the following advantages.

(1) Easy to update product information.

(2) Able to integrate with the purchasing process.

(3) Good search and comparison capabilities.

(4) Provision for globally broad range of product information.

(5) Able to provide timely, up-to-date product information.

(6) Possibility of adding voice and motion pictures.

(7) Cost savings.

(8) Easy to customize.

(9) More comparative shopping.

(10) Ease of connecting order processing, inventory processing, and payment processing to the

system.

Here is an example to show the great significance of online catalogs (source: Efraim Turban, 2001).

With annual revenues of more than $ 5.2 billion, AMP, an electronics components manufacturer, spent more than $ 7 million each year to mail and update 400 specialty catalogs to its distributors all over the world and another $ 800,000 in fax-back phone costs. These catalogs cover about 134,000 electrical and mechanical components.

In the past, AMP had only enough resources to update about one-half of their 400 catalogs each year, so many catalogs had a life-cycle of two years, even though products changed more often than that. However, the estimate of the cost of setting the online catalogs up and running is only $ 1.2 million, roughly one-fifth of the previous printing costs. Of the $ 1.2 million, software and hardware costs were $ 300,000 to $ 400,000, with the remainder spent for language translation and catalog development.

▶ 13.11　M-commerce　移动电子商务

The phrase mobile commerce (M-commerce) was originally coined in 1997 by Kevin Duffey at the launch of the Global Mobile Commerce Forum, to mean "the delivery of electronic commerce capabilities directly into the consumer's hand, anywhere, via wireless technology." Many choose to think of Mobile Commerce as meaning "a retail outlet in your customer's pocket".

Mobile commerce is worth US $230 billion, with Asia representing almost half of the market, and has been forecast to reach US $700 billion in 2017. According to BI Intelligence in January 2013, 29% of mobile users have now made a purchase with their phones. Walmart estimated that 40% of all visits to their internet shopping site in December 2012 was from a mobile device.

The widespread adoption of wireless and mobile networks, devices (handsets, PDAs, etc.), and middleware (software that links application modules from different computer languages and platforms) is creating exciting new opportunities. These new technologies are making mobile computing possible—meaning that when using wireless computing they permit real-time access to information, applications, and tools that, until recently, were accessible only from a desktop computer.

Mobile commerce refers to the conduct of e-commerce via wireless devices or from portable devices, including smart cards. Mobile commerce, also known as m-commerce and m-business, is basically any e-commerce or e-business done in a wireless environment, especially via the Internet. Like regular EC applications, m-commerce can be done via the Internet, private communication lines, or other infrastructures.

M-commerce is not merely a variation on existing Internet services; it is a natural extension of e-business. Mobile devices create an opportunity to deliver new services to existing customers and to attract new ones. It is also sometimes called m-business when reference is made to its broadest definition, in which the e-business environment is wireless. At the core of most m-commerce applications are mobile networks. In today's mobile world, most of the networks rely on either TDMA or CDMA.

There is a reason for the strong interest in the topic of mobile commerce. According to the International Data Corporation, the number of mobile device is projected to top 1.3 billion by 2004. These devices can be connected to the Internet, allowing users to conduct transaction from anywhere. The Gartner Group estimates that at least 40 percent of all B2C transactions, totaling over \$200 billion by 2005, will be initiated from smart wireless devices. Others predict much higher figures because they believe that mobile devices will soon overtake PCs as the predominant Internet access device, creating a global market of over 500 million subscribers. However, others predict a much slower adoption rate.

Since 1999, m-commerce has become one of the hottest topics in IT in general and in EC in particular. Mobility significantly changes the manner in which people and trading partners interact, communicate, and collaborate, and mobile applications are expected to change the way we live, play, and do business. Much of the Internet culture, which is currently PC-based, may change to one based on mobile devices. As a result, m-commerce creates new business models for EC, notably location-based applications.

Although there are currently many hurdles to the widespread adoption of m-commerce, it is clear that many of these will be reduced or eliminated in the future. Many companies are already shifting their strategy to the mobile world. Many large corporations with huge marketing presence—Microsoft, Intel, Sony, AT&T, to name a few—are transforming their businesses to include m-commerce-based products and services. Apple emerged as a world-class company not just because it sells more cell phones than anyone else, but also because it has become the major player in the mobile economy. Similarly, major telecommunications companies, from Verizon to Vodafone, are shifting their strategies to wireless products and services. In Europe alone, over 200 companies offer mobile portal services. In the United States, over 2 million subscribers used General Motors' OnStar in-vehicle mobile services in 2002. DoCoMo, the world's largest mobile portal, with more than 30 million customers in Japan, is investing billions of dollars to expand its services to other countries, via its i-Mode services.

In 2001, a hacker sent an e-mail message to 13 million users of the i-Mode wireless data service in Japan. The message had the potential to take over the recipient's phone, causing it to dial Japan's emergency hotline (1-1-0). NTT DoCoMo, which provides the i-Mode service, rapidly fixed the problem so no damage was done. At the beginning of 2002, researchers in Holland discovered a bug in the operating system used by many Nokia phones that would enable a hacker to exploit the system by sending a malformed SMS message capable of crashing the system. Again, no real damage was done.

Today, most of the Internet-enabled cell phones in operation are incapable of storing applications and, in turn, incapable of propagating a virus, worm, or other rogue program from one phone to another. Most of the Internet-enabled cell phones also have their operating system and other functionality "burned" right into the hardware. This makes it difficult for a rogue program to permanently alter the operation of a cell phone. However, as the capabilities of cell phones increase and the functionality of PDAs and cell phones converge, the threat of attack from malicious code will certainly increase.

Just "because a mobile device is less susceptible to attack by malicious code" does not mean that m-commerce is more secure than e-commerce in the wired world. By their very nature, mobile devices and mobile transactions produce some unique security challenges.

M-commerce's products and services available are stated as follows:

1. Mobile Money Transfer

In Kenya money transfer is mainly done through the use of mobile phones. This was an initiative of a multimillion shillings company in Kenya named Safaricom. Currently, the companies involved are Safaricom and Airtel. Mobile money transfer services in Kenya are now provided by the two companies under the names M-PESA and Airtel Money respectively.

A similar system called MobilePay has been operated by Danske Bank in Denmark since 2013. It has gained considerable popularity with about 1.6 million users by mid-2015.

2. Mobile Ticketing

Tickets can be sent to mobile phones using a variety of technologies. Users are then able to use their tickets immediately, by presenting their mobile phone at the ticket check as a digital boarding pass. Most number of users are now moving towards this technology.

3. Mobile Vouchers, Coupons and Loyalty Cards

Mobile ticketing technology can also be used for the distribution of vouchers, coupons, and loyalty cards. These items are represented by a virtual token that is sent to the mobile phone. A customer presenting a mobile phone with one of these tokens at the point of sale receives the same benefits as if they had the traditional token. Stores may send coupons to customers using location-based services to determine when the customer is nearby.

4. Content Purchase and Delivery

Currently, mobile content purchase and delivery mainly consists of the sale of ring-tones, wallpapers, and games for mobile phones. The convergence of mobile phones, portable audio players, and video players into a single device is increasing the purchase and delivery of full-length music tracks and video. The download speeds available with 4G networks make it possible to buy a movie on a mobile device in a couple of seconds.

5. Location-based Services

The location of the mobile phone user is an important piece of information used during mobile commerce or m-commerce transactions. Knowing the location of the user allows for location-based services such as:

（1）Local discount offers

（2）Local weather

（3）Tracking and monitoring of people

6. Information Services

A wide variety of information services can be delivered to mobile phone users in much the same way as it is delivered to PCs. These services include:

（1）News

（2）Stock quotes

（3）Sports scores

（4）Financial records

（5）Traffic reporting（6）Emergency Alerts

7. Mobile Banking

Banks and other financial institutions use mobile commerce to allow their customers to access account information and make transactions, such as purchasing stocks, remitting money. This service is often referred to as mobile banking, or m-banking.

8. Mobile Brokerage

Stock market services offered via mobile devices have also become more popular and are known as Mobile Brokerage. They allow the subscriber to react to market developments in a timely fashion and irrespective of their physical location.

9. Mobile Browsing

Using a mobile browser—a World Wide Web browser on a mobile device—customers can shop online without having to be at their personal computer. Many mobile marketing apps with geo-location capability are now delivering user-specific marketing messages to the right person at the right time.

10. Mobile Purchase

Catalog merchants can accept orders from customers electronically, via the customer´s mobile device. In some cases, the merchant may even deliver the catalog electronically, rather than mailing a paper catalog to the customer. Consumers making mobile purchases can also receive value-add upselling services and offers. Some merchants provide mobile web sites that are customized for the smaller screen and limited user interface of a mobile device.

11. In-application Mobile Phone Payments

Payments can be made directly inside of an application running on a popular smartphone operating system, such as Google Android. Analyst firm Gartner expects in-application purchases to drive 41 percent of app store (also referred to as mobile software distribution platforms) revenue in 2016. In-app purchases can be used to buy virtual goods, new and other mobile content and is ultimately billed by mobile carriers rather than the app stores themselves.

12. Mobile Marketing and Advertising

In the context of mobile commerce, mobile marketing refers to marketing sent to mobile devices. Companies have reported that they see better response from mobile marketing campaigns than from traditional campaigns. The primary reason for this is the instant nature of customer decision-making that mobile apps and websites enable. The consumer can receive a marketing message or discount coupon and, within a few seconds, make a decision to buy and go on to complete the sale - without disrupting their current real-world activity.

Based on e-commerce, m-commerce is developing so fast that you even cannot expect what kind facilities it may contribute to the development of this world of globalization.

Summary of This Chapter
本章概要

1. 电子商务是进入21世纪后人类活动中一个非常重要的方面。随着电子科技的迅猛发展,电子科学直接影响当代人类的工作、生活、社交等各个方面。国际商务中电子科学的应用越来越广泛。可以说,在当代社会中,没有电子科学的介入,国际贸易交易几乎不可能完成。

2. 电子商务指的是通过简洁、快捷、低成本的电子通信方式,买卖双方不谋面而进行各种商务活动。电子商务包括两个方面:使用电子方式和进行商务活动。电子指互联网及其他各种电子方式。商务主要指产品销售、贸易和交易等其他商务活动。联合国经济合作和发展组织(OECD)认为:电子商务是发生在开放网络上的包含企业之间(B2B)、企业和消费者之间(B2C)的商业交易。

3. 电子商务涉及互联网、内联网和万维网的应用。网络世界的奇妙给国际商务活动带来更多的机遇,同时也带来挑战。电子商务是企业/公司发展、管理策略的一个重要方面。互联网(Internet)是目前世界上规模最大,信息资源最丰富,由数以万计的计算机网络组成的巨型计算机网络。

4. 电子商务的功能主要有:(1)网上广告宣传;(2)信息收集和咨询洽谈;(3)网上买卖;(4)电子支付;(5)电子金融;(6)网上商品和服务传递;(7)交易管理。

5. 电子数据交换(EDI)是一项新的商务技术。国际标准化组织(ISO)认为电子数据交换指的是:利用现代化的计算机和通信技术,将商务或行政事务处理,按照一个公认的标准,形成结构化的事务处理或消息报文格式,从计算机系统到计算机系统的数据传输方法。EDI是远程信息处理技术、数据通信技术和现代网络技术相结合的产物。电子数据交换在国际贸易中应用广泛。它利用存储转发的方式将商业文件,如订单、发票、货运单、报关单、进出口许可证等,按照统一的标准编制成计算机能识别和处理的数据格式,在计算机之间进行传输,以电子手段代替纸面文件,所以它又被称为"无纸贸易"。EDI的作用主要有:(1)贸易无纸化,减少工作中的错误,节约成本,提高工作效率;(2)提高企业管理和服务的质量,提高竞争力;(3)拓展业务空间,获得更多贸易机会。

6. 电子营销(EM)是电子商务的一个重要组成部分。电子营销指通过现代的电子网络手段进行营销活动。电子营销对企业的生存发展有着不可替代的作用。电子营销比起传统的营销手段有"快"和"广"的特点。电子营销组合（7 Ps）是电子营销的中心。

7. 移动电子商务是电子商务的新的衍生品，它将渗透到商务、办公、生活等各个方面。电子商务就是利用手机、PDA 及掌上电脑等无线终端进行的 B2B、B2C、C2C 或 O2O 的电子商务。它将因特网、移动通信技术、短距离通信技术及其他信息处理技术完美的结合，使人们可以在任何时间、任何地点进行各种商贸活动，实现随时随地、线上线下的购物与交易、在线电子支付以及各种交易活动、商务活动、金融活动和相关的综合服务活动等。

▶ New Words and Expressions

alert *a.* 警惕的；活跃的

algorithm *n.* 算法；规则系统

ally *v. & n.* 联合；同盟者；伙伴；助手

animation *n.* 生气；活跃

arena *n.* 活动场所；竞争场所

bilateral *a.* 双边的

bot *n.* （能自动执行特定任务的）机器人程序

browser *n.* 浏览器

browserphone *n.* 浏览器电话

cargo plan （船舶）货物配载计划（图）

caveat *n.* ［法律］终止诉讼申请；（防止误解的）说明

commoditize *v.* 使商品化

compel *v.* 强迫

consecutively *ad.* 按时间顺序地；连续地

coordinate *v. & a. & n.* 调整；（自动数据处理中的）对等检查的；相关检索的；同等级的人/物

cryptography *n.* 密码编制/体系

cumbersome *a.* 麻烦的；拖累的

customize *v.* （按顾客要求）定制；定做；改制

differentiator *n.* 微分器

digitize *v.* 使数字化

directory *n. & a.* 指南；使用手册；工商行名录；号码簿；指导性的；咨询的

disintermediation *n.* 非中介化（指消除商品流通等交易的中间环节）

dissemination *n.* 传播；散布

epoch-making *a.* 划时代的

e-tailing *n.* 电子（网络）零售业

firewall *n.* 防火墙

hyperlink *n.* 超文本连接器；超链接

hypertext *n.* 超文本

in advance of 在……之前

in-bound *a.* 回程的；入站的

interface *n. & v.* 接口；连接装置；界面；使结合；联系

intranet *n.* 内联网

intrinsic *a.* 内在的；本质的

intuitive *a.* 知觉的

inventory *n.* 存货清单；存货

just-in-time ［物流］（为把原材料或零部件的仓储成本降至最低）需要前夕才进货的；适时进货制的

kiosk *n.* 公用电话亭；报亭；售货亭

mall *n.* （车辆不得入内的）步行街

manifest *n.* （货车的）货单；（船舶或飞机的）舱单

millennium *n.* 千年

optimally *ad.* 最适宜地；最佳地

Pacific Rim 太平洋（经济贸易）圈

proposition *n.* 提议；建议；生意

protocol *n.* （条约等的）草案；议定书；［计］协议

realignment *n.* 重组

reintermediation *n.* 再介入

replication *n.* 回答；［法律］（原告的）答辩；复制（过程/品）

repository *a. & n.* （药物）长效的；储藏室；货栈；储藏器；店铺

resource *n.* 资源；办法；对策；资料储备

respondent *n.* （营销调查的）答卷人

retention *n.* 保留

scenario *n.* 方案；设想

sizzle *n. & v.* 发咝咝声；极度兴奋

strain *v. & n.* 紧张

surmount *v.* 克服；覆盖

tenet *n.* 信条；原则

transparency *n.* 透明

undercut *v.* 销价与……竞争

vendor *n.* ［法律］卖主；摊贩

word-of-mouth 口碑

 ## Discussion Questions

1. What is E-commerce?

2. What are the advantages and disadvantages of E-commerce?

3. How can E-commerce be applied in international trade?

4. What is the difference between Internet and Intranet?

5. What does EDI refer to? And what are the functions of EDI?

Chapter 14

International Business Law
国际商法

Objectives
学习目标

To get familiar with international law systems.

熟悉国际法系。

To understand what international business law is.

理解国际商法的实质。

14.1 A Brief Introduction to Civil Law System   大陆法系简介

Civil law (or civilian law) is alegal system originating in Western Europe, intellectualized within the framework of late Roman law, and whose most prevalent feature is that its core principles are codified into a referable system which serves as the primary source of law. This can be contrasted with common law systems whose intellectual framework comes from judge-made decisional law which gives precedential authority to prior court decisions on the principle that it is unfair to treat similar facts differently on different occasions (doctrine of judicial precedent).

Historically, civil law is the group of legal ideas and systems ultimately derived from the Code of Justinian, but heavily overlaid by Germanic, canon-law, feudal, and local practices, as well as doctrinal strains such as natural law, codification, and legislative positivism.

Conceptually, civil law proceeds from abstractions, formulates general principles, and distinguishes substantive rules from procedural rules. It holds case law to be secondary and subordinate to statutory law, and the court system is usually inquisitorial, unbound by precedent, and composed of specially-trained, functionary judicial officers with limited authority to interpret law. Jury trials are not used, although in some cases, benches may be sat by a mixed panel of lay magistrates and career judges.

The term civil law comes from English legal scholarship and is used in English-speaking countries to lump together all legal systems of the jus commune tradition. However, legal

Chapter 14   International Business Law

comparativists and economists promoting the legal origins theory prefer to subdivide civil law jurisdictions into four distinct groups:

- Napoleonic: France, Belgium, Luxembourg, Quebec(Canada), Louisiana(U. S.), Italy, Romania, the Netherlands, Spain, and their former colonies;

- Germanistic: Germany, Austria, Switzerland, Roman-Dutch, Czech Republic, Croatia, Hungary, Slovenia, Slovakia, Bosnia and Herzegovina, Greece, Brazil, Portugal, Turkey, Japan, South Korea, and Taiwan;

- Scandinavian:Denmark, Finland, Iceland, Norway, and Sweden.

- Chinese (except Hong Kong) is a mixture of civil law and socialist law. Hong Kong, although part of China, uses common law. The Basic Law of Hong Kong ensures the use and status of common law in Hong Kong.

Portugal, Brazil, and Italy have shifted from Napoleonic to Germanistic influence, as their 19th century civil codes were close to the Napoleonic Code, whereas their 20th-century civil codes are much closer to the German Civil Code. More recently, Brazil's 2002 Civil Code drew heavily from the Italian Civil Code in its unification of private law; legal culture and academic law now more closely follow the Germanistic tradition. The other law in these countries is often said to be of a hybrid nature.

Some systems of civil law do not fit neatly into this typology, however. ThePolish law developed as a mixture of French and German civil law in the 19th century. After the reunification of Poland in 1918, five legal systems (French Napoleonic Code from the Duchy of Warsaw, German BGB from Western Poland, Austrian ABGB from Southern Poland, Russian law from Eastern Poland, and Hungarian law from Spisz and Orawa) were merged into one. Similarly, Dutch law, while originally codified in the Napoleonic tradition, has been heavily altered under influence from the Netherlands' native tradition of Roman-Dutch law (still in effect in its former colonies). Scotland's civil law tradition borrowed heavily from Roman-Dutch law. Swiss law is categorized as Germanistic, but it has been heavily influenced by the Napoleonic tradition, with some indigenous elements added in as well.

Louisiana private law is primarily a Napoleonic system. Louisiana is the only U.S. state partially based on French and Spanish codes and ultimately Roman law, as opposed to English common law. In Louisiana, private law was codified into the Louisiana Civil Code. Current Louisiana law has converged considerably with American law, especially in its public law, judicial system, and adoption of the Uniform Commercial Code (except for Article 2) and certain legal devices of American common law. In fact, any innovation, whether private or public, has been decidedly common law in origin. Likewise, Quebec law, whose private law is similarly of French civilian origin, has developed along the same lines, having adapted in the same way as Louisiana to the public law and judicial system of Canadian common law. By contrast, Quebec private law has innovated mainly from civilian sources. To a lesser extent, other states formerly part of the Spanish Empire, such as Texas and California, have also retained aspects of Spanish Civil law into their legal system, for example community property.

Several Islamic countries have civil law systems that contain elements of Islamic law. As an example, the *Egyptian Civil Code of 1810* that developed in the early 19th century—which remains in force in Egypt as the basis for the civil law in many countries of the Arab world where the civil law is used—is based on the Napoleonic Code, but its primary author Abd El-Razzak El-Sanhuri attempted to integrate principles and features of Islamic law in deference to the unique circumstances of Egyptian society.

The purpose of codification is to provide all citizens with an accessible and written collection of the laws which apply to them and which judges must follow. It is the most widespread system of law in the world, in force in various forms in about 150 countries, and draws heavily from Roman law, arguably the most intricate known legal system dating from before the modern era. Colonial expansion spread the civil law which has been received in much of Latin America and parts of Asia and Africa.

Where codes exist, the primary source of law is thelaw code, which is a systematic collection of interrelated articles, arranged by subject matter in some pre-specified order, and that explain the principles of law, rights and entitlements, and how basic legal mechanisms work. Law codes are usually created by a legislature's enactment of a new statute that embodies all the old statutes relating to the subject and including changes necessitated by court decisions. In some cases, the change results in a new statutory concept. Other major legal systems in the world include common law, Halakha, canon law, and Islamic law.

Civilian countries can be divided into:

• those where civil law in some form is still living law but there has been no attempt to create acivil code: Andorra and San Marino

• those with uncodified mixed systems in which civil law is an academic source of authority but common law is also influential: Scotland and Roman-Dutch law countries (South Africa, Zambia, Zimbabwe, Sri Lanka and Guyana)

• those with codified mixed systems in which civil law is the background law but has its public law heavily influenced by common law: Louisiana, Quebec, Puerto Rico, Philippines

• those with comprehensive codes that exceed a single civil code, such asFrance, Germany, Greece, Japan, Mexico: it is this last category that is normally regarded as typical of civil law systems, and is discussed in the rest of this article.

The Scandinavian systems are of a hybrid character since their background law is a mix of civil law and Scandinavian customary law and have been partially codified. Likewise, the laws of theChannel Islands (Jersey, Guernsey, Alderney, Sark) are hybrids which mix Norman customary law and French civil law.

A prominent example of a civil-law code would be theNapoleonic Code (1804), named after French emperor Napoleon. The Code comprises three components: the law of persons, property law, and commercial law. Rather than a compendium of statutes or catalog of case law, the Code sets out general principles as rules of law.

Unlike common law systems, civil law jurisdictions deal withcase law apart from any precedence value. Civil law courts generally decide cases using statutory law on a case-by-case basis, without reference to other (or even superior) judicial decisions. In actual practice, an increasing degree of precedence is creeping into civil law jurisprudence, and is generally seen in the nation's highest court. While the typical French-speaking supreme court decision is short, concise and devoid of explanation or justification, in Germanic Europe, the supreme courts can and do tend to write more verbose opinions supported by legal reasoning. A line of similar case decisions, while not precedent perse, constitute jurisprudence constante. While civil law jurisdictions place little reliance on court decisions, they tend to generate a phenomenal number of reported legal opinions. However, this tends to be uncontrolled, since there is no statutory requirement that any case be reported or published in a law report, except for the councils of state and constitutional courts. Except for the highest courts, all publication of legal opinions are unofficial or commercial.

14.2   Codification   法典化

An important common characteristic of civil law, aside from its origins in Roman law, is the comprehensive codification of received Roman law, i.e. its inclusion in civil codes. The earliest codification known is the Code of Hammurabi, written in ancient Babylon during the 18th century BC. However, this, and many of the codes that followed, were mainly lists of civil and criminal wrongs and their punishments. Codification of the type typical of modern civilian systems did not first appear until the Justinian Code.

Germanic codes appeared over the 6th and 7th centuries to clearly delineate the law in force for Germanic privileged classes versus their Roman subjects and regulate those laws according to folk-right. Under feudal law a number of private custumals were compiled, first under the Norman empire (Très ancien coutumier, 1200—1245), then elsewhere, to record the manorial—and later regional—customs, court decisions, and the legal principles underpinning them. Custumals were commissioned by lords who presided as lay judges over manorial courts in order to inform themselves about the court process. The use of custumals from influential towns soon became commonplace over large areas. In keeping with this, certain monarchs consolidated their kingdoms by attempting to compile custumals that would serve as the law of the land for their realms, as when Charles VII of France commissioned in 1454 an official custumal of Crown law. Two prominent examples include the Coutume de Paris (written 1510; revised 1580), which served as the basis for the Napoleonic Code and the Sachsenspiegel (c.1220) of the bishoprics of Magdeburg and Halberstadt which was used in northern Germany, Poland, and the Low Countries.

The concept of codification was further developed during the 17th and 18th centuries AD, as an expression of both natural law and the ideas of the Enlightenment. The political ideal of that era was expressed by the concepts of democracy, protection of property and the rule of law. That ideal required the creation of certainty of law, through the recording of law and through its uniformity. So, the aforementioned mix of Roman law and customary and local law ceased to exist, and the road opened for law codification, which could contribute to the aims of the above mentioned political ideal.

Another reason that contributed to codification was that the notion of thenation-state required the recording of the law that would be applicable to that state.

Certainly, there was also a reaction to law codification. The proponents of codification regarded it as conducive to certainty, unity and systematic recording of the law; whereas its opponents claimed that codification would result in the ossification of the law.

In the end, despite whatever resistance to codification, the codification of European private laws moved forward. Codifications were completed by Denmark (1687), Sweden (1734), Prussia (1794), France (1804), and Austria (1811). The French codes were imported into areas conquered by Emperor Napoleon and later adopted with modifications in Poland (Duchy of Warsaw/Congress Poland; Kodeks cywilny 1806/1825), Louisiana (1807), Canton of Vaud (Switzerland; 1819), the Netherlands(1838), Italy and Romania (1865), Portugal (1867), Spain (1888), Germany (1900), and Switzerland (1912). These codifications were in turn imported into colonies at one time or another by most of these countries. The Swiss version was adopted in Brazil (1916) and Turkey (1926).

United States began codification with New York's "Field Code" (1850), followed by California's Codes (1872), and the federal Revised Statutes (1874) and the current United States Code (1926).

Because Germany was a rising power in the late 19th century and its legal system was well organized, when many Asian nations were developing, the German Civil Code became the basis for the legal systems of Japan and South Korea. In China, the German Civil Code was introduced in the later years of the Qing Dynasty and formed the basis of the law of the Republic of China, which remains in force in Taiwan.

Some authors consider civil law to have served as the foundation for socialist law used in communist countries, which in this view would basically be civil law with the addition of Marxist-Leninist ideas. No matter what it is, civil law was generally the legal system in place before the rise of socialist law, and some Eastern European countries reverted back to the pre-Socialist civil law following the fall of socialism, while others continued using their socialist legal systems. Several civil-law mechanisms seem to have been borrowed from medieval Islamic Sharia and fiqh.

14.3 A Brief Introduction to Common Law System 普通法系简介

1. General Concept

Common law, also known as case law or precedent, is law developed by judges through decisions of courts and similar tribunals, as opposed to statutes adopted through the legislative process or regulations issued by the executive branch.

A "common law system" is alegal system that gives great precedential weight to common law, on the principle that it is unfair to treat similar facts differently on different occasions. The body of precedent is called "common law" and it binds future decisions. In cases where the parties disagree on what the law is, a common law court looks to past precedential decisions of relevant courts. If a similar dispute has been resolved in the past, the court is bound to follow the reasoning used in the prior decision (this principle is known as stare decisis). If, however, the court finds that the current dispute is fundamentally distinct from all previous cases (called a "matter of first impression"), judges have the authority and duty to make law by creating precedent. Thereafter, the new decision becomes precedent, and will bind future courts.

In practice, common law systems are considerably more complicated than the simplified system described above. The decisions of a court are binding only in a particularjurisdiction, and even within a given jurisdiction, some courts have more power than others. For example, in most jurisdictions, decisions by appellate courts are binding on lower courts in the same jurisdiction and on future decisions of the same appellate court, but decisions of lower courts are only non-binding persuasive authority. Interactions between common law, constitutional law, statutory law and regulatory law also give rise to considerable complexity. However, stare decisis, the principle that similar cases should be decided according to consistent principled rules so that they will reach similar results, lies at the heart of all common law systems.

One third of the world's population (approximately 2.3 billion people) lives in common law jurisdictions or in systems mixed withcivil law. Particularly common law is in England where it originated in the Middle Ages, and in countries that trace their legal heritage to England as former colonies of the British Empire, including India, the United States, Pakistan, Nigeria, Bangladesh, Canada, with the exception of Québec where a mix of civil law (on the provincial level) and common law (mostly on the federal level) is used, Malaysia, Ghana, Australia, Sri Lanka, Hong Kong, Singapore, Myanmar, Ireland, New Zealand, Jamaica, Trinidad and Tobago, Cyprus, Barbados, South Africa, Zimbabwe, Cameroon, Namibia, Botswana, Guyana and Israel.

2. Historical Uses

In addition, there are several historical uses of the term that provide some background as to its meaning.

In one archaic usage, "common law" is used to refer to certain customs in England dating to before the Norman conquest and before there was any consistent law to be applied. The English Court of Common Pleas dealt with lawsuits in which the Monarch had no interest, i.e. between commoners.

Additionally, from at least the 11th century and continuing for several centuries after that, there were several different circuits in the royal court system, served by itinerant judges who would travel from town to town dispensing the King's justice. The term "common law" was used to describe the law held in common between the circuits and the different stops in each circuit. The more widely a particular law was recognized, the more weight it held, whereas purely local customs were generally subordinate to law recognized in a plurality of jurisdictions.

These definitions are archaic, their relevance having dissipated with the development of the English legal system over the centuries, but they do explain the origin of the term as used today.

3. Primary Connotations

The term common law has three main connotations and several historical meanings worth mentioning:

Common law as opposed to statutory law and administrative/regulatory law

Connotation 1 distinguishes the authority that promulgated a law. For example, most areas of law in most Anglo-Americanjurisdictions include "statutory law" enacted by a legislature, "regulatory law" promulgated by executive branch agencies pursuant to delegation of rule-making authority from the legislature, and common law or "case law", i.e., decisions issued by courts (or quasi-judicial tribunals within agencies). This first connotation can be further differentiated into (a) pure common law arising from the traditional and inherent authority of courts to define what the law is, even in absence of an underlying statute, e.g. most criminal law and procedural law before the 20th century, and even today, most contract law and the law of torts, and (b) court decisions that interpret and decide the fine boundaries and distinctions in law promulgated by other bodies. This body of common law, sometimes called "interstitial common law," includes judicial interpretations of the Constitution, of statutes, and of regulations, and examples of application of law to facts.

Common law legal systems as opposed to civil law legal systems

Connotation 2 differentiates "common law" jurisdictions and legal systems from "civil law" or "code" jurisdictions. Common law systems place great weight on court decisions, which are considered "law" with the same force of law as statutes—for nearly a millennium, common law courts have had the authority to make law where no legislative statute exists, and statutes mean what courts interpret them to mean. By contrast, in civil law jurisdictions (the legal tradition that prevails, or is combined with common law, in Europe and most non-Islamic, non-common law countries), courts lack authority to act where there is no statute, and judicial precedent is given less interpretive weight (which means that a judge deciding a given case has more freedom to interpret the text of a statute independently, and less predictably), and scholarly literature is given more. For example, the Napoleonic code expressly forbade French judges to pronounce general principles of law.

As arule of thumb, common law systems trace their history to England, while civil law systems trace their history to Roman law and the Napoleonic Code.

The contrast between common law and civil law systems is elaborated in "Contrasts between common law and civil law systems" and "Alternatives to common law systems", below.

Law as opposed to equity

Connotation 3 differentiates "common law" (or just "law") from "equity". Before 1873, England had two parallel court systems: courts of "law" that could only award money damages and recognized only the legal owner of property, and courts of "equity" (courts of chancery) that could issue injunctive relief (that is, a court order to a party to do something, give something to someone, or stop doing something) and recognized trusts of property. This split propagated to many of the colonies, including the United States (see "Reception Statutes", below). For most purposes, most jurisdictions, including the U. S. federal system and most states, have merged the two courts. Additionally, even before the separate courts were merged, most courts were permitted to apply both law and equity, though under potentially different procedural law. Nonetheless, the historical distinction between "law" and "equity" remains important today when the case involves issues such as the following:

● categorizing and prioritizingrights to property—for example, the same article of property often has a "legal title" and an "equitable title," and these two groups of ownership rights may be held by different people.

● in the United States, determining whetherthe Seventh Amendment's right to a jury trial applies (a determination of a fact necessary to resolution of a "common law" claim) or whether the issue will be decided by a judge (issues of what the law is, and all issues relating to equity).

● the standard of review and degree of deference given by an appellate tribunal to the decision of the lower tribunal under review (issues of law are reviewed de novo, that is, "as if new" from scratch by the appellate tribunal, while most issues of equity are reviewed for "abuse of discretion," that is, with great deference to the tribunal below).

● the remedies available and rules of procedure to be applied.

▶ 14.4　Basic Principles of Common Law　普通法系基本原则

In common law legal systems, the common law is crucial to understanding almost all important areas of law. For example, inEngland and Wales and in most states of the United States, the basic law of contracts, torts and property do not exist in statute, but only in common law (though there may be isolated modifications enacted by statute). As another example, the Supreme Court of the United States in 1877, held that a Michigan statute that established rules for solemnization of marriages did not abolish pre-existing common-law marriage, because the statute did not affirmatively require statutory solemnization and was silent as to preexisting common law.

In almost all areas of the law (even those where there is a statutory framework, such as contracts for the sale of goods, or the criminal law), legislature-enacted statutes generally give only terse statements of general principle, and the fine boundaries and definitions exist only in the common law. To find out what the precise law is that applies to a particular set of facts, one has to locate precedential decisions on the topic, and reason from those decisions by analogy. To consider but one example, the *First Amendment to the United States Constitution* states "Congress shall make no law respecting an establishment of religion, or prohibiting the free exercise thereof"—but interpretation (that is, determining the fine boundaries, and resolving the tension between the "establishment" and "free exercise" clauses) of each of the important terms was delegated by Article III of the Constitution to the judicial branch, so that the current legal boundaries of the

Constitutional text can only be determined by consulting the common law.

In common law jurisdictions, legislatures operate under the assumption that statutes will be interpreted against the backdrop of the pre-existing common law and custom. For example, in most U.S. states, the criminal statutes are primarily codification of pre-existing common law. (Codification is the process of enacting a statute that collects and restates pre-existing law in a single document—when that pre-existing law is common law, the common law remains relevant to the interpretation of these statutes.) In reliance on this assumption, modern statutes often leave a number of terms and fine distinctions unstated—for example, a statute might be very brief, leaving the precise definition of terms unstated, under the assumption that these fine distinctions will be inherited from pre-existing common law. (For this reason, many modern American law schools teach the common law of crime as it stood in England in 1789, because that centuries-old English common law is a necessary foundation to interpreting modern criminal statutes.)

With the transition from English law, which had common law crimes, to the new legal system under the U.S. Constitution, which prohibited ex post facto laws at both the federal and state level, the question was raised whether there could be common law crimes in the United States. It was settled in the case of United States v. Hudson and Goodwin, 11 U.S. 32 (1812), which decided that federal courts had no jurisdiction to define new common law crimes, and that there must always be a (constitutional) statute defining the offense and the penalty for it.

Still, many states retain selected common law crimes. For example, in Virginia, the definition of the conduct that constitutes the crime of robbery exists only in the common law, and the robbery statute only sets the punishment. Virginia Code section 1—200 establishes the continued existence and vitality of common law principles and provides that "The common law of England, in so far as it is not repugnant to the principles of the Bill of Rights and Constitution of this Commonwealth, shall continue in full force within the same, and be the rule of decision, except as altered by the General Assembly."

Statutory codification of common law had common law crimes, for example, to create a new cause of action that did not exist in the common law, or to legislatively overrule the common law.

An example is thetort of wrongful death, which allows certain persons, usually a spouse, child or estate, to sue for damages on behalf of the deceased. There is no such tort in English common law; thus, any jurisdiction that lacks a wrongful death statute will not allow a lawsuit for the wrongful death of a loved one. Where a wrongful death statute exists, the compensation or other remedy available is limited to the remedy specified in the statute (typically, an upper limit on the amount of damages). Courts generally interpret statutes that create new causes of action narrowly — that is, limited to their precise terms—because the courts generally recognize the legislature as being supreme in deciding the reach of judge-made law unless such statute should violate some "second order" constitutional law provision (cf. judicial activism).

Where a tort is rooted in common law, all traditionally recognized damages for that tort may be sued for, whether or not there is mention of those damages in the current statutory law. For instance, a person who sustains bodily injury through the negligence of another may sue for medical costs, pain, suffering, loss of earnings or earning capacity, mental and/or emotional distress, loss of quality of life, disfigurement and more. These damages need not be set forth in statute as they already exist in the tradition of common law. However, without a wrongful death statute, most of them are extinguished upon death.

In the United States, the power of the federal judiciary to review and invalidate unconstitutional acts of the federal executive branch is stated in the constitution, Article III sections 1 and 2: "The judicial Power of the United States, shall be vested in one supreme Court, and in such inferior Courts as the Congress may from time to time ordain and establish. ... The judicial Power shall extend to all Cases, in Law and Equity, arising under this Constitution, the Laws of the United States, and Treaties made, or which shall be made, under their Authority..." The first famous statement of "the judicial power" was Marbury v. Madison, 5 U.S. (1 Cranch) 137 (1803). Later cases interpreted the "judicial power" of Article III to establish the power of federal courts to consider or overturn any action of Congress or of any state that conflicts with the Constitution.

14.5 Common Law as a Foundation for Commercial Economies 普通法系:商务经济体的基础

The reliance on judicial opinion is a strength of common law systems, and is a significant contributor to the robust commercial systems in the United Kingdom and United States. Because there is reasonably precise guidance on almost every issue, parties (especially commercial parties) can predict whether a proposed course of action is likely to be lawful or unlawful. This ability to predict gives more freedom to come close to the boundaries of the law. For example, many commercial contracts are more economically efficient, and create greater wealth, because the parties know ahead of time that the proposed arrangement, though perhaps close to the line, is almost certainly legal. Newspapers, taxpayer-funded entities with some religious affiliation, and political parties can obtain fairly clear guidance on the boundaries within which their freedom of expression rights apply.

In contrast, in non-common-law countries, jurisdictions have very weak respect for precedent (example, the U.S. Patent Office), So fine questions of law are redetermined anew each time they arise, making consistency and prediction more difficult, and procedures far more protracted than necessary because parties cannot rely on written statements of law as reliable guides. In jurisdictions that do not have a strong allegiance to a large body of precedent, parties have less a priori guidance and must often leave a bigger "safety margin" of unexploited opportunities, and final determinations are reached only after far larger expenditures on legal fees by the parties.

This is the reason for the frequent choice of the law of the State of New York in commercial contracts.Commercial contracts almost always include a "choice of law clause" to reduce uncertainty. Somewhat surprisingly, contracts throughout the world (for example, contracts involving parties in Japan, France and Germany, and from most of the other states of the United States) often choose the law of New York, even where the relationship of the parties and transaction to New York is quite attenuated. Because of its history as the nation's commercial center, New York common law has a depth and predictability not (yet) available in any other jurisdiction. Similarly, corporations are often formed under Delaware corporate law, and contracts relating to corporate law issues (merger and acquisitions of companies, rights of shareholders, and so on.) include a Delaware choice of law clause, because of the deep body of law in Delaware on these issues. On the other hand, some other jurisdictions have sufficiently developed bodies of law so that parties have no real motivation to choose the law of a foreign jurisdiction (for example, England and Wales, and the state of California), but not yet so fully developed that parties with no relationship to the jurisdiction choose that law. The common theme in each case is that commercial parties seek predictability and simplicity in their contractual relations, and frequently choose the law of a common law jurisdiction with a well-developed body of common law to achieve that result.

Likewise, for litigation of commercial disputes arising out of unpredictable torts (as opposed to the prospective choice of law clauses in contracts discussed in the previous paragraph), certain jurisdictions attract an unusually high fraction of cases, because of the predictability afforded by the depth of decided cases. For example, London is considered the pre-eminent centre for litigation of admiralty cases.

This is not to say that common law is better in every situation. For example, civil law can be clearer than case law when the legislature has had the foresight and diligence to address the precise set of facts applicable to a particular situation. For that reason, civil law statutes tend to be somewhat more detailed than statutes written by common law legislatures—but, conversely, that tends to make the statute more difficult to read (the United States tax code is an example). Nonetheless, as a practical matter, no civil law legislature can ever address the full spectrum of factual possibilities in the breadth, depth and detail of the case law of the common law courts of even a smaller jurisdiction, and that deeper, more complete body of law provides additional predictability that promotes commerce.

14.6 About Corporate Law and Its History 公司法及其历史

Corporate law (also "company" or "corporations" law) is the study of how shareholders, directors, employees, creditors, and other stakeholders such as consumers, the community and the environment interact with one another. Corporate law is a part of a broader companies law (or law of business associations). Other types of business associations can include partnerships (in the UK governed by the Partnership Act 1890), or trusts (like a pension fund), or companies limited by guarantee (like some community organizations or charities. Under corporate law, corporations of all sizes have separate legal personality, with limited liability or unlimited liability for its shareholders. Shareholders control the company through a board of directors which, in turn, typically delegates control of the corporation's day to day operations to a full-time executive. Corporate law deals with firms that are incorporated or registered under the corporate or company law of a sovereign state or their subnational states. The four defining characteristics of the modern corporation are:

- Separate legal personality of the corporation (access to tort and contract law in a manner similar to a person)

- Limited liability of the shareholders (a shareholder's personal liability is limited to the value of their shares in the corporation)

- Shares (if the corporation is a public company, the shares are traded on a stock exchange, such as the London Stock Exchange, New York Stock Exchange, Euronext in Paris or BM&F Bovespa in Sao Paulo)

- Delegated management: the board of directors delegates day-to-day management of the company to executives

In many developed countries outside of the English speaking world, company boards are appointed as representatives of both shareholders and employees to "codetermine" company strategy. Corporate law is often divided into corporate governance (which concerns the various power relations within a corporation) and corporate finance (which concerns the rules on how capital is used). A major contributor to company law in the UK is the Companies Act 2006.

1. Definition

The word "corporation" is generally synonymous with large publicly owned companies inUnited States. In United Kingdom, "company" is more frequently used as the legal term for any business incorporated under the Companies Act 2006. Large scale companies ("corporations" in business terminology in the US sense) will be PLC's in the United Kingdom and will usually have shares listed on a Stock Market. In British legal usage any registered company, created under the Companies Act 2006 and previous equivalent legislation, is, strictly, a particular subcategory of the wider category, "corporation". Such a company is created by the administrative process of registration under the Companies Act as a general piece of legislation. A corporation, in this British sense, can be a corporation sole which consists of a single office occupied by one person e.g. the monarch or certain bishops in England and Wales. Here, the office is recognized as separate from the individual who holds it. Other corporations are within the category of "corporation aggregate" which includes corporate bodies created directly by legislation such as the Local Government Act 1972; universities and certain professional bodies created by Royal Charter; corporations such as industrial and provident societies created by registration under other general pieces of legislation and registered companies which are the subject matter of this article.

In the United States, a company may or may not be a separate legal entity, and is often used synonymously with "firm" or "business". A corporation may accurately be called a company; however, a company should not necessarily be called a corporation, which has distinct characteristics. According to Black's Law Dictionary, in America a company means "a corporation — or, less commonly, an association, partnership or union — that carries on industrial enterprise".

The defining feature of a corporation is its legal independence from the people who create it. If a corporation fails, its shareholders will lose their money, and employees will lose their jobs, though disproportionately affecting its workers as opposed to its upper executives. Shareholders, however owning a part piece of the company, are not liable for debts that remain owing to the corporation's creditors. This rule is calledlimited liability, and it is why corporations end with "Ltd." (or some variant like "Inc." and "plc"). In the words of British judge, Walton J., a company is...

"...only a juristic figment of theimagination, lacking both a body to be kicked and a soul to be damned."

But despite this, under just about every legal system in existence and as per international norms, corporations have the same legal rights and obligations as actual humans. Corporations can exercise human rights against real individuals and the state, and they may be responsible for human rights violations. Just as they are "born" into existence through its members obtaining a certificate of incorporation, they can "die" when they lose money into insolvency. Corporations can even be convicted of criminal offences, such as fraud and manslaughter.

2. History

Although some forms of companies are thought to have existed duringAncient Rome and Ancient Greece, the closest recognizable ancestors of the modern company did not appear until the second millennium. The first recognizable commercial associations were medieval guilds, where guild members agreed to abide by guild rules, but did not participate in ventures for common profit. The earliest forms of joint commercial enterprise under the lex mercatoria were in fact partnerships.

With increasing international trade, Royal charters were increasingly granted in Europe (notably in England and Holland) to merchant adventurers. The Royal charters usually conferred special privileges on the trading company (including, usually, some form of monopoly). Originally, traders in these entities traded stock on their own account, but later the members came to operate on joint account and with joint stock, and the new joint stock company was born.

Early companies were purely economic ventures; it was only a belatedly established benifit of holding joint stock that the company's stock could not be seized for the debts of any individual member. The development of company law in Europe was hampered by two notorious "bubbles" (the South Sea Bubble in England and the Tulip Bulb Bubble in the Dutch Republic) in the 17th century, which set the development of companies in the two leading jurisdictions back by over a century in popular estimation.

But companies, almost inevitably, returned to the forefront of commerce, although in England to circumvent the Bubble Act 1720 investors had reverted to trading the stock of unincorporated associations, until it was repealed in 1825. However, the cumbersome process of obtaining Royal charters was simply insufficient to keep up with demand. In England there was a lively trade in the charters of defunct companies. However, procrastination amongst the legislature meant that in the United Kingdom it was not until the *Joint Stock Companies Act* 1844 that the first equivalent of modern companies, formed by registration, appeared. Soon after came the *Limited Liability Act* 1855, which in the event of a company's bankruptcy limited the liability of all shareholders to the amount of capital they had invested. The beginning of modern company law came when the two pieces of legislation were codified under the *Joint Stock Companies Act* 1856 at the behest of the then Vice President of the Board of Trade, Mr Robert Lowe. That legislation shortly gave way to the railway boom, and from there the numbers of companies formed soared. In the later nineteenth century depression took hold, and just as company numbers had boomed, many began to implode and fall into insolvency. Much strong academic, legislative and judicial opinion was opposed to the notion that businessmen could escape accountability for their role in the failing businesses. The last significant development in the history of companies was the decision of the House of Lords in Salomon v. Salomon & Co. where the House of Lords confirmed the separate legal personality of the company, and that the liabilities of the company were separate and distinct from those of its owners.

In a December 2006 article, *The Economist* (an English-language weekly news and international affairs publication owned by The Economist Newspaper Ltd. and edited in offices in London.) identified the development of the joint stock company as one of the key reasons why Western commerce moved ahead of its rivals in the Middle East in post-renaissance era.

Summary of This Chapter
本章概要

大陆法系(civil law system)一词中的"大陆"两字指欧洲大陆,故又称为欧陆法系,亦称为市民法(civilian law)、罗马法系、民法法系(civil law)、法典法系、罗马日耳曼法系,是受罗马法影响而成立的法律系统,是与英美法系(普通法系)并列的当今世界两大重要法系之一。这个法系现在主要由欧洲大陆的国家(例如法国、意大利、德国、荷兰等)以及受其影响的日本、中国大陆(包括中国台湾)等地采用。主要历史渊源是古时罗马帝国(Roman Empire)的法律,其后在欧洲中世纪的后期(即是文艺复兴以前,约12至15世纪),罗马法在欧洲大陆又再度受到重视。到了18世纪,欧洲大陆的许多国家都颁布了法典,尝试列出各种法律分支的规范。因此欧陆法系又称成文法。

大陆法系以成文法为主,通常不承认判例法的地位(但也有例外,如法国行政法就承认判例法);具有悠久的法典编纂的传统;在法学理论上崇尚理性主义,倾向于建构,重视逻辑,抽象化的概念体系;在司法审判中传统上要求法官严格按照法条审判,以三段论为最重要的推理模式。强调公、私法的区别。(这些法系的国家通常都有完整、独立的民法典)

大陆法系是指欧洲大陆大部分国家19世纪初以罗马法为基础建立起来的,以1804年《法国民法典》和1896年《德国民法典》为代表的法律制度,以及其他国家或地区仿效这种制度而建立的法律制度。它是西方国家中与英美法系并列的、渊源久远和影响较大的法系。法系是根据若干国家和地区基于历史传统原因,在法律实践和法律意识等方面所具有的共性而进行的法律的一种分类,它是这些具有共性或共同传统的法律的总称。

(1)在罗马全盛时期,罗马统治者以武力扩大其版图,强行适用罗马法,被征服地区的居民也因罗马法的发达和完备而自愿采用罗马法,使罗马法成为"商品生产者社会的第一个世界性法律"。

(2)日耳曼人入侵罗马后,日耳曼法采取属人主义原则,使罗马法得以保存。日耳曼人建立的国家编纂的法典受罗马法影响。公元9世纪,随着封建制度的发展,法律的属人主义不再适用,罗马法与日耳曼法融合。

(3)12世纪后,罗马法复兴运动兴起,罗马法研究同社会实际需要相结合,成为西欧大陆国家具有权威的补充法律。经过改造和发展的罗马法成了欧洲的普通法,具有共同的特征和法律传统,从而奠定了大陆法系的基础。

(4)资产阶级革命取得胜利,西欧许多国家的资本主义制度确立并巩固以后,适应资本主义经济、政治、文化的发展以及国家之间的交往,这些国家的法律制度相互间的联系和共同特征获得进一步发展。首先在法国,以资产阶级革命为动力,在古典自然法学和理性主义思潮的指导下,在罗马法的直接影响下,开创了制定有完整体系的成文法的模式。法国法典成为欧洲大陆各国建立自己的法律制度的楷模,标志着近代意义上大陆法系的模式的确立。随后德国在继承罗马法、研究和吸收法国立法经验的基础上,制定了一系列法典。德国法典成为资本主义从自由经济到垄断经济发展时代的典型代表。

(5)由于以法国和德国为代表的大陆法适应了整个资本主义社会的需要,并且由于它采用了严格的成文法形式易于传播,所以19世纪、20世纪后,大陆法系越过欧洲,传遍世界。

普通法系(common law system),又称英美法系,是指以英国普通法为基础发展起来的法律的总称。它首先产生于英国,后扩大到曾经是英国殖民地、附属国的许多国家和地区,包括美国、加拿大、印度、巴基斯坦、孟加拉、马来西亚、新加坡、澳大利亚、新西兰以及非洲的个别国家和地区。到18世纪至19世纪时,随着英国殖民地的扩张,英国法被传入这些国家和地区,英美法系终于发展成为世界主要法系之一。英美法系中也存在两大支流,这就是英国法和美国法。它们在法律分类、宪法形式、法院权力等方面存在一定的差别。

英国从11世纪起主要以源于日耳曼习惯法的普通法为基础,逐渐形成了一种独特的法律制度,再加上仿效英国的其他一些国家和地区的法律制度,西方国家中出现了与大陆法系并列的一种历史悠久和影响较大的法系,又称普通法系、英国法系、判例法系。

1066年诺曼底公爵威廉征服英国以前,英国各地施行的是盎格鲁—撒克逊的习惯法;东北部则施行入侵的丹麦人传入的北欧条顿人习惯法。诺曼人在英国建立以国王为中心的封建土地制度,逐步形成王权专制国家,在历史上第一次设立权威极大的御前会议(王国法院),以其判例作为普通法适用于全国,并由国王派出的巡回法官在各地宣传和施行这些法律。狭义的普通法即指这类判例法。

英国判例法中还包括一种它所特有的衡平法。这是从14世纪开始发展的一种与普通法并行的、主要适用于民事纠纷的法律原则和诉讼程序。由于民商事关系的发展,传统的普通法的严格限制有时无法适应需要,英王允许臣民在无法从普通法法院获得公平处理时,由大法官以衡平(又称公平或良知)原则予以处理,命令或禁止民事被告人从事一定的行为。其后,设立独立的衡平法院(又称大法官法院),发展了一套抽象的衡平法准则。由于当时大法官多由僧侣担任,所以实际多是按照教会法和罗马法的某些原则来审决案件。最初主要用以处理因程序欠缺或迟延等所产生的争讼,之后逐渐发展至实体法方面。19世纪末调整法院体系时,取消衡平法院,审判权统一归于普通法法院,但高等法院仍设有由衡平法院演变而来的大法官庭,在审判实践中也不时援用衡平原则,给予衡平救助。在其他英美法系国家中,有的仍保留衡平法的某些效力,甚至还存在个别的衡平法院。

▶ New Words and expressions

admiralty *n.* 海事法;海事法庭;海军部;海军上将的职位

affiliation *n.* 附属;从属关系;友好关系;加入;联盟

appellate court 上诉法院;高等法院

as per 按照;依据,如同

attenuate *v. & a.* 使减弱;使纤细;变纤细;变弱;减弱的;稀薄的;细小的

bench *n.* 法官席;法官;(英国议会的)议员席;长凳子

behest *n.* 命令;要求,吩咐

Chancery *n.* (英)大法官法庭;(美)衡平法院;档案馆;大臣官邸

codify *v.* 编成法典;使法律成文化

compendium *n.* 纲要;概略

converge with 与…收拢在一起

Court of Common Pleas 普通诉讼法庭;民诉法院

custumal *n.* 惯例;习惯法汇编;惯例书

delineate *v.* 描绘;描写;画…的轮

discretion *n.* 自由裁量权;谨慎;判断力;判定;考虑周到

enactment *n.* 制定,颁布;通过;法令

entitlement *n.* 权利;津贴

extortion *n.* 勒索,敲诈

hybrid *n. & a.* 混合;混合物;混合的

inquisitorial *a.* 询问的;严格审问的

Islamic *a.* 穆斯林的;伊斯兰教的

indigenous *a.* 本土的;土著的;国产的;固有的

in deference to 遵从;服从;顺从;有鉴于;考虑

jurisdictions *n.* 司法管辖区

jurisprudence *n.* 法律体系;法学及其分支;法律知识;法院审判规程

legislature *n.* 立法机关;立法机构

lex mercatoria 商人习惯法;商法

litigation *n.* 诉讼;起诉

magistrates *n.* 裁判官;地方法官(magistrate 的复数);治安官;地方行政官

manorial *a.* 领主的;庄园的;采邑的

mechanism *n.* 机制;原理,途径;进程;机械装置;技巧

merged into 并入;结合

minor *n.* 未成年人

ordain *v.* (上帝、法律等)命令;判定;注定;颁布命令

ossification *n. & v.* 僵化;骨化;成骨;管理

overlaid *v.* 覆盖;遮掩;在…上覆盖(或铺、涂)

pledge *n.* 保证

prevalent *a.* 流行的;普遍的,广传的

precedential *a.* 有先例的;优先的

proceeds from 从……产生;从……出发;起因于

promulgate *v.* 公布;传播;发表

pursuant to 依照,按照,依据

revert *v. & n.* 回复;重提;返祖遗传;归还;使回复原状;恢复原状者

set forth 陈述;提出;出发;陈列;宣布

stare decisis 遵循先例;(拉)根据过去判例

statutory *a.* 法定的;法令的;可依法惩处的

subordinate to 从属于;服从

tort *n.* 侵权行为

tribunal *n.* 法庭;裁决;法官席

trusts *n.* [贸易] 信托;照管

verbose *a.* 冗长的;累赘的;啰嗦的

unbind *v.* 不受约束;释(解)放;解开(过去式 unbound 过去分词 unbound)

underlie *v.* 成为……的基础;位于……之下

(过去式 underlay 过去分词 underlain)

vitiate *v.* 损害

without reference to 不论;不考虑;置……于不顾;没有提及

➤ Discussion Questions

1. How many law systems are there in the world?

2. What is the difference between Common Law System and Civil Law System?

3. What are the fundamental principles of Common Law System?

Chapter 15 | International Payments 国际支付

Objectives
学习目标

To understand the importance of international payments.

理解国际支付的重要性。

To have a general view of common modes in international payments.

了解国际支付方式概况。

15.1 The Significance of International Payments 国际支付的意义

It is well-known that international payment is the most important in the international trade in that the seller's greatest interest is to get the money. Only after the seller has received the full sum of money without claims can we say the transaction is concluded and will the seller feel at easy. In other words, getting paid to the seller's utmost satisfaction is the most important aspect of international trade; on the other hand, the buyer's first obligation is to pay the money or to promise to pay the money for the goods he buys from the seller. Otherwise, all the effort that is put by the seller into marketing(research), pricing, physical distribution, documentation and so on would be for nothing.

Of the 3Ps (payment, price, packing) of international trade, learners of international trade need pay most attention to payment. How, when and where to pay is of mutual interest, which should be discussed, negotiated before the contract is signed by and between the seller and the buyer. Payment terms, which will be discussed later in this chapter should be clearly specified in the contract. Therefore, both the seller and the buyer have to acquaint themselves with international payment methods and the relevant things such as foreign change rate, the role of banks, etc.

15.2 Risks in International Payments 国际支付风险

Chances are that sellers who is not sure that payment can be surely obtained will run into difficulty and likewise that buyers who is not sure that goods in good condition can be received will also get into trouble. Both the seller and the buyer bear the risks in getting paid and paying. International trade has been growing fast, though. Whoever does business must run some risk. Basically speaking, the more risks one bears, the more profits he may get, which, to some extent, is true.

Practically, there are four chief methods of payment commonly adopted in international trade, each offering different levels of security and risk to both the seller and the buyer. The four chief methods are: *prepayment* (*CWO*), *documentary Letter of Credit*, *documentary collections* and *open account trading*. What method is to be adopted depends on the relationships between the seller and buyer. Both parties have to fully understand the payment terms agreed and the obligations that the arrangement entails. The following figures (Figure 15.1 and Figure 15.2) show the risks either party bears:

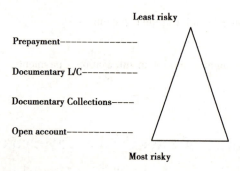

Figure 15.1 Payment Risks to the Seller (Exporter)

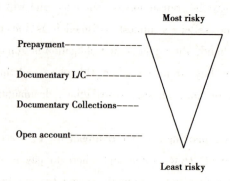

Figure 15.2 Payment Risks to the Buyer (Importer)

▶ 15.3 Terms of Payment 支付条件

Terms of payment are actually what is mentioned just above, namely, the four chief methods of payments and some others. The seller is especially cautious about the terms of payment, because when selling goods to the customer in a different country it is essential to safeguard oneself against the risks. By risks we mean not only the physical risks of loss, damage or delay of the goods in transit but other risks of non-payment, force majeure, conflict of different laws and the like. Terms of payment normally need repeated discussion by both the seller and the buyer before the terms are put down in the Contract. Terms of payment range from "cash with order" at one end to "open account" at the other. Here again the terms are listed in the order of least risk for the seller:

CWO (cash with order)

Part-cash with order—balance due on notice of readiness to ship

Documentary letter of Credit

Documentary collections (D/P: documents against payment

D/A: documents against acceptance)

O/A (open account)

Other payment mechanisms like consignment sales or countertrade

15.4 The Importance of a Contract in International Payments 合同在国际支付中的重要性

A contract is a legal binding agreement between two persons, or more than two persons (whether natural persons or juristic persons such as partnerships, companies or other corporations) under which the parties acquire certain rights against each other, and undertake certain obligations (either to perform certain acts or to show forbearance in certain matters) according to the terms of the agreement.

By contract, here we mean the contract signed by and between the seller and the buyer in international trade. This contract is the core of an international transaction in that not only the seller and the buyer have to comply with the contract, but also other parties involved in the transaction such as banks will refer to it and all the other documents are based on this contract. In other words, the terms and conditions in other documents as in an L/C must be in exact agreement with those stipulated in the contract; otherwise, the "assembly line" of the transaction will be bottlenecked. For instance, if something like a figure in the L/C is different from that in the contract, slight as it may be, the bank will not accept the L/C.

In the contract, payment terms like "documentary letter of credit", "D/P", "D/A" are clearly stated.

15.5 Letter of Credit 信用证

A letter of Credit (L/C) is just a document issued by a bank in the importer's home location. The issuing bank of the L/C gives its authority to another bank or banks in an overseas country (usually in the exporter's home location) to provide funds to the named holder of the L/C (the beneficiary) against the reimbursement by the issuing bank.

Both the seller and the buyer are willing to accept the documentary L/C, because: from the perspective of the seller, he can be assured that he will be paid by the bank which is a trustworthy and solvent paymaster in his own country if only he presents the stipulated documents to it. Besides, the seller, when necessary, can use the documentary credit arrangement to purchase raw materials he needs and the like so as to manufacture goods for export. What's more, the seller can take legal action against the local bank in the event that the bank fails to honour the credit when the documents specified in the contract of sales are presented; on the buyer's part, he can raise credit with the help of the documents from the bank and it is not necessary for him to have his own funds available to pay the seller .

Letters of credit are governed by the "autonomy principle", which means that when the essential documents are presented the issuing bank have the obligation to pay the beneficiary of the letter of credit despite such issues as breach of contract, defective goods, non-performance or any other factor, but fraud is the exception. The letter of credit is a kind of an independent contract between the parties to it. The seller and the buyer both must meet the terms of it so that payment can be made against compliant documentation.

The following parties are involved in a letter of credit:

(1) The applicant;

(2) The issuing bank (opening bank);

(3) The advising bank (notifying bank);

(4) The confirming bank;

(5) The beneficiary;

(6) The paying bank (drawee bank);

(7) The negotiation bank.

Types of Letter of Credits   信用证的种类

Letters of credits can be categorized into different types according to their functions or features. Businessmen choose the category which they find appropriate for import and export financing. The following are some types of the L/C:

(1) Documentary Letter of Credit

A documentary letter of credit stipulates that payment is to be made, bill of exchange is to be accepted or negotiated against documentary drafts or requisite documents such as commercial invoice, shipping documents, insurance policy, inspection certificate, certificate of origin, packing list and the like, all of which evidence that goods are shipped and are in transit.

Documentary L/C is commonly used in international trade payments. As already mentioned above, the L/C in this book refers to the documentary L/C. With documentary L/C, the importer feels it safer to pay money, because the exporter must present the requisite documentation, one of which is the Bill of Lading which is the document of title to the goods.

（2）Clean Letter of Credit

Clean L/C refers to the L/C according to which the issuing bank makes payment against only the draft drawn by the beneficiary or some ordinary documents which do not include the important shipping documents. Clean L/C is not commonly used in international trade, because if clean L/C is used, the importer runs greater risk.

（3）Revocable Letter of Credit

A revocable L/C refers to the L/C that may be cancelled or amended by the bank that is supposed to make payment without obtaining the agreement of the beneficiary. So the exporter is not in favour of a revocable L/C which is less reliable than irrevocable credits. It is possible that the L/C may be cancelled at any time up to the point where the exporter presents the requisite documents to the advising bank and demands payment. The exporter may have shipped the goods before he gets to know that the L/C has been cancelled.

A revocable L/C is rarely used. It may be used in the trade between affiliated and subsidiary companies, or where the goods are to be shipped in a series of consignments and the importer wants to examine the quality of the first consignment and cancel the credit if the goods do not satisfy him.

（4）Irrevocable Letter of Credit

An irrevocable L/C is the one that cannot be revoked or amended by the issuing bank without the consent of the parties that are involved in the L/C. Almost all letters of credit used in practice nowadays are irrevocable. It is very clear that an irrevocable L/C gives the exporter more security, but may have disadvantages for the importer.

（5）Confirmed Letter of Credit

When a bank upon the authorisation or request of the issuing bank adds its name to the undertaking already given by the foreign bank involved in the L/C, the L/C becomes a confirmed one. The confirming bank is usually in the exporter's country.

By confirming the L/C, the confirming bank undertakes the same liabilities and responsibilities as the issuing bank to pay, or to accept or negotiate bills. A confirmed L/C is usually irrevocable. So a confirmed irrevocable L/C gives the exporter more advantages or security, as he has now two banks (one is the issuing bank which is located in the importer's country, the other is the bank—usually the advising bank—that is located in his own country) to guarantee that he can get payment or negotiate the bills.

The steps of the flow chart arestated as follows：

（1）The applicant (importer) and the beneficiary (exporter) sign a contract of sale.

（2）The applicant approaches a local bank to apply for opening an L/C.

（3）The issuing bank (opening bank) issues an L/C and sends it to the advising bank (notifying bank).

（4）The advising bank informs the beneficiary of the opening of the L/C.

（5）The beneficiary presents the documents to the negotiation bank for the negotiation of the draft.

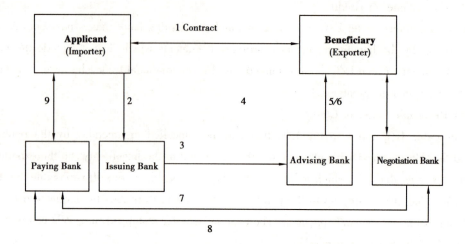

Figure 15.3   Flow Chart of Irrevocable Documentary L/C

（6）The negotiation bank negotiates the draft.

（7）The negotiation bank asks the paying bank to reimburse it.

（8）The paying bank reimburses the negotiation bank.

（9）The paying bank asks the applicant to pay money to it for the documents. With the documents, the applicant can fetch the goods.

15.6   Collection   托收

In international payments another common way to settle payments is by collection whereby the exporter first ships cargoes to get necessary documents and entrusts banks as intermediaries to collect the money for the goods.

Banks, working as the agents of the principal, provide service only. They undertake no liabilities or responsibilities for making payment or the authenticity of the documents.

15.6.1   Definition of Collection   托收的定义

According to the *Uniform Rules for Collection*, the definition of collection is described as follows:

（1）"Collection" means the handling by banks, on instructions received, of documents in order to:

① obtain acceptance and/or, as the case may be, payment or

② deliver documents against acceptance and/or, as the case may be, against payment, or

③ deliver documents on other terms and conditions.

（2）"Documents" means financial documents and/or commercial documents:

① "financial documents" means bills of exchange, promissory notes, cheques, payment receipts or other similar instruments used for obtaining the payment of money.

② "commercial documents" means invoices, shipping documents, documents of title or other similar documents, or any other documents whatsoever, not being financial documents.

The definitions can be defined in other words as follows:

Banks that have received instructions from the customer deal with financial documents and/or commercial documents for the purpose of obtaining acceptance or making payment, or of delivering commercial documents against acceptance and/or payment or on other terms and conditions.

Collection exposes exporter to more risks, because the exporter ships the cargoes first before obtaining the payment. When the goods arrive at the destination, they might be refused or the importer may find fault with the goods. If this happens, the exporter has to deliver the goods in the hand of the importers with loss of profit or transport the goods back, but that involves charges. It is very clear that collection provides more security to the importer.

15.6.2　Parties Involved in Collections　托收的有关方

The parties in relation to collection are the importer, the exporter, and the banks, all of whom are named differently according to their functions.

(1) Principal

"Principal" is the client who entrusts a local bank to handle the operation of collection. The client is usually the exporter who draws a B/E (or does not draw it dependent on the terms and conditions of the transaction). Therefore, the principal is normally the drawer of the B/E. It is customary that the principal must fill in a collection application form in which he gives clear instructions for collection. These instructions will be copied onto the collection order which must be sent together with a bill for collection. The principal has the legal obligations to compensate the bank for any expenses and responsibilities arising from foreign laws or usages.

(2) Remitting Bank

"Remitting bank" is the bank which the principal entrusts to handle the operation of collection. Remitting bank is normally a local bank in the exporter's country. Remitting bank will usually write out the collection order based on the principal's instruction in the collection application form.

A remitting bank, strictly speaking, does not have legal obligation to check documents in order to ensure the correctness of the document. Nevertheless, the remitting bank should pay attention to the following points:

1) Whether the documents mentioned in the collection order/instruction have been presented.

2) If the documents are in sets, it must be assured that no member of the set is missing; otherwise, the holder of the missing document may claim the goods.

3) The bills of exchange should be drawn correctly and the shipping documents should be in good order.

4) The Incoterms like FOB, CFR or CIF that are used should be paid attention to, as different terms demands differently. For example, CIF demands that an endorsed insurance document should be presented together with the set of documents to cover at least the full invoice price.

(3) Collecting Bank

"Collecting bank" is the bank which is entrusted by the remitting bank to collect money from the payer, who is usually the drawee of the B/E. The collecting bank is normally a bank in the payer's country. The collecting bank in the buyer's country could be the issuing bank under a documentary L/C.

(4) Payer (Drawee)

"Payer" is the person who is the drawee of the B/E according to the collection order/insturction. The payer is normally the importer.

(5) Presenting Bank

"Presenting bank" is the bank that presents the B/E and/or documents to the drawee and collect money from the drawee. Presenting bank is usually the collecting bank, which is not always the case, however. For example, when the payer is not in the same area as the collecting bank or it is not convenient for the payer to deal with the collecting bank for some reason, a bank in the payer's area, rather than the collecting bank, is entrusted to present the B/E and/or documents to the payer to collect the money.

(6) Case-of-Need (Principal's Representative)

"Principals representative" is the person who is nominated by the principal to act as case-of-need in the cases where there appear non-acceptance and/or non-payment. The representative, who is on behalf of the principal, takes charge of the goods in respect of storage, sales and so on in the place where payment is to be made.

If the principal needs a representative, he should give clear instructions in the collection application form. The collection order/instruction must bear such instructions. If the principal fails to do so, banks will not accept any instructions from the case-of-need.

15.6.3 Clean Collection and Documentary Collection 光票托收与跟单托收

(1) Clean Collection

Clean collection refers to the collection which is made with financial documents only. In other words, by clean collection, it is meant that financial documents such as a B/E are presented to the bank which is entrusted by the principal for collection without commercial documents such as a B/L which is title to the goods. Clean collection is not often used except for the case where a small amount is to be collected. It is chiefly used for "open account" transactions or services.

The operation processes of clean collectionare described as follows:

1) The exporter sends the documents which evidence that goods are shipped or air forwarded direct to the importer.

2) The exporter sends the bill or note to the local bank (the remitting bank) to ask for collection.

3) The remitting bank sends the bill to the collecting bank in the importer's country.

4) The presenting bank (either the collecting bank itself or another bank) presents the bill for collection. The presenting bank acts in accordance with the collection order/instruction as well as the "Uniform Rules for Collection".

5) With payment collected, the presenting bank sends the payment to the remitting bank.

6) The remitting bank credits the account of the exporter with relevant sum after deducting necessary charges that should be borne by the exporter.

(2) Documentary Collection

Documentary collection refers to the collection which is made together with commercial documents as well as financial documents or which is made with commercial documents only. It can be seen that in either case, commercial documents are required to accompany the collection. With commercial documents, the payer enjoys more security, because he pays money on condition that commercial documents such as a B/L should be presented to him. In this way, the payer obtains title to the goods. On the other hand, the bank also has more security, because when the bill is dishonoured, the bank holds the documents of title to the goods.

In international trade, documentary collection is most often used. So when we speak of collection, we usually refer to documentary collection. The documentary collection provides security for the parties by means of controlling the shipping documents which include any document of title to the goods.

There are two types of documentary collection:

(1) D/A (Documents against Acceptance) (The word "acceptance" is a technical term here)

(2) D/P (Documents against Payment)

1) D/A

When the presenting bank presents the documents (the document of title to the goods included) to the importer, the latter must accept the bill before he gets the documents. (Please refer to the following chapter about "accept"). D/A may be used when the situation is the buyer's market and when the buyer is reliable.

The following are the operation steps of D/A:

① The principal approaches the remitting bank for collection. After he finishes filling in the collection application form, he gives it to the remitting bank together with the B/E and the shipping documents.

② The remitting bank produces the collection order/instruction based on the instructions of the collection application form and sends it to the collecting bank together with the B/E and the shipping documents.

③ The collecting bank presents the B/E and documents to the importer who writes on the B/E the word "accepted" and the date on which he accepts the B/E as well as his signature. Afterwards, the importer gives the B/E back to the bank in exchange for the documents.

④ The importer pays money when the bill matures.

⑤ The collecting bank informs the remitting bank that payment is effected and transfers the account to the remitting bank.

⑥ The remitting bank hands over the payment to the exporter.

The following flow chart may help readers understand it better:

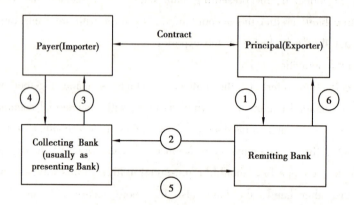

Figure 15.4   Flow Chart of D/A

From the above it can be seen that the exporter runs greater risk. He has to spend money on production and distribution of the goods in the time lag between placing the order and the final delivery. Besides, the exporter has to bear a further credit period based on the term of the B/E.

The exporter, however, can discount the B/E in order to get money earlier. Please refer to the following chapter about "discount" of a B/E.

2) D/P

By D/P, it is meant that the principal gives the B/E and the shipping documents to the bank and entrusts the bank to collect the payment from the importer on condition that the importer effects payment. Otherwise, the shipping documents shall not be released to the importer. In the following circumstances, D/P may be used:

First, the market situation is in the seller's favour(the seller's market). In such situation, the seller does not worry about selling out the goods.

Secondly, the seller is not sure of the buyer's reliability or of the stability of the buyer's country's political and economic situations.

Thirdly, the seller hopes to get a loan from the bank in the interval between shipment and payment. When the bank keeps hold of the documents of title to the goods and a sight bill, the seller may find it easier to get a loan from the bank.

On the other hand, so far as the buyer is concerned, D/P is also an improvement as compared with "cash with order". The buyer doe not have to pay when placing the order. His fund is not tied up. He does not pay until the collecting banker approaches him for payment.

D/P is further divided into two types: D/P at sight and D/P after sight.

D/P *at sight*: when the presenting bank presents the B/E and the shipping documents to the importer, the latter should make payment immediately to get the shipping documents.

D/P *after sight*：when the presenting bank presents the B/E and the shipping documents to the importer, the latter should accept the B/E and make payment on the maturity date of the B/E so as to get the shipping documents from the collecting bank.

15.7　Bill of Exchange　汇票

Bills of exchange, which are a key form of negotiable instruments, enjoy a wide range of uses in commercial, financial and banking transactions. More often than not, bills of exchange are traditionally used in international trade in which the bills of exchange offer written evidence of the financial obligations underlying trade transactions.

Further, bills of exchange have grown into a very flexible instrument in the areas of finance and banking. For example, bill discounting and acceptance credits. The B/E is proof of the importer's obligation to pay.

Generally speaking, in simple words, a bill of exchange is actually a piece of paper with words and sum of money on it. It is used to transfer money from one person to another one instead of the actual money itself.

To be accurate, *a bill of exchange is an unconditional order in writing addressed by one person to another, signed by the person giving it, requiring the person to whom it is addressed to pay on demand, or at a fixed or determinable future time, a sum certain in money to, or to the order of, a specified person or to bearer.*

15.7.1　Parties toa Bill of Exchange　汇票有关方

Basically, there are three key parties to a B/E：

(1) The drawer;

(2) The drawee;

(3) The payee;

Besides the above three parties, there might be additional parties：

(4) Acceptor;

(5) Holder;

(6) Bearer;

(7) Discounter;

(8) Endorser;

(9) Endorsee.

15.7.2　Types of Bills of Exchange　汇票种类

There are many types of bill of exchange. The following are some more important ones：

(1) Sight Bill of Exchange

A sight B/E is usually defined as follows：

A bill which is expressed to be payable on demand, or at sight, or on presentation; and a bill in which no time for payment is expressed.

In other words, a sight B/E is the B/E that is payable the moment the B/E is presented to the drawee of it. A sight B/E is used in the case where the exporter wants to sell goods to the importer for immediate payment. When a sight B/E is presented to the drawee, the presentation will itself trigger the settlement process unless the B/E is dishonoured.

（2）Usance /Time/ Term /Tenor Bill of Exchange

A usance B/E is the one that is payable at a stipulated period of time after sight or after date. The date on which the drawee/acceptor sights the B/E is considered the date on which the B/E is accepted. The acceptor adds the date to his acceptance. In this way the date of payments is fixed. The date on which payment should be effected is called maturity date of the B/E. So a B/E that is payable at 60 days is not a sight B/E but a usance B/E.

Usually, in the eye of law, a bill ceases to be a B/E if it bears an uncertain due date such as "180 days after inspection of the goods on the buyer's premises", or "after sight", or "on or before arrival of vessel" and so on.

（3）Clean Bill of Exchange

A clean B/E is the one that is not accompanied by any commercial documents, especially not accompanied by the shipping documents. The drawer of a clean B/E may be a business, an individual, or a bank. The payee may be a business, an individual, or a bank.

In international trade, a clean B/E is usually used where the export is not of goods but of a service or used in respect of commission, the remainder of the payment and so on. A clean B/E is used where no shipment is involved or where the shipping documents have for some reason been sent separately to the buyer.

Only when the importer is considered to be trustworthy or "open account" is in use can a clean B/E be used. Generally speaking, clean Bs/E are not often used.

（4）Documentary Bill of Exchange

A documentary B/E is the one that is accompanied by commercial documents like the invoice, B/L, and insurance policy. When a documentary B/E is presented to the drawee for payment or for acceptance, the drawee will not effect the payment or acceptance unless the shipping documents are also presented to him.

A documentary B/E is welcomed by both the importer and the exporter in that both have more security. Therefore, in international trade, a documentary B/E is most often used in international settlement.

（5）Commercial Bill of Exchange

A commercial B/E refers to the B/E we have been discussing. The definition previously provided gives a clear picture of it.

The drawer of a commercial B/E may be a business or an individual and the payer may be a business, an individual or a bank. In international payments, the drawer of a commercial B/E is normally the exporter, who draws a B/E for the purpose of getting payment for the goods he sells. A commercial B/E is usually accompanied by shipping documents.

(6) Banker's Bill of Exchange

A Banker's draft is a cheque that is drawn by a bank upon another bank. In other words, a banker's draft is an order to pay a sum of money (a draft) drawn payable to order (if drawn to bearer it is not a valid banker's draft) by a bank as drawer on the same bank as drawee.

It can be seen from above that the drawer and the payer of a banker's draft are both banks. Such being the case, there is little risk that the banker's draft will not be paid because of shortage of funds. However, it is possible that a banker's draft might be dishonoured since no bank would pay once it had reliable knowledge that the draft was in the wrong hands.

In international payments, after a banker's draft is issued, it is normally given to the remitter (usually the importer) for him to send to the bank nominated by the exporter. Usually, the draft is sent together with a letter or a copy of the invoice if the payment is concerned with a consignment of goods. On the other hand, the bank which draws the draft must send a notification of payment to the overseas paying bank so that the latter can check the draft presented to it. Occasionally, the draft may be sent to the beneficiary on behalf of the customer.

15.8　Promissory Note　本票

A promissory note is sometimes used in international trade especially when the settlement is made by means of remittance. A promissory note is:

An unconditional promise in writing made by one person to another, signed by the maker, engaging to pay, on demand or at a fixed or determinable future time, a sum certain in money, to or to the order of, a specified person or to bearer.

Before the promissory note is received by the payee (beneficiary), the note is considered inchoate (i.e. incomplete). As soon as the promissory note is delivered, it becomes a bona fide note. Promissory notes are often used in "Forfaiting" arrangements. (Please refer to the following chapter about fortfaiting.)

(1) Contents of a Promissory Note

According to the law concerned in this country, a promissory note usually should include the following items:

1) The words "Promissory Note".

2) Unconditional promise to pay the amount of money.

3) The name of the payee.

4) The date of making the promissory note.

5) Signature of the maker.

If a promissory note does not indicate the places of making payment and making the promissory note, the business quarter of the maker of the promissory note is taken as the places of making payment and making the promissory note.

（2）Types of Promissory Notes

Promissory notes can be divided into the following sorts：

1）General promissory note：the maker of a general promissory note is a business or an individual, so it is also called "commercial promissory note".

2）Banker's promissory note：the maker of a banker's promissory note is a bank.

3）Sight promissory note：payment should be made when the promissory note is sighted.

4）Term promissory note：promise to make payment at a fixed or determinable future time.

A general promissory note can be a sight promissory note or a term promissory note；whereas a banker's promissory note is always a sight one.

（3）Liabilities of the Parties

There are usually two parties to a promissory note：the maker and the payee. The maker of a promissory note is just the payer of it. A promissory note can be endorsed, so there may be another party：the endorser.

1）Maker

The maker of a promissory note is the principal debtor. He engages that he will pay the promissory note within the tenor. A maker of a promissory note must realize that in whose favour he is making the promise.

2）Endorser

A promissory note can be endorsed in the same way as an "ordinary" bill of exchange or cheque.

The endorser is liable to pay the promissory note or compensate the holder (or any subsequent endorser) for non-payment provided that the necessary proceedings in dishonour have been taken.

15.9   Cheque   支票

（1）Definition and Contents of Cheques

A cheque is bill of exchange which is drawn on a banker and is payable on demand. In other words, a cheque is an unconditional order signed by the drawer who entrusts the bank or other financial organisations to pay a sum certain in money to the payee or the bearer of it. It is a special piece of paper which is used to transfer money from one person to another instead of using the actual money itself.

Normally a cheque should include the following：

1）The word "Cheque".

2）Entrustment of paying unconditionally.

3）A fixed sum of money.

4）The name of the payer.

5）The date of drawing the cheque.

6) The drawer's signature and the stamp.

The drawer writes the cheque which is usually a pre-printed form provided by his bank and gives the cheque to the payee who either cashes it or pays it into his own account.

(2) Parties to a Cheque

A cheque normally may involve the following parties:

1) The drawer, whose account will be debited.

2) The drawee (a bank where the drawer has an account).

3) The collecting bank (the payee's bank which collects/obtains payment for its customer from the paying bank—the drawer's bank).

4) The paying bank where the drawer has an account.

When a customer cashes a personal cheque at his own bank, the bank is both the paying bank and collecting bank.

(3) Types of Cheques

Usually a cheque is asight instrument. Money should be paid the moment the cheque is presented. This kind of cheque is an uncrossed one as compared to the crossed cheque.

Crossed cheque: a crossed cheque is the one on the corner of which two parallel lines are printed. A crossed cheque cannot be cashed. Money is transmitted only through the banks. Crossed cheques will normally be paid by the paying bank if they are presented by a collecting bank. A cheque can be crossed by the drawer, the payee or the collecting bank.

15.10 Remittance 汇付

(1) Mail Transfer (MT)

A mail transfer is an authenticated order in writing addressed by one bank to another instructing the bank to whom it is addressed to pay a sum certain in money (namely, a definite amount of money stated on the document) to a specified person or beneficiary, or when a specified person or beneficiary applies for it.

The importer, when choosing to send a payment by mail (usually by airmail), gives instructions to the remitting bank by filling an application form in which the following are normally included:

1) The amount in a certain currency, e.g. in USA Dollars, or in RMB.

2) The name and the detailed address of the exporter, the beneficiary.

3) The name and branch of the bank and the account number (if known).

4) Clear instructions about who is to pay the charges of the transfer.

The payment can be remitted either to the beneficiary's account with a bank or with an instruction to a bank to notify and pay the beneficiary.

(2) Telegraphic Transfers (TT)

If a payee wants to send a payment more quickly, he may do so by requesting a telegraphic transfer which will be sent by telex or cable. But TT is more expensive than MT.

The instructions sent to the banks are the same as for an MT. Besides, the same methods of reimbursement are involved. The stages of MT and TT are the same except that MT is concerned with post while TT is concerned with telegraphic means such as telex or cable. The following flow chart indicates the operation stages of MT and TT.

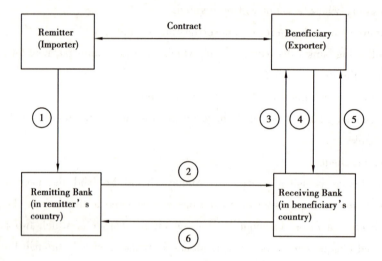

Figure 15.5　Flow Chart of MT and TT

Here are some explanations about the above flow chart.

The remitter and the beneficiary have signed a contract which stipulates that money is to be paid through MT or TT. The stages are described as follows:

1) The remitter approaches a local bank to apply for remittance. He must fill out an application form to give instructions to the remitting bank.

2) The remitting bank, after getting money from the remitter, sends MT or TT advice to the receiving bank by post or by telegraphic means. In the case of TT, the remitting bank normally also sends cable confirmation by airmail to the receiving bank for it to check the documents.

3) The receiving bank notifies the beneficiary of the payment after checking the documents from the remitting bank.

4) The beneficiary gives the receipt to the receiving bank before he obtains the payment to evidence that payment has been received by him.

5) The receiving bank, after obtaining the receipt from the beneficiary, transfers payment to the beneficiary.

6) The receiving bank sends the beneficiary's receipt to the remitting bank and asks the remitting banks to reimburse it.

TT is most often used, as payment can be sent more quickly.

(3) Remittance by Banker's Demand Drafts

A banker's draft is a cheque issued by a bank upon another bank. This draft is normally a sight draft. The importer (remitter) obtains a banker's draft from the issuing bank and sends it to the beneficiary. The following flow chart describes the stages of paying by a banker's draft.

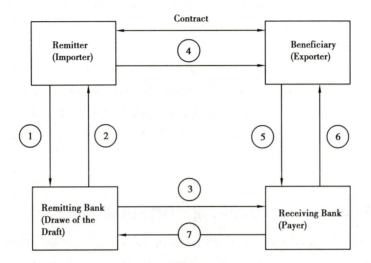

Figure 15.6   Flow Chart of a Banker's Draft

Here are some explanations about the flow chart:

1) The remitter approaches a local bank to apply for remittance by a banker's draft. He must fill in the application form. The remitter's account will then be debited. (Please refer to Figure 5.3 about application for foreign draft.)

2) The remitting bank (issuing bank) draws a draft and gives it to the remitter.

3) The remitting bank sends a notification to the receiving bank. The remitting bank will normally send a notification to the bank that is drawn on to tell the bank such information as the amount, the name and the date of the payee of the draft.

4) The remitter sends the banker's draft to the beneficiary, the exporter. The draft is normally sent together with a letter or copy of the invoice if the payment is concerned with a consignment of goods. Occasionally, the bank will send the draft on behalf of the remitter, but the bank is not liable if the draft is lost in transit.

5) The beneficiary endorses the draft and presents it to the receiving bank for payment. When receiving the draft, the beneficiary (payee) just pays the draft into his account with his bank (receiving bank) if it is drawn in the local currency and upon a local bank. But if the draft is drawn in a foreign currency and/or drawn on a bank in another country, the beneficiary has to ask his bank to send the draft for collection and gets the payment in due course. If the beneficiary has a foreign currency account in the currency in which the draft is drawn, he may request to pay the draft into that account.

6) The receiving bank checks the documents and pays the beneficiary.

7) The receiving bank then notifies the remitting bank of the payment and asks for reimbursement.

Besides the banker's draft, promissory notes or cheques are sometimes used in this way instead. It must be emphasized that the exporter must be quite sure that he can get the payment before he delivers the goods. It is likewise very important to the exporter that the date of remittance should be included in the contract.

(4) SWIFT Transfers

As mentioned above, instructions can be sent by post, by telex or by cable, but if banks concerned are members of SWIFT, banks will choose to send instructions through SWIFT system instead. They will send a SWIFT message instead of an airmail letter, and an urgent SWIFT message instead of a telegraphic transfer. The procedures of SWIFT transfers are similar to those of MT and TT.

15.11   International Factoring   国际保理

Factoring is normally used when an international transaction is based on an open account basis. The exporter runs more risks when dealing on an open account basis. In order to have security to get payment or, in other words, to reduce the risks, the exporter tends to use factoring. Factoring is often used for the sake of the exporter.

Factoring is a procedure whereby a factor (a special company or a bank) takes over the debtors (sales) ledger of a firm and, for an agreed fee, undertakes responsibility for the accounting records, invoicing and collection of payment that is due.

Factoring occurs when an exporter sells the importer's debt to a factor (in his own country) to get money of an agreed percentage of the invoice value. He can get money when the credit term comes to an end or when the invoice for the transaction is raised.

Many factoring companies are concerned with banks. By buying the book debts of a client (exporter) at a price and arranging collection, the factoring company (factor) transfers the exporter's burden of status inquiries, credit control, and foreign exchange risk from the exporter's shoulders to its own. Sometimes, it may attend to shipping or forwarding of the goods.

Factoring has been traditionally used more often in the industries like steel stockholding, timber, engineering and textiles. But factoring is beginning to be used in other industries like manufacturing. Besides, suppliers of raw materials, components and consumer goods tend to use factoring.

A factor's services are often proper for businesses that manufacture goods or sell services which are complete at the time of invoicing. If the goods or services have been delivered or completed by the time the invoice is issued, a debt actually exits. So the factor can finance the invoice and it does not have to make large reserves against the potential need to recourse the debt to the exporter when the importer fails to make payment.

However, it must be born in mind that factoring is not a panacea or in other words, it is not a powerful key to unlock all kinds of locks, but an appropriate package of services to meet real needs.

It offers credit assessment, a hands-on approach to collections and assured payment, which will be discussed later.

(1) Parties to Factoring

Normally, the parties involved in factoring are: exporter, importer, original factor and foreign factor.

1) Exporter

The exporter, who is also called a client (of the factor), approaches a factor to apply for factoring when he is going to deal with an importer on the basis of open account term.

2) Importer

The importer is the customer of the factor in his own country and he agrees to the exporter's idea to use factoring facilities which help him in the transaction.

3) Original Factor

The original factor is the factor in the exporter's country. The original factor accepts its client's application and provides the factoring service. A factoring agreement has to be signed by and between the factor and the client (exporter).

(2) Foreign Factor

The foreign factor is the factor in the importer's country. The foreign factor is entrusted by the original factor to provide detailed information such as the reliability, the credibility to the original factor. Besides, the foreign factor helps to collect money.

(3) Advantages and Disadvantages of Factoring

It is clear that factoring can facilitate international transactions by providing the exporter security to get payment when the transaction is based on the open account term. As far as the importer is concerned, with factors to act as the intermediaries, the transaction agreement based on open account term is more likely to be arrived at. In this way, the importer can enjoy the advantages of the transactions on the basis of open account term.

Factoring also becomes a valuable alternative to the traditional overdraft, because by securing as much as 80 percent of the value of outstanding invoices, the liquidity is restored and the assets represented by debtors liberated to provide further finance, without formal limits.

In addition, by using factoring, a company might not necessarily raise money secured on its own property. The company can be financed without recourse to external sources of capital and without using the company's own equity. This is especially beneficial to the company which is developing at a critical stage.

Factoring facilities are especially appropriate for fast-developing and profitable companies which are managed by managers willing to contract out sales ledger administration and credit management in the same way as they lease premises or company cars.

1) Advantages of Factoring to the Exporter

As mentioned above, factoring is used when the transaction is based on the open account, which is most risky to the exporter. The greatest advantage of factoring to the exporter is that the exporter has more security to get the payment. The factoring service benefits help exporters to control the risks from the growing demand for open account trading terms. Factoring provides a higher level of credit protection. The advantages that factoring brings to the exporter are listed as follows:

A. The exporter may have access to get to know the reliability and the payment ability of the importer through factors.

B. The exporter can overcome language, time zones and culture barriers. By using factoring, the foreign factor who is in the importer's country and speaks the same language as the importer can more easily and conveniently contact the importer with no language or culture obstacles. Otherwise, the exporter would have to contact the importer with much difficulty.

C. The exporter who uses factoring does not have to get involved in the complicated and difficult claim procedures, which it is the factors' responsibility to deal with.

D. The exporter may have more chances to conclude a transaction. This is especially true when the market of the goods involved is a buyer's market. Besides, factors may either have their own offices overseas or are members of FCI, through which exporters are likely to compete in overseas markets on the same terms as local suppliers.

E. The exporter can avoid foreign exchange risks. The factor can make advances in foreign currencies.

F. Delays in making payment are reduced. Since the factor will pay the exporter in advance, the latter can get funds earlier, thus increasing the exporter's cash flow.

G. Discounts to importers to induce them to pay quickly can be reduced.

H. Analysis of sales statistics is provided by the factor.

2) Advantages of Factoring to the Importer

A. The importer need not tie up his funds and therefore the cost of importation is reduced.

B. The importation procedures are simplified, so efficiency is improved.

C. The price of the goods might be higher, but it is not so high as doing the business under L/C.

3) Disadvantage of Factoring

Factoring might be expensive for a smaller exporter. The cost of factoring can be classified as follows:

A. The cost of service.

Any service offered should be charged, which is reasonable and understandable in the business world. The cost of using factoring may be relatively higher compared with other types of export finance. The charge for service is normally 1% or 2% and sometimes 3% of the total invoice value. The factoring charge varies according to the average invoice size, the expected sales volume and the credit rating of importer.

B. The cost of finance

The costs include a discount charge above bank base rates for finance. An advance will normally be charged at about 3 per cent above base rate, on a day-to-day basis. It is normally higher than the usual interest rate by 1.5 percent to 2 per cent.

Nevertheless, exporters tend to use factoring for the advantages mentioned above. And they may try to get compensation to some extent from other ways like raising the price a little.

Summary of This Chapter
本章概要

1. 在国际贸易的三个 P (payment, price, and packing) 中，国际支付 (payment) 最为重要，因为进口商不可能在没有把握的情况下，贸然将货款付出；同样道理，出口商若没有把握收到货款，绝不会轻易发货。因此，进口商和出口商都十分重视国际支付，使用不同的支付条件直接影响贸易双方的成交欲望。

2. 进口商与出口商都承担一定的风险。支付方式的不同对双方的风险有直接影响。预付货款 (prepayment) 对进口商风险最大，因为货款一旦放出，进口商就处于非常被动的地位；相反，出口商处于主动地位。同样的道理，若支付条件是赊账 (open account, O/A)，出口商处于非常被动的地位，因为进口商有可能拒付货款，或对货物挑剔以达到降低需付货款的目的。所以，选择支付方式至关重要，选择何种支付方式主要取决于双方的贸易关系以及当时的客观因素。

3. 选择货币需要慎重。国际贸易中，可以选用进口商或出口商国家的货币，也可以选择第三个国家的货币，由进出口双方商定。货币有"硬通货"和"软通货"之分，所谓硬通货，指国际上普遍具有信心接受其作为进行交易的货币。硬通货必须是政治稳定的货币，其币值稳定或有升值趋势，并可以自由兑换。相反，所谓软通货指的是不被国际社会接纳的货币，其币值不稳定，信用较差，软通货易受贬值影响，所以难以兑换成外币。

4. 信用证是国际支付中最重要的付款方式。最常用的信用证种类是跟单信用证。信用证业务中，银行起着关键的作用。因为出口商不会轻易发货，进口商也不会贸然付款，银行作为中间人发挥担保的作用。信用证是开证银行应客户的申请要求，向另一方开具的载有一定金额，在一定期限内凭符合规定的单据付款的书面保证文件。

5. 信用证所涉及的当事人主要有：开证申请人、开证 (银) 行、通知 (银) 行、受益人、议付银行、付款银行、保兑银行等。开证申请人简称为开证人，通常是进口商。买卖双方签订了买卖合同后，买方有义务以卖方为收益人开立信用证。开证银行是应开证人的申请要求开立信用证的银行。开证行开立信用证后便承担了付款责任。开证行的担保代替了申请人的担保，换言之，银行信用代替了商业信用。通知行通常是出口商所在地的银行。通知行在收到了开证行寄来来的信用证后，通知受益人信用证已经开立，以便让出口商 (受益人) 装运货物以及准备必需的单证。受益人通常是出口商。当通知行通知受益人信用证已经开立后，受益人必须根据信用证条款装运货物，备妥有关单证，如：装箱单、提单、商业发票、保险单 (根据支付条件而定) 等。议付银行指的是买进向它提交的跟单信用证项下的出口商汇票的银行。议付行又被成为押汇银行、购票银行或贴现银行。受益人在装运了货物后，备妥有关单证，便到议付行议付，取得货款。同时，受益人有义务通知进口商货物已经发运，以便进口商准备收货。付款行是开证行指定代行信用证项下付款或承担汇票付款的银行。换言之,付款行即在所规定的单证被出示时向受益人付款的银行。付款行一般是开证行,也可能是被指定的第三家银行。保兑行指的是对信用证进行保兑(confirm)的银行。通知行或付款行通常被要求对跟单信用证加以保兑,该银行就成为了保兑行。保兑行承担了和开证行一样的担保付款的责任。

6. 信用证通常包括以下内容:(1)信用证号码。(2)信用证开立日期与地点。(3)信用证种类。(4)所依据的合同。(5)信用证的主要当事各方。(6)信用证金额。(7)货物的名称、数量、规格、包装、单价、价格条款等。(8)运输条款:装运港和目的港名称,装运时间,是否允许分批装运或装船。(9)有关汇票的规定。(10)有关装运单证的规定。(11)特殊条款。(12)对议付行的指示。(13)开证行的印章或签字。(14)信用证是否遵循《跟单信用证统一惯例》。

7. 信用证种类。信用证种类有很多,主要有:(1)可撤销信用证和不可撤销信用证。可撤销信用证指的是在信用证有效期内不通知受益人,便可对信用证进行修改或撤销的信用证。这种信用证在国际贸易实践中很少使用。不可撤销信用证指的是在信用证有效期内,未经受益人同意,不得撤销或修改的信用证。通常不可撤销信用证上都标明'不可撤销信用证'字样,即使没有标明该字样,也一般视其为不可撤销信用证。(2)保兑信用证与未保兑信用证。保兑信用证指的是经过出口商所在地的银行(通常是通知行)保兑的信用证。对出口商而言,保兑信用证经由两家银行担保货款的支付。未保兑信用证指未经过银行保兑的信用证。未保兑信用证只有开证行担保货款的支付。当开证行资信很好、实力很强或成交金额不大时,通常使用未保兑信用证。(3)即期信用证与远期信用证。即期信用证指的是当所规定的单证被提示给银行时,并且在信用证条款皆符合要求的情况下,银行立即付款给受益人的信用证。该信用证有利于出口商,可使出口商迅速获得货款。远期信用证指的是在所规定的单证被提示后的一定时期内保证付款的信用证,可分为银行承兑远期信用证和延期付款信用证。(4)跟单信用证与光票信用证。跟单信用证指的是凭跟单汇票或仅凭单据付款、承兑或议付的信用证。这些单据指的是代表货物所有权的、或者证明货物已经装船的货运单据,如:提单、商业发票、保险单、产地证书、装箱单等。光票信用证指的是开证行仅凭受益人开具的汇票或简单收据而无须附带货运单据付款的信用证。在国际支付中,光票信用证使用很少,因为进口商在没有获得代表物权的运输单据时付款,就会承担很大的风险。(5)备用信用证是开证行对受益人承担一项义务的凭证。备用信用证与其他信用证最大的区别就是:买卖双方都不希望用到它。备用信用证是在买方未履行付款义务时充当"后备"的作用,备用信用证只有在开证申请人未履行其付款义务时使用。备用信用证已被国际商会归类于跟单信用证,使用于《跟单信用证统一惯例》。但是,跟单信用证用于一笔具体的交易的支付,是在合同当事人根据合同履行合同义务过程中的支付。

8. 托收是国际支付手段中四种常用的方式之一。国际商会第522号出版物《托收统一规则》给托收的定义是:托收是指由接到委托指示的银行办理金融单据和/或商业单据,以便取得承兑或付款,或凭承兑或付款交出商业单据,或凭其他条件交出单据。

9. 托收的当事方通常是:委托人,托收行,代收行及付款人。委托人通常是卖方,他开出汇票或不开出汇票委托银行向国外付款人收款。托收行是接受委托人的委托、转托国外银行向国外付款人代为收款的银行。代收行是托收行的代理人,它是接受托收行的委托向付款人收款的进口地银行。付款人通常就是进口方。

10. 需要时的代理人(case-of-need):托收业务中,出口委托人为防止因付款人拒付而发生无人照料货物的情况,在付款地事先指定好代理人。该代理人的权限一般在托收委托书中有明确规定。当付款人拒付时,需要时的代理一般被授权代为照料货物和处理仓储、转售或运回等事宜。

11. 托收分为光票托收和跟单托收。光票托收指的是金融单据托收,而不伴随商业单据委托银行代收款项的一种托收结算方式。跟单托收指金融单据伴随商业单据的托收,或商业单据不伴随金融单据的托收。根据跟单托收,出口商先行装运货物,出具以进口商为付款人的跟单汇票或不带汇票的装运单据,交给当地的银行,由该银行寄往进口地的代收行,向进口商收取货款。跟单托收又分为以下三种:(1)即期付款交单(D/P at sight):出口商出具即期汇票,通过银行向进口商提示,进口商见票后即期付款以取得装运单据。(2)远期付款交单(D/P after sight):出口商出具远期汇票,由银行向进口商提示汇票和装运单据,进口商承兑汇票。进口商于汇票到期日或汇票到期日之前付款以获得单据。远期付款交单具有付款交单和承兑交单的一些特点,在实际业务中,远期付款交单较少使用。(3)承兑交单(D/A):进口商承兑汇票(在汇票上签字)出口商才发放单据(由代收行发放)。进口商在汇票上签字承诺在以后的某日(通常是 30 天、60 天、90 天)付款。承兑交单只使用于远期汇票的托收。

12. 托收委托书(collection order)是由出口商准备的重要文件。托收委托书上载有详细的跟单托收条款和条件。出口商在准备托收委托书时必须十分仔细,不能有任何错误,因为银行完全是按照托收委托书行事。

13. 金融单据指汇票、本票、支票、付款收据等。商业单据指发票、运输单据、货物所有权单据(如提单)等。

14. 托收对进口商有利,但对出口商风险大。在付款交单条件下,有可能买方或其银行拒付,尤其是在行市下跌时更是如此。按照付款交单方式,买方付款前不能获得代表货物所有权的单据。在承兑交单的方式下,问题可能更大。买方承兑汇票后,便获得代表货物所有权的单据。卖方于是承担更大的风险。卖方一般不太愿意接受付款交单或承兑交单,除非卖方对买方的资信深信不疑。但是,国际贸易中使用付款交单或承兑交单有时很有必要,例如:为扩大出口。特别是推销新产品或滞销产品,为了贯彻对外贸易政策,尤其是为了促进与发展中国家的贸易。

15. 根据《托收统一规则》,银行在托收业务中,仅提供服务,不提供信用。托收方式与汇付方式相同,皆属于商业信用性质。出口商委托银行的货款收取成功与否全凭进口商的信用。

16. 国际商会制定出版的《托收统一规则》是一项国际惯例。该惯例没有法律的强制性。不过,若在托收指示中明确规定以该规则为准,该《规则》对各有关方具有约束力。

17. 国际支付中,很少用现金结算,一般都是采用票据作为结算工具。票据是以支付金钱为目的的证券。可转让票据指通过背书或交付而进行转让流通的凭证。汇票、本票、支票是完全可流通转让票据(证券)。票据是非现金结算工具,它能代替货币使用。准可转让票据指不能转让但具有可转让票据某些特点的票据。常见的准可转让票据有:提单、仓单(准许货物出仓库)及信托收据(进口商收到付款交单汇票,但无力在货到时付款的情况下给银行的单据。银行先付款给出口商)。

18. 汇票是无条件付款命令,由出票人出具给受票人,命令其即时或在指定时间交付一笔数目的款项给收款人。汇票在国际贸易中被广泛使用。出口商通常以出票人身份要求进口商支付款项给出口商本人或其银行。

19. 汇票的种类:(1)跟单汇票(documentary draft):指汇票在流转使用过程中随附各种装运单据(主要包括提单、商业发票或保险单)的汇票。跟单汇票是国际贸易中使用非常广泛的汇票,因为跟单汇票适应国际贸易买卖双方很难交付实际货物的特点,通常进行单据买卖。出口商出具跟单汇票的目的是:在买方未支付货款或未承兑汇票之前,通过手中掌握的单据,掌握货物所有权。如果买方拒付,就拿不到代表货物所有权的单据,也就无从提货。跟单汇票的使用较好地体现单据与货款对流的原则,对交易双方都有利。(2)光票(clean draft):光票指在流转过程中不附带任何装运单据的汇票。国际贸易中通常不使用光票。光票往往用来支付小额费用,如佣金、样品费、运杂费和广告费等。(3)商业汇票(commercial draft):商业汇票是由卖方向买方开出的、用以索取货款的无条件支付命令书。商业汇票的出票人是商业企业、个人、公司,付款人可以是商业企业,也可以是银行。商业汇票一般有随附单据,并可以背书转让。收款时,通过当地银行委托国外银行向买方收款。(4)银行汇票(banker's draft):银行汇票是由银行签发,以另一银行为付款人的汇票。进口商在当地银行购买银行汇票自行邮寄或携带给国外收款人。银行汇票一般是光票,可以通过背书转让。(5)即期汇票(sight draft):指持票人出示汇票时受票人必须立即付款的汇票。这种汇票通常在票面有这样的内容:见票即付(at sight pay to…),要求即付(on demand pay to…),提示即付(on presentation pay to…)。(6)远期汇票(time draft):指受票人承兑后不必立即偿付,而在承兑后规定期限到时,才须支付的汇票。这种汇票在汇票上会注明:见票后30或60……天付款(at 30/60…days after sight)。(7)通融汇票(accommodation draft):指因出票人资信较差,而由其他人承兑或背书作为担保人的票据。一家资信地位较差的公司,如果由自己开立汇票,不易为他人接受,难以流通,使资金得不到融通。经它与另一家资信地位很好的公司商妥,由该资信很好的公司开立、背书或承兑的票据,从而起到直接承担或保证支付票据上款项的责任,以使票据容易为他人所接受,由此可以融通资金。这种汇票对开票人来说,并没有商品买卖的实际交易行为为基础,只是为了帮助他人融通资金而开立的票据。(8)商业承兑汇票(commercial acceptance draft):指付款人为工商企业或个人承兑的远期汇票,出票人通常也是工商企业或个人。(9)银行承兑汇票(banker's acceptance draft):指以银行为付款人的远期汇票,经付款人承兑后就成为银行承兑汇票。这是在银行应进口商请求开立远期信用证时,出口商发货后据以开出的汇票。经付款银行承兑后,这种汇票可以随时贴现(discount)出售,取得票款。它是国际金融市场上广泛流通的票据。

20. 汇票运作:(1)出票(to draw):出票是将汇票作为支付工具结算货款的一种程序。它是指出票人在汇票上填写付款人、付款金额、付款日期和地点以及受款人等项目,经签字交付给受款人的行为。进出口业务中贷款大都采用逆汇法通过银行结算,即出口商在货物装运后主动开出汇票向进口商索取货款。出口商开出汇票就作为要求付款的凭证。受款人在我国指中国银行。(2)见票(sight):见票是将汇票作为支付工具进行货款结算的一种程序。当持票人把汇票提交给付款人,要求其承兑和付款时,付款人看到汇票就叫见票。如果被提示的是即期汇票,付款人见票后必须立即付款;如果被提示的是远期汇票,付款人见票后办理承兑手续,待汇票到期时付款。(3)提示(presentation):指持票人将汇票提交给付款人要求其承兑或付款的行为。(4)承兑:指付款人对远期汇票表示承担到期付款责任的行为。付款人在汇票上写明"承兑"字样,并注明承兑日期以及签字,然后交还给持票人。(5)拒付(dishonor):指国际贸易中当持票人提示汇票要求付款人承兑或付款时,付款人拒绝承兑或付款的行为。(6)背书(endorsement):指在汇票、支票、提单等有价证券的背面上签名,表示同意转让的行为。背书通常由持票人在汇票的背面或粘单上签名,或者再加上受让人(transeree)即被背书人(endorsee)的名称,并把汇票交给受让人。背书分空白背书(blank endorsement)和特别背书(special endorsement)。空白背书又被称作不记名背书,指背书人只在汇票上签名,但不注明被背书人。特别背书又被称作记名背书,指背书人在汇票背面签名并注明被背书人或其指定人。如:"付给……银行或其指定人"(Pay… bank or order)。(7)有追索权和无追索权(with recourse, without recourse):当汇票遭到拒付时,持票人可向其前手(prior party),即他之前的背书人及出票人,行使汇票的追索权,将已经付出的票款从背书人或出票人那里索回,这就叫有追索权。出票人及背书人为了避免受到追索,可在汇票上注明不受追索的字样,即使转让的汇票被拒付时,持票人也无权向其背书人或出票人追索票款,这就叫无追索权。(8)贴现(discount):贴现是指远期汇票承兑后尚未到期,由银行或贴现公司从汇票票面金额中扣除按照一定贴现率计算的贴现息后,将净款付给持票人,从而贴进票据的行为。

21. 汇票内容:汇票上必要的内容通常是:标明"汇票"的字样,无条件支付委托,应支付的金额,付款人名称,收款人名称,出票日期,出票人签章。汇票内容若不完全,该汇票无效。在实际业务中,汇票还包含付款日期、付款地点和出票地点等内容。

22. 支票(cheque):一般来说,支票是以银行为付款人的即期汇票。支票是银行存款客户向他开立账户的银行签发的,授权银行即期支付一定数额的货币给一特定人,或其指定人,或持票人的无条件书面支付命令。支票必备的内容有:(1)标明"支票"的字样;(2)无条件支付命令;(3)应支付的金额;(4)付款银行名称和地点;(5)收款人名称或其指定收款人;(6)出票日期和地点;(7)出票人名称及其签章。必备内容缺一不可,否则该支票无效。

23. 划线支票(crossed cheque):划线支票即转账支票,它只能作为银行转账用,不能提取现金。

24. 本票(promissory note):本票是出票人对另一个人无条件支付一定金额的承诺。本票必备内容:(1)标明"本票"的字样;(2)无条件支付承诺;(3)应支付的金额;(4)收款人名称;(5)出票日期;(6)出票人签章。必备内容缺一不可,否则该本票无效。

25. 本票分为一般本票和银行本票,一般本票分为即期和远期两种。银行本票只有即期的。银行本票是光票。在中国,本票仅指银行本票。工商企业和个人不能出立本票。

26. 拒付证书(protest):指由付款的公正人(public notary)所出示的证书,证明汇票或支票持有人提示承兑或付款时,付款人拒绝承兑或拒付的事实。

27. 订货付现(cash with order, CWO):订货付现指进口商向出口商订货时必须支付货款。这种方式对进口商来说风险较大。为了减少风险,可以采取订货支付部分货款方式(P-

CWO),这样,进口商便掌握了一定的主动权,从而风险减少。

28. 货到付款(cash on delivery,COD):货到付款指成交的货物抵达进口商指定的目的地后货款才支付。这样,进口商风险很小,但对出口商风险很大,因为,一旦货物被拒收,出口商将承担很大损失。

29. 记账/赊账交易(open account,O/A):记账方式指将应收款项记入买方账内,然后按约定期限进行结算。具体方式是:卖方在货物装运后,即将货运单据寄给买方,货款则借记买方账户,然后按约定期限,由买方将账款通过银行汇交卖方,或由卖方开具汇票向买方收款。采用这种支付方式,对卖方风险很大。

30. 汇付(remittance):汇付即汇款。按照这种方式结算货款,卖方将货物直接交给买方,由买方径自通过银行将货款汇交卖方。汇付一般涉及以下当事方:(1)汇款人(remitter):在国际贸易中汇款人通常是买方。(2)汇出行(remitting bank):汇出行指接受汇款人的委托或申请,汇出款项的银行,通常是进口商所在的本地银行。(3)汇入行(receiving bank,paying bank):汇入行指受汇出行委托,解付汇款的银行。汇入行通常是出口商所在地的本地银行,它一般是汇出行的代理行。(4)收款人(payee):收款人是出口商。

31. 汇付种类:(1)信汇(mail transfer,MT):指买方将货款交给银行(汇出行),要求汇出行以信件委托汇入行付款给卖方的一种汇款方式。(2)电汇(telegraphic transfer,TT):指买方要求汇出行以电报或传真或电传,委托汇入行付款给卖方的一种汇款方式。(3)票汇(demand draft,DD):指买方向本地银行(汇出行)购买银行即期汇票自行寄给卖方,由卖方收款人凭票直接向付款行或委托当地银行,通过其在付款行所在地的分行或代理行,向付款行收取款项的一种汇款方式。

32. 采用 SWIFT 电汇方式:SWIFT 的意思是:"环球银行财务电讯协会"(Society for Worldwide Interbank Financial Telecommunication,SWIFT)。采用该方式电汇款项有三大优点:(1)安全可靠;(2)高速度低费用;(3)自动加核密押,它为客户提供快捷、标准化、自动化的通信服务。加入 SWIFT 的中国银行有:中国银行(识别代码:BKCHCNBJ),中国工商银行(识别代码:ICBKCNBJ),中国农业银行(识别代码:ABOCCNBJ),中国投资银行(识别代码:IBOCONBJ),交通银行(识别代码:COMMCNBJ),中国建设银行(识别代码:PCBCCNBJ),中国人民银行(识别代码:PBOCCNBJ),中信实业银行(识别代码:CIBKCNBJ)。

33. 采用 CHIPS 电支付方式:CHIPS 的意思是:纽约清算所银行间支付系统。是非常重要的国际美元支付系统。只有该系统的成员才能通过该系统支付和收款。

New Words and Expressions

accept *v.* 承兑

advise *v.* 通知;建议

beneficiary *n.* 受益人

claiming bank 索偿行

clean collection 光票托收

clean L/C 光票信用证

collecting bank 代收行

confirmed L/C 保兑信用证

confirming bank 保兑行

documents against acceptance (D/A) 承兑交单

documents against payment (D/P) 付款交单

documentary collection 跟单托收

documentary letter of credit（L/C）跟单信
用证

D/P at sight 即期付款交单

D/P after sight 远期付款交单

factor *n. & v.* 保理商；为…… 保理

flow chart 流程图

hard currency 硬通货

irrevocable L/C 不可撤销信用证

issuing bank 开证行

negotiation *n.* 议付；谈判；协商

paying bank 付款行

presenting bank 提示（汇票）银行

principal *n.* 委托人

present *v.* 提示（提交汇票等）

protest *n. & v.* 拒付证书；拒付

revocable L/C 可撤销信用证

sight L/C 即期信用证

SWIFT L/C 环球银行财务电讯协会信用证

time L/C 远期信用证

validity *n.* 有效期

Discussion Questions

1. Which mode of payment means the greatest risk to the exporter?

2. What is an L/C?

3. Why is factoring used in international business?

4. What is the difference between a draft and a cheque?

References　参考文献

1. Bagozzi R P. Marketing Management. New Jersey：Prentice Hall，1998.

2. Ball D A. International Business：Introduction and Essentials. 5th ed. Burr Ridge，USA：RWIN，1993.

3. Ballou R H. Business Logistics Management. 4th ed. New Jersey：Prentice-Hall Inc.，1999.

4. Belkaoui A R. International and Multinational Accounting. London：The Dreden Press，1994.

5. Bennett R，Blythe J. International Marketing：Strategy Planning，Market Entry & Implementation. London：Kogan Page Limited，2002.

6. Black D. Financial Market Analysis. 2nd ed. Chichester，John Wiley & Sons，Ltd.，2000.

7. Bodie Z. Essentials of Investments. New York：McGram-Hill Higher Education，2001.

8. Choi F D S. Handbook of International Accounting. New York：John Wiley & Sons，Inc.，1991.

9. Choi F D S. International Accounting. 4th ed. New Jersey：Prentice Hall，2002.

10. Maximo V. et al. Global Finance. 2nd ed. New York：Addison-Wesley Educational Publishers，Inc.，1998.

11. Bradley F. International Marketing Strategy. 3rd ed. Prentice Hall，1999.

12. Buckley A. The Essence of International Money. 2nd ed. London：Prentice Hall，1996.

13. Caves R E. Multinational Enterprises and Economic Analysis. 2nd ed. Cambridge：Cambridge University Press，1996.

14. Clark E. International Finance. London：Chapman & Hall，1993.

15. Clark T R D，Smith T. Towards A Theory of International Services：Marketing Intangibles in a World of Nations. Journal of International Marketing，1996，4（2）：9-28.

16. Coyle J J. The Management of Business Logistics：A Supply Chain Perspective. 7th ed. Mason，Ohio，South-Western：Thomson Learning，2003.

17. Czintota M R. Global Business. 3rd ed. Ohio：South-Western Thomson Learning，2001.

18. Czinkota M R，Ronkainen I A，Moffett M H. International Business：Update 2003. Mason，Ohio，South-Western：Thomson Learning，2003.

19. Dalrymple D J，Parsons L J. Basic Marketing Management. New York：John Wiley & Sons，Inc.，1995.

20. Daniels J D，Radebaugh L H. International Business：Environment and Operations. 9th ed. London：Prentice Hall，2001.

21. Finney M J. International Tax Planning. 2nd ed. Surrey，England：Tolley Publishing Company

Ltd., 1993.

22. Foot M, Hook C. Introducing Human Resource Management. Essex: Pearson Education Limited, 2002.

23. Frain J. Introduction to Marketing. 4th ed. London: International Thomson Business Press, 1999.

24. Gibson H D. International Finance: Exchange Rates and Financial Flows in the International Financial System. London: Longman, 1996.

25. Gourdin K N. Global Logistics Management. Oxford: Blackwell Publishers Ltd., 2001.

26. Grosse R, Kujawa D. International Business: Theory and Managerial Applications. Chicago: IRWIN, 1995.

27. Gourdin K N. Global Logistics Management. Oxford: Blackwell Publishers Ltd., 2001.

28. Hays R. Principles of Auditing: An International Perspective. London: McGraw-Hill Publishing Company, 1999.

29. Hill C W L. Global Business Today. Boston: Irwin McGraw-Hill, 1998.

30. Jackson T. International HRM: A Cross-cultural Approach. London: SAGE Publications Ltd., 2002.

31. John R. Global Business Strategy. London: International Thomson Business Press, 1997.

32. Johnson J C, Wood D. Contemporary Logistics. 6th ed. New Jersey: Prentice-Hall Inc., 1996.

33. Jones C P. Investments: Analysis and Management. 8th ed. New York: John Wiley & Sons, Inc., 2002.

34. Kahal S E. Introduction to International Business. London: Mcgraw-Hill Book Company, 1994.

35. Kotler P. Marketing Management. 11th ed. New Jersey: Prentice Hall; Person Education International, 2003.

36. Krugman P R. Currencies and Crisis. London: The MIT Press, 1993.

37. Lambert D. Fundamentals of Logistics Management. Boston: The McGraw-Hill Companies, Inc., 1998.

38. Luo Y D. Multinational Corporations in China. Copenhagen: Copenhagen Business School Press, 2000.

39. McDonald F, Burton F. International Business. London: Thomson, 2002.

40. Matthews C. Managing International Ventures: The Route to Globalizing Your Business. London: Kogan Page Limited, 1999.

41. Melvin M. International Money and Finance. 6th ed. New York: Addison-Wesley Educational Publishers, Inc., 2000.

42. Mendenhall M. Global Management. Cambridge, Massachusetts: Blackwell Publishers, 1995.

43. Moffett M H. Fundamentals of Multinational Finance. Boston: Pearson Education. Inc., 2003.

44. Morgan G. Images of Organization: The Executive Edition. 1st ed. San Francisco: Berrett-Koehler Publishers, Inc., 1998.

45. Nobes C, Parker R. Comparative International Accounting. Essex, England: Prentice Hall, 2002.

46. Nunning J H. Multinational Enterprises and the Global Economy. England: Addison-Wesley Publishers Ltd., 1993.

47. Piggott J, Cook M. International Business Economics：A European Perspective. 2nd ed. England：Addison Wesley Longman Limited，1999.

48. Postma P. The New Marketing Era. New York：McGraw-Hill，1999.

49. Punnett B J, Ricks D A. International Business. 2nd ed. Cambridge，MA：Blackwell Publishers Inc.，1997.

50. Radebaugh L H, Gray S J. International Accounting and Multinational Enterprises. 5th ed. New York：John Wiley & Sons, Inc.，2002.

51. Roberts C. International Financial Accounting：A Comparative Approach. 2nd ed. England：Prentice Hall，2002.

52. Rodrigues C. International Management：A Cultural Approach. St. Paul，MN：West Publishing Company，1996.

53. Rugman M A, Hodgestts M R. International Business. 3rd ed. England：FT Prentice Hall，2003.

54. Sharpe W F. Investments. New Jersey：Prentice Hall Inc.，1999.

55. Slack N, Chambers S, Johnston R. Operations Management. 3rd ed. England：Pearson Education Limited，2001．

56. Stonehouse G. Global and Transnational Business：Strategy and Management. West Sussex，England：John Wiley & Sons, Ltd.，2000.

57. Taggart J H, McDermott M C. The Essence of International Business. London：Prentice Hall，1993.

58. Valdez S. An Introduction to Global Financial Markets. 3rd ed. London：Macmillan Business，1997.

59. Walton P. International Accounting. London：International Thomson Business Press，1998.

60. 麦克唐纳. 世界贸易体制[M]. 叶兴国，译. 上海：上海人民出版社，2002.

61. 查尔斯 W L. 国际商务：全球市场竞争[M]. 周健临译. 北京：中国人民大学出版社，2002.

62. 冯宗宪，Vong E. 国际商务[M]. 西安：西安交通大学出版社，1999.

63. 董光祖. 新编实用国际贸易辞典[M]. 北京：经济科学出版社，1997.

64. 加雷恩·琼斯. 工商导论——公司如何为人创造价值[M]. 北京：人名邮电出版社，2007.

65. 杰夫·马杜拉[美]. 商学导论(Introduction to Business)[M].北京：人民邮电出版社，2008.

66. 翁凤翔. 国际商贸实践[M]. 杭州：浙江大学出版社，2004.

67. 翁凤翔. 国际支付精要[M]. 杭州：浙江大学出版社，2004.

68. 翁凤翔，陈建平. 国际商务法规英语[M]. 上海：上海交通大学出版社，2015.

69. 翁凤翔，孟广君. 国际商务英语阅读[M]. 上海：上海交通大学出版社，2015.

70. 徐德志. WTO 协定文本与世界商道通则[M]. 广州：广东旅游出版社，1999.

71. 薛求知，刘子磬. 国际商务管理[M]. 上海：复旦大学出版社，2004.

72. 周汉民. 中国走进 WTO[M]. 上海：文汇出版社，2001.